ADVANCED
ROAD BIKE
MAINTENANCE

Published 2011 in Germany by Delius Klasing Verlag, Siekerwall 21,
D - 33602 Bielefeld with the title "Die Rennrad-Werkstatt für Profis"
© Moby Dick Verlag, ABC Straße 21, 20354 Hamburg

This English-language edition first published in July 2013

A catalogue record for this book is available from the British Library.

ISBN 978 0 85733 388 9

Library of Congress control no. 2013932258

Published by Haynes Publishing, Sparkford, Yeovil, Somerset BA22 7JJ, UK.
Tel: 01963 442030 Fax: 01963 440001
Int. tel: +44 1963 442030 Int. fax: +44 1963 440001
E-mail: sales@haynes.co.uk
Website: www.haynes.co.uk

Haynes North America Inc.
861 Lawrence Drive, Newbury Park,
California 91320, USA.

Printed in the USA by Odcombe Press LP,
1299 Bridgestone Parkway, La Vergne, TN 37086.

Translated by Claudia Brinkmann

Photo credits: Matthias Borchers, Cannondale, Franz Faltermaier,
Uwe Geißler, Markus Greber, Georg Grieshaber, Dr. Michael Heidelbach,
Robert Kühnen, Daniel Kraus, Thomas Niedermüller/Getty Images,
Thomas Streubel, Daniel Simon, Dirk Zedler

Front cover image: Photograph by Guy Harrop. Custom-built Specialized S-Works SL4 Roubaix
courtesy of Rock & Road, Yeovil. Park Tool workstand and tools courtesy of Madison.co.uk
*Please note equipment shown for illustrative purposes only – always refer to bike and workstand
manufacturers' recommendations when mounting a bike on a workstand*

**While every effort is taken to ensure the accuracy of the information given in this book, no
liability can be accepted by the authors or the publishers for any loss, damage or injury
caused by errors in, or omissions from, the information given.**

ADVANCED
ROAD BIKE
MAINTENANCE
The practical handbook

Dirk Zedler
Thomas Musch

UPGRADING | SET-UP | CARE | MAINTENANCE | PROBLEM-SOLVING | REPAIR

Contents

WHEELS AND TYRES

DRIVETRAIN AND BRAKES

Contents

MAINTENANCE AND REPAIRS

TIPS FOR TRAVELLING, PRE-COMPETITION CHECKS AND WINTER

THE AUTHORS   303

Dear readers and road-bike lovers,

Advanced Road Bike Maintenance contains a plethora of tips and advice, and contains much information learned over the past few years, in part due to the rapid development taking place in the field of road-bike components. All these tips and tricks have been gathered and published in this book, which covers most current components offered by Campagnolo, SRAM and Shimano, including the latest Shimano electronic gearshift system, Di2. This practical book, in conjunction with the manufacturers' tried and tested maintenance and care instructions, is a treasure trove for both the road-bike novice, and experienced road-bike enthusiast who are already familiar with the technical details of their bikes.

When carrying out the described maintenance jobs, keep in mind that – despite all efforts to keep the information current – the detailed instructions might not always apply exactly to your specific bike. Variations to models, and changes due to continuous product development, cannot easily be catered for, even if we endeavour to take into account any differences and exceptions as comprehensively as possible. Therefore, please adhere to the assembly instructions provided by your bike's manufacturer at all times.

Please also bear in mind that the instructions given in this book are not absolute gospel. Your own experience and skills might dictate a different way of going about things, or may make the use of additional tools necessary. For this reason, and in the interest of your own safety and the reliable operation of your bike, do not challenge yourself too hard. If in doubt, make enquiries, or ask your local specialist retailer for advice!

To that effect, we hope you will enjoy reading this book, and wish you many successful hours working on the most fascinating piece of sports equipment to be propelled by muscular power!

Thomas Musch and Dirk Zedler

Workshop set-up

Neatly placed tools and equipment are a visual treat and make working on your bike a pleasure. Here are a few useful tips for a successful workshop set-up.

It is five minutes past two on a Saturday afternoon. The training squad is assembled and ready to go. Actually, not quite. "Hold on a minute, I just have to quickly adjust my headset." You can hear cycling shoes clacking on the stairs down to the basement, and then a long silence – until finally a loud moaning sound emerges from the workshop, disturbing the peaceful Saturday lunchtime setting: "Where's the 5mm Allen key?"

Everyone is familiar with this scenario, and we all laugh about it, except for the person who is rummaging around in his workshop without success. The 5mm Allen key – or, more precisely, the hex key or hexagon socket – is the mother of all cycling tools. Since you basically need it for all sorts of jobs on a regular basis, it is common to own more than one, but alas it never shows up exactly where it is needed. Moreover, disorderliness and waiting training buddies are not the only nuisances when it comes to tools. If you bury the expensive vernier calliper or thread tap thoughtlessly under old bike parts and other tools on the worktop, it quickly becomes useless scrap metal. Therefore the motto is: while the others are busy making jokes, we are going to tidy up.

If you intend to set up the ideal home workshop, you need a free area on a wall and at least the same amount of space in front of it.

This is the best way to work on the bike – which is placed or suspended in this space – and not become claustrophobic. The area must also be sufficiently lit. The dim light of a 25W bulb dangling from the ceiling might be just enough for pumping up a tyre, but certainly not for truing a wheel. It is absolutely essential to have a fluorescent tube or – even better – two tubes installed in the workshop area.

For many of the jobs you will carry out, you will need a sturdy worktop at a comfortable height. For sawing, filing and drilling, a vice, which is mounted securely on the worktop, is indispensable. If you're a perfectionist, you could go to a specialist supplier and get yourself a professional workbench, with built-in storage cabinets. Sturdy, second-hand desks, which authorities and companies regularly sell off for very little money, can be almost as sturdy and quite practical, too. If the top surface of the table is too thin, and sags when under load, it can easily be reinforced by fitting a suitable wooden panel on top. The wood should have a smooth surface, but it is wise to avoid synthetic material, or veneer, since such surfaces are easily chipped. Another alternative is to re-use old kitchen cabinets, and perhaps wooden worktops.

If only a limited amount of space is available in your workshop-to-be, a board with the following approximate dimensions can serve as an emergency table – 300mm wide and 30 to 40mm thick. You can use the space even more efficiently if you fit this board on hinges fixed to the wall, enabling you to fold it away when not in use.

Workbenches and desks with drawers provide additional storage space for the many tools and small bike parts that you will need. You could divide the drawers into compartments using small wooden strips. This will prevent the parts from sliding around when opening and closing the drawers. Alternatively, your DIY shop will have ready-made plastic partitioning systems, which can be adjusted to your requirements. If you store screws, nuts, washers, valve caps, etc, in these compartments, life will be much easier when you need to do a repair job on your bike.

Prevent screws from coming loose – various thread-lock compounds for jobs on the bike.

Frequently used tools, like Allen keys, screwdrivers and pliers, however, are most accessible when hanging on a wall. DIY stores provide special racking systems for this purpose, featuring flexible and versatile hooks. Constructing your own tool wall is of course cheaper and often more practical, plus it is much more fun.

The heart of the action is, of course, the bike itself. It makes most sense to suspend it from a special workstand. This enables you to work at a height where you are not required to bend your knees and squat when carrying out work. Furthermore, cranks and wheels can be turned freely this way. For the DIY mechanic, the mid-range Home Mechanic PCS10 model offered by Park Tool for around £150 is a very good choice. This stand is height-adjustable, of good quality and is also good value for money. Park Tool produces a range of workstands to suit all budgets, as do several other manufacturers but bear in mind that, as with all tools, generally the quality is reflected in the price.

A workstand is not the only way to

The Home Mechanic PCS10 from Park Tool serves DIY mechanics well.

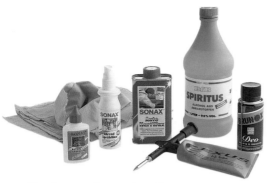

Cleaning, greasing, waxing, oiling – a range
of protective products is a must.

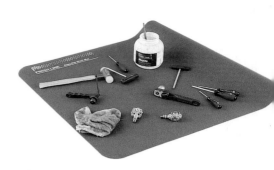

Keeps the floor and worktop clean – the professional
roll-up protective mat.

suspend your bike, of course. You can also
suspend it from the ceiling. You can build your
own basic and space-saving mounting device
using the following components, available from a
DIY store: galvanised chains, 3 ceiling hooks and
3 plastic-coated hooks for suspending the bike
from the saddle and handlebars. One hook can
be fitted to the ceiling above – or more slightly
behind – the location where you wish to suspend
the saddle. The two hooks for the chains which
hold the handlebars, however, should be fixed at
a reasonable distance from each other to the left
and right of the handlebars. The wheels will turn
without moving the bike when suspended if the
supporting chains run at an angle from the
ceiling to saddle and handlebars. In order to
prevent handlebars and forks turning repeatedly
in relation to the frame, you can fix the front
wheel to the frame down-tube using a strap.

Dirt and oilstains on the floor are a constant
nuisance, especially when you end up finding
traces of residue from your workshop in your flat
or house, having transported them via the soles
of your shoes. You can prevent this by placing a
large piece of cardboard, or a generously sized
leftover piece of carpet under the workstand.
Alternatively, you can be more professional using
a special protective mat. It's good practice to
sweep the floor and workbench clean after
repairing your bike, and you will win favour with
your spouse/partner/housemates!

A further detail to consider before starting
work is a supply of clean cloths for cleaning dirty
parts. For example, cotton rags cut out of old
t-shirts, or linen cloths, are easy to use and

absorb liquids well. Cloths made from synthetic
materials (such as old cycling jerseys) are not
really suited to this purpose, as they tend to
smudge rather than clean.

A few further items should be part of the
standard equipment in your workshop: shoe
boxes or plastic ice-cream cartons can be used
to store lubricant cans, chain oil and grease,
wax (to prevent corrosion) and solvent (for
degreasing and removing glue residues), as well
as adhesives.

An essential requirement in every good workshop – a
sturdy track pump featuring a pressure gauge.

Your tool wall

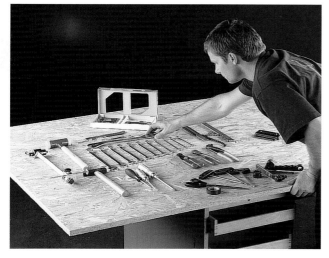

1 Lay out the tools on the wooden panel. Put the tools you use most frequently in the centre, in order to have quick and easy access to them. When laying them out, ensure there is sufficient space between the individual tools. Note also that some tools will find their own positions when the panel is installed. Pliers that hang from below the hinge open up and spread out a little unless they have a safety catch. Adjust the fastening points once all tools have adopted their final position.

2 Use suitable screws to fit the panel, depending on the type of wall to which it is being secured. Use suitable wall-plugs, and make sure that you drill the wall with the correct size hole for the plugs. Screwdrivers, Allen keys and similar items can be hung on a panel fitted at right–angles to the panel using a metal bracket. Sort flathead screwdrivers and Phillips screwdrivers according to size and in separate rows. When drilling the holes for the tool blades to pass through, make them half a millimetre larger than the external dimensions of the blade.

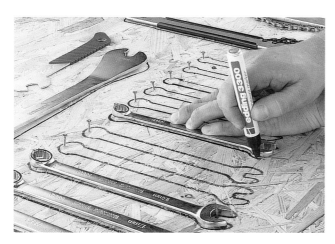

3 Before finally attaching the tool panel to the wall, using at least four solid screws, draw the outline of each tool on the panel. This foolproof marking method helps to instantly identify at a later stage if tools are missing or put back in the wrong place.

Tools and equipment

Which tools do you need when working with the current high-tech road bikes? The following information will help you to choose the best tools to help you to maintain your bike.

Modern bikes are designed in such a way that only a small number of tools are required even for regular maintenance work – and these can even be taken on a ride in most cases. The only catch here is that you have to select carefully. The widespread and annoying inconvenience in the bike industry is that neither standardised dimensions, nor size designations are used, resulting in differences from country to country – a phenomenon that is rooted in history and has not yet been eradicated. Therefore, the comprehensive toolkits offered by Elite, Park Tool and others, seem quite tempting. These sets are presented in practical foldout tool rolls or boxes, and give the impression that they

provide the necessary specialist tools as well as standard items. However, it is worth checking the requirements for your specific bike, as unless you are likely to be working on a range of different bikes featuring components from different manufacturers, these toolkits may contain far more specialist tools than you are likely to need. If one or more tools are not useful to you, you might be better off buying the specialist tools individually.

In addition to the specialist tools, a basic toolkit is required, including spanners, screwdrivers, etc. In many cases, specialist tools can only be used in conjunction with standard tools. When buying basic tools, you should pay special attention to quality and dimensional accuracy. If a screwdriver does not fit a screw exactly, or the tool material is too soft, the screw is easily damaged.

Without a doubt, good-looking, high-quality tools are a joy to own and use, but they don't come cheap. Therefore you should give careful thought to what is really necessary. Riders who only ever want to adjust the brakes and change a tube in a case of emergency will be fine with a basic kit. A small number of additional items will allow you to perform bigger maintenance tasks, for example adjusting and greasing the headset and hub bearings, or replacing cables. The most comprehensive toolkit will enable you to replace parts and fully assemble a bike, provided that the bearing seats and threads in the frame have been prepared appropriately, and the headset cups have been pressed into position.

Basic equipment

The toolkit for riding on the road
When you're out and about on a ride, or when you're on your way to a training camp, a small selection of tools might be sufficient if you have chosen it carefully. A small kit might fit into your saddle bag or jersey/jacket pocket. Multi-tools are particularly clever items. Ideally, a multi-tool should feature Allen (hexagon) keys ranging from 2.5 to 8mm, flat-bladed and Phillips screwdrivers, a chain tool and, for many modern road bikes, a Torx key (for example for aligning the brake pads in newer Campagnolo sets) as a minimum. The affordable multi-tools offered by Park Tool, Cool Tool and Topeak are to be recommended, and although cheaper versions are available, the price usually reflects the quality. Bear in mind that a good multi-tool can make the difference between continuing or abandoning a ride if trouble occurs miles from home!

Although many combination tools come with both tyre levers and a spoke key, in most cases a better choice would be to buy two separate tyre levers and a separate spoke key. The Spokey spoke key, which comes in various sizes, is a good choice, as it fits securely around all sides of the nipple, preventing the common problem of

Multi-tools should only be used in emergencies on the road.

rounding off the flats – particularly important when dealing with aluminium nipples. On aerodynamic wheels, the spoke nipples are often integrated into the rim, making it necessary to select the correct specific tools for repairing an out-of-true wheel.

Standard equipment

Tools for maintenance
The disadvantage of modern bikes with ever-more gears is the rapid wear and tear on the chain. Special chain checking tools, such as the Caliber 2 by Rohloff or the CC2 by Park Tool will indicate precisely when a new chain is required.

A chain-rivet tool will make it easier to

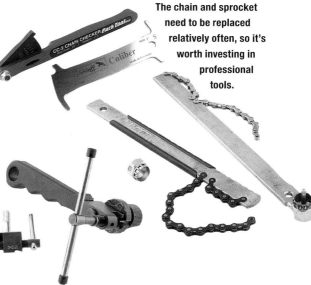

The chain and sprocket need to be replaced relatively often, so it's worth investing in professional tools.

15

Ring spanners and open-ended spanners are nice to look at, however, are rarely needed on a road bike.

replace the chain (compared to a multi-tool). For modern, narrow chains without a removable connecting link or special rivet pin, the Revolver 3 tool by Rohloff is indispensable.

The cassette lockring can be unscrewed using an appropriate tool in conjunction with a ratchet or a spanner, while counterholding the cassette with a chain whip. It is necessary to unscrew the cassette lockring in order to remove the cassette from the freewheel body.

Many bike parts have nuts or screws featuring a hexagonal head. An appropriate socket set is useful for dealing with these fixings. Open-ended spanners and ring spanners are also recommended, or combination spanners which feature an open-ended spanner at one end, and a ring spanner at the other. Wherever practical, ring spanners are preferable, as they grip the fixing over a

larger surface area, which means there is less wear and tear on the fixing's surfaces.

On some bike parts, the spanner flats are very narrow, for example on certain pedals. This means that the standard spanners cannot easily be used for these components. The pedals, in particular, can be removed more easily using special pedal spanners, which feature a longer lever. This is usually preferable to using a hex key in the end of the pedal spindle, or a standard spanner (if it fits). The Park Tool pedal spanner has a particularly long arm, which is beneficial as you can place your hands at a safe distance from the chainring sprockets.

A pair of cone spanners will be needed for wheel hub adjustment, and for some classic headsets. Cone spanners by Tacx are comfortable tools – the plastic covering protects your hands, and the long handle helps when applying force. Classic headsets are becoming increasingly rare, but if you are riding them, you have to make precise adjustments and apply a great deal of force to prevent them from becoming loose and being destroyed. Elite offers an adjustment set which goes easy on the hands because it features plastic edges. In many cases it makes sense to tighten the cone locknut using a standard open-ended spanner, since this features a wider jaw area than a cone spanner and hence leaves fewer ugly imprints on the surfaces.

When fitting brake and gear cables, cable cutters – as offered by Shimano or Park Tool – ensure that the outer casings are not squeezed

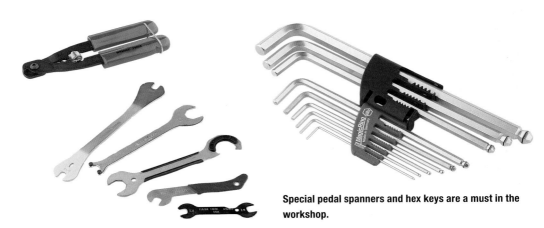

Special pedal spanners and hex keys are a must in the workshop.

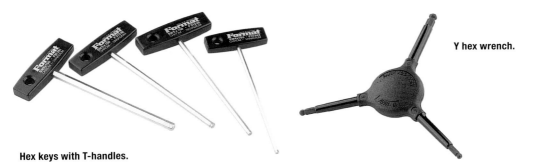

Y hex wrench.

Hex keys with T-handles.

or damaged, and prevent the inner cable from fraying.

Riders who enjoy working on their bike often, will quickly find the limits using multi-tool Allen (hex) keys. The compact design of multi-tools prevents optimum access to some fixings. In addition, there is the risk that all fixings are tightened to the same torque, since similar-sized keys are used. It is possible to overtighten small screws and also to find that it is not possible to apply sufficient force to tighten larger-diameter screws.

Separate hexagon-key sets can provide more leverage, and reversible keys are available featuring spherical heads at one end, which allow force to be applied to a fixing at a slight angle. These sets often feature a single handle, into which different keys can be slid. For final tightening, use a normal key rather than a spherical-ended key wherever possible, otherwise fixing and tool will suffer. The particularly practical key set offered by Wiha comes with an integral spring washer on the spherical end of each key which makes it possible to use these keys to fit screws into recessed holes.

The Park Tool ball-head Y hex wrench AWS-8 is useful to complement a multi-tool when out on the road, as it offers the advantages of three separate hex keys, providing greater flexibility and the ability to apply more torque than a multi-tool.

An optimum range of hexagon keys would ideally include both keys with spherical ends and standard T-handle keys, but your budget may not stretch to this. As ever, buy the best tools you can afford.

Screwdrivers should ideally have a blade

shaft that runs the full length of the tool – in order to loosen a very tight or seized screw, you should be able to give the screwdriver a whack using a hammer without worrying too much. Using a hex key which has flats where the key meets the handle, high torque can be applied via an open-ended or ring spanner. Jewellers' flat-bladed and Phillips screwdrivers may be useful for changing bike computer (and heart-rate monitor) batteries, and also come in handy when hub grease seals or similar items need to be removed.

Screwdrivers.

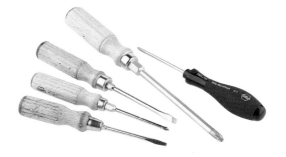

Bottom-bracket tools.

Derailleur tools.

Additional equipment

Overhaul and parts renewal

Affordable, basic crank pullers are available, and you will need a suitable open-end spanner to turn the puller spindle. Park Tool produces a range of crank pullers with integral handles, which avoids the need to use a separate spanner to turn the spindle.

A wide range of tools is available for removing and refitting the various types of bottom-bracket bearings, almost universally now of the renewable cartridge type, from affordable basic tools to professional tools with integral pullers.

Since cartridge bearings became widely popular, adjusting bottom-bracket bearings had become a thing of the past for a while. However, with the introduction of the Dura-Ace bearings which Shimano offered between 1997 and 2003, it became necessary to think again. The lock ring must be tightened using a suitable peg spanner. Park Tool offers a spanner which engages with the lock ring around its entire circumference, thus preventing the sensitive aluminium part from getting scratched.

If you're unfortunate enough to drop your bike on its right side, or even if the bike falls when stationary, it's very easy for the derailleur hanger to get bent. Using a suitable special alignment tool, you can easily and accurately bend it back.

You may also need circlip pliers to remove circlips from certain bearing assemblies. Circlip pliers are relatively cheap and usually come with fittings to cover internal and external circlips.

Always use torque wrenches to adhere to the recommended tightening torques for sensitive parts. This ensures safety and reliability. Cheap 'dial indicator' torque wrenches can provide approximate values only – it is always

Long-nosed pliers and circlip pliers.

Torque wrenches.

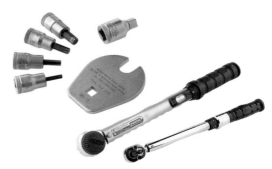

Soft-faced mallet and hammer.

best to use a quality 'click-off' torque wrench.

Hexagonal bits in sizes of 4, 5, 6 and 8mm are essential, and in some cases you may also need a 15mm open-ended spanner to remove the pedals.

A good socket set is invaluable. As well as using sockets to unscrew and tighten fasteners, suitable-sized sockets can also be used as a mandrel when pressing bearings into position. The choice is between ¼-, ⅜- and ½-inch square-drive sockets, depending on the socket size and use. Drive adaptors and extensions are available to allow sockets to be used with different-sized ratchets or with torque wrenches.

Occasionally, a soft-faced mallet may be required to help to loosen stubborn fixings or bearings. Obviously a mallet should be used sparingly, and care must be taken not to damage components.

When setting up a bike or a bike computer, various dimensions, such as the height of the frame and saddle, the distance between the handlebars and the saddle, as well as the wheel circumference, will be needed. You may also need to measure spoke thicknesses, bearing diameters, etc. So, in addition to an accurate tape measure, a vernier calliper may prove a useful tool.

Socket set.

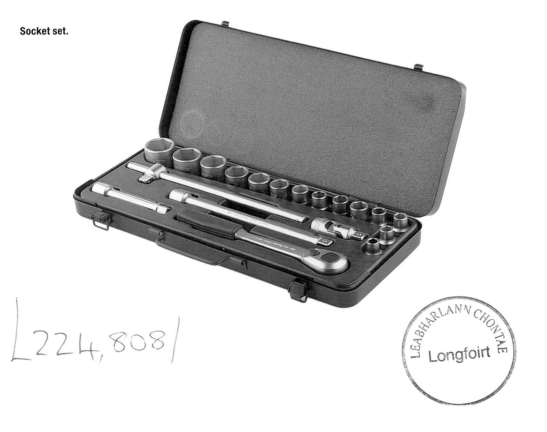

Torque

Using a torque wrench and ensuring tightening torques are correct

Tight is followed by off. This flippant insight into the abrupt end of the life of a screw, commonly used amongst mechanics, has become more and more valid in bike-enthusiast circles. The drive to reduce weight to a minimum also applies to screws. Where solid, steel 8mm-diameter screws used to hold the fort, nowadays we are often dealing with small and delicate titanium screws, commonly with diameters of 5mm.

There is a thin line between a reliable 'tight fitting' screw and the risk of it breaking off. For this reason, manufacturers would be advised to pay more attention to the rules concerning the use of screws. For example, the following simple rule of thumb, used by many design engineers, is often neglected: For aluminium materials, the suggested depth of engagement for a screw is at least 1.4 times its diameter.

A degree of force is needed to move a rusty screw, while a new screw, lubricated with high-grade assembly grease, hardly provides any resistance. With a few exceptions, all the screws on your bike should be greased, unless the manufacturer explicitly suggests that screws are fitted 'dry'. Also bear in mind that the parts do settle over time. When assembling components, remember that the individual items move and 'self-adjust' when in operation – clearances reduce, and screws can loosen. For this reason, it's advisable to re-check that fixings are still tight a short while after fitting them.

Hint

- Always reset (zero) a torque wrench after using it, and when storing the wrench, as otherwise the integral spring may stick or weaken, and the torque set may no longer be accurate. It's a good idea to rotate the setting collar backwards and forwards a few times if the wrench hasn't been used for a while, to redistribute the internal lubricant.

Handling fixings correctly

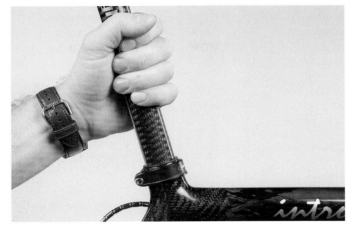

1 Check the condition of all relevant components before tightening any fixings. All parts must be a hundred per cent compatible. In the case of the seat post, it should slide into the seat tube effortlessly; however, there should be no noticeable play. If the seat post and/or the frame are made of carbon, no grease must be applied, otherwise it may not be possible to fit the post tightly, which could be dangerous, and may cause damage to the seat post.

2 Before tightening screws/bolts and nuts, check whether the fixings are of the correct length. As a classic example, the sleeve nut for the brake calliper bolt is often too short for mounting on a carbon fork. So, count the number of threads. The nut needs to screw onto the bolt at least six full turns, otherwise a longer nut or bolt will be needed.

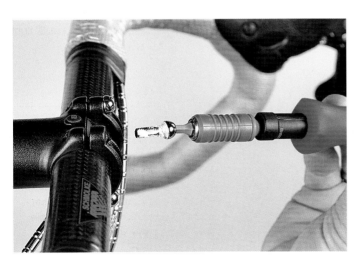

3 You need to grease most of the screws on the bike in order to reduce friction and corrosion. It is important to apply lubricants not only to the threads, but also to the area below the screw head, as this is where extreme levels of surface pressure can occur, which may damage a part's surface.

Handling fixings correctly (continued)

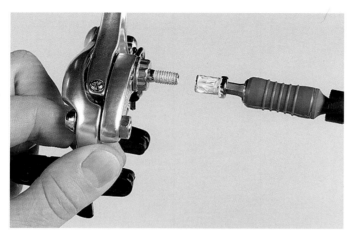

4 Do not grease screw threads to which thread-locking compound has been applied, for example brake calliper mounting bolts. In this particular case, we recommend (for metal frames) that you only grease the outside of the sleeve nut. However, always grease bottom-bracket bearing cups, even if the threads have thread-locking compound applied.

5 Screw heads are often inaccurate, as manufacturers aim to keep manufacturing costs down. Often, screw heads do not offer sufficient contact area for the tool, hence the tool must be used carefully in order to prevent damage to the screw head and cross threading.

6 To achieve the correct torque when using a torque wrench, hold the wrench at the grip on the handle, and apply smooth, gradual pressure until the wrench indicates the appropriate figure, clicks or releases itself. In order to ensure that the actual torque, rather than the screw's static friction, is being measured, it is advisable to loosen the screw by at least one turn, then retighten to the appropriate torque using the wrench.

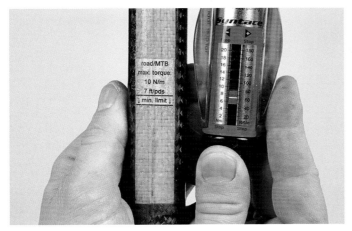

7 Often, recommended torque-wrench settings are provided as a torque range, or a single figure may be given, in which case this figure is the upper limit. Tighten to the upper limit in gradual stages; tighten to about two thirds of the maximum value, then loosen the fixing by half a turn before retightening. Repeat this process, gradually tightening to the upper torque limit.

8 When tightening fixings, watch for any warning signs. When tightening clamp fittings, if the two clamped surfaces close so far that they touch, the screw force no longer has a clamping effect – it now deforms the parts. Always check the security of the components when working with small torque values.

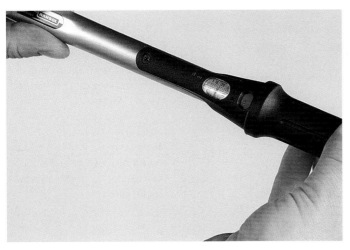

9 Check the tightness of fixings after around 150 miles and every 1,500 miles after this. Always zero the torque wrench when you have finished using it, in order to cut down on wear and tear and to preserve accuracy. It's a good idea to rotate the setting collar backwards and forwards a few times if the wrench hasn't been used for a while, to redistribute the internal lubricant.

Torque settings

To ensure the safe operation of your bike, screws, bolts and nuts need to be tightened carefully and checked regularly. A "click-off"-type torque wrench is best suited for this purpose. Tighten gradually, in stages, to the specified maximum torque (ie, in increments of about 0.5Nm). In between stages, keep checking the tightness of the component. Do not exceed the maximum torque specified by the manufacturer!

When working with parts for which no figures are available, take care not to overtighten. Adhere to the specified figures, and always check the instructions provided by the component manufacturers.

Hint

● Some components have torque figures printed-on to them, or cast in to their surface. Always use a torque wrench and do not exceed the specified maximum torque! If you are not a hundred per cent sure, or have queries, contact your local bike dealer for advice.

The following table provides an approximate guide to tightening torques for various components. Always check against the component manufacturer's recommended figure.

Recommended torque settings

System	Component	Shimano* (Nm)	SRAM/Avid** (Nm)	Campagnolo *** (Nm)
Rear derailleur	Derailleur to hanger	8–10	5–7	15
	Cable clip	5–7	5–7	6
	Pulleys	2.5–3		
Front derailleur	Clamp to frame	5–7	5–7	5 (Clamp) 7 (Direct assembly)
	Cable clip	6–7	5	5
Brake levers	Clamps to handlebars	6–8	6–8	10
Gearshift levers	Clamps to flatbars			6
Hub	Quick-release lever	5–7.5		
	Bearing locknut	15–17		
	Cassette lockring	30–50	40	40 (11-spline) 50 (10-spline)
Pedal cranks	Square			32–38
	Shimano Octalink	35–50		
	Shimano Hollowtech II	12–15		
	Isis		31–34	
	Gigapipe		48–54	
	Splined			42
	Ultra Torque			42–60
Chainwheels	Chainwheel securing bolts	8–12	12–14 (Steel) 8–9 (Alloy)	8

System	Component	Shimano* (Nm)	SRAM/Avid** (Nm)	Campagnolo *** (Nm)
Bottom bracket	Square	50–70		70
	Shimano Hollowtech II, SRAM Gigapipe	35–50	34–41	
	Octalink	50–70		
Pedal	Pedal spindle	35–55	47–54	0
Shoe	Cleat	5–6		
Brake	Brake calliper	8–10	8–10	10
	Cable clip	6–8	6–8	5
	Brake pad attachment	5–7	5–7	8
	Brake block holder attachment	1–1.5		
Seat post	Clamp	20–29		18–22

The figures given are those specified by the component manufacturers. Always refer to the latest manufacturer's recommendations:

* http://techdocs.shimano.com/techdocs/index.jsp

** www.sram.com

*** www.campagnolo.com

Recommended torque settings for disc brakes

Component	Shimano (Nm)	Avid (Nm)
Brake calliper mounting to frame/fork	6–8	9–10 (IS adaptor) 8–10 (Brake calliper)
Brake lever mounting to handlebars	6–8	
One-bolt clamp		4–5 (Juicy 5)
Two-bolt clamp		2.8–3.4 (Juicy 7/Carbon)
Hose-to-lever and hose-to-calliper securing screws	5–7	5
Brake hose connection piece on brake calliper	5–7	
Reservoir cap	0.3–0.5	
Grub screw (vent hole)	4–6	
Brake disc mounting (6-hole)	2–4	
Brake disc mounting (Centre lock)	40	

Bearing and assembly grease

Details of the different types of grease. Not all lubricants are suitable for any task

Not all types of grease are the same. This may sound obvious, but it is a point that a lot of cyclists consider relatively unimportant. Riders often use one single lubricant on their bike, regardless of whether they need to grease a screw or lubricate bearings. They seem to be unaware of the fact that different lubricants are designed to fulfil various different requirements. The different colours used for lubricants hint at different characteristics, but they do not reveal exactly what they are suited for. In so-called rolling bearings (headset, pedals, bottom bracket, hubs, freehub) little balls or needles rotate and generate very high point-loads or linear-loads. The lubricant is required to withstand this high pressure, and at the same time remain on the contact surfaces, as they need to remain lubricated at all times. This is the domain of specialised types of bearing grease.

Screw threads and clamp bolts, as featured on the seat post, require a lubricant that separates the contact surfaces and protects them. The worst-case scenario is when a thread seizes. When this happens, the contact surfaces have been damaged so much that they combine or "cold-weld". Aluminium parts, in particular, which are softer than steel screws, as well as titanium, which has a high coefficient of friction, need to be treated using special assembly paste or special grease.

Neither type of lubricant should be applied to carbon components. Wrongly greased parts will not tighten as designed. In some cases, screws may have to be tightened to such an extent that the carbon fibres may get crushed and damaged, in which case it is virtually guaranteed that they will break at a later stage.

On the other hand, not lubricating carbon parts is not an ideal answer either. One solution is the assembly paste for carbon and aluminium made by Dynamic. This product has tiny plastic granules added to a relatively runny carrier component. These granules slightly penetrate the surface of the carbon, thereby increasing the friction in the joint and enabling a low-torque fastener to be used. However, the high pressure and shear forces of a tight screw or bolt can grind and crush the granules.

A test involving a carbon seat post

demonstrated that – using Dynamic paste – the screw's required tightening torque could be nearly halved, compared to mounting it 'dry', ie without lubricant. Using standard grease or a standard assembly paste you need to tighten the screw by applying more than twice the force in order to safely fasten the post. The same was true of an aluminium seat post. For this reason, Dynamic paste (or a similar product such as Finish Line, Tacx Dynamic or Fiber Grip) is recommended for mounting handlebars and seat posts made from carbon, or for mounting handlebar stems on carbon steerer tubes, but keep in mind that all other types of lubricant and grease are unsuitable for carbon parts!

Lubricating and greasing correctly

1 Grease the screws evenly, both the screw thread and the head's contact surface. You can achieve the best results using a paintbrush.

2 Dismantle the expander cone and bolt for adjusting the headset; paint the lubricant thinly on the contact surfaces of the components, on the inside, and also on the screw (left-hand photo). Reassemble the components and thoroughly wipe off any excess lubricant.

3 Also thinly grease the main threads. This will reduce internal friction, and also allows for easy and precise adjustment of the headset.

4 In order to avoid annoying 'cracking' noises, thinly lubricate the inner surfaces of the seat post clamp and the outer surface of the seat tube.

5 When using cartridge bottom brackets, apply the assembly paste not only to the external threads of the bearing cups, but also to the contact surfaces of the cartridge unit and the crank splines.

6 Any screw threads and discs which are part of the crank puller mechanism should be lubricated on both sides. If you disregard this, a lot of friction may build up in the system when it is released.

Using carbon assembly paste correctly

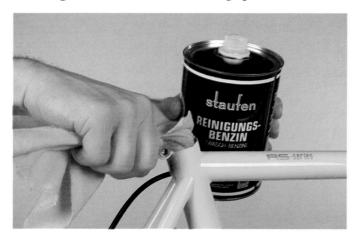

1 Degrease the appropriate surfaces of the parts to be assembled, using solvent or cleaning alcohol.

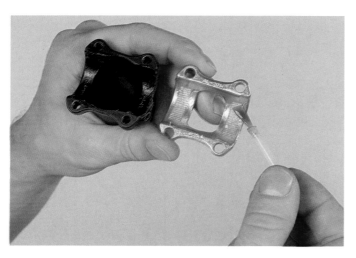

2 Paint the assembly paste on the contact faces of handlebar stem, stem face plates and the carbon handlebar itself. Remember that all relevant screws should be carefully lubricated, too.

3 Apply paste to the steerer tube and handlebar stem clamp, to help to prevent crushed carbon steerer tubes and loosening headsets.

4 Apply assembly paste to the inner surfaces of the seat tube and the seat post itself. Grease the clamp bolt, and fit the post.

Where bearing grease is required

1 Non-sealed bearings can be filled up with bearing grease. There is no need to use the grease sparingly, as an excess of grease does not have any noticeable braking effect thanks to the bike wheel's relatively low rotational speed.

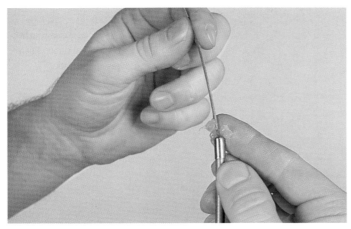

2 Before fitting gear and brake cables into their sheathing, carefully clean any dirt off the inner cables and run them through your greased fingers while threading into the cable outer.

Position yourself!

Saddle, handlebars and pedals are the contact points between the rider and their bike, and in order for the rider to adopt the best possible riding position, the seat post and the handlebar stem also have to be mounted and adjusted correctly. This chapter contains all the information you need to set your bike up to give you the most comfortable and efficient riding position.

When you see a professional racing cyclist in action, it often looks as if they have virtually become one with their bike. It seems as if they are sitting 'in' their bike. Moving grip from the top to the lower part of the handlebars, accessing the brakes, rising out of the saddle to pedal 'standing up' – all this looks harmonious and very natural. The stretched legs, the stationary position of the pelvis, the arms at a slight angle, enabling fast reactions at all times – rider and

bike in perfect harmony. This intimate connection between rider and bike is obviously a result of using the bike frequently and clocking up several thousand miles per year. Another reason is that racing cyclists adjust and check their positioning on the bike extremely meticulously, and this is one of the habits of professional cyclists that is truly worth adopting for amateur riders.

Considering how differently individual humans are designed, a standard adjustment method does not exist. However, there are a few guidelines to be adhered to.

The overall goal is to produce the optimum pedalling action. You should straighten your knees as much as possible at the bottom of the pedal stroke, so that you do not have to tilt your pelvis to the side when the pedals reach the lowest point of the pedal circle. You can check the saddle height by sitting on the saddle and putting the heel of your foot (in cycling shoes) on the pedal – which must be at the lowest point of its circle – with your leg almost fully straightened. Ideally, the shoe cleat should engage with the pedal with the knee still at a slight angle.

Finding the right position

If you are a newcomer to a racing bike, don't be tempted to try to copy the consistently aerodynamic riding position sported by the professionals. The consequence after your first ride could be pains in the neck, wrists and backside. You should be able to comfortably grip all necessary handlebar positions, ie, the upper handlebar (top tube), the lower handlebar (bottom tube) and the brake levers, over a long period. If you find that you always leave your hands on the upper handlebar (top tube) and ride with your elbows stretched out, thereby transferring each bump on the road surface through to your brain, this is a clear indication of the handlebars being set too low and the stem (reach) being too long. To begin with, it is advisable to have the stem set as high as possible. The top part of the saddle should only be slightly higher than the upper part of the handlebars (top tube). Seasoned professional riders, however, have their saddle set about 10 centimetres higher than their handlebars.

The best way to determine the correct horizontal distance between saddle and handlebar is by placing your hands on the lower handlebars (bottom tubes). This position is the most suitable from an aerodynamic point of view. Here, ideally your upper arm and forearm are at a right-angle to each other, while the knees almost touch the elbows when pedalling. If your knees actually touch your elbows, this means the stem is too short – unless you deliberately want to sit upright using the upper handlebar

(top tube). While on a ride, you can check your riding position by briefly looking sideways into a large shop window.

Using your multi-tool, you can also make changes to your riding position while you're out and about. However, it is safer to adjust your bike in the workshop, where you can use a torque wrench to tighten the fixings to the recommended torque.

Handlebar facts

Back in the days when names like Merckx and Gimondi or Poulidor represented the majority of handlebar makes for road bikes, the choice was not that difficult. In the meantime, the shapes available have become more complex and the range available more extensive. From an objective point of view, handlebars fulfil a very straightforward job. However, in the worst-case scenario, an unsuitable model can reduce the rider's enjoyment by causing hand and back pain. Therefore, you need to choose handlebars very carefully to suit your own personal preference.

The current variety of shapes and dimensions available for road-bike handlebars should mean that most riders can find components to allow them to achieve a perfect riding position on the bike. Apart from the width, the two important handlebar dimensions are 'reach' and 'drop'. These two dimensions indicate the depth and height of the handlebars (see sidebar). Generally, the handlebars available can be divided into three categories: 'classic', 'anatomic' and 'ergo'. The first of these is still very popular among professional cyclists. Featuring a consistent radius and tube diameter, the 'classic' handlebar is flexible to handle and grip, and accessing the brake levers from the

Dimensions for the three basic handlebar shapes

CLASSIC

Manufacturer	Models	Reach	Drop	Size*
3T	Rotundo	83mm	139mm	m
Deda	Newton Shallow, Campione	80mm	135mm	m
FSA	Traditional (Energy only)	90mm	145mm	l/m
Ritchey	Classic	82mm	135mm	m

ANATOMIC

Manufacturer	Models	Reach	Drop	Size*
Deda	Newton , Big Piega, Mara, Sfida	110mm	135mm	m
Ritchey	Logic/Superlogic/Evo Biomax	125–144mm	72–82mm	s/m/l
Syntace	Racelite	100mm	136mm	m
	Racelite 2 Carbon (XL)	100/110mm	145/151mm	m/l
	Racelite CDR (XL)	90/100mm	129/133mm	s/m

ERGO

Manufacturer	Models	Reach	Drop	Size*
3T	Ergonova	89mm	128mm	s
	Ergosum	77mm	123mm	s
Deda	Presa, Fluida, Nuova Sfida, Zero 100	80mm	135mm	m
FSA	New Ergo (numerous models)	80mm	150mm	m/l
	Compact (numerous models)	80mm	125mm	s
Ritchey	Curve	73mm	128mm	s

*suitable for the following hand sizes: l=large hands, m=medium-sized hands, s=small hands

lower part of the handlebar (bottom tube) is easiest on this model. However, the range of 'classic' handlebars on offer is more limited than that available for other types.

The most widespread type is the anatomical ('anatomic') shape featuring changing radii and straight handlebar grips. In addition, this design is optimised for the positioning of gearshift/brake levers. The most recent variant, called the 'ergo' or 'wing' shape, is an attempt to combine the benefits of both 'classic' and 'anatomic' handlebars, featuring a radius which increases towards the ends of the handlebars. The curvature of the tubes also determines how well the shift/brake levers fit on the handlebars. Depending on the reach, the handlebars and grips provide an almost flat contact surface for the rider's hands.

Contributor: Jens Klötzer

K-Force by FSA featuring Ergo shape: handlebar ends horizontal, brake levers vertical – smooth transition in shape along bar length.

The most important handlebar dimensions

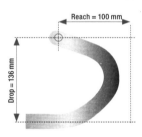

The Rotundo by 3T features the Classic shape. If the combination of the handlebar position and levers is not comfortable, you can try turning the bars slightly upwards while moving the levers slightly downwards.

WIDTH Normally measured between the outer edges of the handlebar ends. Handlebar width should correspond to the width of the rider's shoulders. Note that FSA specifies the width of its handlebars between the handlebar-end tube centres. On some compact handlebar types, the handlebar bottom tubes are angled slightly outwards. Keep this in mind when looking at manufacturers' dimensions!

REACH Measured horizontally from the centreline of the top tube to the furthest-forward front edge of the handlebars.

DROP Measured vertically, from the centreline of the top tube to the centreline of the bottom tube.

DIAMETERS The diameter of the handlebar stem (the centre of the top tube) must match the diameter of the clamp. Common sizes are 26.0 and 31.8mm (oversize), but there are one or two exceptions, such as the Deda oversize measurement, which is 31.7mm.

The Biomax handlebars offered by Ritchey feature a particularly distinctive Anatomic shape.

Fitting the seat post

1 Bear in mind that all seat posts have a maximum extended length – you cannot simply pull a seat post out of the frame seat tube as far as you wish and hope for the best! Always observe the label or markings on the seat post specifying the maximum extended length. The lower end of the seat post, inside the seat tube, should reach at least down as far as the frame's top tube. A seat post that does not extend far enough down into the frame can cause the frame to break due to the high leverage.

2 When working with a carbon seat post and/or frame, use a suitable carbon assembly paste, which will increase the friction in the clamp, reducing the required clamp-bolt torque. This reduces wear and tear on the post and the frame.

3 Tighten the seat-post clamp bolt using a torque wrench. Start by applying half the torque specified by the manufacturer. If no specifications are available, start at 2.5Nm.

4 Try twisting the saddle relative to the frame in order to check the clamping action. If the post can be rotated, increase the torque by 0.5Nm and check again. Never exceed the specified torque. If no figure is specified, we recommend a maximum of 5Nm.

5 When fitting the saddle, never move it so that the clamp is positioned at the very front or rear of the saddle rails. If the saddle rails are positioned with their curvature against the clamp, this can cause stress fractures, resulting in the rails breaking suddenly. If there is a scale on the saddle rails, slide the clamp only within the limits of the scale. When fitting a saddle without a scale on the rails, leave at least 10mm between the ends of the clamp and the start of the curvature at the front and back of the saddle rails.

6 Seat posts are available not only in different lengths but also to cater for various saddle mounting positions. A 'cranked' seat post can provide up to around 40mm rear offset for the saddle position, reducing the need to slide the saddle rearwards on its rails.

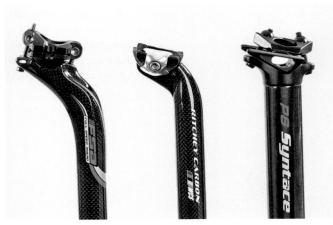

Seat posts featuring single saddle-clamp bolt

1 The saddle angle is adjusted via a curved, toothed, two-piece clamp, which clamps the saddle rails to the seat post. The finer the tooth pattern on the clamp plates, the better. A central bolt clamps the parts together.

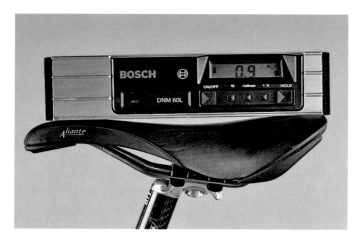

2 You do not need to completely remove the clamp when fitting the saddle. With the clamp bolt in position in the seat post, slacken the bolt by a few turns, then twist the upper clamp plate in order for it to slide over the saddle rails. Now rotate the upper clamp plate back into position so that the recesses in the clamp plates fit over the saddle rails. Use a spirit level on the upper surfaces of the saddle to check the saddle angle.

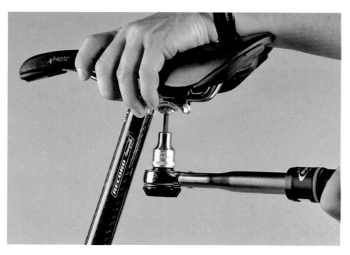

3 Once the upper surface of the saddle is horizontal, slowly start tightening the clamp bolt using a hex key, ensuring that the toothed clamp plates lock together. Check that the clamp plates are correctly engaged, with the teeth locked together, then tighten the clamp bolt to the torque specified by the manufacturer.

Seat posts featuring two saddle-clamp bolts

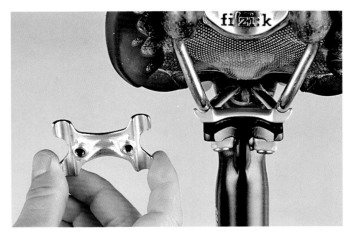

1 This type of clamp is generally stronger than the single-bolt type. To fit the saddle, first undo both clamp bolts sufficiently to be able to remove the upper clamp plate. First position the seat rails on the lower clamp plate, then place the upper plate back over the rails.

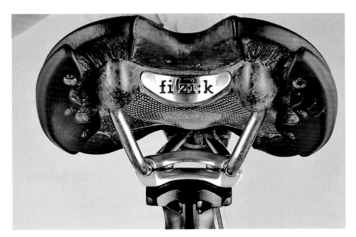

2 Grease the threads and heads of the clamp bolts, then tighten them, working alternately between the two bolts so that the seat rails are clamped evenly on both sides. Hold the saddle and the clamp in position while tightening the bolts, and if the clamp plates are toothed, make sure that the teeth on the two plates are securely engaged.

3 Using a torque wrench, tighten both clamp bolts to the specified torque. Again, tighten the two bolts evenly, working alternately on both sides. Start by tightening to half the specified torque, before progressively tightening fully.

Seat posts featuring yoke-type clamp

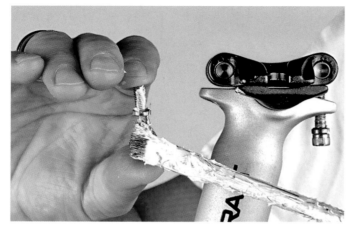

1 This type of clamp features a sliding lower clamp plate, with an upper clamp plate secured by two bolts, one at the front of the clamp, and one at the rear. The angle of the saddle is adjusted using the clamp bolts – tightening the front screw lowers the nose of the saddle, while tightening the rear screw lowers the rear of the saddle. Make sure that the clamp bolts' threads and heads are greased. With the clamp bolts loose, slide out the lower clamp plate then slide the saddle into position, making sure that the saddle rails engage with the recesses in the upper clamp plate.

2 Slide the lower clamp plate back into position, then alternately and gradually tighten both clamp bolts, constantly checking the angle of the saddle. If you need to adjust the saddle angle, slacken the front bolt and tighten the rear bolt to raise the nose of the saddle, or vice versa to lower the nose. Once you are happy with the saddle angle, tighten the clamp bolts to the manufacturer's specified torque.

Hints

- Saddle clamps shorter than 40mm are prone to put above-average stress on lightweight saddle rails made of titanium, titanium tube or carbon, therefore there is a high risk that the rails may break! Sharp edges may also damage the rail material.
- Using a torque wrench, check that the saddle-clamp bolts are still tight after 100 to 200 miles, and every 1,000 miles after this.
- Check that the saddle still flexes. Some 'tall' rack clamps can allow the underside of the saddle to 'bottom-out' on the top of the clamp, which can be very uncomfortable! By ensuring that there is a 20mm gap between the underside of the saddle and the top of the

clamp, the saddle will still flex under load, and will be comfortable to sit on.
- Always observe the maximum extension length for the seat post. The lower end of the seat post, inside the seat tube, should reach at least down as far as the frame's top tube.
- The scope for adjustment varies according to the type of saddle and the saddle clamp. Always observe the manufacturer's fitting recommendations, and never fit the saddle with the clamp positioned at the extreme front or rear of the saddle rails.

Seat posts featuring partly covered yoke clamps

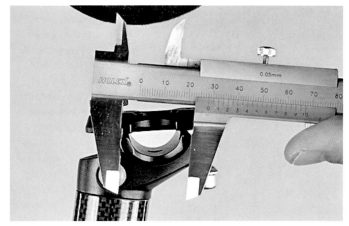

1 With this design, the front clamp bolt is positioned exactly on the seat post's vertical central axis. This has the advantage that the saddle can be moved further backwards, compared to other clamp types. The disadvantage is that the front clamp bolt is difficult to reach, as it is positioned under the saddle. Slacken both clamp bolts sufficiently to enable you to pull out the lower clamp plate.

2 Slide the saddle into position, engaging the rails with the recesses in the top clamp plate, then slide the lower clamp plate into position, and tighten the front clamp bolt. Tighten the rear clamp bolt until the lower clamp plate sits firmly on the saddle rails. If you need to adjust the saddle angle, slacken the front bolt and tighten the rear bolt to raise the nose of the saddle, or vice versa to lower the nose. Once you are happy with the saddle angle, tighten the clamp bolts to the manufacturer's specified torque.

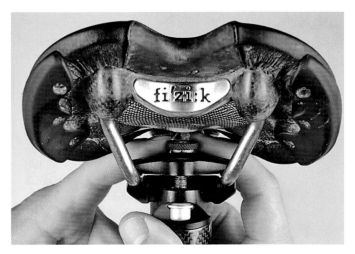

3 Make sure that the clamp bolts are screwed sufficiently into the clamp and seat post, as the clamp might fail otherwise. This is difficult to achieve with this type of post, as you cannot see the threads of the front bolt. In order to be safe, count the number of turns when tightening the bolt. The bolt should be screwed in by at least six full turns.

Adjusting the saddle position

1 Slacken the seat-post clamp bolt by two or three turns. Now the post should be easy to move. If it does not move, do not apply force, otherwise the seat post may suffer damage. Instead, try slackening the clamp bolt further. If the post still does not move, you may have to send the bike back to the dealer. Adjust the seat-post height, depending on your requirements.

2 From above, look over the saddle nose and the top tube down to the bottom bracket. If these three points are on the same front-rear centreline, you can tighten the seat-post bolt. If adjustment is required, turn the saddle and post as necessary, then retighten the seat-post clamp bolt in accordance with the manufacturer's instructions, taking care not to overtighten.

3 Grasp the saddle firmly at its front end and try to twist it relative to the frame. If you succeed, despite having locked the post clamp, you need to remove the post once again and repeat the process. As described earlier in this chapter, it's a good idea to grease the metal seat posts when fitting to metal frames, but as a rule of thumb, mount carbon seat posts without using grease – use a carbon assembly paste instead.

Fitting the handlebar stem

1 Instead of sliding the saddle a long way rearwards, you can often use a longer handlebar stem in order to make the riding position more comfortable. Stems come in lengths from approximately 60 to 140mm.

2 With carbon forks, it is not good practice to increase the stem height using a large number of spacer rings. Many manufacturers recommend that you use spacer rings to a maximum depth of 50mm with carbon forks.

3 The better option is to flip the stem. Almost all current stems are "reversible" and can be mounted either way up. The result is a difference in handlebar height of approximately 15 to 35mm, depending on the stem length.

Fitting the handlebar stem (continued)

4 If this does not provide a suitable handlebar height, you can consider stems that deviate from the classic angles. A 17-degree stem at a length of 120mm will raise the handlebars by approximately another 20mm, compared to a 6-degree stem turned upwards.

5 If changing, or adjusting, the stem, ensure that the brake and gear cable lengths allow for a longer, higher or reversed stem featuring a different angle. Make sure that the cable reaches between the front brake/gear lever and the cable stops on the frame are adequate. Move the handlebars from side-to-side in order to check that the rear brake/gear cables are long enough. You may need to fit new, longer cables.

6 When fitting the handlebars and the stem, liberally apply assembly paste. Apply to the clamping area on the fork steerer tube, to the stem clamp surfaces, as well as the clamping area on the handlebars, the stem handlebar clamp and the stem cover. When tightening the clamp bolts use the same process described previously for the seat post.

Fitting brake lever hoods/grips

1 Completely release the gearshift levers by repeatedly pushing the levers to move the chain to the smallest chain ring and smallest rear sprocket. This is the only way to fully release the tension from the cables in order to position them correctly for refitting.

2 Slide the grip backwards over the lever body and fold up the rear of the grip.

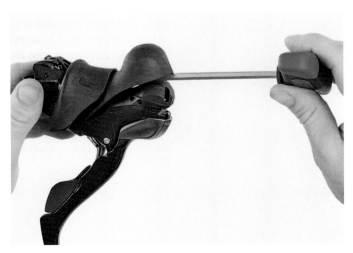

3 Slide a long hex key under the grip to engage with the lever clamp bolt. Turn the bolt anti-clockwise to release the clamp.

Fitting brake lever hoods/grips (continued)

4 When working with carbon components, liberally apply carbon assembly paste to the clamping surface on the handlebars, the clamp and the clamping surfaces of the lever assembly.

5 Slide the clamp on to the handlebars in the correct position (Campa clamps feature an arrow indicating the top of the clamp). Position the clamp and the grip at the exact position where the lever is to be fitted. Lightly tighten the clamp bolt using a hex key.

6 Modern handlebar shapes lend themselves to aligning the top part of the grip with the top of the handlebar top tube. For the finishing touch, align the two grips – this could be done using a straight edge or spirit level against the handlebar lower tubes.

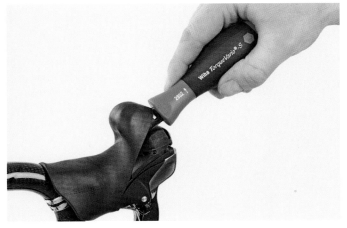

7 Tighten the clamp bolt to the manufacturer's specified torque using a torque wrench. If you do not know the specified torque, generally, the upper limit for carbon handlebars is 6 Nm. Do not exceed this torque.

8 Check for a tight fit by attempting to turn the grip on the handlebars. If the grip is not tight, gently increase the torque for the clamp bolts, but be careful, as if the screws are too tight, it is very easy to damage the handlebars. Try using a little more carbon paste or, if in doubt, choose a different type of handlebars altogether.

9 Pull the rubber cover to the front, thereby enabling access to the gear cable. Push the gear cable through the opening at the bottom part of the grip until it emerges through the top part.

Fitting brake lever hoods/grips (continued)

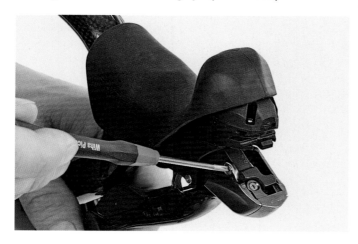

10 When working with the latest Shimano grips, you will need to remove a trim plate in order to insert the brake cable. Simply remove the securing screw and take off the trim plate. Similarly, if the trim plate is scratched during a fall, it can easily be replaced.

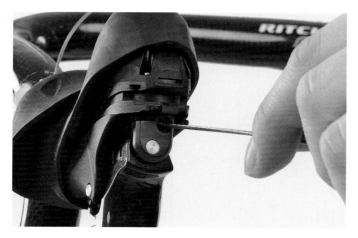

11 For all models, pull the brake lever and slide the brake cable through the opening (with the lever pulled). Pull the cable through until it reaches the opening of the grip. Slide the cable outers (the end without the end cap) on to the brake cables. When fitting Shimano and SRAM gear cable outers, you need to fit a metal end cap facing towards the grip. This is not the case with Campagnolo cables.

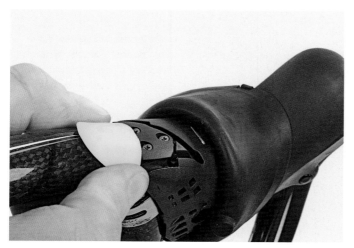

12 Route the cables as you would like them to run along the handlebars. Check whether a step, or edge, is present between the handlebars and the upper end of the grip. If necessary, cut-to-size pieces of handlebar tape or a silicone pad in order to cushion the step.

Adjusting the handlebar angle

1 Slacken the bolts at the front of the stem faceplate by two or three turns. You should now be able to turn the handlebars without any resistance. Position the handlebars so that they point slightly downwards. The upper edges of the brake levers (covered by the grips) should be horizontal and should not point downwards.

2 Once the handlebars are aligned, check that they are still aligned centrally in relation to the faceplate. Most handlebars have alignment marks for this purpose, which should be visible on both sides of the stem. Once the handlebars are correctly positioned, tighten the faceplate screws evenly top and bottom.

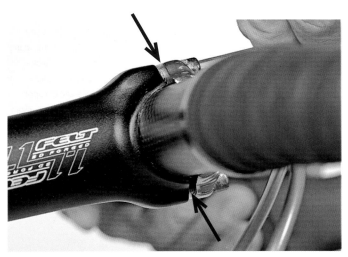

3 The gaps between the stem faceplate and the stem, at the top and bottom, should be equal. Tighten the clamp bolts. If a torque-setting range is specified, start at the lower end. If the stem faceplate has four clamp bolts, tighten them in a diagonal sequence. Once the bolts have been tightened, attempt to turn the handlebars downwards using heavy pressure. If the handlebars move, increase the torque on the clamp bolts, taking care not to overtighten them. If this does not work, degrease the handlebars and the stem, and apply carbon assembly paste.

Adjusting the handlebar angle (continued)

4 If you have a threadless fork steerer tube, you can only adjust the handlebar height using spacer rings between the upper headset bearings and the stem. Slacken the stem clamp bolts until the stem can be turned slightly on the steerer tube – usually slackening the bolts by two or three turns will be enough. Completely remove the top expander bolt and end cap. Note that once the expander bolt has been removed, the fork will be loose, and if the bike is suspended, the fork might suddenly drop out of the frame!

5 Take a look at the position of the stem in relation to the steerer tube. The upper edge of the steerer tube should always be positioned approximately 2–3mm below the upper edge of the stem, otherwise it is not possible to adjust the headset.

6 Pull the stem off the steerer tube. You can now swap the spacer rings from below the stem to above, and vice versa. The order of the spacers is not important, but don't add or remove any spacers (the overall 'pack height' must remain the same), and place at least one thin spacer below the stem in order to prevent it from pressing directly on the upper headset bearing.

7 Slide the stem on the steerer tube. Fit the stem end cap and refit and lightly tighten the top expander bolt. Lift the front wheel until the wheel spins freely, and check that the steerer tube/forks turn freely from left to right. Tighten the expander bolt gradually until you feel an initial resistance.

Useful tip

Numerous spacers above the stem do not look very appealing. Instead, have the fork shortened once you have established your riding position.

8 Rest the front wheel on the ground, and apply the front brake. Place some weight on the saddle, and push the bike forwards and backwards with one hand, checking with your other hand whether there is any play between the steerer tube/forks and the frame. If there is any noticeable play, I means that there is still play in the headset bearings. If necessary, tighten the expander bolt a little more, then check that the steerer tube/forks still turn freely. Repeat this procedure until there is minimal play in the headset bearings, but the tube/forks still turn freely.

9 When you are happy that the headset bearings are correctly adjusted, align the stem straight ahead and evenly tighten the clamp bolts. Tighten the clamp bolts to the manufacturer's specified torque. On completion, check that the stem is secure, and does not turn in relation to the steerer tube – you can do this by holding the front wheel between your knees and trying to turn the handlebars from side to side.

Fitting shoe cleats

1 Stand in a relaxed and comfortable position, paying attention to the natural position of your feet, since this is the foot position to aim for when your shoes are engaged with the pedals. Most people find that their heels point slightly in towards each other and their feet adopt an open 'V' shape with toes pointing slightly outwards.

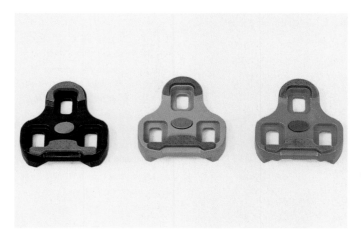

2 It is down to your own personal preference whether you prefer your feet to be firmly fixed in one position in the pedal, or whether you prefer some sideways flexibility (the ability to move your heels). Look offers cleats featuring 0 degrees (black), 4.5 degrees (grey) and 9 degrees (red) of heel movement. Shimano also offers a fixed version (red) and a flexible one (yellow). Time cleats all have a degree of flexibility built in.

3 All these cleat systems fix to the shoes in the same way, using the three-hole Look standard pattern. When fitting cleats, always ensure that each cleat sits flush with the curvature of the sole of the shoe. If there is a gap between the sole and the cleat, the cleat may deform in use, which can cause problems engaging and releasing from the pedal.

4 Lay the main body of the cleat in position on the sole of the shoe, then fit the screw plates, making sure that they are positioned to allow the screws to fit easily and engage with the threads in the shoes. Tighten the screws two or three turns – ideally using your fingers. The screws should provide no resistance during this process.

5 Initially, position the cleat so that the securing screws are in the middle of the elongated holes in the screw plates. Use a set-square positioned against the rear edge of the cleat so that you can clearly see the angle of the cleat relative to the shoe. Adjust this angle to suit your own preference, bearing in mind your natural foot position when standing, as mentioned previously.

6 If you ride with your heels turned heavily inwards, you should position the shoe towards the outside of the pedal in the area where the ball of the foot is. This gives more flexibility for the heel. Therefore, in this case, the cleats should be positioned towards the inside edge of the shoe. When you are happy that the cleats are correctly positioned, progressively tighten the screws, ideally to the specified torque.

Fitting shoe cleats (continued)

7 Once all the cleat screws are tight, working on each pedal in turn, lock your shoe into the pedal and check that neither your heel nor your ankle make contact with the pedal crank.

8 Check that your foot position is comfortable, and also make sure that the ball of your foot is in a central position above the pedal-spindle axis. If adjustment is required, loosen the cleat once again and re-align as necessary.

9 In order to check that the cleat position is the same for both shoes, hold the soles of the shoes against each other, as shown. When the cleats are held flush with each other, the shoe heels should meet exactly.

Speedplay cleats

1 If you have Speedplay-compatible shoes, with the appropriate special holes in the soles, it is possible to mount Speedplay cleats directly on to the sole. If you have Look-compatible shoes, you can still fit Speedplay cleats using a stainless-steel adaptor plate. If you currently have Look-type cleats fitted, first remove them, taking care not to lose the small components.

2 When fitting Speedplay cleats to Look-compatible shoes, first fit the adaptor plate to the sole of the shoe, checking for any gap between the adaptor plate and the sole. Use the various adaptor pieces and wedges provided in the Speedplay mounting kit to eliminate any gap between the plate and the sole of the shoe. Work from the front to the rear of the plate. The plate must not be able to move on the sole of the shoe.

3 The Speedplay Zero model cleat enables you to set large angles of freeplay (heel movement). Each cleat has two adjuster screws positioned on the outside edge of the shoe. The front screw adjusts the 'inwards' freeplay inwards, towards the pedal crank, and the rear screw adjusts the 'outwards' freeplay. Bear in mind that if you opt for a large amount of 'outwards' freeplay, you will need to twist your foot through a significant angle to release your shoe from the pedal.

Tyres, tubes and valves

If breakdown statistics existed for road bikes, the flat-tyre phenomenon would be in first place by a large margin.

There are many possible causes for tyre damage; problems often originate internally in the system comprising the tyre, inner tube, rim tape and wheel rim.

The interaction of these four components is complex, as they have to meet multiple and partially contradictory requirements. The wheel/tyre combination needs to be as lightweight and aerodynamic as possible, roll smoothly, provide good grip on the road surface, have good shock absorption and on top of this should be robust and long-lasting.

The most important factor in avoiding flat tyres is ensuring correct tyre pressure. If the tyre is not pumped up firmly enough, a puncture can be an imminent threat when riding over road imperfections at fast speed, the inner tube getting squeezed between tyre and rim tape. This is typically indicated by two small oblong holes in the inner tube the width of the wheel rim – also known as a 'snake bite'. Therefore, checking the tyre pressure before every ride – ideally using a track pump with a pressure gauge – is a must. Frame pumps or mini-pumps are less suitable, as it is more difficult to achieve the required pressure, and the gauges on these pumps are often inaccurate. The tyre size and the weight of the rider determine the ideal tyre pressure.

Generally, the following rule-of-thumb can be applied: optimum pressure (bar) is rider's body weight (kg) divided by ten. For example, a rider weighing 65kg should aim for a tyre pressure of 6.5bar (95psi). Lighter riders can achieve a good compromise by staying slightly below the maximum pressure specified on the tyre wall by the tyre manufacturer – perhaps by one or two bar. However, if the tyre pressure is less than 5bar, the puncture risk increases. Heavier riders should take advantage of the maximum possible specified pressure. Pumping up tyres beyond the recommended limit does not offer any benefits, as it does not make them roll more smoothly. Instead, comfort will suffer and the risk of the tyre coming off the rim increases.

Layering information

In order to protect against exterior damage, there should be as many layers of canvas under the tyre tread as possible. Three canvas layers are standard, but the protection improves if another one or two layers of nylon mesh or Kevlar fabric are added. The term Kevlar, however, can be misleading. It often denotes the foldable version of a tyre which, instead of wire bracing, contains bracing made from Kevlar. In most cases, using this material also means that the tyre is around 50g lighter.

Inner tubes come in various different types of material, but butyl (rubber), which can easily be recognised by its black colour, is the best compromise, due to its well-balanced properties. The inner tube size must be compatible with the tyre size, otherwise there is the risk that the tube could be damaged while fitting, or may become overinflated to achieve the correct tyre pressure, therefore becoming prone to punctures. A vast range of inner tubes is available, from different manufacturers and in different price ranges, featuring different-strength tyre walls and different valve lengths. Standard tubes weigh around 100g; lighter tubes, weighing less than 80g, are generally more prone to punctures. When buying tubes, pay attention to the valve length, especially if your bike is fitted with aero wheel rims. If your wheels require tubes with long-reach valves, and your tyre repair kit contains a tube with a short valve, you may be forced to call it a day if you suffer a puncture and you don't succeed in repairing the tube.

Rim tape provides protection for the tube, keeping the delicate tube away from spokes, nipples and the sharp edges of the rim. Fabric tape, secured with paste, is a tried and tested option. Plastic 'endless' tape also works well, but only if it has the same width as the base of the rim. Rim tape made from rubber or insulating tape is not suitable for road-bike tyres!

Have you practised yet?

In order not to be caught unawares while out on a ride, it is advisable to practise removing the tyre and changing the tube at home – and also when the tyres are in perfect condition. At the same time, you can check the base of the rim for sharp-edged areas, as well as checking that the rim tape is correctly positioned. These are two important details, which, unfortunately, are often overlooked by manufacturers.

A too large and sharp-edged valve hole in the rim cut out the valve from the inner tube.

This inner tube was mounted on a smooth rim without rim tape and has burst where the valve reinforcement meets the valve.

Tools and materials
Tyre levers, pump, file, screwdriver, rim tape, insulating tape, valve extensions

Removing and refitting a wheel

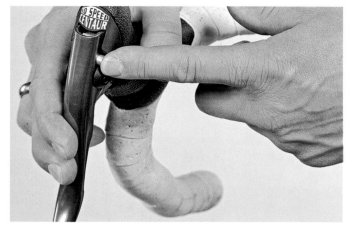

1 First, release the brake calliper, so that the brake pads clear the tyre. With Campagnolo brakes, use the small locking pin in the Ergopower shift/brake lever for this purpose. Pull lightly on the brake lever and push the pin from the inboard end of the lever outwards.

2 If you are a Shimano rider, pull the release lever (situated on the brake calliper) upwards, so that the brake pads clear the tyre.

3 To remove the wheel, pull the quick-release hub lever while simultaneously supporting your hand with your thumb.

Front wheel

1 When removing the front wheel, loosen the nut on the opposite side to the quick-release lever by a few turns in order for the hub spindle to slide from the dropout in the fork.

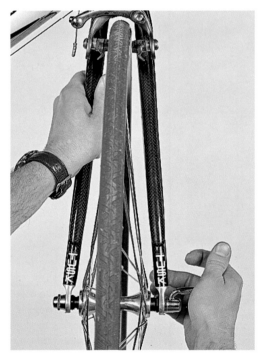

2 When refitting a front wheel, position yourself in front of the bike, hold the fork still, and position the fork dropouts over the hub spindle. The quick release lever should be on your right. Tighten the quick-release hub nut a little, until the lever provides considerable resistance when it is pushed closed, and check that the wheel rim is positioned in the middle of the fork. Check that the wheel is secure, then refit the locking pin, or push down the brake lever, as appropriate, to bring the brake pads back into position.

Hints

- Practising works wonders! Have a go at removing and refitting the wheel even if it is not an emergency.
- The clue is in the term 'quick release' – they should clamp securely, as well as being positioned to quickly gain access.
- Whenever refitting wheels, check the brakes before continuing the ride. Do not forget to lock the brake's quick release mechanism.

Wrong

Right

Rear wheel (front-facing dropouts)

1 Before opening the quick release lever, shift the chain to the smallest sprocket and the smallest chain ring – this is the best way to ensure that the chain does not get in the way while you are removing and refitting a wheel. Racing cyclists do this on the move, by the way, since it saves time!

2 Open the quick-release lever. Hold the frame at the seat post or at the top at the seat stays and lift up the rear wheel. Lightly tap the wheel from above and towards the front of the bike. The wheel should slide out of the dropouts and can then be removed from the chain.

3 In order to fit the rear wheel, position yourself behind the bike and to the side and grip the left seat stay. Lift the frame sufficiently that you can lift the rear wheel into position, hooking the chain onto the smallest sprocket.

4 Grip the rear derailleur at its front edge and, using your thumb, push on the derailleur cage in order to extend the mechanism to allow the wheel hub spindle to slide up into the dropouts. Keep hold of the frame and pull the wheel spindle fully into the dropouts. Check that the wheel rim is positioned centrally between the rear seat stays, then lock the wheel and the brake quick-release mechanisms.

Rear wheel (rear-facing dropouts)

1 If the dropouts face towards the rear, it is easier to remove the rear wheel with the bike suspended from a work stand. While on a ride, it is useful to lean the bike saddle against a fence or a wall. Operate the shift mechanism to move the chain to the smallest sprocket, and open the brake and wheel quick-release levers. Hold the rear end of the bike and pull the wheel backwards out of the dropouts, then guide the hub spindle forwards and downwards past the rear derailleur.

2 If this procedure does not work in one smooth movement, rest the wheel on the floor and grip the rear derailleur at the front of the mechanism. Use your thumb to push down on the derailleur cage, extending the mechanism against the spring tension. This should create a gap, through which the hub spindle, including quick release nut, can pass if you push the wheel from behind, for example using your knee.

3 When refitting, extend the rear derailleur against the spring tension, as described in step 2, and position the chain on the smallest sprocket. It is important to prevent the derailleur mechanism from moving inwards towards the centre of the frame. Hold the rear wheel between your knees, and guide the frame, first forwards, then downwards and lastly backwards again, enabling the hub spindle to slide fully into the dropouts. Check that the wheel rim is positioned centrally between the rear seat stays, then lock the wheel and brake quick-release mechanisms.

Removing the tyre and inner tube

1 Unscrew the valve cap, slacken the valve nut (at the top of the valve) and push the valve pin until all the air has escaped from the tube. Push together the sides of the tyre casing around the entire wheel circumference so that the tyre is resting against the lowest point of the base of the rim.

2 Slide a tyre lever under the tyre beside the valve. When working on the rear wheel, work on the opposite side to the cassette – this way you can avoid injury if you hand slips. The blunt side of the lever must point towards the tube. Lever the tyre over the side of the rim before inserting the second tyre lever approximately 10cm away from the first. Lever the side of the tyre over the rim as before.

Hints

- The best way to avoid punctures is to ensure that the tyre pressures are correct. Check the pressures once a week.
- Many punctures occur because of problems originating inside the wheel/tyre, for example when rim tape slides and exposes the sharp edges of the spoke holes.
- When fitting tyres, use plastic tyre levers to avoid damaging the tube and tyre.

3 Hold the first lever tight and slide the second lever under the side of the tyre around the entire circumference. If you have difficulty moving the second lever, pull it out, and try refitting a further 10cm away from the first lever. Pull the tube out sideways, but leave the valve in position in the rim: this way you will find the damaged area of the tube more easily.

Fitting a new inner tube

4 Inflate the old, punctured, tube (with the valve still in the rim), and place the pumped-up tube near your ear. You will hear a hiss as air escapes from the location of the damage. If the hole is on the side of the tube facing the rim, faulty rim tape, a ridge on the rim or a splinter introduced during manufacture may have caused the damage. If the hole is on the side facing the road, a sharp-edged object is likely to have punctured the tyre. Two oblong holes on the side of the tube suggest that it has been pinched due to shock-loading, or under-inflation. Remove the damaged tube.

5 Pump up the replacement tube slightly until it adopts a round shape. Check that there are no foreign objects (thorns, metal slivers, etc) on the inside of the tyre wall. To minimise the chance of dirt getting inside the tyre, do not rest the rim on the floor any longer but on your shoes instead. Place the valve into the valve hole, and slide the tube into the tyre, working on both sides. Do not stretch, bend or fold the tube during this process.

6 Once the tube is neatly positioned in the tyre, press the tyre's side wall over the braking surface of the rim, using your fingers. Start opposite the valve and evenly work your way along both sides.

Fitting the tyre

7 Slide the tube into the tyre evenly, taking care not to crush the tube. When you get to the point where 20 to 30cm are left, rest the rim on the tips of your toes, with the valve at the top of the rim, pointing down.

8 Using both hands, pull the tyre downwards in the direction of the valve using a reasonable amount of force. Hold the tyre on the rim in this position and support the wheel in your groin area. Push the side of the tyre fully on to the rim.

9 If you cannot manage this by hand, check that the tube is positioned fully inside the tyre, as a precautionary measure. Then fit two tyre levers with the rounded sides facing the tube. Using both levers, lift the tyre over the rim flange. If this does not work, the tyre is presumably too small for your rim. Try a tyre from a different manufacturer.

Fitting the tyre (continued)

10 Lightly push the valve into the tyre. This should release the tube from under the wheel rim if you trapped it during fitting. Pump up the tube just enough that it still has room to move around slightly inside the tyre.

11 Slide the tyre back and forth from the edge of the rim around its entire circumference, and inspect it to check that the tube is not trapped anywhere between the tyre and the rim. Pump up the tyre fully once you are satisfied all is well. The maximum recommended tyre pressure is specified on the label, or moulded into the rubber sidewall of the tyre.

12 Finally, lightly spin the wheel, while keeping an eye on the raised bead at the bottom of the tyre sidewall. The top of the bead should be an even distance from the rim edge all the way around the tyre. If this is not so, deflate the tyre again and check the positioning of the tyre, as the likely cause is an inner tube trapped between the tyre and rim, which is rapidly likely to lead to a puncture.

Useful tips for tubeless tyres

1 When using tubeless tyres, the valve nut needs to be checked for tightness on a regular basis. If the valve nut is loose, the tyre will quickly lose air.

2 When fitting tubeless tyres, the tyre and the rim flanges must be lubricated on both sides using a special solution. Generally, washing up liquid diluted with water will do the job. This is the only way the tyre will slip into its seat and become airtight.

3 Fitting tubeless tyres is similar to fitting clincher tyres. With the valve fitted, push the tyre down on to the base of the rim as far as possible, using your hands and no tools. Align the tyre evenly around its circumference.

Useful tips for tubeless tyres (continued)

4 Using a mini pump to pump up tubeless tyres when mounting for the first time is a fruitless exercise. Your chances are not much better using a track pump, but it is possible to use a track pump for topping up the air when tubeless tyres have lost a little pressure. Only an electric compressor, or possibly a CO_2 cartridge, can deliver the sudden rise in pressure required to settle the tyre onto the base of the rim neatly and tightly to provide an airtight seal. There will be a clearly audible bang as the tyre settles on to the rim.

5 **Useful tip:** Use sealant/repair spray to inflate the tyre when out and about. This should guarantee that you can repair a punctured tubeless tyre. Slide the nozzle on to the valve. Hold the bottle so that the nozzle sits neatly on the valve, then depress the plunger (if applicable) and wait for approximately two minutes for the spray to fill the tyre. Pull the can away from the valve with one sudden, smooth movement. Ride the bike for a few miles to distribute the latex spray evenly inside the tyre.

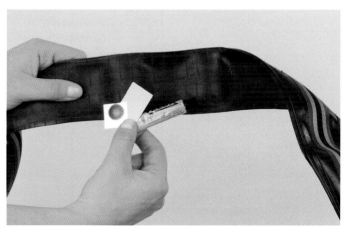

6 When repairing holes on the inside face of the tyre, you can use the same method as used for a tube. If you have used repair spray previously, this will have to be thoroughly removed from the damaged area, otherwise the patch will not adhere properly and will not last. Re-inflate the tyre afterwards using the repair spray. If the damage is only minor, it should be sufficient to use the spray only. Practise using the spray at home, as it is not quite as easy as you may think to handle!

Gluing on tubular tyres – preparation

1 New wheel rims can be very smooth, carbon rims even come clear lacquered, in order to provide a good surface for the glue to stick to, the surface should be roughened slightly using emery cloth. Clean any grease or oil from the base of the rim using a suitable solvent. Allow any solvent residue to evaporate fully before fitting the tyres.

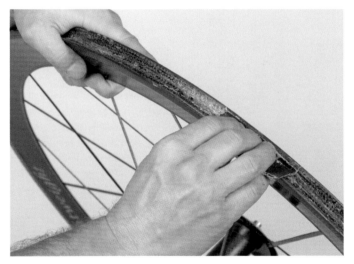

2 If the rims have had tyres glued to them previously, any remaining glue residue must be even and smooth. If it is not, use emery cloth to provide an even surface.

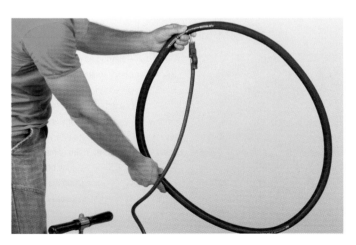

3 Lightly inflate the tyre and insert the valve through the hole in the rim. Starting at the valve, push the tyre evenly into the wheel rim – as described on page 64, step 6 onwards.

Gluing on tubular tyres - preparation (continued)

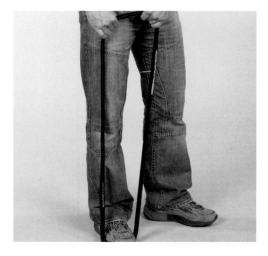

4 If it is not possible to slide the tyre on to the rim or if it requires a lot of force, you may have to stretch the tyre first, as shown, in order to ensure a good fit. After stretching, check again whether the tyre can be slid on to the rim without excessive force.

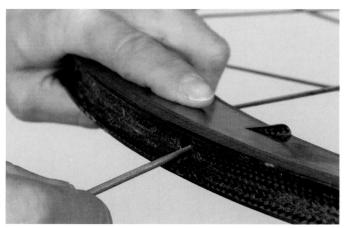

5 With the tyre fitted, spin the wheel and check that it runs true. For example, if there is a ridge on the valve hole on the inside of the rim, this can lift the valve and tyre, and lead to vertical run-out of the tyre and vibration. Gently remove any burrs from the valve hole, or reduce any ridge using a round file. Insert the file from the tyre side of the rim, and not from the hub side, otherwise the fibres of the carbon weave might fray. Seal the filed area afterwards with clear varnish or superglue.

6 Check the valve length. The valve stem must protrude from the rim by at least 10 to 15mm in order for the pump nozzle to fit.

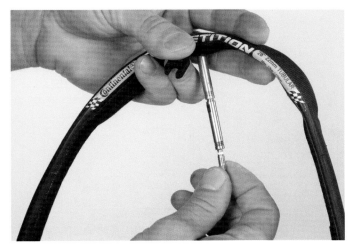

7 If necessary, fit a valve extension. Extensions are supplied by many wheel manufacturers as part of the package. If the original valve end (containing the valve pin) can be removed, screw-on extensions are the best choice for extending the valve. When using valve extensions which are screwed on to the end of the valve, either the knurled valve nut needs to be left unscrewed, or the extension unscrewed to access the valve nut every time the tyre is inflated.

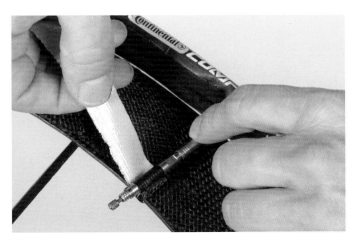

8 In order to prevent annoying rattles as the wheel rotates, wrap a few layers of tape around the valve stem where it contacts the valve hole in the rim. However, make sure that the valve still fits through the hole!

9 Before fitting the tyres, ideally, 'park' the prepared new tyres, fully inflated, fitted to the rims for a few days. This will make final fitting easier.

Gluing on the tyre

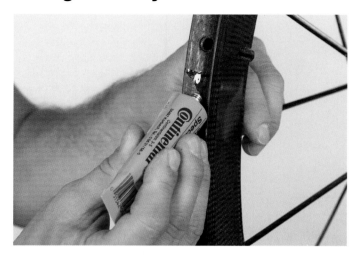

1 The easiest way to apply the glue is by fitting the wheel to a wheel jig, or mounting it in an old fork clamped in a vice. If you are experienced at applying the glue, you will be able to apply it straight from the tube. Otherwise a paintbrush with stiff bristles will make the job easier.

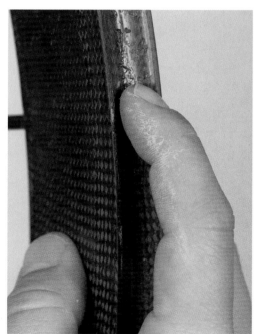

2 With liquid tyre glue, you will need to apply several layers to create a good adhesive bed. Spread the tyre glue evenly, and as thinly as possible, around almost the entire circumference of the rim. Leave an area of five to ten centimetres opposite the valve free from glue to make it easier to remove the tyre again at a later date.

3 Allow the glue to dry until it loses its sticky liquid feel when pressing a finger against it. This can take a few hours.

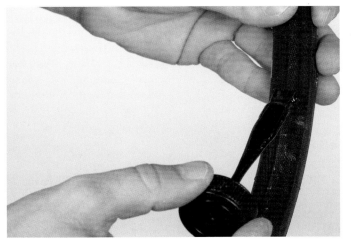

4 Once the glue has lost its stickiness, using the same procedure, add another two thin films of glue to the rim, and finally one layer to the protective strip on the tyre (again, leave an area opposite the valve free from glue). Leave the rim and the tyre overnight.

5 Before fitting the tyre, apply a final layer of glue to the rim. Also apply a layer of glue to the protective tape on the tyre. After allowing the glue to dry briefly, rest the rim on the ground, with the valve hole facing upwards. The section of the rim opposite the valve should be free of glue, so the surface of the tyre and rim should be clean at that point. Lightly inflate the tyre until it just begins to take its shape, then fit the valve through the valve hole and press it firmly against the rim.

6 Try to avoid the sides of the tyre touching the bed of adhesive, otherwise your tyre will look smudgy right away. Using both hands, grasp the tyre approximately 10 to 15cm to the right and left of the valve, then stretch it hard between your hands and pull hard downwards on to the rim.

Gluing on the tyre (continued)

7 Work the tyre progressively into the base of the rim. By twisting the tyre slightly, it should work evenly into the rim. Continue like this at a steady pace until you have about 20cm left to go at the bottom of the wheel.

8 Repeat the procedure to stretch the tyre, again starting at the valve, pulling the tyre down until you reach the section yet to be fitted. Keeping the tyre taut by holding your fingers against the rim and your thumbs on the tyre, brace the wheel against your hips. Heave the tyre with both thumbs into the base of the rim.

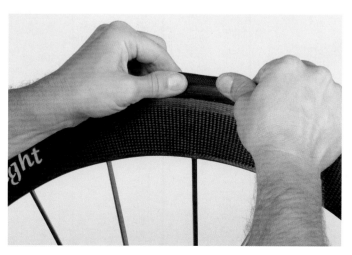

9 When the tyre is fully seated in the rim, it needs to be centred, as it will rarely run true straight away. Clamp the wheel in the jig or forks again and spin it. If the tyre does not run true, or if it moves visibly to the side at any point, lift it up at that exact point, twist it a little to true it, and release it again.

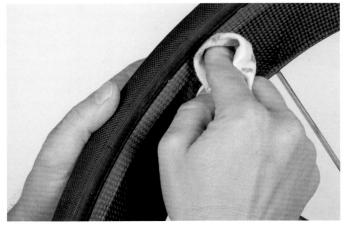

10 Using cleaning alcohol, wipe any adhesive residues off the side of the rim and the tyre sidewall. Once you are happy that the tyre runs true and smoothly, remove the wheel from the jig or forks and inflate the tyre to approximately half its recommended pressure.

11 Lean your hands on the ends of the hub spindle and quick release levers and roll the wheel a few metres along the ground. As you roll the wheel, vary the pressure between the vertical and an angle on either side of the wheel. Roll the wheel vertically and also for a few turns in an inclined position. Make a final check to ensure that the tyre still runs true, then inflate it to the maximum recommended pressure. Wait at least eight hours, and ideally a whole day, before riding on the wheel for the first time.

Removing a glued-on tyre

Starting opposite the valve (in the area which you left free from glue), apply pressure to the tyre until a gap opens between the tyre and rim. Slide a plastic tyre lever into this gap and use it to lever off the tyre.

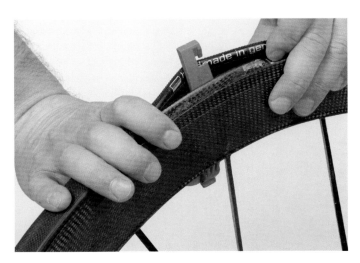

Valves

1 Most riders know by now that the valve on a road-bike tyre needs to be unscrewed in order to be able to inflate the tyre. However, often it proves difficult, if not impossible to inflate the tyre because the valve pin sticks, preventing air from passing freely.

2 Valve nuts have both advantages and disadvantages. In cases where the valve hole in the rim matches the valve diameter, they are essentially unnecessary. Valve nuts can be helpful when inflating a tyre, as they prevent the valve from being pushed inwards, often damaging the tube in the process. You can always screw on a valve nut when inflating the tyre, and unscrew it again afterwards.

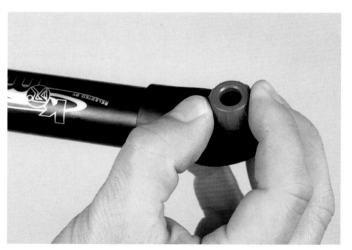

3 If the air escapes from the sides of the valve when operating the pump, the rubber sealing ring in the pump head is likely to be worn or damaged. This can usually be overcome by turning the seal retaining ring on the pump head, as this squeezes the pump rubber and ensures that the hole in the rubber fits around the valve body tightly again.

4 Pump rubbers inevitably wear out, and generally they can be replaced on most hand and track pumps. Try to make sure that you have one or two spare rubbers just in case you need them.

5 Punctures are often caused when the tube is squeezed while riding over a bump or a pothole. The best way to avoid this is to check regularly that the tyre pressures are correct. As mentioned previously, the rule of thumb here is tyre pressure equals rider's weight (plus any extra luggage) – divided by 10 – in bar. The maximum recommended tyre pressure is usually printed on the type label or on the side of the tyre by the manufacturer.

6 Slight air loss is not necessarily a sign of a damaged tube. Often air can escape if the valve pin is not seated correctly. Check whether the valve is fully seated using a suitable valve tool, or small pliers if necessary, but be careful not to bend the valve pin!

Valves (continued)

7 If a foreign object hits the valve, it is very easy for the valve pin to become damaged. This particular problem often occurs during transport when the wheels are removed. Always use valve caps when transporting your bike parts.

8 Some rims feature valve holes that are larger than the diameter of the valve, causing the valve to sit at an angle. Do not pull on the valve to straighten it. Instead, release the air from the tyre, and remove one side of the tyre from the rim. Re-align the tube, making sure the valve is straight, then refit the tyre.

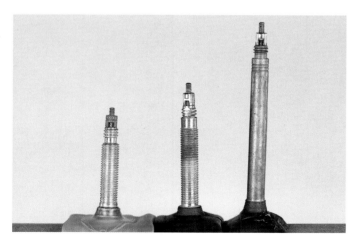

9 Rims vary considerably in terms of sidewall thickness. Almost all manufacturers now offer tubes with different-length valves, ranging from 35 to 65mm. In order to be able to inflate the tyre properly, the valve should protrude roughly 20mm from the rim (when measured to the end of the valve pin). If necessary, valve extensions can be fitted to most tubes, and some tubular tyres.

10 The best solution (on the right) is an extension that screws in between the end of the valve (valve pin) and valve body. With this type of extension, the valve can be operated in the usual way when inflating the tyre. Less practical (left), are extension tubes that are screwed on to the end of the valve. These do not generally seal as well, and the knurled section of the valve pin can become stuck in the extension tube – if this happens, push the knurled nut in using a spoke or similar.

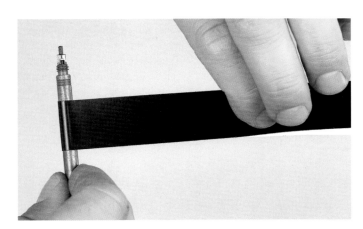

11 The long valves fitted to aero rims have a tendency to move against the edge of the hole in the rim with each rotation of the wheel, thus causing a tedious rattling noise. To prevent this, apply two to three layers of insulating tape around the valve body where it touches the rim.

Checking rim tape

1 Deflate the tyres and remove them. Check that the rim tape sits evenly in the base of the rim and covers all the spoke holes. It should sit evenly in the base of the rim, without riding up on to the side of the rim.

2 The rim tape should be free from tears, splits and folds. Tape made from polypropylene, in particular, may become brittle. Often the valve may be too big for the hole in the tape or the profile of the tape may be wrong. Replace any tape that is faulty.

3 If the valve is not correctly aligned in the rim, do not try to pull it into place. Deflate the tyre, remove one side of the tyre from the rim, and align the tube. In addition, rim tape with a hole that fits snugly around the valve can be used to keep the valve in a vertical position.

Checking new rims

1 Tube valves can literally be punched out by sharp-edged valve holes in the rim. On new rims, remove any burrs from the edge of the valve hole using a file or a sufficiently large drill, and smooth the area with emery cloth.

2 Check new rims thoroughly. Remove any burrs or sharp edges using a triangular scraper or a countersink bit. Also check any join lines or manufacturing marks on the rim, as sharp edges are capable of cutting open the side of the tube or tyre.

3 On rims with no spoke holes, apply a strip of rim tape approximately 10cm long above the valve bore. This will protect the tube and its valve area from the sharp edge of the valve bore.

Continuous rim tape

1 Plastic tape must match the width of the base of the rim exactly. The spoke holes will then be covered, and the tape will sit evenly on the rim. The tape's valve hole must not be larger than that of the rim.

2 Using a screwdriver, push the edge of the continuous tape in to the valve hole in order to prevent it slipping. Starting at the valve, lay the tape in place. Push it completely into the base of the rim. Take care not to bend or fold the tape.

3 It is possible that if the tape is too narrow, or too long, it may slide during fitting. Check that the tape is perfectly seated, and tight, before fitting the tyre.

Glued-on rim tape

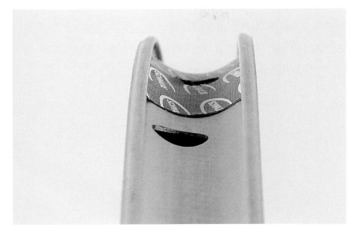

1 Rim tape that is glued on must exactly match the width of the base of the rim. Therefore, check the width of the tape before you glue it on to the clean and grease-free rim.

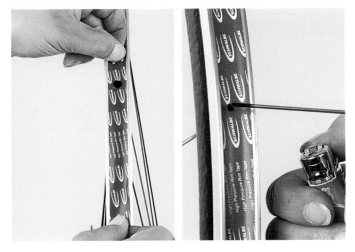

2 Start at the valve. Fit the tape tightly, and make sure that it is centred on the base of the rim. The ends of the tape should overlap by at least one to two centimetres. The overlap – ie the double-layer taping – in this area is particularly important if the pre-cut valve hole is too large. Where there is double-layer taping, you need to cut the valve hole yourself. Do not cut into tape, as the hole may tear. The best way to make the hole in the tape is to heat up an old spoke and melt a hole.

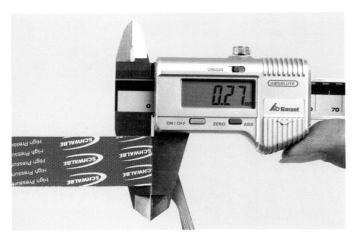

3 Always begin fitting the tyre to the opposite side of the rim to the valve, then work towards the valve evenly from both sides. If it is difficult to fit the tyre by hand, and you have to use tyre levers long before you reach the valve, this may be a sign that the tyre and the rim are not compatible, or that the rim tape is too thick. In this case, fit thinner tape.

Puncture repair tricks

Nothing is easier than repairing a puncture, right? One would have thought so… The difficulty is getting the details right. This chapter describes the right way to do it and how to prevent punctures in the first place.

Find the position of the hole, and inspect the damage before repairing the tyre. Remove any foreign objects in the tyre casing, or more damage will be caused as soon as you start riding.

Repairing the tyre using patches and liquid adhesive ('rubber solution') is occasionally referred to as 'vulcanisation'. However, this is incorrect, since vulcanisation usually requires the presence of heat and sulphur. The adhesive simply sticks the patch to the tube in the conventional way.

When buying a repair kit, you should make sure that the patches match the size of the tube. Small and very thin patches are available specially for road bikes. These are barely noticeable when fitted, and therefore the tyre will run evenly. Cleanliness is vital when repairing punctures. Some tubes and tyres are supplied pre-treated with talc or silicone, and the tubes themselves can have a very shiny finish, but any of these factors can reduce the effectiveness of glued repairs. The area to be repaired should always be roughened using emery paper or similar, and very shiny tubes should be cleaned using an alchohol-based cleaner.

Impatience when repairing a puncture is counterproductive, as the glue needs time to dry.

Bear in mind that a puncture repair kit will not last forever, as glue deteriorates and the patches can become brittle over time. Ideally, replace the repair kit every year.

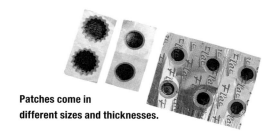

Patches come in different sizes and thicknesses.

Hints

- Tyre deflation is usually caused by something simple, for example the valve pin may not be screwed tightly into the valve.
- Check the glue in your puncture repair kit on a regular basis. Even an unopened tube may dry up after one or two years!!

Repairing an inner tube

1 This patch is too big. It would fit all the way around the tube. Only the smallest patches are suitable for road-bike tubes.

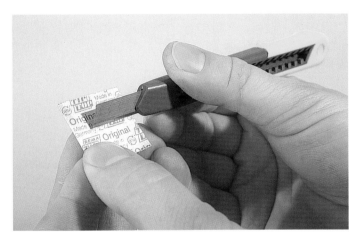

2 When using older patches, scratch the aluminium carrier foil a little and warm up the patch with your hand. The foil will then come off more easily.

3 Align the patch over the hole and mark the edges of the carrier foil on the tube. Cut the carrier foil to a square shape – this will make alignment easier when fitting the patch later on.

Repairing an inner tube (continued)

4 Thoroughly roughen the area to which the patch will be applied. Do not touch this area afterwards, and try to keep everything clean.

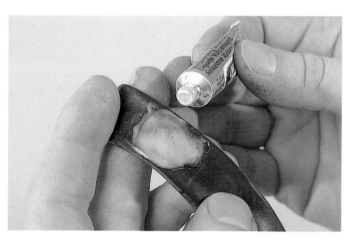

5 Apply glue to the tube, and spread evenly using the tube.

6 Leave the glue to dry for around five minutes, until the glue has a satin finish, at which point the patch can be applied.

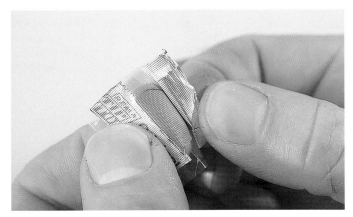

7 When using older patches (as shown in the image), separate the foil from the patch. When working with newer patches, read the instructions – these are usually removed from the aluminium foil complete with the transparent carrier film.

8 Align the patch with the marks made on the tube previously. Press the patch on to the tube as hard as possible. When out on a ride, a pump can serve as a support underneath the tube. If you're at home, you could put the tube on a table and roll a round object over the patch. Pressure should be applied from the centre of the patch outwards. The amount of pressure applied when fitting the patch will determine the quality of the repair.

9 To complete the repair, the patch needs to be folded to tear the perforations of the carrier film. If the carrier film is removed starting from the centre of the patch, there is very little risk of the patch lifting from the tube. The carrier film must be removed in order for the solvents to evaporate. Ideally, allow the glue to dry overnight before fitting the tube. When the repair is dry, pump up the tube and check for air leaks.

Wheels

Wheels have always featured cutting-edge technology – nowadays they define the overall look of the bike almost more than the shape and colour of the frame. This chapter explains the complex technology of wheels, and offers useful assembly and maintenance tips.

It used to be straightforward. If you wanted a first-class wheel, you went to an experienced wheel builder and asked them to build you a wheel to your specfications, hand-built with carefully chosen spokes, hubs and rims. Their quality used to depend on the skills of the wheel builder and your choice of components.

In the mid-'90s, the French manufacturer Mavic – then the market leader as far as high-quality rims were concerned – started to produce complete wheels built from compatible hubs, spokes and rims. Other manufacturers also discovered that it was more profitable to offer complete wheels than individual components. The result was that the market for so-called 'system' wheels grew rapidly. At the same time, the choice of available rims for hand-built wheels shrank.

Nowadays, Mavic still offers a handful of classic rim models such as the Open Pro rim, but modern, machined rims with widely spaced spoke holes, as used in the Ksyrium series, are as difficult to obtain 'off-the-shelf' as their matching hubs or spokes – unless they are bought as replacement parts.

Yet there are still good arguments in favour of hand-built wheels, for example their unique look, certain performance features and, often, their cheaper price. Conventional hubs are offered by many manufacturers, and there is no shortage of different spoke types either. There is a narrower choice of rims, but if you search hard, you will find everything you need – from 16-hole carbon rims to ceramic-coated aluminium rims. On-line wheel suppliers often offer a vast range of component choices. They also often provide detailed information on the weight of rims and spokes. What is not so obvious is the performance of the wheels in terms of rigidity or aerodynamics.

In a comparative test carried out in spring 2011, *Tour* magazine compared several hand-built wheels to 'system' wheels, testing many different criteria – including a comprehensive aerodynamics test in the wind tunnel. The result was surprising, in that a hand-built wheel came out on top, particularly in the aerodynamics category. This shows what is possible when you choose the individual parts carefully.

In other areas, however, the system wheels demonstrated their strengths. A typical wheel of this type, like the Ksyrium SR by Mavic, achieves the best back-wheel ridigity with a low overall weight of 1449g, these wheels featuring a mixture of compatible hubs, rims and three different spoke types (aluminium blade, aluminium round and carbon). Overall, this test clearly demonstrated that system wheels come out on top more frequently in the rigidity and weight categories – provided the designers developed the wheel as an actual system.

Nevertheless, the hand-built wheels featured in this test provided many arguments in favour of bespoke wheels. Hand-built wheels can look fantastic, and some spokes even feature their own unique sound! Front wheels with silver spokes have become a rarity in times where black is used everywhere. Exclusive spokes can help to make a unique wheel which stands out from the crowd. Additionally, carefully chosen wheel components can be chosen to cater for special requirements, such as their suitability for all-weather or rainy conditions. Ceramic-coated rims, for example, provide consistent braking and avoid the aluminium residue produced when braking in wet conditions, which often ends up smeared over the entire bike. Not only does the bike remain clean, but ceramic-coated rims are much harder wearing than their pure aluminium counterparts.

If you look at overall performance, hand-built wheels can certainly hold their own. Excellent aerodynamics, rigidity and braking performance can all be achieved using hand-built wheels, but system wheels often provide the ideal combination of low weight and rigidity. Riders who know exactly what they want, or who prefer a bespoke solution, will be able to order wheels to match the colour scheme of their bike. In terms of warranty, hand-built wheels will usually win over system wheels. Some wheel builders may offer warranties of five years or more against spoke breakage, and mass-production manufacturers offering system wheels cannot compete with this.

Text: Robert Kühnen

Hints

- Aerodynamics is a big issue with wheels. Air resistance is more significant than rolling resistance from around 10mph onwards. From around 15mph, it accounts for two-thirds of the total resistance.
- The rigidity of the rear wheel is particularly noticeable when riding out of the saddle, especially when sprinting. The rigidity of the front wheel is more noticeable when steering at high speed. Stiffer wheels are usually more resilient and will usually last longer.

Tools and materials

Spoke key, wheel jig, possibly socket spanners or wheel-specific centering tools, sprocket puller, chain whip, cone spanner, Allen key or brand-specific bearing tools and soft faced mallet, masking tape or insulating tape, bearing grease, and possibly specialist freewheel grease.

Checking play

1 Check the wheel-bearing play with the bicycle suspended on a stand. Hold the frame or fork in one hand and move the rim slightly backwards and forwards using your other hand. If the rim tilts slightly sideways, the bearing play needs to be adjusted. However, before getting your tools out, check that the wheel quick-release mechanism is tight.

2 Bearings that have been adjusted too tightly, with insufficient freeplay, can suffer serious damage. If the spindle does not appear to rotate freely, with minimal freeplay, you need to remove the wheel and remove the quick release mechanism. Turn the hub spindle and check that it runs true.

3 On some hubs, the bearing play tightens up when the quick-release lever is pushed into place to secure the wheel, which can result in the bearings running too tightly. To compensate for this, place washers or nuts the same thickness as the fork blades on the quick-release spindle either side of the hub, then push the quick-release lever closed to tension the hub.

Adjusting the hub bearings

1 Traditionally, hubs are equipped with conical bearing cones. Working on the opposite side of the hub to the freewheel, fit a cone spanner of the correct size for the cone flats and hold it tight, bracing your fingers against a couple of spokes. Fit the second spanner to the cone locknut in such a position that when slackening the locknut the second spanner moves away from the first spanner, avoiding a collision between your hands and the spokes! This is important, as in most cases the locknut will suddenly slacken.

2 Hold on to the spindle on the opposite side of the hub, and use a cone spanner to gradually tighten the cone that you have just slackened, tightening by quarter-turn increments at the most. Keep turning the spindle and checking the amount of play in the bearings. If the bearings cannot be adjusted using this method because the cone does not run true on the spindle, the spindle will need to be straightened or renewed.

3 If the degree of play is satisfactory and the bearings are running smoothly, clamp the opposite end of the spindle in a vice, fit the cone spanner to the cone and tighten the locknut using the second cone spanner. Be careful not to hurt your fingers – you can pull the spanners towards each other by hand. Fit the quick release components. With the quick release tensioned, turn the wheel. If the bearings have tightened up, you will need to repeat the procedure.

4 If you intend to clean and grease the hub bearings, you need to unscrew the locknut and the bearing cone completely from the spindle. When removing them, make a careful note of the exact sequence and orientation of any washers and spacers. These ensure the correct alignment of the wheel.

5 Turn the wheel over and hold the hub body over the worktop, or over a small container to catch the bearings. Pull the spindle slightly upwards so that the ball bearings fall out, taking care not to lose any. Collect the ball bearings before pulling out the spindle completely and removing the remaining ball bearings from the other side. It is important to keep them separate since the ball bearings on each side of the hub may have different diameters.

6 Clean the spindle, cones and ball bearings using an absorbent cloth. It is normally not necessary to use a special degreaser. Apply fresh grease to all bearing surfaces. Insert the ball bearings on the same side of the spindle from which you removed them. Carefully slide in the spindle to prevent the ball bearings from falling out. Insert the ball bearings on the remaining side and adjust the hub as described in steps 2 and 3.

Hub bearings on Mavic hubs

1 On Mavic wheels, adjusting the bearings is child's play, as the wheel can remain in the frame. You need a special cone spanner which is usually included when you buy the wheels.

2 Engage the four pins on the cone spanner with the holes in the cone, and carefully turn it clockwise, in small steps. Constantly check the play. Once you are happy with the adjustment, remove the wheel from the frame, and check the play again.

3 If you feel that the bearings are too tight, slacken the cone again by one turn (using the Mavic cone spanner). Remove the wheel and remove the quick release components. Working on the side of the spindle with the adjustable cone, give the spindle a light tap using a soft-faced mallet. This will release the preloaded tension. Afterwards, re-adjust the play as described previously.

Hub bearings on system wheels

1 The bearings on many system wheels can be adjusted with the wheels mounted in the frame – as an example, see the Zipp wheel shown. To carry out adjustment, unscrew the adjusting ring pinch-bolt using a hex socket. Slacken the pinch-bolt by one or two turns.

2 Tighten the adjusting ring a little, either by hand or using a cone spanner. Keep checking the play. Tighten the pinch-bolt again in order to lock the adjusting ring. If the adjustment has not changed, try repeating the procedure on the other side of the hub. If the hub has been overtightened, the procedure as described in step 3 opposite should solve the problem.

Hub bearings on DT Swiss hubs

1 Many manufacturers use DT Swiss hubs for their wheels. They are easily recognisable, as they require hardly any tools to remove and refit the components. Just remove the wheel and the quick release, and remove the cassette.

2 Remove all dirt and grease from the sprocket teeth, and check the condition of the freehub. Some cassettes can dig into the freehub and leave grooves and bulges. Any damage should be carefully smoothed out using a file. Afterwards, refit the cassette.

3 Fit the freehub side of the spindle into a vice. Grip the wheel with both hands, at the spokes close to the hub, and pull upwards. This should release the end cap from the spindle.

4 Pull off the freehub and remove the two rings, the two springs and the guide sleeve from the hub body. Take note of the alignment and the order of the components to ensure correct refitting. The smaller-diameter end of the spring faces towards the lock washers.

5 Clean all the components, and the inside of the hub using an absorbent cloth. If necessary, brush off any old lubricant from the surfaces using an old toothbrush. Apply specialist DT Swiss grease evenly to all parts of the freewheel and the inside of the hub.

6 Too much grease can result in the freewheel not working properly. Reassemble the parts in the reverse order to that noted during dismantling, and refit the freewheel body by gently twisting it. You will notice the end cap clicking into position. Check the operation of the freewheel by turning it, checking that it locks when attempting to rotate it clockwise.

Build your own wheel

Despite the trend towards system wheels, there are still arguments in favour of the hand-built wheel. These include their long lifespan, competitive price and good component availability. This chapter provides a complete DIY wheel-building guide.

As mentioned in the previous chapter, hand-built wheels can be individually fine-tuned according to the rider's weight and the wheel's intended use. Lightweight riders can assemble very lightweight rims with only a few spokes without running into problems; quick-starting heavyweights will need sturdy rims with a high profile and probably a 36-spokes hub.

Before you can select spokes of the correct length, you need to determine the brand and type of wheel rim to use, as well as the hub. Your bike dealer is then often in a position to tell you, based on experience, how long the spokes need to be. If this is not the case, you will have to measure the hub and rim and then calculate the spoke length using a formula that requires some mathematical knowledge.

It is easier to determine the spoke length by means of appropriate computer programs. Spoke manufacturer DT Swiss, for example, offers a good program on its website (www.dt-swiss.com). If you know how to use the spreadsheet software Excel, you could use it in combination with a simple spreadsheet table offered on T&S's website (www.tunds.com).

The spoke manufacturer Sapim also provides a small program on its website (www.sapim.be) for calculating spoke lengths. Whizz Wheels is a company producing bespoke wheels. On their website, www.whizz-wheels.de, you can find a wheel calculator which allows you to combine various wheel components in a very simple way. At the initial planning stage, for example, you can determine how much the completed wheel set will weigh.

When you finally get down to assembling and truing the wheel, it is important to understand the mechanical context. It is a widespread misunderstanding to think that the spokes support the rim – something they can't actually do. Spokes can be bent and bowed when you grip their ends and squeeze them together. Using a newly spoked wheel as an example, you can easily simulate the movements and forces that occur during the ride, yet are almost invisible.

In its initial state, the hub is suspended relatively centrally to the rim. If you put downward weight on the hub, the upper spokes will tighten up and the lower ones will initially be under less stress, but then they will bend. Hence the lower spokes can hardly contribute anything in terms of bearing the weight carried by the hub. When the wheel is tensioned, any load that the lower spokes cannot deal with will be redistributed among the remaining spokes, adding to the load they have to bear. As a wheel turns, each spoke is progressively loaded one after the other, and at the lower part of the wheel, where the rim is slightly flattened due to the road surface, the load will be less.

To keep the hub central, each spoke must be equally pretensioned – so each spoke pulls outwards on the hub with the same force. This means that a properly pretensioned wheel is capable of bearing enormous weights in a radial direction. It is less able to deal with lateral loads, however. To demonstrate this, have a look at the loosely spoked wheel once again. If you push the hub to the side, you will see how the spokes on one side take up the tension. However, there is a relatively large amount of travel before tension builds up. This is due to the fact that the spokes run at an angle between the hub and the rim. The more acute the angle is, the less resistance the spoke can produce to side loads.

The situation at the rear wheel is even more complicated than that at the front. Firstly, the spokes on the cassette (drive) side are clearly positioned much more steeply than those on the opposite side. If the spoke tension is the same on both sides, the rim will run in a central position in relation to the hub flanges, but not in relation to the entire hub – as a result of the weaker lateral forces caused by the acute angle. For this reason, the spokes on the drive side need to have considerably more tension.

The second challenge for the rear wheel comes from the motive forces that the spokes must transmit from the hub to the rim. If you turn the example wheel's hub as the chain would do, the 'cable' spokes that point almost tangentially towards the rear are tensioned, while the remaining spokes are free from tension. As a general rule, motive forces oscillate, resulting in this cyclical load being superimposed on the varying stresses produced by continuous rotation of the wheel.

As you can see, the spoke tension is at least as important for a long-lasting wheel as the quality of the individual components. With

Hints

- Some professional wheel builders weld the spokes together at the intersection points. The argument in favour of doing this is a more even load distribution around the wheel; however, the large amount of work involved and the fact that it is difficult to repair are definite downsides.
- Braided spokes are no more than an aesthetic touch. There are no technical reasons for doing this.

every rotation of the wheel, each spoke is stressed and then released. The spoke can only cope with this alternating load for a decent length of time if the basic tension is so high that the spoke itself is still tensioned even in the worst-case scenario, when it is stressed to its limit. Spoke tension being too low is the number one spoke killer.

For a better overview, count the spokes first before laying them out, ready to be fitted. This is particularly important for the rear wheel, as the spoke lengths for the drive side (right) and the opposite side (left) differ by a few millimetres.

Tools

Twist drill or countersink bit, spoke key, truing stand or truing gauge, perhaps socket wrench or wheel-specific truing tools, truing block, spoke tension gauge, possibly threadlock adhesive

Planning and choosing spokes

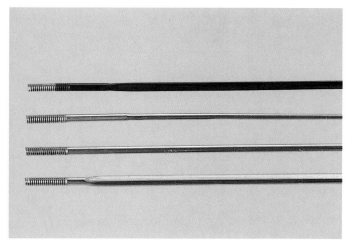

1 Plain-gauge spokes are perhaps the poorest choice. Double-butted spokes – ie, spokes whose middle area has been thinned out – can deal better with loads, as this gives the spokes more elasticity and decreases the risk of breakage at the nipple thread and hub flange. These spokes are also lighter. Blade (or 'aero') spokes are generally only used in combination with stiff, deep-profile rims and a reduced number of spokes.

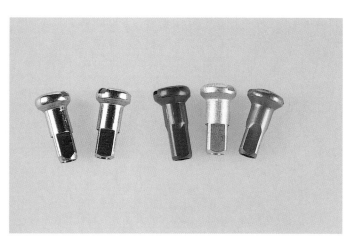

2 Brass nipples are the most common choice, as they offer the best compromise between weight, longevity and rigidity. Note that nipples for 1.8mm spokes can look similar to those for 2.0mm spokes. Aluminium nipples are nice and colourful and are a few grammes lighter, but they also have disadvantages, as they tend to seize up inside the rim hole and on the spoke thread, and the flats are more easily damaged.

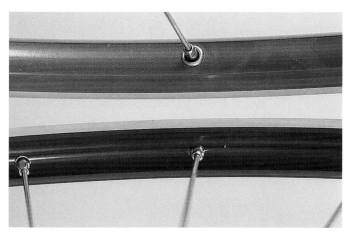

3 Eyelets in the rim holes increase the weight by a few grammes as well, but they do simplify the spoking and truing process. This is particularly true when you need to re-true at a later stage – you will learn to appreciate their advantages. Aluminium nipples in combination with rims without reinforced nipple holes are the least suitable combination for daily use.

Planning and choosing spokes (continued)

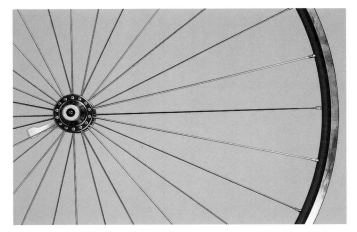

4 You can spoke front wheels radially (without overlapping the spokes) for cosmetic and aerodynamic reasons. This type of spoking is not really suitable for rear wheels, since the motive forces cannot be transmitted continuously. It is common to use the three-cross pattern for rear wheels. Before you think about spoking the front wheel radially, you should check with the hub manufacturer whether their product is suited to this option. Some manufacturers offer special radial hubs as part of their range.

5 Spokes typically have a diameter of 2.0mm. There are also spokes featuring 1.8mm diameter. Although the 1.8mm spokes are lighter in weight, they have a lower tensile strength and tend not to seat as accurately in the hub flange – the photo shows this by means of the greater clearance between the spoke and the hole. 2.34mm spokes seat perfectly in standard hub bores and are a good choice for very high loads.

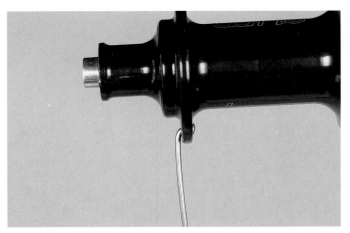

6 Not all spokes sit closely against the hub flange – yet this is essential for long life. Reasons for a poor fit are the spoke curvatures being too shallow and/or the hub flanges being too thin. In this case, try different spokes.

7 If the spoke and the hub do not match very well, washers fitted between the spoke flange and the inside of the hub will improve the situation. These prevent harmful movement between the hub and the flange.

8 Check whether the holes in the rim have been deburred. Often you will still find machining residue. Deburr the holes by hand using a twist drill or a special countersink bit. In the case of eyeleted rims you only need to deburr to the necessary depth to prevent the inner tube from being damaged in this area at a later stage.

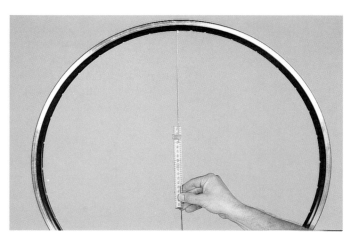

9 Here's a useful technique for determining the rim diameter. Shorten two spokes (cut at the hub end) to exactly 250mm. Screw nipples on to the spokes so that the spoke end is flush with the slot in the nipple. Insert the two spokes in two holes in the rim that are opposite each other, and measure the distance between the hub ends of the spokes using a rule. This figure plus the spoke lengths (500mm) will give you the figure for the diameter in question.

Measuring and checking

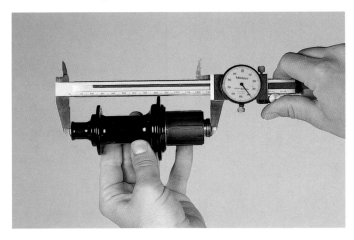

10 Measure the widths on the hubs between the faces that contact the forks, ensuring that any relevant locknuts or sleeves are in place. On road bikes, the nominal dimension for the back-wheel hub is 130mm; hubs for mountain bikes are 5mm wider. The back-wheel hub has an asymmetrical design, whereas the front-wheel hub is symmetrical. On the front wheel, the distance between the clamping surfaces is 100mm.

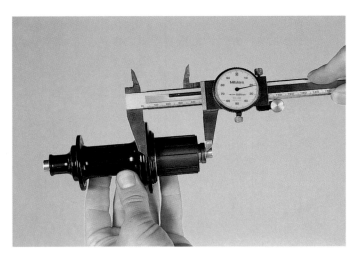

11 On both sides of the hub, measure the distance from the centre of the flange to the outside of the clamping surface on the spindle. For precise results, you should place the vernier calliper on the flange so that the calliper body is parallel to the spindle. Align the calliper jaw with the outer face of the clamping surface, then read the measurement.

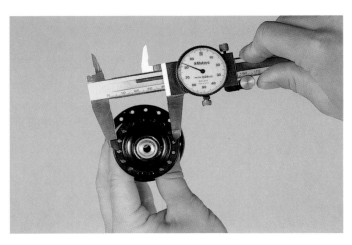

12 Measure the diameter of the hole circle on the hub flange. Measure between the centres of two opposite holes. Take the measurement on both sides of the hub, as the flange diameters may vary.

Fitting and tensioning spokes

13 If you are using aluminium nipples, grease them on the outside, particularly at the rounded head contact surface. Another option is to lubricate the eyelets or the nipple contact surfaces on the rim using a paintbrush.

14 On the cassette (drive) side, insert a spoke into every second hub hole, starting from the outside and working your way inwards. When spoking the front wheel, start on the side on which the lettering ends. This ensures that the lettering will be legible by the rider at a later stage, and it will usually match the alignment on the rear wheel hub.

15 Turn the rim so that the lettering on the label faces towards you and is legible. Take the first spoke and insert it into the hole to the left of the valve hole. If you are aiming for perfect aesthetics, you should take the second or third spoke that was threaded through, in the direction of the wheel rotation, after the lettering on the hub body. Using this method guarantees that the lettering on the hub will align with the valve when the wheel is completed.

Fitting and tensioning spokes (continued)

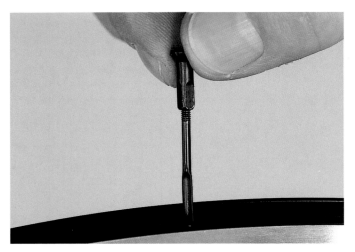

16 Take a nipple and screw it on to the spoke by hand until only about four of the spoke's threads protrude at the nipple's bottom end.

17 Take the next spoke and insert this in the fourth hole in the rim, counting from the first. This means that three holes remain spoke-free between the two spokes. Once you have inserted spokes in this way around the entire circumference of the wheel, starting at the drive side, check once again that there is an even distance between the spokes.

18 Turn the wheel around, ensuring that the opposite side of the hub is now facing you. Insert the spokes from the outside towards the inside of the hub, starting on the opposite side to the holes that are already used on the drive side, and offset clockwise by one hole. Again, every second hole should remain spoke-free.

19 Take the spoke that points towards the valve hole, which is offset slightly clockwise in relation to the opposite spoke. Then guide it into the rim hole on the right of the valve hole – ie, the valve hole should be between the two spokes, with no other spoke holes between the two spokes 'empty'. Again, use your fingers to fit a nipple until only four threads are showing.

20 Continue inserting the spokes in a clockwise direction, ensuring that you insert a spoke to the right of every already fitted spoke on the opposite side of the hub. When you have inserted the last spoke, you should have pairs of spokes fitted around the entire circumference of the wheel. Insert the remaining spokes from the drive-side through the flange, this time starting from the inside to the outside. When you finish this process and all the spokes have been inserted, turn the wheel around once again, making sure that the drive side is now facing you.

21 Turn the hub body in the opposite direction to that of the wheel's later direction of rotation. The spoke on the left-hand side of the valve hole should be 'turned away' from the valve hole! This will prevent the spoke sitting on the inside of the hub flange from becoming the driving spoke. The spokes fitted in the next step – the spokes fitted to the sprocket side of the hub in step 20 – can withstand the oscillating motive forces better in the long run.

Fitting and tensioning spokes (continued)

22 Take one of the spokes not yet fitted to the rim, and place it over two of the already fitted spokes in an anti-clockwise direction. Then thread the spoke through below the third spoke. Insert the spoke thread through the hole to the left of the two already fitted spokes. This will leave a gap next to the following spoke in an anti-clockwise direction.

23 Since from now on you will no longer be able to use your fingers to screw on the nipples, fit and tighten them using a screwdriver. Sometimes it is easier to insert the nipple in the rim first and use the screwdriver to hold it, before then inserting the spoke.

24 On rims with deep profiles, a spoke tool is a tried and tested means of fitting the nipples into the rim. DT Swiss or Sapim are two companies that offer these tools. The tools clamp the nipples, and prevent them from slipping and disappearing into the rim cavity.

25 Continue using this 'twice over, once under' method for all the spokes on the drive side. Once the final spoke has been fitted to the rim with the nipple, check again that the spoke pattern is correct. Check that for each set of three spokes, between the spokes on the drive side there is always one spoke from the opposite side of the hub!

26 Now insert the spokes for the opposite side through the flange, again working from the inside of the hub out. Here, a certain degree of resistance may need to be overcome, however this will be kept to a minimum if you bend the spokes slightly between the hub flanges, ensuring that they 'dive' into the flange's spoke hole more or less straight.

27 Turn the wheel around yet again, so that that drive side is facing away from you. Continue applying the 'twice over, once under' method on this side, too, as previously. However, on this side the spokes are crossed in a clockwise direction. It should not be possible to fit a spoke to the wrong hole at this stage, as there is not much choice left.

Fitting and tensioning spokes (continued)

28 Finish off by inserting the last available spoke into the rim and fitting its nipple. Before the truing process, check the spoke pattern once again, and ensure that no spokes have been missed out by accident and that all are correctly positioned.

29 When you have verified that everything is in the correct position, the spokes to the left and right side of the valve should be lined up parallel to each other. You will then be able to place the pump on to the valve without running into problems.

30 A second and much more important point to consider is that the 'cable' spokes' curvatures need to be located on the outside on both sides, so that their flanges point towards each other.

Truing the wheel

1 Select the correct spoke key: tools with small contact surfaces or too-large jaw gap can easily damage the nipple's flats, rounding them off. Good spoke keys grip the nipple on three sides, and contact the nipple over a considerable area while fitting it closely.

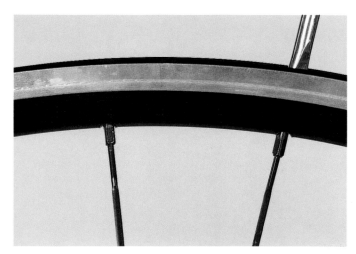

2 On a newly spoked wheel with loose spokes you now have a final opportunity to grease the nipples' rim-contact area. Grease reduces friction, which means that the nipples will not become embedded in the rim. Continue turning the nipple on to the spoke threads with a screwdriver or special tool, until the nipple's bottom edge just about covers the last thread.

3 You can speed the process up by using a special spoke key, where the tool fits snugly in the spoke hole in the rim to hold the tool while you are quickly screwing in the nipple.

Truing the wheel (continued)

4 Once all the nipples have been screwed in evenly, use the spoke key to gradually apply tension. Apply the 'right-hand' rule to find the direction of rotation – also if you need to re-tighten later on. Grip the spoke with your right hand so that your thumb points towards the spoke – then the remaining fingers on your hand will point in the direction in which you need to turn the nipple to tighten the spoke. Since the nipple is held by the rim, the spoke is tightened.

5 With the wheel fitted to a truing jig, fit the spoke key to one of the spokes next to the valve hole, and turn the nipple half a turn. Then fit the key to the next spoke along and increase the tension here as well. Continue this method for all the spokes until you have reached the valve hole again. If the spokes are still loose, you need to go around once more. Never apply more than half-a-turn of tension at a time!

6 When all the spokes have been lightly tensioned, check the rim's position in relation to the hub. If you carried out all the steps according to the instructions, the front wheel should be fine. This does not apply to the rear wheel, however, as here the rim will be positioned asymmetrically in relation to the hub. If you have a professional truing stand, you will notice the incorrect positioning immediately (see photo with rim misaligned to the right).

7 If your truing stand does not provide the facility to check the rim offset from the hub, you will need a centring gauge. Follow the manufacturer's instructions, and place the gauge on the rim, adjusting the measuring probe to the hub.

8 Turn the wheel over and fit the gauge to the opposite side of the hub. You will notice a gap on the measuring probe or on the rim, which indicates the discrepancy. Do not be surprised if the difference is quite large; this measurement is a 'zero-offset' figure. The actual offset is half the visible difference. In the scenario shown in the picture, you would need to move the rim away from the drive side.

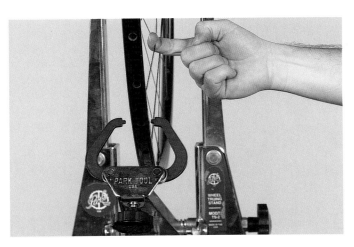

9 Use one finger to pull a single spoke to the outside and observe the gap that is created between the rim and the pointer on the truing stand. If the rim is moving in the desired direction, you have identified the side whose spokes you need to tension further.

Truing the wheel (continued)

10 Another option is to push two spokes together on one side. This also causes the rim to move to the side. Again, start on the spoke located directly at the valve hole and then, one by one, tension the nipples on every second spoke, applying a quarter turn each time.

11 Tension the spokes so that the rim is centred in relation to the hub, and the spokes feel taut all around the wheel.

12 Grip two opposing pairs of spokes approximately at their middle and push them together. Do this all the way around the wheel. This has the effect of pulling the spoke flanges into the hub and the nipples into the rim, while settling the spokes.

13 Even slight decreases in spoke tension will result in the wheel no longer running true. Adjust the pointer on the truing stand so that the rim just touches it when you turn the wheel. The lateral run-out is largest where the rim comes closest to the pointer. This is the place where further tensioning is required – on the opposite side of the hub, and applying quarter-turns at the most. To prevent blade spokes from twisting, counterhold them with a slotted block.

14 If the wheel runs true, without any significant lateral run-out, reposition the truing stand's pointer below the rim in order to check radial run-out. Turn the wheel, observe the gap between the pointer and the rim, and look for the largest deviations. Some spokes do not run true at the connection to the hub, since this is where they have been ground. This type of radial run-out towards the hub is often minimal and cannot be remedied.

15 Push together the pair of spokes located where the rim gets closest to the pointer. It is important to observe that it is only by tensioning a spoke pair running to opposite sides of the hub that you can correct the radial run-out without introducing massive lateral run-out. Tension particularly carefully and in small steps. If the rim runs true, check again for radial and lateral run-out and adjust once more if necessary.

Truing the wheel (continued)

16 Place the hub on to a wooden block on a solid surface. Grip the rim with your hands on opposite sides and push it downwards. This will produce creaking noises, however the rim should only move slightly. Repeat this process all the way round the rim's circumference from both sides. If you re-check the radial and lateral run-out thoroughly afterwards, the spokes will barely need to settle any further during running in.

17 A dial gauge will make truing jobs easier. It can be mounted on the truing stand by means of a magnetic base. The gauge should be positioned with its dial roughly in the middle of its measuring range. Turn the wheel in the jig and look for the position that is roughly at the centre between the runouts to the left and right. Turn the adjusting ring on the dial gauge to zero the pointer. If you now move the wheel slowly, you will see the pointer move away from the zero position. Identify the spoke that causes the pointer to move, then adjust the tension in the spoke slightly. Keep turning the wheel and retensioning the spokes until the pointer eventually only moves by 0.2mm to each side at the most.

18 If you are an experienced wheel builder, you will have a natural feeling for how high the spoke tension needs to be. You can find out what an ideally tensioned wheel feels like by gently pressing spoke pairs together. You could also carry out the sound test, which give you an idea of the tension. Spoke tension gauges such as those offered by DT Swiss or Braun (see www.zentriboy.de) are much more precise.

19 Once everything is perfectly adjusted, and the wheel runs true, apply some liquid (medium-firm) thread-lock adhesive (eg, Sapim or DT Swiss products) to the threads of each spoke. Then spin the wheel. The adhesive will penetrate the gap between the spoke and nipple and dry off and harden. This will prevent the nipples from working loose.

Gearshift mechanism

Modern gearshift mechanisms offer a large number of gears. However, they are very sensitive to adjustment. This chapter explains how to adjust the gears on your road bike properly.

In the bike shop or during a test ride, it's easy to get very enthusiastic when you discover how perfectly modern road bikes operate and how easy they are to use. However, after a few rides on your new bike, the gears often start to operate less smoothly. The chain can become reluctant to switch to the next sprocket, and it might make rattling noises or even fall off the chainrings altogether when switching gears.

The cause of all this is the cables. Inner cables are prone to stretching, while the cable outers are not, which means that the cables effectively move out of adjustment. Fortunately, these minor faults can be remedied in a few minutes, provided you are familiar with how the gearshift mechanism works. On a bike gear system, it is at the lever where the act of engagement takes place; the rear derailleur only responds to the instructions transmitted by the cable. When the rider pulls the gear lever, the lever pulls in the cable and then releases it again when the push of a button switches down the gears. This causes the spring in the rear derailleur to move the chain on to a smaller sprocket. If the tension in the cable is too high, it will switch down to a smaller sprocket reluctantly, or not at all. The tension in the cable determines how the rear derailleur lines up with the sprockets, and the tension is adjusted via an adjusting screw.

The rear derailleur features three additional adjusting screws that normally need not be touched. Two of these limit the rear derailleur's range of movement towards and away from the wheel. They also ensure that the chain does not fall between the sprockets and the frame and that the rear derailleur does not get caught in the spokes. Both these problems could result in damage to your bike, and a suddenly locked wheel could even result in a fall. You should check these adjustment screws if your bike falls over, if you have a crash, or when fitting a different rear wheel.

In order to adjust the gearshift mechanism, you either need an assistant to help you lift the back wheel off the ground, or a workstand in which the bike can be suspended while still operating the drive mechanism.

If your adjustments are not successful, and you do not end up with smooth performance, you should check whether the external cables have been bent or are too long. Both these factors increase the friction between the cable inner and outer, and therefore they can affect gearchange performance. Gear cables which rub directly against the frame in the bottom-bracket area also produce unnecessary friction – over time, they dig themselves into the paint, resulting in metal rubbing on metal. The consequence of this is a loss of precision when switching gears.

After making any adjustments, always check that the switching mechanism is working properly when the bike is stationary. To do this, try switching through all the gears at different speeds. Afterwards, we recommend that you go on a test ride somewhere free of other vehicles, since potential problems will only show up when the bike is under load, for example when the frame is flexing slightly.

If you still cannot identify the cause of the problem, despite all your efforts, the last resort is to take the bike to a dealer. There are many more

potential reasons why the gearshift mechanism may not work properly. For example, the chain might be too short or too long, or the distance between the rear derailleur and the cassette could be wrong. Another possibility is a bent derailleur hanger, the bottom-bracket spindle might be too long, or the frame may have been incorrectly aligned.

Tools and materials
Hex keys, flat-bladed screwdriver or Phillips screwdriver

Adjusting the rear derailleur

1 Move the chain to the smallest chainring and the smallest sprocket until there is no more movement in the levers. The gear cables are then completely free from tension. Look at the rear derailleur from behind. Its guide pulley should now be positioned exactly below the smallest sprocket. The chain is then routed in a straight line. If this is not the case, you need to adjust the derailleur (outer stop) position using the limit screw.

2 The limit screws on rear derailleurs are often marked 'H' for high gear and 'L' for low gear. In this case the high gear stands for high transmission ratio (small sprocket). Turn the screw clockwise to move the rear derailleur towards the wheel and anti-clockwise to move it away from the wheel. Count the screw turns so that you can turn it back to its original position in case you turn the wrong screw and the rear derailleur does not move.

3 Check the inner stop. Turn the cranks slowly, and gently push the rear derailleur towards the inside until the chain has climbed on to the largest sprocket. It should not be possible to push the derailleur further inwards, otherwise the chain could get caught between the chainring and the spokes, or the derailleur cage might collide with the spokes. Both situations can lead to crashes, falls and major damage.

4 Adjust the travel on the rear derailleur by adjusting the second limit screw until the chain runs reliably on the largest sprocket. Keep turning the crank, and release the rear derailleur so that the chain runs back on to the smallest sprocket.

5 Screw in the cable tension adjustment screws completely at the rear derailleurs, and, where applicable, also at the cable guide on the frame or steerer tube (see photo no. 7 on the next page and no. 4 on page 125). The gear cable should not hang loosely, but should be slightly tensioned.

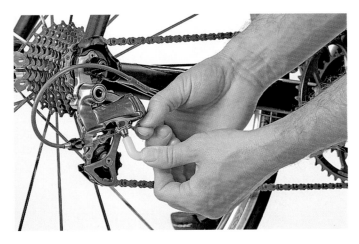

6 If this is not the case, slacken the cable clamp bolt on the rear derailleur, but do not remove it completely. While doing this, hold on tightly to the gear cable. With the cable under slight tension, tighten the clamp bolt, noting that the cable must still be positioned in the guide slot in the rear derailleur and in the bolt's washer. Then tighten the clamp bolt again.

Adjusting the rear derailleur (continued)

7 Now turn the cranks, and switch one gear higher. The chain should climb to the next sprocket immediately. If it does not, increase the cable tension slightly, then switch back to the smallest sprocket and unscrew the adjustment screw on the rear derailleur by half a turn anti-clockwise. Check the switching mechanism again. If the chain does not move, you need to turn the adjustment screw another half turn anti-clockwise.

8 If the chain does climb up to the next sprocket, switch back and check if it can also move down. When the chain is on the second or third sprocket, look at the rear derailleur from behind. The chain should run straight down from the sprocket on to the guide pulley; it should not rub against any of the neighbouring sprockets. If switching from the smallest to the next biggest sprocket runs smoothly, gradually switch through all the gears. When you get to the biggest sprocket, however, you should take care that the chain does not overshoot – this is a risk if the limit screw has not been adjusted correctly. When the chain is on the largest sprocket, check the inner stop position again by gently pushing the rear derailleur towards the spokes by hand and turning the wheel.

9 In order for the gearshift mechanism to function as well as possible, there should be one chain link of clearance between the derailleur top guide pulley and the sprocket at all times, and two links must be exposed between the sprocket teeth and the pulley as well. The rear derailleurs offered by Shimano and SRAM feature a screw for adjusting this clearance, which acts on the derailleur hanger. To check the set up, turn the cranks backwards, and check that the guide pulley does not touch the sprockets.

10 If there is still not enough clearance, you can shorten the chain by one link. To check the correct chain length, carefully switch to the largest chainring. With the chain running on the largest chainring and the smallest sprocket, the derailleur guide pulleys need to be aligned vertically one above the other.

11 The adjustment screws on Campagnolo rear derailleurs differ from those on Shimano and SRAM models. On Campagnolo components, the limit screws are positioned on the outside face of the mechanism. The rear screw sets the inner stop position, while the front screw sets the outer one.

12 On Campagnolo rear derailleurs, you can adjust the gap between the guide pulley and the sprockets by means of a screw located at the bottom of the derailleur, very near the guide pulley's axle.

Adjusting the front derailleur

1 Move the chain to the biggest sprocket and the smallest chainring. Check the alignment of the derailleur outer guide plate with the biggest chainring. There should be 1–3mm clearance between the outer face of the guide plate and the chain. The bottom edge of the plate should be positioned approximately 2mm above the chainring throughout. In addition, the outer guide plate should be parallel to the chainrings. Note that the teeth on modern chainrings are shaped differently in places, which can be misleading.

2 If one of these conditions is not met, you need to loosen the front derailleur clamp bolt by one to two turns and then adjust the position of the derailleur. Afterwards, retighten the clamp bolt and check the alignment again.

3 Move the chain to the smallest chainring, and check how the derailleur inner guide plate sits in relation to the chain. The chain should not rub, yet the clearance must be as small as possible. Adjust the clearance using the limit screw located on the inside of the derailleur. If this is difficult to access, swing the derailleur cage slightly outwards by hand. Then screw in the limit screw step by step.

4 The cable tensioning screw on the bottom tube or the steerer tube needs to be screwed in fully, and the gear lever released, before you can check whether the cable is correctly tensioned. It should only be possible to pull the cable a short distance away from the bottom tube before the front derailleur starts moving. If this is not the case, hold the front derailleur tight and unscrew the cable clamp screw. Tension the cable and tighten the clamp bolt, noting that the cable must still be positioned in the guide slot in the derailleur and in the bolt's washer. Switch to one of the centre sprockets at the rear.

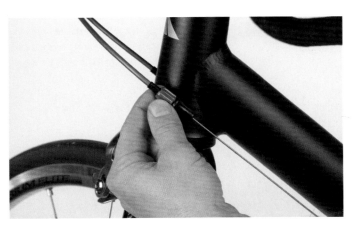

5 Move the chain to the biggest chainring. If the chain does not climb up, this is due to insufficient cable tension, or the fact that the limit screw has been screwed in too far. Tension the cable by turning the tensioning screw on the steerer tube or bottom tube by half a turn anti-clockwise. Try again to switch to the biggest chainring. Keep tensioning the cable for as long as is necessary until the chain switches over successfully.

6 Leave the chain on the biggest chainring and switch to the smallest sprocket at the rear. The clearance between the front derailleur and the chain must be as small as possible to prevent the chain from coming off. Shift to the smallest sprocket again and turn the limit screw in by a quarter turn. Then switch up to the largest sprocket again and turn the cranks. Repeat this as often as is required until the clearance is correct. Finally carry out a thorough check to ensure that everything is working correctly.

Special features of Campagnolo rear derailleurs

1 The most important adjustment is to the end stop which sets the extreme inner position. Slowly turn the cranks and push the rear derailleur inwards by hand. Turn the rear Phillips screw clockwise to move the derailleur towards the wheel. The front screw determines the outer-stop position.

2 To adjust the clearance between the top guide pulley and the sprocket teeth, use the adjusting screw on the underside of the derailleur.

3 Turn the screw to set the clearance. This can be difficult, as Campagnolo rear derailleurs have limited compatibility with derailleur hangers positioned a long way back. When adjusting the front derailleur, with the chain on the largest chainwheel, the derailleur inner guide plate should be parallel to the chain rings, with 1–2mm clearance between the outer guide plate and the chain.

Special features of SRAM derailleurs

1 Adjust the inner-stop position using the large upper adjusting screw. This aluminium screw will accept a 2.5mm hex key.

2 Adjust the distance between the upper guide pulley and the tips of the sprocket teeth using the 2.5mm hex key on the adjuster screw at the rear of the derailleur. Due to the roller cage's different pivot point, the clearance needs to be larger (6mm) than on Campagnolo and Shimano components.

3 The clearance between the outer guide plate and the chain should be 1 to 3 millimetres, with the chain on the largest chainring (not smallest chainring as shown here).

Special features of Shimano Dura-Ace 7900 derailleurs (1)

1 The Dura-Ace 7900 front derailleur no longer features fine adjustment for the clearance between the derailleur guide plate and the chain. The components are manufactured so that all gears can be switched without the chain rubbing against the guide plate. Although the chain should never run on the biggest chainring at the front and the biggest sprocket at the rear simultaneously, this position is necessary to make adjustments.

2 Adjust the cable tension at the cable end on the bottom tube or, depending on the individual model, by using the adjuster on the end of the cable outer. Adjust the cable so that the chain just no longer rubs against the front-derailleur inner plate.

3 Switch down from the biggest to the smallest chainring and then check the cable. The cable should have a generous amount of slack. Change gear a few times. In order to shift the chain to the biggest chainring, switch through all the positions on the lever until the chain engages with the biggest ring. If the lever tends to slip back and does not engage properly, the cable tension might be still too high.

Special features of Shimano Dura-Ace 7900 derailleurs (2)

1 The inner end stop position is set by the rear, bottom Phillips screw. In principle, this is the same method as used by Campagnolo and SRAM, but it has the advantage that it enables you to look at the guide pulley's position in relation to the sprocket directly from the rear while making the adjustment.

2 Switch to the smallest sprocket (not largest, as shown here) and turn the cranks. Turn the Phillips screw located in the dropout until the tips of the guide pulley's teeth no longer touch those of the sprocket.

3 What all manufacturers' models have in common is that the inner adjustment screw adjusts the inner stop. Switch to the smallest chainring. Then adjust the screw so that the chain just no longer rubs against the front derailleur's inner guide plate. The ideal clearance is 0.5mm or less.

Shimano Di2 groupsets

The advantages of the 'Di2' electronic groupset offered by Shimano in terms of shifting speed and precision are well known. Another benefit is that the components are very easy to fit. In this chapter, we show you the important steps.

The Di2 system has had a significant impact on the road-bike world, especially as it is now offered at a reasonable price for an increasing number of racing cyclists, as a variant of the Ultegra middle-class groupset. Technology fans desperately want it, but purists fear that, in the long run, the increasing use of electronic equipment may make the bike unnecessarily complicated, expensive and prone to faults. The electronic models differ from the mechanical groupsets by featuring different shift/brake levers as well as front and rear derailleurs with servo motors which are operated via the shift levers. The shifting method is identical to that of mechanical groupsets, however, the circuits and the forces involved in switching are kept to a minimum. A rechargeable battery supplies the power. This battery is secured on an aluminium bracket on the bottle-holder holes and sits below the bottle itself. Levers, battery and derailleurs are connected by means of a two-part cable harness, which is available in two versions and three lengths – both as an external cable, or as a version for installation inside the frame.

The electronic groupset is almost designed for routing the cables internally. The bike will look tidy, and the cables are protected against damage. In contrast with interior Bowden cables, which are susceptible to friction, the electric cables can be guided around a thousand corners without a problem – this is an ideal solution for time-trial bikes in particular. When fitted externally (which is very much the second-best solution), the cables are guided in self-adhesive cable channels, with the frame's cable guides remaining unused.

The performance of this system is simply stunning. The front derailleur, in particular, excels above all the other components, switching quickly, precisely and powerfully under all conditions. The electronically controlled front derailleur adjusts itself automatically so that the chain never drags. It even allows for extreme chain skew, although this is not advisable due to the poorer efficiency and higher wear and tear it entails. If you deliberately switch slightly further or less than required, the shifting mechanism is still secure, regardless of how quickly or how hard you pedal. The chain will never fall between the sprockets and the frame or the chainrings and bottom bracket.

The 7.4V lithium-ion battery is extremely reliable. A *TOUR* test produced the surprising result that the derailleur switches 15,000 times before the battery runs out of steam. And even when there is no power left at the front, the rear derailleur can still be switched through another 50 times before the power runs out altogether. This is a protective function determined by the control system. The rear derailleur will complete

Hints

- Fitting the cables is complicated, and choosing the right cable set depends on the bike type and frame. You can find several instruction manuals and parts lists on Shimano's website.
- When you have finished fitting, test ride the bike in a vehicle-free area and test the gearshifting mechanism.

roughly 20,000 switching operations, with 1,500 to 2,500 miles being the typical average riding distance reached.

A status indicator informs the rider how much charge is left in the battery in four stages. At 43 per cent capacity, a flashing green light is shown. At 12 per cent, this changes to a permanent red light. At 3.5 per cent you will see a flashing red light. This last warning almost always gives you enough time to get back home to recharge, even if you are on an extended ride. But you should really charge the battery when the permanent red light starts to show. Even a quick charging session of about 15 minutes should be enough in the event that you discover the low status only minutes before you are ready to go for a ride.

It takes a maximum of two hours for the empty battery to fully recharge. Longer charging will not improve its capacity. One of the downsides to the otherwise convincing overall concept is that there is no trickle-charging feature for maintaining the battery. To be fair, a worn-out battery can be replaced, of course, just as with any other rechargeable battery system.

Robert Kühnen

Tools
Allen key

Fitting wiring looms

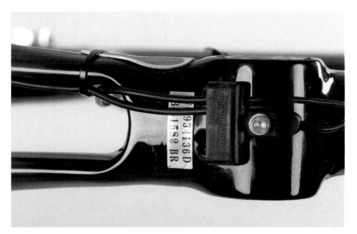

1 With external cables, the central connector in the cable harness is positioned below the bottom bracket. A special guide system, which holds the cables for the front and rear derailleurs, is fitted here.

2 The control unit is fitted just below the handlebars. The two thin cables from the shift levers are joined here. Only fit these parts approximately to begin with.

3 Route the cables to the front and rear solenoids. Pay attention to the stickers with the labels 'RD' for the rear derailleur and 'FD' for the front derailleur. Using cable ties, secure the cable harness to the frame in such a way that tyres, cranks and your feet do not get caught in the harness or rub against it.

Battery check

1 You can check whether the battery still has enough charge by pressing on one of the rocker switches on the brake lever for a few seconds. If the lamp lights up green, there is still enough charge in the system. If it does not, you need to charge the battery.

2 Fold the cover back and press the button on the power pack on the bottom tube. Using your other hand, pull out the rechargeable battery from its bracket. In order to fit the battery again after recharging, you need to press the button again and slide the battery back into position.

3 Tests have shown that the battery supplies energy for approximately 1,500 miles – after this the front derailleur will no longer operate. The rear derailleur will still work for another few miles before running out of steam as well. Recharging the battery takes about two hours.

Switching mechanism and front derailleur

1 To begin with, turn the cranks gently and press one of the switching buttons several times, until the chain is positioned on either the largest or the smallest sprocket. Adjust the limit screw in order to prevent the chain from travelling beyond the sprocket. Use the same method to set the opposite limit of travel for the derailleur.

2 At the rear, switch to the largest sprocket. At the front, switch to the smallest chainring. Turn the cranks backwards slowly and check that there is a small clearance between the upper derailleur guide pulley and the largest sprocket. If this is not the case, turn the adjuster screw at the back of the derailleur to adjust the gap.

3 With the chain still on the largest sprocket and smallest chainring, adjust the front derailleur via the outwards-facing screw. The inner chain guide plate needs to be positioned as close as possible to the chain without touching.

Synchronisation

1 Switch to a medium gear. Press the button on the front switch below the handlebars until the control light is illuminated red. Now you can fine-tune the adjustment of the rear derailleur. Turn the cranks and listen to the chain.

2 If you can hear noises while the chain is turning, press the front lever. Every time you press, the rear derailleur moves inwards by 0.1mm. If the noise becomes louder, you need to press the rear lever.

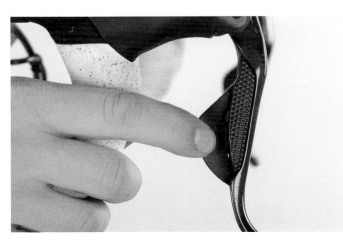

3 Each time the rear lever is pressed, the rear derailleur will move outwards in increments of 0.1mm. When the chain is running quietly, press the button on the switch below the handlebars again. Now the red light will go off. Finally, switch through all gears to check that they are working properly.

Off topic: Gearing for steep gradients

1 You can assemble an extremely capable transmission system for steep gradients (hills, mountains...) very affordably by purchasing a 10-speed mountain bike chain, an MTB cassette and a road-bike gearing system with a long cage length. To fit these components, first remove your old chain, and disconnect the cable from the rear derailleur. Pull the rear derailleur slightly rearwards and remove the securing bolt completely.

2 Remove the wheel and remove the quick-release skewer. Fit a chain whip to the largest sprocket to counterhold the cassette. Fit a suitable special socket to the cassette locking ring, then unscrew the locking ring using a wrench.

3 Remove the cassette and the special spacer ring for road-bike sprockets. Clean the contact surfaces and threads of the freehub body thoroughly and regrease it afterwards, applying thin and even layers of grease.

4 Slide on the MTB cassette components. The sprockets' interior profile is asymmetrical, meaning that they can only be fitted in one position. The markings on the individual sprockets indicate the correct direction of rotation.

5 Grease the threads and the contact surfaces of the cassette locking ring and position it carefully. Turn the ring two or three turns by hand at first, then use a torque wrench to tighten it to 40Nm. Check that the locking ring has been securely tightened.

6 Clean the rear derailleur hanger and grease the threads. Hold the rear derailleur slightly turned to the rear, and then gently screw the securing bolt into the derailleur hanger, a few turns by hand. Afterwards, tighten the bolt to a torque of 8–10Nm. Fit the rear wheel.

Off topic: Gearing for steep gradients (continued)

7 Release the gear lever fully to release all tension from the cable. Turn back all adjusting and end-stop screws. Connect the cable to the rear derailleur. All external sleeves and fittings belonging to the cable must be positioned neatly in the guides, and the cable should be slightly tensioned. Protect the gear cable against splayed ends using a crimped-on end cap.

8 Place the chain on the biggest chainring, with the lettering on the chain on the right (outside) when looking in the direction of travel. Guide the chain through the front derailleur and over the smallest sprocket, and then through the rear derailleur. Pull the chain together at the bottom. When in this position, the rear derailleur's pulleys should be aligned vertically one above the other.

9 When the chain is set on the smallest chainring and smallest sprocket, it should remain slightly tensioned. On the other hand, when the chain is on the biggest chainring and the biggest sprocket, the rear derailleur cage must not be fully tensioned. Shorten the chain using the appropriate tool.

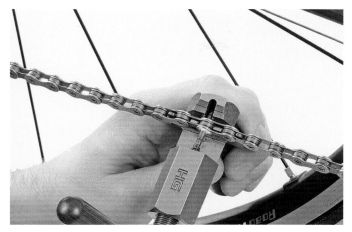

10 Briefly cast an eye over the chain to establish whether it is the correct length, before fitting a new rivet or a new split-link, as applicable.

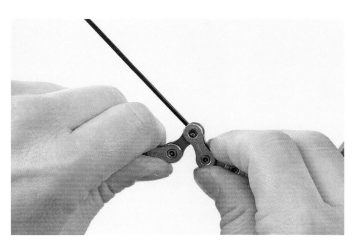

11 The reconnected chain link must move freely. If you push the links together by hand, the tension in the rear derailleur should cause the chain to fully retighten. Otherwise, move the chain perpendicular to the running direction or retighten the rivet slightly to free the link.

12 At the end of this process, where applicable, use the pliers to break off the guide pin on the chain rivet. Adjust the rear derailleur's outer end stop, the cable tension and, above all, the inner end stop, in order to prevent the rear derailleur or the chain from colliding with the spokes. Adjust the clearance between the upper guide pulley and the sprocket as described previously.

Chains

In terms of efficiency, the road bike's power transmission is second to none. However, it needs to be meticulously fitted and maintained.

More gears, a better gearshift mechanism – the drive trains offered by component manufacturers are getting more and more sophisticated, hence the demand for high-tech chains. Chains need to be narrow, flexible, suitable for climbing, durable and should also have low friction. For these exacting requirements to be fulfilled, it is vital that the chain is correctly fitted.

As a general rule, drives with chains from the same manufacturer as the other drivetrain components on the bike work most reliably. Without the correct tools, fitting a new chain is risky. If you want to avoid buying specialist tools, you are better off having the chain fitted at your local bike shop. Using a chain with renewable 'split-links', such as the SRAM Powerlink will make the process easier, as no tools are required for removing the chain.

The chain must never ever be opened again at the point where the connecting pin (or the connecting link in case of SRAM chains) sits! A new rivet pin or connecting link should always be used when refitting the chain.

If the chain you have had fitted up to this

point has worked well, you can use its length as a reference for the new chain. Otherwise, you can determine the length by fitting the new chain over the largest chainring and the smallest sprocket, and through the derailleur mechanism. The correct length is achieved when the rear derailleur pulleys are positioned vertically one above the other. In most cases, new chains are too long and will need to be shortened. On Shimano and Campagnolo chains, to shorten the chain you will need to take out a few inner and outer links, and you should only do this on the end of the chain that finishes with an inner link. On SRAM chains, you will need to shorten the chain by a further half-link as the connecting-link halves must be positioned opposite each other.

Tools and materials
Riveting tool and suitable rivet pins (or connector links), measuring tools, chain grease, cloth

Shimano chains

1 The latest Dura-Ace chain by Shimano is asymmetrical. On the inner face, all links have holes. The embossed marks on the outer face of the chain point in the direction of rotation. Shorten the chain, using Shimano chain tool TL-CN-27 or TL-CN-32. Make sure that one end of the chain finishes with an outer link, and the other with an inner link – shorten the chain by half a link more than necessary so that the new rivet can be fitted between an inner and an outer link.

2 With the chain in position, slide the greased rivet pin through the chain links. Make a final check to ensure that you have the correct chain length, before pushing the rivet into position using the correct Shimano chain tool (riveting tool) for ten-speed chains. Turn the tool spindle until you can feel and hear that the rivet has fully engaged. You will notice that the force necessary to turn the spindle reduces immediately. Stop turning now!

3 Check that the riveted chain link moves freely and check that the new rivet protrudes to the same extent on both sides. The chain must be fully tensioned by the tension of the rear derailleur, and the links around the new rivet must move freely. If this is not the case, you need to move the chain slightly, or possibly press in the rivet a little further. On completion, break off the rivet guide pin using pliers.

11-speed chains by Campagnolo

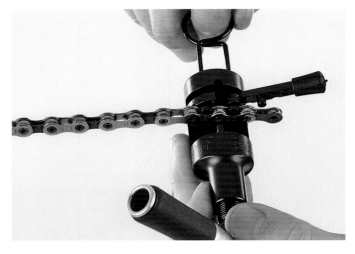

1 Using Campangnolo tool UT-CN 300, for 11-speed chains, shorten the chain. Pull the safety pin out of the riveting tool and push the small lever outwards. Insert the chain into the riveting tool and secure it using the pin. Turn the spindle until the old rivet has been pushed completely out of the chain.

2 Slide the new, greased rivet, with the guide pin, through the chain from the inside face towards the outside. Check the chain length once again, before applying the riveting tool, in its unlocked position, to the inside face of the chain.

3 Secure the chain by sliding the safety pin into the riveting tool. Turn the tool spindle evenly until the rivet engages with the chain. At this point the resistance will reduce. Stop turning! Remove the riveting tool and check that the rivet protrudes by about a tenth of a millimetre from the outer face of the chain.

4 If the link does not move freely, you need to readjust the riveting tool and check again. If everything fits neatly and the link moves freely, insert the rivet's protruding guide pin into the tool and break it off. Slide the safety pin into the riveting tool once more.

5 Secure the chain in the tool once more, and make sure that the conical tip of the tool spindle is centred on the rivet. Turn the tool spindle slightly forwards (applying some force) to expand the end of the rivet. The rivet should still protrude from the outer face of the chain by around 0.1mm.

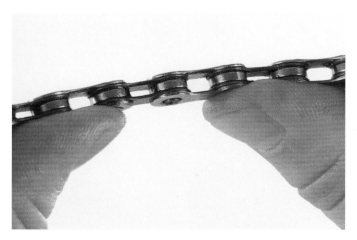

6 By pushing the links together by hand, check that the riveted area moves smoothly. The chain must be fully tensioned by the tension of the rear derailleur, and the links around the new rivet must move freely. If this is not the case, bend the chain gently backwards and forwards and from side-to-side until the rivet is no longer stuck and moves freely.

11-speed chains by Campagnolo (continued)

7 If you need to split the chain again, you must **not** do this at the point where the new rivet has been fitted, as this would render the chain unsafe, even if you fitted another new rivet using the riveting tool. Even if the chain were split in a different place, one of the outer links may break.

8 Instead, you need to shorten the chain by the length of the 'HD-Link' spare part, including the two outer links and two rivets. The HD-Link is then fitted. Combined with the new rivets, the new outer links should ensure that the chain holds reliably.

SRAM Red chains

1 In accordance with SRAM's recommendations for determining the chain length, fit the chain over the largest chainring and the largest sprocket – avoiding the rear derailleur! You need to add a full link to this length, including an internal link and split-link parts. This will produce the same chain length as using the classic method, where you guide the chain over the large chainring and the smallest sprocket while keeping the rear derailleur pulleys in a vertical position.

2 After determining the correct length, guide the chain over the smallest sprocket and the smallest chainring, and then through the rear derailleur. Grease the pins of both parts of the split-link.

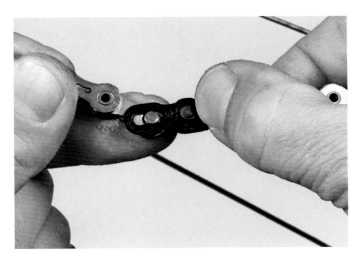

3 Slide both parts of the split-link into the front and rear sections of the chain, so that they are positioned opposite each other. Bring together the ends of the chain and insert the pin with the grooves into the opposite outer link, press slightly and pull the chain links apart to lock them together.

4 Turn the chain backwards until the connecting link is positioned in the upper chain run. Step on the pedal and push it in order to lock the chain. There must be an audible clicking noise. Check whether the link moves freely and try out all gears for a final check.

Rim brakes

Who brakes, loses. This is a popular saying amongst cyclists. Not only is it popular, it is also incorrect. The truth is that without brakes you will not get very far. However, only brakes that work perfectly guarantee that you reach your destination at all – and that you are among the first to arrive. This is due to the fact that the more efficiently the brakes work, the later you can brake when going into a bend, thereby losing less time. Therefore the saying should be "Who brakes last, wins".

It is not always the brake pads that are responsible for the brakes becoming less effective. Sometimes, it is only that the braking surface on the wheel rim is dirty. The best way to clean rims and brake pads is to use a cloth and cleaning alcohol. Afterwards, remove a thin layer of rubber from the tops of the brake pads using abrasive paper. If the brake calliper moves only hesitantly, the pivots and cables are likely to be dirty. In this case, you need to remove the entire brake. So, it makes sense to prevent this problem in the first place by occasionally cleaning the brakes with water and a little washing-up liquid. When you have dried them, apply a few drops of thin oil to the joints and spring caps in order to ensure the smooth operation of the brake. With the bike resting in a stable position, pull the brake levers several times so that the oil is distributed and reaches the bearings.

Scratchy noises during braking are mainly due to deposits in the pads. As well as small stone particles, some of the very hard constituents of a brake pad are capable of pulling aluminium particles from the rim, causing little aluminium lumps to build up on the pads over time. The consequences of this are that it becomes increasingly difficult to apply the brakes precisely, and that the braking surface wears down more quickly.

In most cases, normal wear and tear of brake pads becomes evident when the braking power decreases and you need to pull the levers closer to the handlebars for effective stopping power. This happens gradually and is not noticeable at first. In extreme cases, the lever has to be pulled right against the handlebars. Get into the habit of checking the brake operation regularly.

Worn out brake pads need to be replaced immediately, otherwise the brake shoe may damage the rim. With deep rims, the small tabs designed to make fitting the wheel easier pose a particular risk. You should also replace the pads if the pad and rim materials are not compatible. This can often be the case even with wheels that have come straight from the factory. For example, if the pad is made from a material that is too hard and the rim from one that is too soft, the rim will wear considerably faster.

Different manufacturers offer different types of pads: Campagnolo and Shimano each provide a selection of pads for uncoated black or coloured anodised rims featuring a relatively soft surface. There is a second type of pad which improves stopping power in rainy conditions, particularly with hard-anodised aluminium rims, which can be recognised by their dark grey colour. Manufacturers of aftermarket pads have a range of options on offer, including special pads for rims with a ceramic coating.

The increasing popularity of carbon wheels has once again highlighted the issue of brake pads. The commonly used rubber pads that achieve such good braking results on aluminium rims are usually unsuitable when it comes to carbon rims. Also, carbon rims require special pads because in comparison to aluminium rims they allow for dramatically lower braking forces.

Hints

- Regularly check that the brake levers operate freely, and check the adjustment of the brakes.
- Clean dirty rims using a cloth and some cleaning alcohol. After cleaning the rims, remove a thin layer of material from the tops of the brake pads using abrasive paper.
- Regularly check the pads for contamination, which can gradually wear out the rims.
- Have you just fitted new pads? Test the brakes while riding the bike in a safe area away from traffic in order to check that they work properly and to familiarise yourself with the potentially different braking action.

Tips for cantilever brakes

- Try different types of brake blocks. The braking force may vary depending on the combination of the brake blocks and the type of rim.
- Strong braking forces cannot be achieved when unstable forks or rear stays are so flexible that they bend. Reinforcement brackets are useful to prevent this.
- Allow sufficient time for the job. Adjusting a cantilever brake perfectly is a puzzle which requires a great deal of patience!

Component manufacturers such as Campagnolo, Shimano and SRAM, as well as companies producing accessories (such as Cool Stop and Corima) have started offering specialist carbon brake pads. Additionally, wheel manufacturers have started to equip their carbon wheels with specialist pads more frequently as a factory standard fitment. However, this does not always solve the inherent problem with carbon wheels, which is that the braking action is easily reduced, especially in wet conditions.

Tools and materials

Set of hex keys, torque wrench, screwdriver, vice, pipe wrench (Campagnolo pads), open-end spanner, soft soap, abrasive paper, cleaning alcohol

Checking the brakes

1 Pull the brake lever and observe when the pads touch the rim. After a third of its travel (at the latest) the lever should have produced resistance. If the point of resistance occurs any later, turn the ring on the adjusting screw, and while doing so, observe the clearance between the pads and the rims. As a general rule, the clearance should not be more than 1–2mm in case an emergency stop is required.

2 If the available adjustment is not sufficient, release the cable clamp screw at the calliper and tighten the cable slightly. Pay attention to the fact that the inner cable needs to be clamped in the groove provided in the clamp plate. Tighten the clamp screw to a torque of between 6 and 8Nm (Shimano and SRAM) or 5Nm (Campagnolo). Also check the brake mountings on the frame and the fork, tightening the securing bolts to a torque of between 8 and 10Nm (Shimano and SRAM) or 10Nm (Campagnolo).

3 Check whether the brake pads are positioned symmetrically on each side in relation to the rim. The distance should be identical on both sides. On Shimano and SRAM models, turn the hex screw on top of the brake and check the brake synchronisation. On Campagnolo models, the very small adjuster screws are positioned on the sides of the braking mechanism.

Adjusting lever reach: Shimano

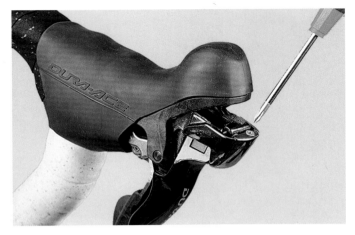

1 Open the quick-release lever on the brake calliper. Pull the brake lever gently, and completely remove the crosshead screw from the top of the lever. Then remove the cover (pulling it forwards and downwards). Now the access hole for making adjustments can be reached.

2 Pull on the lever gently and turn the screw in the access hole clockwise. Keep releasing the lever at intervals and check whether you can reach the lever comfortably from the bottom handlebar tube. If this is not possible, tighten the screw a little more. Repeat the same adjustments on both brakes. On completion, close the quick-release levers on both brakes.

3 The adjustment has an impact on the brake's free travel. Check that there is still free travel on both brake levers, and also whether the rims can still turn freely between the brake pads. Make appropriate readjustments on the cable tensioning screws at the brake callipers until both brake levers have the same amount of free travel – this should be a maximum of a quarter of the overall travel to the handlebars.

Adjusting lever reach: SRAM

1 You can adjust the lever reach on the gear and brake levers. Fold the rubber grip cover rearwards and release the gear lever completely. Push the gear lever to the inside again and then pull it slightly towards the handlebars to enable access to the adjuster. The adjuster features a small hole.

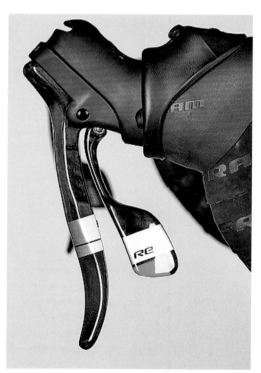

2 Using a pointed tool, push the adjuster element inside and select one of the six options for positioning the lever closer to the handlebars.

3 Then use a 3mm hexagonal key to position the brake lever closer to the handlebars (turning the adjuster to the right). The lever may just about touch the gear lever. Check that the brake lever still has a small amount of freeplay before the brakes begin to operate. Gently release the cable.

Replacing the pads

1 The easiest way to renew the pads is by removing them completely. Open the quick-release lever and release the brake body, then slacken the pad securing screws.

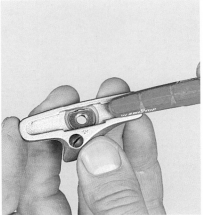

2 On Shimano and SRAM pads, loosen and remove the hexagonal screw on the outside of the holder. Pull out the pad, noting the exact shape and the direction of the orientation arrows. Slide a pad suitable for your rim (and of the correct shape) into the holder. The best way to secure the pad is using a new screw, complete with lock washer.

3 When mounting the pad holders on the brake, align them carefully. The closed ends of the holders need to face towards the front of the bike, and the open ends towards the rear. This ensures that the pad is pushed into the holder while braking, not pulled out! The curvature of the pad should also be suited to the shape of the rim.

Replacing the pads (continued)

4 A concave washer sits between the pad holder and the brake body, which allows the pad to be adjusted precisely to the braking surface. Lightly tighten the screw so that the angle of the pad can be adjusted, then slide the pads to the correct height. The pad should not protrude beyond the top or bottom of the braking area on the rim.

5 Pull the brake lever to hold the pads against the rims, making a final check to ensure that they are aligned correctly, then tighten the screws using a torque wrench (5–7Nm for Shimano and SRAM pads, 8Nm for Campagnolo). If the brakes squeak, position the pads at a slight angle, so that the front of the pads contact the rim first. You will need to adjust and secure the pads by hand.

6 Close the quick-release lever and check the distance between the pads and the edges of the rim, as well as the correct operation of the brake. Make any necessary adjustments to the brake lever travel or the pad positions as described previously.

Special features of Campagnolo brakes

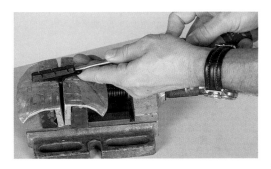

1 Replacing the pads for Campagnolo brakes is a bit more complicated, as the pads are secured by screws, but are a very tight push-fit in the bracket. Clamp the pad bracket, complete with securing screw, in a vice, and push the pad out by about 1cm using a screwdriver.

2 Grasp the pad and pull it from the bracket in an upward direction.

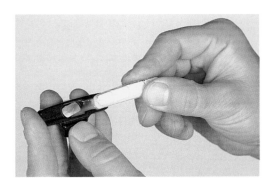

3 Apply some liquid soap on the contact surfaces of the metal bracket and also of the new pad and, using your hands, push the pad in as far as possible.

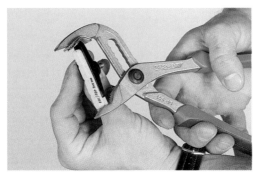

4 To push the pad fully into the bracket, a pipe wrench can be used or, alternatively, use a vice. Protect the edge of the pad bracket from damage using a strip of cardboard.

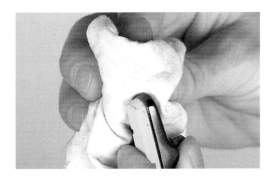

5 After fitting, carefully wash the entire pad using water. The soap needs to be removed completely from the pads in order for the brakes to work efficiently.

Cantilever ('cross') brakes – general

1 For optimum braking efficiency, the force must be transferred from the brake cable to the brake bodies as efficiently as possible. The smaller the angle between the cable runs to the two brake bodies, the greater the ability to apply the braking power to the pads; however, braking power is reduced when the mounting points on the frame and the fork flex away from each other.

2 On all cantilever brakes a flat triangular cable bracket transfers the force from the brake lever to both brake bodies, via the cables. With the newer generation of cantilever brakes (pad and cable attachment are positioned above the brake body pivot point – not as in this image!) the '90-degree rule' applies – the moment that the brake pads touch the rim, the cable run should form a right angle to an imaginary line through the pivot point of the brake arm and point where the cable attaches to the brake body.

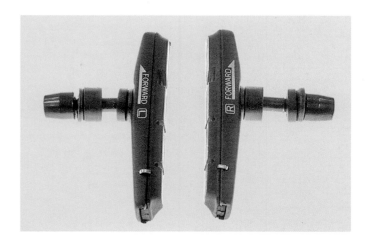

3 The brake pad holders are secured to the brake arms using a hexagonal nut. The initial adjustment of the brake pad position depends on the different thicknesses of the spacers positioned on the brake pad studs. If you mount the thin spacer on the inside, between the pad and the brake arm (on the left in the picture), the cable attachment point on the brake arm will be in a higher position than if the thick spacer is used between the pad and brake arm (on the right in the picture).

Cantilever brakes – lever adjustment

1 The more the pad wears, the closer the cable attachment point on the brake body moves towards the handlebars. Check the degree of freeplay at the brake levers regularly, as this should not be more than a quarter of the entire lever travel. If necessary, make readjustments directly at the auxiliary brake levers on the handlebars. Turn the adjuster on the cable at the lever anticlockwise to reduce the cable tension (freeplay).

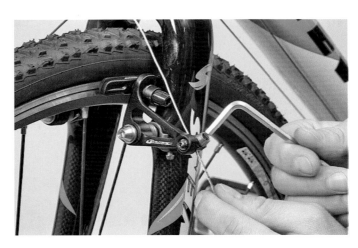

2 If no auxiliary brake levers are fitted, make adjustments at the cable adjuster on the fork or the frame. Release the locknut and turn the slotted adjusting screw in an anticlockwise direction to reduce the cable tension (freeplay). When you are happy with the freeplay, hold the adjusting screw and tighten the locknut.

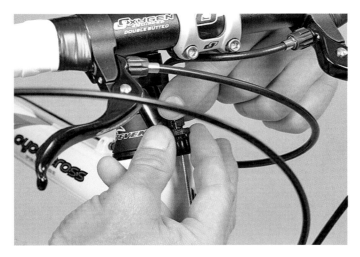

3 If you have exhausted both adjustment options, do not adjust the 'straddle' cable at the brake body without due consideration. It is possible that the pads have worn down so far that they will slide into the spokes from the edge of the rim if the straddle cable is effectively shortened. Therefore, check first that the pad is still thick enough to make full contact with the braking area on the rim.

Cantilever brakes – pad position adjustment

1 Slacken the pad securing nut. The pad can be adjusted horizontally or vertically in relation to the edge of the rim as well as at an angle to the wheel's radius. The pad must touch the edge of the rim with its entire surface area. There must be a gap between the top edge of the pad and the tyre. This is to ensure that the pad holder does not touch the tyre as the pads wear down.

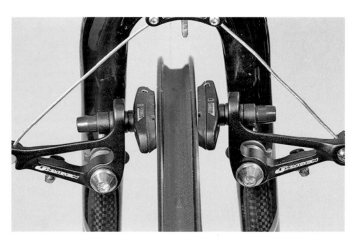

2 Position the pads in relation to the rim at a slight angle so that there is about 1mm clearance between the rear ends of the pads and the rim when the front edges of the pads contact the rim. This ensures that the pads are gently pulled towards the rim when the rim begins to decelerate. This slight angling of the pads also prevents the brakes from squeaking. Lightly tighten the securing nuts once adjustment has been made.

3 Push each brake pad and arm against the rim with one hand, while finally tightening the securing nut to the manufacturer's recommended torque. Finally, check that the pads are in the correct position.

Cantilever brakes – adjusting the cable yoke

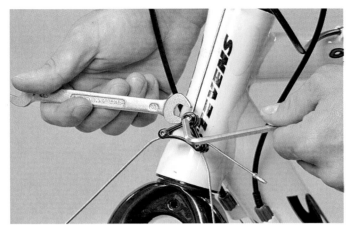

1 Release the central screw on the cable yoke mechanism by one or two turns. You can then slide the yoke down the main cable. You can only slide the yoke upwards on a preset brake if the straddle cable is also slackened. In order to do this (see the model in the picture), you need to release the cable at the brake arm and also at the two small hex screws on the yoke.

2 Now you can adjust the straddle cable and hence the mechanism. Try out different length settings for the straddle cable, and different height settings for the yoke until you have determined your preferred setting. Once you are happy with the adjustment, gently tighten the cable clamp screw on the brake body and the main cable clamping screw on the yoke. Gently pull on the brake, and observe the point at which the pads make contact with the rim. Also note the cable position.

3 Once everything is adjusted to your satisfaction, tighten the cable clamp screws on the brake body and the cable yoke to the manufacturer's recommended torque. Move the straddle cable into position in the yoke until the pads are positioned symmetrically in relation to the rim. Pull the brake lever several times, then tighten the two small straddle-cable clamp screws on the yoke. For final fine adjustment, you can adjust the each brake body spring preload using the tensioning screw on the body.

Disc brakes

Since the International Cycling Union (UCI) lifted the ban on disc brakes on cyclocross bikes, there has been an increase in the number of mass-produced bikes featuring disc brakes, and the range of aftermarket disc brakes has increased. This chapter explains how to fit and maintain them.

A round metal disc, brake pads on either side, plus a mechanism that moves the pads together towards the braking surface. This is the basic principle of a disc brake – pretty simple! According to this definition, however, the rim of a bike wheel provides the largest potential disc brake on the bike. This is essentially correct, but the pros and cons of the 'traditional' calliper brake system versus disc brakes vary depending on the bike on which they are to be used.

The main advantage of a disc brake is that it sits in the middle of the wheel and hence is relatively well protected against dirt. Due to their smaller circumference, disc brakes can also be applied faster. The result is that with disc brakes the braking effect is of a very high standard, but they can still be applied precisely and evenly, and their efficiency is not significantly affected by wet conditions. A further advantage of disc brakes is that they do not cause wear on the wheel rims.

For these reasons, disc brakes have been standard fitment on mountain bikes for several years. They have recently started to appear on cyclocross bikes, having finally been legalised by the UCI, and on some road bikes. Despite the reservations of many traditionalists, there is every indication that this more modern, improved braking technology has its advantages for road bikes. This means that, in the future, the annoying issues of melting carbon rims, rim failures due to the heat generated by extreme braking, and the altogether poorer braking performance that carbon wheels display may be soon be laid to rest.

Both hydraulically operated and mechanically (cable) operated disc brakes are available, but the former are the benchmark. Disc brakes are characterised by an initial pressure point which is easy to detect when the pads contact the disc, providing good feedback and control when braking. The problem road cyclists have had so far is that the brake levers offered by the component manufacturers are designed to operate with cables. Yet this is soon to change. Currently, however, you will have to make do with converters from aftermarket suppliers. These convert the cable movement into hydraulic pressure to operate the brake pads. Before considering buying a converter kit, check that your disc-brake system and the converter kit use the same type of fluid. Some hydraulic braking systems are designed for use with mineral oil and some with DOT brake fluid – never mix the two, as they are not compatible.

Mechanical disc-brake systems do not fully exploit the potential that disc-brake technology has to offer. Due to cable-friction issues, and the slightly elastic quality that the cable system therefore features, the operation of cable disc brakes is not as direct and accurate as that possible with hydraulic brakes. This means that cable systems cannot provide braking performance to match hydraulic systems, and it is necessary to compensate for pad wear using an adjusting screw (hydraulic brakes are self-adjusting). However, some of the mechanical brakes are in fact compatible with

the brake levers offered by Campagnolo, Shimano and SRAM, and hence can be fitted without the requirement to modify the operating levers. For this reason alone, disc brakes already have the edge on the Cantilever or Mini-V brakes featured on many cyclocross bikes.

Tools and materials

Hex keys, torque wrench, long-nose pliers, gloves (to protect against the sharp burrs on the brake pads)

Readjusting and pad replacement (Shimano mechanical disc brakes)

1 You can compensate for pad wear using the two adjustment screws provided. Turn the screws clockwise, in small steps, to bring the pads closer to the disc. Look from the outside through the viewing window and use the hex key to adjust the inner pad first. With the lever in its rest position, the pad must not touch the disc.

2 Now adjust the outer pad by turning the outer adjuster screw clockwise. While making the adjustment, keep pulling the brake lever to check the operation of the mechanism. With the brake lever released, the pad must not touch the wheel. At the lever, you should notice resistance at the latest when the lever is pulled half-way.

3 In order to check or renew the brake pads, remove the wheel. Slacken the pad adjusting screws. Pull the retaining clip from the pad retaining pin, then unscrew the pin using the hex key. Remove the pads. Fit the new pads using a reversal of the removal process. On completion, check the pad adjustment as described previously.

Assembly (Shimano mechanical disc brakes)

1 Fit the brake disc to the hub body, ensuring that its direction-of-rotation mark corresponds with the direction of rotation of the wheel. Tighten the locking ring using a cassette locking-ring tool and a torque wrench. Tighten the locking ring to the specified torque (Shimano 40Nm).

2 Fit the mounting adaptor for the brake calliper on to the fork lugs, using the screws supplied with the adaptor. Push the adaptor in the direction of the wheel rotation and tighten the screws to the specified torque (Shimano 6–8Nm).

3 Position the brake calliper on the adaptor and fit the securing screws, lightly tightening them so that the calliper can still slide a little on the adaptor. Fit the brake cable, routing it carefully from the brake lever to the calliper.

Assembly (Shimano mechanical disc brakes) - continued

4 Tighten the inner-cable clamp bolt at the calliper to the specified torque (on Shimano cables 6–8Nm), then fit the wheel.

5 Pull the brake lever vigorously. The brake calliper will move towards the optimum position in relation to the brake disc. Once the calliper position has stabilised, tighten both securing screws to the specified torque.

6 Using a hexagon key, loosen the adjuster screw for the inner pad by about half a turn (on Shimano pads by two clicks). This ensures that there is some play between the inner pad and the disc.

7 Pull the brake lever towards the handlebars ten times, applying as much force as possible. During this process, the cable outer is compressed, the inner cable stretched and the entire brake mechanism settles in.

8 The next step is to readjust the cable at the calliper to ensure the lever travel suits your requirements. In order to do this, use an open-end spanner to loosen the locking nut and turn the knurled nut anticlockwise. When you have finished adjusting, hold the knurled nut and tighten the locking nut again using an open-ended spanner.

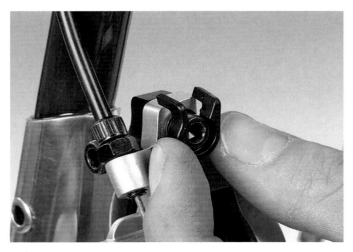

9 Finally, check that the brake disc runs freely and that the pads are positioned parallel to the disc. Fit the retaining clips over the securing screws.

Cables

In the age of hydraulics and wireless radio communication, Bowden cables seem slightly antiquated. However, when mounted correctly and maintained well, cables will work precisely and are long-lasting.

The new electronic groupsets offered by Shimano, the Dura-Ace Di2 and Ultegra Di2, show how great a degree of switching precision is possible using cables and electronics. Yet, not only will it take some time for the new technology to become widespread, but neither is it compatible with every type of bike. Anyone aiming to build a classic steel or titanium bike will have to keep using conventional technology as far as gear and brake operation is concerned. As an aside, internally routed cables, which used to be proof of impressive frame construction skills on classic steel frames, are now increasingly found on modern carbon frames.

- Gear and brake cables differ considerably – you should neither swap nor mix them. Gear inner cables are slimmer and have a distinctly smaller end fitting. Gear cable outers are reinforced longitudinally with wire; this makes the cable outers stiffer so that they flex as little as possible when changing gears. The brake cable outers, however, are helical-shaped and reinforced with wire, which makes them more flexible.
- Some shift/brake levers offer you the choice between routing both cables to the front of the handlebars or routing one cable to the front and the other to the rear. Which option to adopt depends mainly on the handlebar type.
- On small frames (perhaps up to 54cm) it may be advantageous to cross the cables in front of the steerer tube. In this case, the front derailleur cable runs to the right side of the bottom tube and the rear derailleur cable to the left. You need to then cross the cables below the bottom tube once more. This prevents the gear cables from bending between the handlebars and the cable brackets on the frame.
- In order to prevent excessive friction on the cables in the area of the bottom bracket, special plastic guides can be used. These are now fitted as standard by most frame manufacturers, or at least they come as part of the bike package. The guides are often packaged with the gearshift and brake levers.

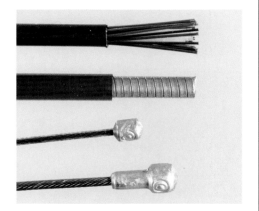

Comparison of gear and brake cables

- Pay attention to the position of the handlebar stem when routing the cables – the stem should be at its highest setting, otherwise you will not be able to adjust the handlebar height upwards at a later date unless new cables are fitted as well.
- The lengths of the gear cable outers need to be adapted to suit the individual bike. However, the length of the short piece of the cable outer which leads from the chain stay to the rear derailleur does not need to be altered. Cable outers with an end fitting at one end only should be fitted with the end fitting at the bottom-bracket end.

Running gear and brake cables through the inside of the frame tubes can drive even experienced mechanics towards a nervous breakdown at times, for example when a cable disappears into the interior of a carbon-monocoque frame.

For this reason, when working with internally routed cables, you should never completely remove the original cables from the frame. When performing repairs, or fitting new cables, leave the cable outer or the inner cable inside the tube. This enables you to ensure that, when refitting the original or new cables, the routing is correct.

Even when fitting external cables on the frame tubes, with cable guides which have been glued, soldered or welded on, care is required in order to ensure that everything goes smoothly. It only takes a frayed cable, a poorly positioned cable clamp or an edge that a cable rubs against, to have a dramatic impact on the precision of the gearshift mechanism or the operation of a brake.

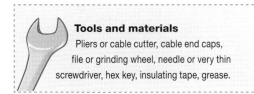

Tools and materials
Pliers or cable cutter, cable end caps, file or grinding wheel, needle or very thin screwdriver, hex key, insulating tape, grease.

Fitting gear and brake cables

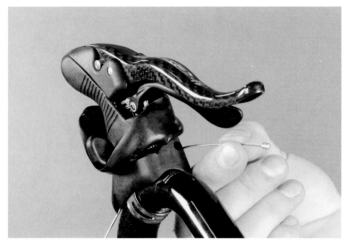

1 Fold back the rubber covers on both brake levers. Release the gear lever completely in order to be able to insert the cables correctly into the gearshift lever mechanism. Thread the cable through the gearshift lever mechanism – this must be possible without the need for undue force.

2 Pull the brake lever towards the handlebar, then slide the cable through the brake lever arm and through the hole at the back towards the handlebar. The nipple on the end of the cable must fit neatly into the cable housing in the lever. Shimano levers can be moved furthest if you release the gear lever first and then push it completely to the inside – in the same way as when you change gear.

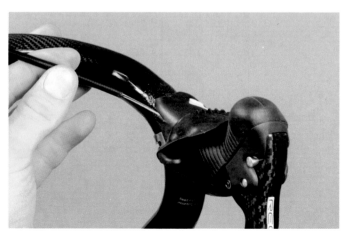

3 Slip on the brake cable outer and slide this into the brake lever from the handlebar side until it is resting against the stop. Use the same method to fit the gearshift cable outer. No cable end caps are used on the cables shown here! Note that on Shimano cables grease has been applied inside the end caps (from the side with the lettering) – therefore, the lettering should point towards the levers.

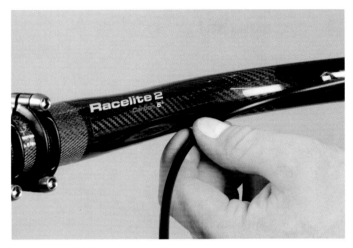

4 Lay the cable outers along the crossbar of the handlebar, as far as the thickened area of the bars near the centre. This is where the handlebar tape will come to an end at a later stage in the process, and the cable will surface from being covered by the tape. Fix the cable outers in position on the bars using adhesive tape. Make sure that the brake cable outer is well clear of the front brake.

5 Push the brake calliper arms against the wheel rim and hold the cable outer next to the end fitting on the calliper in order to determine the final length. Be careful not to bend or fold the cable outer. Mark the correct length of the cable outer so that you can shorten it to the correct length.

6 When determining the length of the cable for the rear brake, move the handlebars fully to the right-hand side in order to determine the maximum required length. Even with the handlebars in this extreme position, the cable still needs to have some play at the steerer tube without being bent or getting caught in the headset.

Fitting gear and brake cables (continued)

7 Turn the handlebars from the extreme right to the extreme left. The cable must continue to move freely, and the outer must not be taut or impede any other cable. The cable outers of both gear cables usually need to be the same length. Run the two gear cables to the cable guides on the frame bottom tube. Hold both cables tight in this position.

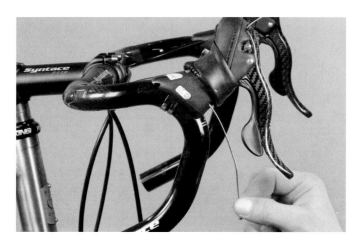

8 Pull all the inner cables from the cable outers again, taking care not to bend or kink them. The cable inners need to be withdrawn from the outers sufficiently to be safely outside the area where you will apply the cutting tool.

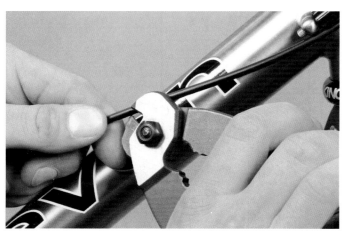

9 Cut the cable outers to the required length, using a special cable cutting tool, such as those offered by Shimano or Park Tool, or very sharp pliers. Check that the cable outers have been cut off cleanly at a right-angle and sit correctly in the cable guides on the frame.

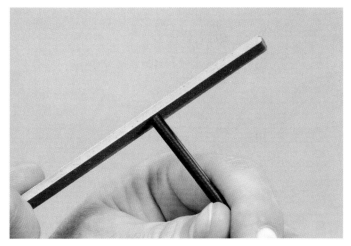

10 If this is not the case, file the end of the cable outer until it fits into the cable guide – do this at right-angles to the cable run. Using a grinding wheel will be faster, but you need to take care, since the cable-outer friction-reducing plastic lining tends to melt on the inside as a result of the heat produced. If necessary, cool the cable down with water. Make sure the cable outer's original round profile is restored if it was squeezed and deformed during the shortening process.

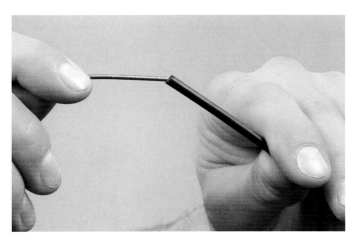

11 Clear the end of the inner plastic tube in the cable outer using a suitable-diameter sharp object, such as a partially ground spoke or the end of a bradawl.

12 While it is possible to fit the cable outers without end caps at the gear levers and brake callipers, end caps are essential at the rear derailleur and at the guides on the frame. Pull the end caps from the cut-off cable pieces, and refit them to the ends of the cable outers on the bike.

Fitting gear and brake cables (continued)

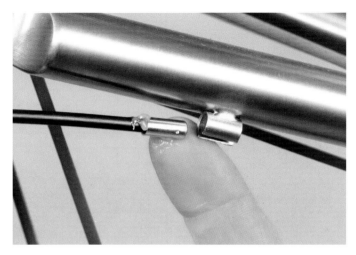

13 To prevent creaking and corrosion, apply a little grease to the cable end caps, the cable guides on the frame and also the brake callipers.

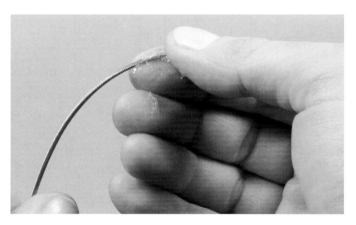

14 Thinly lubricate the inner cables. Do this by pulling them through some bearing grease on your thumb and index finger and then pushing them through the cable outers and the end caps (where applicable) as far as the brake or derailleur.

15 Slide the cable outers fully into the cable fixings on the gear and brake levers and into the guides on the frame. Fix the cable outers to the handlebars in two to three places, using a few layers of tightly wrapped insulating tape, before starting to fit the handlebar tape.

16 Secure the ends of the cable inners using the clamp screws. Adjust the brakes and the gearshift mechanism, and check once again that all cables are correctly routed and fitted into all cable guides and end stops.

17 Pull the brake lever hard several times towards the handlebar. Operate the gearshift mechanism to move through all the gears several times as well. The inner cables will stretch and the cable outers will be slightly compressed. Eventually the cable travel will increase, and readjustment will be necessary.

18 Using the cable cutter, shorten the inner cables to leave a length of approximately 3cm beyond the ends of the cable clamp screws. Fit end caps to the ends of the cables to prevent the inner cables from fraying.

Frame-tube interior-mounted cables

1 First, loosen the cable clamp screw at the rear derailleur, front derailleur or the brake. Leave the inner cable in position and try to pull the cable outer out of the frame slightly. If necessary, remove the cable outer end fitting and remove the cable-cover plate from the frame.

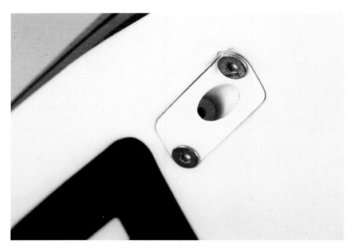

2 If cable guides are fitted to the frame, the cable outer will run up to the cable guide, and only the inner cable will run inside the frame tubes. There may or may not be a cable-guide duct inside the frame tube.

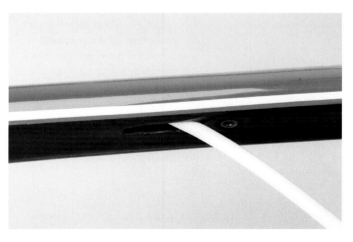

3 If the cable outer runs through the whole length of the frame, check whether the cable runs in a duct in the frame. If this is the case, consider yourself lucky. Otherwise replacing the cable will be slightly more complicated.

Replacing the cables when the cable outer does not run through the frame tubes

1 If the inner cables run through the frame without a cable outer, there is a risk that new cables will be almost impossible to route through the frame. To make the job easier, slide a piece of plastic tube over the cable inner, starting at the back of the frame, before removing the old cables. Keep pushing the tubing through the frame until it protrudes from the front cable hole.

2 If this is not successful, attach a length of strong thread (at least as long as the cable) to the rear end of the inner cable and secure it with a layer of adhesive tape. Pull out the inner cable slowly and evenly towards the front, pulling the thread into position in the frame as you go. Once the cable inner has been pulled completely out of the frame, detach it from the thread, and leave the thread in place in the frame to help fitting of the new cable. Measure the length of the old cable, and if necessary cut the new cable to the same length. Using the same method as previously, use the thread to pull the new cable into position in the frame.

3 If the inner cable does not slide from the frame freely using the thread, use an old cable instead of the piece of thread. At the ends of the two cables, for the final couple of centimetres, reduce both cable thicknesses to half the normal number of strands (by cutting off stands using wire cutters), interlink them and solder them together. Proceed as described in step 2 above, pulling the old cable from the frame, and leaving the piece of old cable in position to aid fitting of the new cable. Use the old cable to pull the new cable into position in the frame, soldering the ends of the cables if necessary, as previously.

Replacing the cables when a continuous cable outer is present

1 Leave the entire cable outer inside the frame and, working at the front of the cable, pull the inner cable from the cable outer.

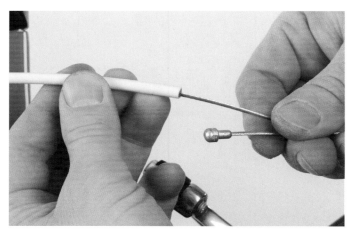

2 With the inner cable completely removed, push an old inner cable through the cable outer, starting at the back. Once the old cable inner is in position, hold on to the old cable, and then pull the cable outer out of the frame towards the front, leaving the cable inner in position in the frame.

3 Now slide the new cable outer on to the front of the section of inner cable left in place in the frame – this ensures that it will be routed correctly through the frame. With the cable outer in place, fit any necessary end caps, the pull out the old inner cable, and insert the new inner cable in its place.

Fitting cables for the first time

1 Not every frame manufacturer includes internal guide tubes for the cables. If these are not fitted, missing, or if the cable was pulled out too quickly too soon, a length of relatively stiff wire may help you to guide new cables into position, such as a wire from a Shimano Positron gearshift system.

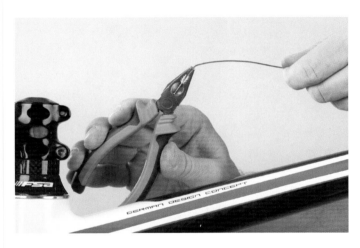

2 Bend the tip of the stiff wire round slightly, as this will make it easier for the end of the wire to find the exit hole at the rear of the frame tube more easily. You can then guide the wire along the frame so that the tip is near the exit hole in the frame.

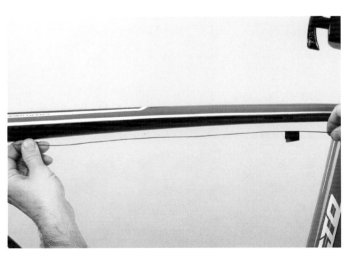

3 Hold the wire against the tube, with the front end of the wire aligned with the cable exit hole at the front of the frame tube. Mark the position of the rear cable exit hole on the wire, using adhesive tape. From the rear of the frame, guide the wire in as far as the tape, until the tip of the cable protrudes from the front exit hole. If the wire does not emerge from the front exit hole, try to catch the wire using a suitable tool – for example a loop made from thin cable ties.

Bottom bracket

There is now a wide range of bottom-bracket types, with different frame manufacturers having different preferences to suit their designs.

For many years there were various 'standard' features of a bike that you could rely on. These included the outside diameter of the tubes, the headset diameter and the design of the bottom bracket bearing. All this has changed dramatically over the past few years.

When welded aluminium frames were introduced about 20 years ago, the tube diameters increased enormously, and the carbon forks that emerged in the late '90s required stronger steerer tubes. The bottom bracket bearings, however, remained unaffected for a

The dimensions at a glance

Name	Dimensions for road bike (width/inner diameter)	Dimensions for MTB (width/inner diameter)
Italian thread	70mm/36mm x 24tpi	
BSA thread	68mm/1.370" x 24tpi (right side, left-hand thread)	73mm/1.370" x 24tpi (right side, left-hand thread)
BB 30	68mm/41,96mm	73mm/41,96mm and 85mm/41,96mm
Shimano Pressfit	86.5mm/41mm	92mm/41mm
SRAM Pressfit 30	68mm/46mm	73mm/46mm
FSA BB 386 Evo	*Dimensions unknown at the time of writing*	

long time. Up until a few years ago they featured a thread, which was either Italian or English (BSA/BSC). They had roughly the same diameter, the difference being that with the BSA thread there is a left-hand thread on the right side. The advantage of this design is that the bearing cup does not have the tendency to unscrew itself in use. Therefore, the BSA thread was the uncontested market leader for a long time.

The disadvantage of this standard was that the bearing cups were narrow and the spindle diameter was limited. It was Shimano who first developed a new bottom-bracket system, followed by Campagnolo. They used bearings which were screwed into the thread in the frame, but which were positioned externally, against the housing. The bearing width, and the distance between the bearings increased, and as a result there were fewer problems with bearing wear.

Cannondale then created a standard which they called 'BB30'. This kept the BSA housing dimensions, but does not need a thread. At first, the new standard was only accepted with some hesitation, but it gained more and more momentum when manufacturers like FSA produced an increasing number of bearings and cranks compatible with it.

Nowadays, the dam seems to have been breached. More and more manufacturers are producing bottom brackets to their own standards. Shimano's BB Pressfit, which is offered for mountain bikes and road bikes, sticks to the familiar bearing arrangement, however, the bottom bracket housing needs to be 86mm wide – instead of 68mm as before – and also threadless. Then the bottom bracket assembly can be pressed in. The advantage of this system is that it is easier to fit, and the wider bearing housing offers more options to the design engineer for enabling the smooth transfer of power.

Other designs are similar in principle, although dimensions vary.

In the face of all this choice, in terms of dimensions, it is good to see that there are adaptor sleeves for a lot of these designs, which will accept bearing shells with a BSA thread, which means we are almost going back in time.

Introduction (all bottom brackets)

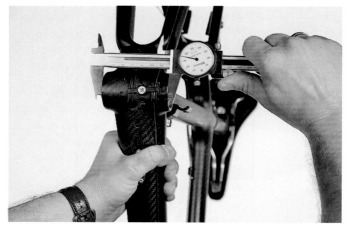

1 When buying the replacement bottom bracket parts, pay attention to the model. This is determined by the bottom-bracket thread. Two versions are common and you can distinguish them from the width of the housing – the 68mm BSC type is most widely used. Its designation in inches is 1.370 x 24tpi. The right-hand bearing cup features a left-hand thread.

2 The housing of the rarer Italian type (see picture) is 70mm wide. The right-hand thread on both sides has the designation 36 x 24tpi. The first figure represents the thread's outer diameter in mm, the second the number of threads per inch. Check that the thread is neatly cut and free from metal shavings.

3 On cartridge bearings by Campagnolo and Shimano (from the 2005 season, only in groupsets below Ultegra), the right-hand surfaces of the housing must be smoothly machined, for which the manufacturer or dealer is responsible. For Shimano bottom brackets in Ultegra and Dura-Ace 10-speed groupsets, both surfaces need to be smooth. Remove any paint residue on the inner surfaces or inside the thread.

Fitting Shimano Dura-Ace or Ultegra bearings

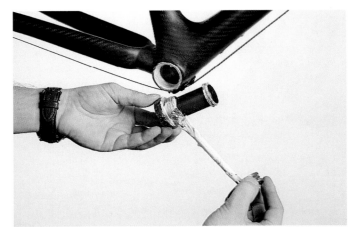

1 Using a cloth, wipe the thread in the housing in the frame clean, or blow it clean using compressed air. Grease the entire area around the threads, and the housing and bearing contact surfaces, using high-quality assembly grease to prevent corrosion. Bearing grease is not suitable here. Make sure you also grease the other side of the assembly, which fits on the left-hand side of the housing.

2 First, carefully position the right-hand bearing cup on the housing and rotate it until the thread engages. If you do not manage to achieve this straightaway, rotate the bearing slightly in the opposite direction of that required to screw it into the threads, applying slight pressure. The moment the threads are positioned correctly in relation to each other, you will notice that the bearing gently snaps into place. Screw in the bearing unit by a few turns by hand. This should be possible without applying any force. If not, the housing has not been properly prepared.

3 Screw in the cup on the opposite side in the same way. Use the appropriate bottom-bracket tool, and first tighten the right-hand bearing cup, using a torque of 30–50Nm, then tighten the left-hand bearing cup. Shimano supplies this tool as a standard part of its bottom-bracket kit – it resembles an open-end spanner. Unfortunately, it is difficult to apply an accurate, high torque using the tool. You are better off using a torque wrench.

Fitting Dura-Ace or Ultegra bearings (continued)

4 Apply a thin layer of bearing grease to the spindle and slide it into position, pushing it in from the right-hand side. The spindle should glide in, almost as if it is being 'sucked in'. However, it should not stick. If the spindle does not slide into position smoothly, do not apply force. If necessary, have the threads checked or re-cut by your dealer.

5 Check that the sealing ring in the housing is correctly aligned and seated. Apply a thin layer of assembly grease to the inside face of the left-hand crank and also to the sealing ring. When sliding the crank onto the spindle, the splines must engage correctly – there is a 'master spline', so the crank will only fit in one position.

6 Grease the spindle end screw, and the screw thread and the screw head contact surface on the spindle and crank. Fit the screw in the adjusting tool provided by Shimano for this purpose, and screw it in. As soon as the screw engages, the job is actually done – you do not need to tighten it any further. The recommended torque is 0.4–0.7Nm – almost negligible.

Campagnolo Ultra Torque system

1 Wipe the thread clean, or blow it clean using compressed air. Grease the entire area around the threads, and the housing and bearing contact surfaces, using high-quality assembly grease to prevent corrosion. Bearing grease is not suitable here.

2 First, carefully position the right-hand bearing cup and turn it anti-clockwise. The threads in the cup and the housing must engage, and the cup must not be positioned at an angle. If you do not manage to achieve this straightaway, rotate the bearing slightly in the opposite direction of that required to screw it into the threads, until you feel it begin to engage with the threads. Now screw in the bearing in the correct direction by hand. This should be possible without applying any force. If not, the housing has not been properly prepared.

3 Screw in the opposite bearing cup in the same way (noting that this has a right-hand thread!). Tighten each cup until the inside face of the cup sits against the surface of the housing in the frame.

Campagnolo Ultra Torque system (continued)

4 Campagnolo provides a special tool with each crank. Use this to tighten the right-hand bearing cup first, to a torque of 35Nm, then tighten the left-hand cup. Unfortunately, the Campagnolo tool does not have a torque function, so in order to tighten the components properly, you will need to apply a considerable amount of force.

5 Apply a thin layer of grease to the bearing cup in the frame, then apply assembly grease to the surfaces of the spindle and the bearing cups on the cranks. Slide the drive-side spindle into the housing, from the right-hand side. The spindle should glide in, almost as if it is being 'sucked in'. If the spindle does not slide into position smoothly, do not apply force – carefully check the alignment of the components.

6 Campagnolo supplies a securing clip as part of the package. Its function is to secure the bearing in the cup. Check the positions of the small holes for the clip, positioned in a groove running round the outside of the bearing housing.

7 Fit the securing clip to the groove, engaging the ends of the clip with the holes. Once one end has engaged, press on the other end until it snaps into its hole.

8 Once the clip has been fitted, check that the crank is sitting tightly in the bearing. To do this, try to pull the crank outwards.

9 Apply bearing grease to the bearing surfaces and spindle on the left-hand crank. Slide the thin, wave washer onto the shaft and position it over the shoulder on the shaft. Then slide the crank assembly into the bearing cup.

Campagnolo Ultra Torque system (continued)

10 Turn the cranks so that one is positioned vertically upwards, and the other downwards, then push the left-hand crank gently into the frame, and turn it gently backwards and forwards until the teeth on the two spindle halves firmly engage.

11 Grease the threads and head contact surface of the spindle end screw. Slide the screw on to the tool supplied along with the Campagnolo kit, or on to a 10mm hex key, and screw it in by hand.

12 Fit the Campagnolo tool to the torque wrench using a 10mm socket. Counterhold the crank, and tighten the screw to a torque of 42Nm. Wipe off any excess grease.

Fitting BB30 bearings

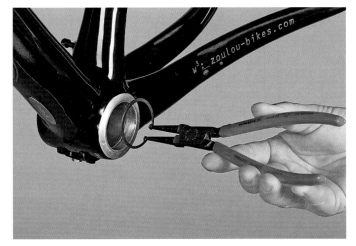

1 Clean the housing in the frame, and check for any burrs. The two grooves running round the outside of the housing must be free from dirt. Lightly grease the groove, then pretension the circlip using circlip pliers.

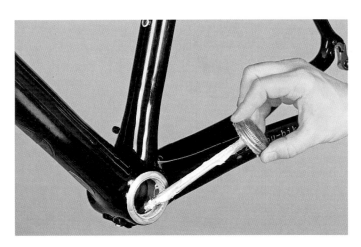

2 Fit the circlip into the groove, making sure that it is fully engaged. Check its fit by engaging the pliers in one of the holes in the circlip and trying to turn it. If the circlip is not seated properly, it will jump out. If it is fitted correctly in its groove, it will rotate smoothly when pushed with the circlip pliers.

3 Apply assembly grease to the bearing seats and the locking ring, and also the bearing's outer cup. Do not use carbon paste or similar lubricant, or the bearings will creak when riding.

Fitting BB30 bearings (continued)

4 Dismantle the special tool. The bolt-shaped part of the tool (see arrow) is positioned against the frame to pull the bearing into position. The bearing is push-fit in the housing. Before using the tool, clean and lubricate the tool's thread.

5 Press one bearing cup in at a time. Slide the threaded part of the tool through the housing in the frame so that the end of the tool fits neatly against the end of the housing. Then slide the bearing cup into position over the threaded rod, followed by the remaining part of the tool. Apply light pressure with your hand to push the bearing cup into position, then screw the nut onto the end of the tool, and turn it by hand to draw the bearing cup in a little further. Make sure that the bearing cup slides in straight, holding the opposite end of the tool, then unscrew the nut a few turns, again by hand.

6 Take the 32mm open-ended spanner and tighten the nut further. Make sure that the bearing cup is drawn into the housing without tilting. When there is significant resistance as the spanner is turned, the bearing cup has reached its final position against the shoulder in the housing.

7 Fit the bearing cup on the other side in the same way. When the tool is fitted from the side to which the bearing cup has already been fitted, the end of the tool should fit securely against the frame housing. If this is not the case, this means that the first bearing cup has not been pressed in far enough and needs to be pressed in slightly further.

8 A spring washer must be slid onto the chain-ring end of the spindle. This spring washer is designed to pre-tension the bearings, preventing axial play. The spring washer is fitted in conjunction with two aluminium washers. Before fitting the spindle, fit the spring washer and the first aluminium washer, with the smooth side of the washer pointing outwards, away from the bearing.

9 Grease the spindle and push it into the frame, complete with the spring washer and the first aluminium washer. Ensure that the washers do not tilt. When fitting these components, there may be some degree of resistance, and you may need to push the assembly into position using your hand. If this is unsuccessful, you could tap the assembly into position using very light blows from a soft-faced mallet.

Fitting BB30 bearings (continued)

10 Fit the second aluminium washer, also with its smooth side pointing outwards, away from the bearing. Grease the contact faces of the spindle and the crank, as well as both internal and external threads. Fit the crank to the spindle, and screw in the crank securing bolt. Make sure that the bolt does not cross-thread. Once the crank is engaged with the spindle, tighten the securing bolt to the specified torque, using the torque wrench.

Removing BB30 bearings

1 Unscrew the crank securing bolt, anticlockwise, until the crank is released from the spindle by the integrated puller. Hold the frame, and release the spindle assembly by gently tapping with the soft-faced mallet.

2 The three-part special tool can remove one bearing cup at a time. Dismantle the tool and then clean and lubricate the thread. The housing in the frame should also be clean to enable the tool to grip properly.

3 Insert the puller legs into the bearing and manoeuvre it so that both legs are in contact with the bearing cup. Screw the puller body onto the thread so that the closed end points outwards.

4 Fit the nut to the tool. The tool needs to be positioned concentrically with the bearing. Counterhold the nut using the 32mm open-end spanner, and use a hex key to turn the puller shaft anti-clockwise until the bearing is pulled from the housing.

Hints

- You can modify frames to accept BB30 bearings by using the sleeves for classic BSA bearings. This may be necessary when the original bearings no longer fit the frame properly. These sleeves, offered by several manufacturers (such as Cannondale, FSA and Reset), slide or press into the frame. They are then secured in the frame by the bearing cups. If the fit is not good enough, you will have to glue in the sleeve using a suitable medium-strength metal adhesive, such as one of the adhesives offered by Loctite.

- An exploded view of the components makes fitting simpler. If no such drawing is supplied with the bearings, you could search the manufacturers' internet sites – they often provide manuals to download.

- Check the tightness of the screws after riding for about 100 miles. After this, check them every 1,000 miles.

Fitting Pressfit BB86 bearings

1 In principle, Pressfit bearings are identical to screw-fit bearings, with the obvious exception that they are a press fit! The frame needs to be suitable for Pressfit bearings, and must feature a special 86.5mm-wide bottom bracket housing of appropriate diameter. In order to fit the bearing, you will need a special Shimano tool.

2 Position the two plastic bearing cups by hand, push the tool's threaded rod through the frame, and screw on the end of the tool until both ends of the tool contact the bearing cups. The inside edges of both cups need to fit into the housing slightly, and the outer edges must sit parallel to the surfaces of the tool. Using a ring spanner, counterhold the nut on the tool.

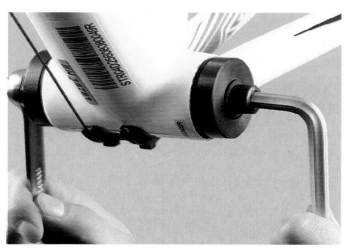

3 Engage a hex key with the other end of the tool, and turn the threaded rod slowly and evenly. The bearing cups should slide in evenly without tilting. Keep turning the threaded rod until both cups sit against the shoulders in the housing. Once you feel the resistance on the tool increase, remove the tool and slide in the crank/spindle assembly. This spindle should turn smoothly.

Removing Pressfit BB86 bearings

1 To remove the bearings you will need the Shimano special puller tool, featuring claws that spread apart. If you use any other tools, you run the risk of damaging the frame. Under no circumstances mount the frame on a workstand, suspended by a frame tube or seat post, to carry out these jobs!

2 Slide the tool in from one side. Slide it in until it protrudes slightly from the other side, then hold the three claws and slide the tool in further. During this process, the claws are spread apart until they sit securely on the bearings. Tighten the tool a little to ensure that it fits securely.

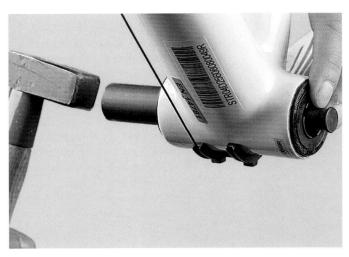

3 In order to remove the bearing, hold the frame tightly with one hand, then apply a few cautious taps to the tool, using a hammer. Keep tapping until the bearing is released. If you do not succeed by applying gentle taps, tap harder, but ask somebody to help you hold the frame (so the frame structure does not get damaged). Repeat the process to remove the bearing on the other side.

Fitting conventional cartridge bearings

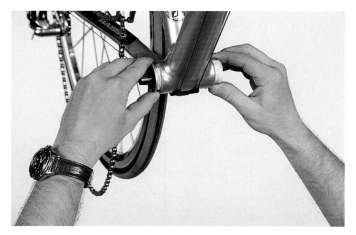

1 Prepare the bottom bracket for fitting the bearings, then screw in the left-hand cup (whose inside surfaces should also be well greased) until it engages with the cartridge.

2 Guide the bottom bracket tools into engagement with the bearing cartridge's splined shaft, starting on the right-hand side, and screw the cartridge into the housing using an open-end spanner. If you feel significant resistance, you will be better off using a torque wrench with a hexagon bit from this point onwards. Tighten the cartridge to a torque of 70Nm (Campagnolo), or 50–60Nm (Shimano), then repeat the procedure for the left-hand side.

3 The discussion as to whether or not grease should be applied to the surfaces of the square spindle is as old as this type of component. Campagnolo and Shimano recommend that grease is not used. Presumably the manufacturers fear that the crank may actually bind on the spindle due to the thickness of the grease, but, if you reduce the tightening torque, this risk is minimised. However, without grease, there is no protection against corrosion.

4 After you have tightened both sides, check that the bearing operates smoothly. If you notice any binding, or the bearing does not run smoothly, you need to remove it and thoroughly clean (or re-cut) the threads in the right-hand side of the housing. If this does not fix the problem, Campagnolo recommend that the left-hand bearing cup is fitted without grease, but using thread-lock compound on the threads, and tightened to a torque of 30Nm. However, this will make removal of the bearing at a later stage more difficult.

5 Our experiences with greased square-section spindles and reduced torque have been positive throughout. However, the tightness of the crank securing bolt should be checked regularly using a torque wrench. Once you have decided on whether or not to use grease, slide both cranks onto the spindle.

6 The crank securing bolts offered by the two main manufacturers already feature bolt security measures (such as thread-locking compound). This protection against the bolts coming loose makes sense, however, not using grease means that there is no protection against corrosion. It is recommended that even if the bolt threads are left dry, the surface under the head is greased. Tighten the bolts to 32–38Nm for Campagnolo components, or 35–50Nm for Shimano components.

Headset

In recent times, the traditional quill stem on road bikes has almost universally given way to the Ahead stem. This also has an impact on how to fit and maintain the headset.

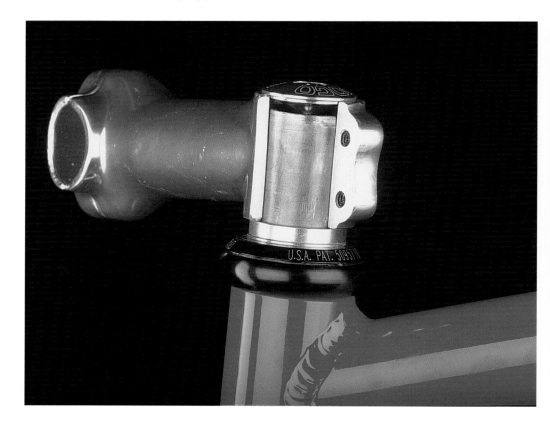

The headset is one of the bike's fastest-wearing components, since it is exposed to constant shocks while riding. Add to this the water and dirt contamination that can find its way past the seals to the interior of the headset over time, thinning out the lubricant which ensures smooth steering, and you have a recipe for heavy wear. If you want to establish whether the headset bearings are still running smoothly, pull the front brake, hold the lower bearing with two or three fingers and your thumb, and push the bike forward and backward. If the fork and bearing shell move against each other, then there is

excessive play in the bearings, which needs to be adjusted. Now hold the bike up high by its top tube, lifting the front wheel off the ground. If you now lightly touch one of the handlebar ends, the front wheel should leave its central position and tilt to the side. If this does not happen, check first whether the brake/gear cables are obstructing the movement, or whether the bearing itself is dragging. The very durable roller-type bearings, by the way, never run as smoothly as ball bearings. If it is possible to turn the front wheel sideways from left to right without applying great force, but the wheel then snaps

On an Aheadset, the end cap presses on the stem, which then determines the play in the bearings.

into place in the centre position, this means that the bearing components are already worn or damaged. However, in most cases only the lower bearing will be worn, as the impact force occurs mainly from below.

Before you organise a replacement, you should cast an eye over the headset components to determine the exact parts you require. The parts you will require will depend on the headset type. On classic ball-bearing types, you should at least replace the entire lower bearing.

Always take thorough measurements of your old headset before organising replacement parts. Bearing shells and fork crowns are available in different diameters. With quill-stem headsets, in addition, you need to check the height of the bearings – especially if you intend to fit a different make of headset, or a later model of your current type. The height should be measured starting at the lower edge of the bearing cup on the fork, up to the top edge of the upper cup on the frame tube. If the new bearing is shorter than current one, you will need to shorten the steerer tube, or it will not be possible to adjust the headset. If the new bearing is higher than the current one, the locknut may no longer fit onto the steerer tube, in which case you will need a fork with a longer tube.

Ahead technology

The most striking difference between the Aheadset system and the quill-stem system is

Hints

- Noises (eg cracking!) are often a result of inadequate lubrication. On forks with metal steerer tubes, you can apply assembly grease to the tube, between all parts of the headset and the spacers. With carbon forks no grease should be used between steerer tube and stem nor between the expander cone and the inside of the steerer tube, or it will not be possible to clamp the parts securely. With carbon forks, you need to be particularly careful to ensure that the grease is applied only to the metallic components of the headset, the clamp or the contact surfaces of aluminium spacers.

- If you continue to experience play in the bearings, this is often due to a lack of friction between the stem and the steerer tube or insufficient grip being exerted by an expander cone in the steerer tube. On carbon components, apply a thin layer of carbon assembly paste to the clamping areas – this should help to improve the friction between the components, whilst protecting the carbon material. Also check that there is a 2–3mm cap between the end cap and the top edge of the stem, otherwise it will not be possible to adjust the bearing play.

- If you experience resistance while steering or notice play with the handlebars in certain positions, this may be due to the bearings not fitting correctly, for example if the upper and lower bearings in the frame are not aligned with each other due to manufacturing faults or unsuitable bearings.

- Various different bearing diameters and angles are available. You can often find the exact bearing specification stamped on the headset's outer ring (see photo). If markings are visible, you can consult the FSA information on bearings. Most bike dealers use this information for headset bearing sizes.

This is not what it should look like! The sharp-edges on the stem have produced indentations on the carbon steerer tube.

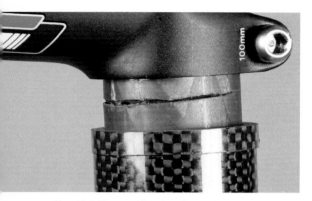

How big? The exact headset dimensions are usually specified on the outer ring.

Hints

- With most headsets, it is recommended that the stem does not press directly onto the top bearing. You should therefore put at least a thin spacer under the stem.
- Do not use any external clamps to take the weight when adjusting the headset. Clamping mechanisms with a close fit which are based on the cone principle are more suitable. These clamps also stiffen the tube from the inside, preventing the stem from damaging the fibrous material.
- If you saw too much off carbon forks, you will not be able to extend them again. Therefore, insert more spacers below the stem to begin with (yet no more than 50mm altogether) – this will enable you to find your seating position more easily.

that the stem does not fit down inside the fork steerer tube, but instead slides over the top of the steerer tube to form the top part of the headset. The essential idea behind the Ahead technology is to keep it simple. With the Aheadset, the end cap pushes the stem down on the steerer tube to apply pressure to the bearings, thereby providing adjustment of the freeplay.

In order to be able to adjust the headset, there must be a gap between the top edge of the fork steerer and the bottom edge of the cap – otherwise the cap would sit directly on the tube, preventing the stem from being pushed downwards. A gap of approximately 2mm is enough, but if the steerer tube needs to be cut, the cut must be at an exact right-angle to the tube. If the gap between the end of the tube and the end cap is much more that 2mm, the surface area of the stem which supports the steerer tube will be reduced.

It can be difficult to build up enough confidence to shorten the steerer tube. Adjusting the handlebar height afterwards is only possible if you use spacers. These spacers are fitted onto the steerer tube between the stem and the headset top bearing. When you need to adjust the height, you can swap the spacers from bottom to top. Angled stems provide another solution for adjusting the height of the handlebars.

Flip-flop stems, which can be reversed, are ideal for adjusting handlebar height. Reversing

them allows for two handlebar heights. The larger the angle of such a stem, the bigger the difference in height between the two positions. Stems with a 17-degree angle result in a very large difference in handlebar height when reversed, and are not suitable for fine-tuning. You can recognise flip-flop stems easily because of their symmetrical clamping area shape – the top and bottom edge of the clamp must be parallel to each other.

Tools
Various hex sockets, torque wrench, assembly grease, carbon assembly paste, cloth

Checking the headset

1 Apply the front wheel brake and place the fingers of your other hand on the gap between the frame and the top headset ring. Put weight on the saddle and push the bicycle gently forward and backward. If the gap between the headset ring and frame changes, there is too much clearance in the headset. Repeat this test with the wheel positioned at right-angles to the frame.

2 In order to check for freedom of movement, lift the bike up by its top tube by approximately 20cm. Lightly touch the handlebar – it should start turning from the central position by itself until either the brake cable touches the frame or the handlebar touches the top tube. Check this action on both sides.

3 If the handlebar does not turn fully to both sides, try releasing the cables and then try again. Investigate any cracking or grinding noises. Often, they are only due to dry or corroded cables in the frame guides. If this is the case, apply lubricating oil. If this does not solve the problem, check that the fork runs freely at the bottom bearing, and that there is sufficient freeplay at the top bearing. Make sure that any spacers are evenly seated.

Adjusting the headset

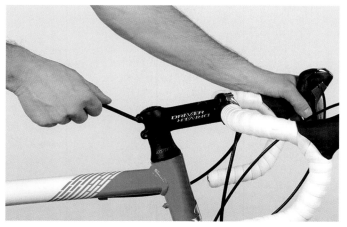

1 Loosen the clamping screws on the side of the stem, turning them two to three turns. It is not necessary to unscrew them completely.

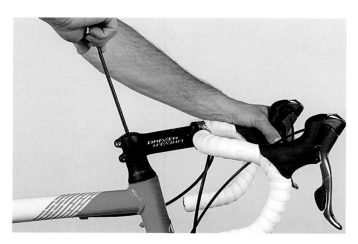

2 Readjust the headset freeplay by turning the expander bolt positioned at the top of the stem. If you turn the bolt clockwise, play will decrease, and if you turn anticlockwise, play will increase. It is important to remember that the screw should not be fully tightened – it is used for fine-tuning! Only use quarter-turns, and keep checking the freeplay between each adjustment, as described previously.

3 Once you are satisfied with the degree of play, realign the stem in relation to the front wheel. To do this, look over the frame to align the stem and the front wheel. The handlebar should now be exactly at right-angles to the direction of travel.

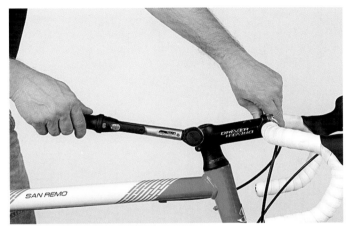

4 Retighten the stem clamp screws again, according to the manufacturer's recommendations. Use a torque wrench, and if no recommended torque figures are provided, increase the torque incrementally, starting at 4Nm. Increase in steps of 0.5Nm until the stem is clamped securely to the fork (next photo).

5 In order to check that the stem is securely clamped, wedge the front wheel between your knees, take the handlebars in your hands and try to twist them away from the stem, applying moderate force.

Headset maintenance

6 If you want to carry out maintenance on the headset, if noises occur despite having adjusted it correctly, or if steering is unsatisfactory, you will need to remove the fork. Remove the front brake from the fork assembly, and remove the front wheel. Loosen the stem clamp screws and hold on to the fork from now on.

Adjusting the headset (continued)

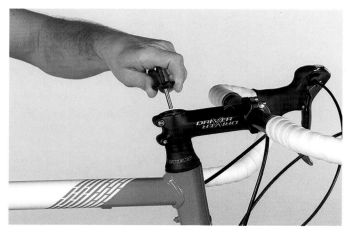

7 Undo the top expander bolt completely, and remove the end cap. First, pull off the handlebars, complete with the stem, and carefully suspend them in such a way that the frame, levers, handlebars and stem are not at risk of damage.

8 Remove the spacers, the trim cap and the upper, slotted bearing cup. Take note of the positions of all parts, and lay them out in order, wiping them clean with a cloth.

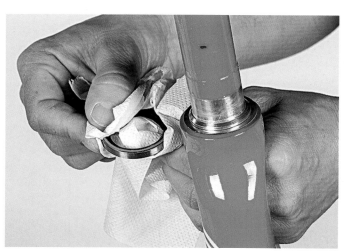

9 Pull the forks from the frame in a downward direction. Wipe all parts clean. Check that the bottom bearing cup sits correctly, is undamaged, and that the steerer tube is free from scratch marks. Remove the headset and wipe the grease from the bearing surfaces on the frame. Check that the headset is easy to turn and that there is no play, and also check that all the components are free from dirt and contamination. Check the bearing surfaces for wear and damage.

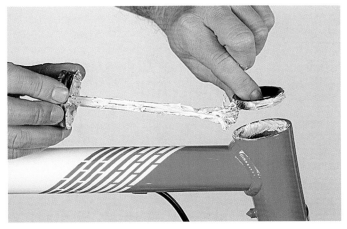

10 When assembling, grease the bearing components generously. The grease will provide an additional seal for the bearings. Wipe off any excess lubricant after assembling the components. On carbon steerer tubes, no grease must come into contact with the tube's upper clamping area.

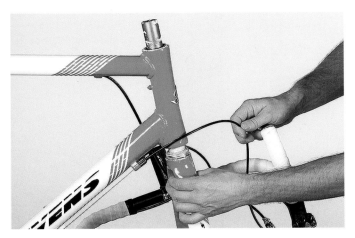

11 Take note of the order in which the parts are assembled, and place the bottom bearing on the seat at the top of the fork. With sealed bearings, the bevel of the outer ring normally points towards the frame, and that of the inner ring points towards the seat on the fork. Fit the fork into the frame's head tube from below.

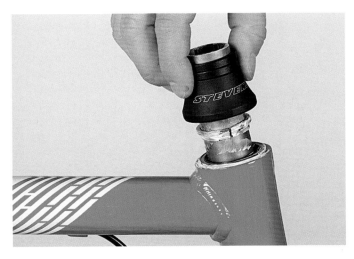

12 Slide the upper bearing (generously greased), the slotted bearing cup, the spacers and the end cap fully onto the steerer tube, avoiding freeplay. Then slide the stem onto the steerer tube and fit the end cap. Adjust the headset as described previously.

Choosing the right stem for carbon steerer tubes

1 Stems where the clamping load is applied in one specific area are unsuitable for use with carbon steerer tubes, as if the steerer is clamped at one single point, the carbon is easily damaged.

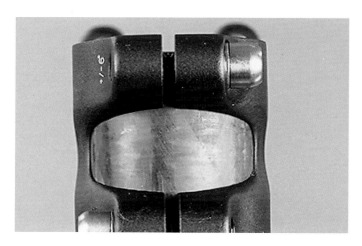

2 Stems featuring a large number of screw recesses, or a wide slit at the clamping point are equally unsuitable, as it is easy to deform and damage the steerer tube.

3 Stems with a large hole where the horizontal tube meets the upright (see arrow) opposite the clamp are best avoided too. The tube is likely to be only supported by perhaps a few millimetres at the top edge of the stem, or not at all in the worst-case scenario!

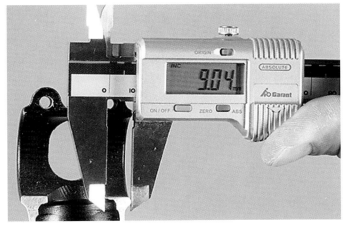

4 To be able to adjust the headset or replace the end cap, the stem's top edge must protrude 2–3mm above the top edge of the steerer tube. Also measure the thickness of the stem's collar (see cross-section of the stem in photo) – it should be at least 7mm thick at the top and bottom.

5 In general, it is always best to use stems specifically designed for use with carbon steerers. You can identify whether they are suitable by checking that they come with a clamp featuring a narrow slot, or symmetrically positioned outer clamping bolts, with sufficiently large steerer contact areas at the top and bottom end of the stem.

6 Once you have found a suitable stem, check that the steerer contact surfaces inside the stem are free from ridges. Every now and again some products slip through quality control processes despite featuring slight ridges, which may damage the carbon. If this is the case, replace the stem. If this is not possible, smooth over critical areas using fine abrasive paper.

Fitting the stem

1 Release the expander bolt and then push it down. Some end-cap/expander bolt assemblies are released in this way and then can be pulled out, complete with the end cap. Note that the fork will have come loose after releasing the expander bolt. If you cannot pull out the end cap/expander bolt as a complete unit, unscrew the end cap or the expander bolt fully and remove both. The actual clamping mechanism will remain inside the steerer tube and needs to be removed separately.

2 Slide the new stem – with the clamping screws slackened – on to the steerer tube to test the fit. It must be possible to slide the stem on, without using excessive force, and there must be no play in the stem. The top edge of the steerer tube must be approximately 2–3mm below the top edge of the stem. If necessary, insert one or more spacers to achieve this.

3 Remove the stem again and clean the clamping areas of both the stem and steerer tube, removing any dirt and grease with cleaning alcohol or solvent. Apply carbon assembly paste to the area on the steerer tube where the stem is to be secured. Fit the fork, and clamp the stem on loosely – just so it holds the fork enough to prevent it from falling out under its own weight.

4 Take the headset expander mechanism apart and check for any burrs or ridges which could prevent the parts from sliding smoothly against each other. Remove any such burrs using a file and/or emery cloth. Apply a very thin layer of grease to the areas that come into contact with each other, the threads, and the undersides of the screw heads. Make sure the outside faces of the components are free from lubricant, otherwise the mechanism will lose its clamping effect.

5 Apply carbon assembly paste to the inside surfaces of the steerer tube where the expander cone fits, and to the contact surfaces of the expander cone. Loosely fit the expander components together, before sliding the assembly into the steerer tube. Slide the expander cone in until the end cap is firmly seated. Tighten the expander bolt. This will adjust the freeplay and loosely secure the stem. Caution! What you are doing here is adjusting the freeplay – tightening the expander bolt will not secure the forks/stem solidly in position.

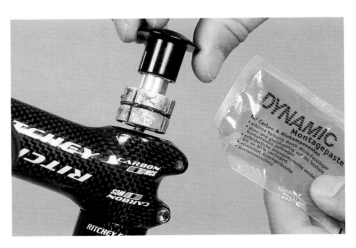

6 On mechanisms where the expander is screwed in first and the bearing is then adjusted separately, you will need to slacken the expander bolt by about two to five turns (depending on the type) after pretensioning the expander cone. Then slide in the complete assembly, stopping when the end cap is securely seated.

Fitting the stem (continued)

7 Remove the end cap again, then refit the expander bolt and tighten to approximately 3–4Nm. Refit the end cap again, and adjust the bearing freeplay by carefully tightening the expander bolt.

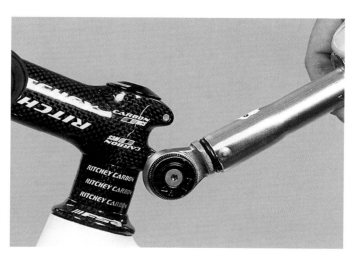

8 If you followed the above procedure, you should not need to apply much effort to tighten the stem clamp screws. Tighten the screws to the specified torque. After tightening, wedge the front wheel between your knees and try twisting the handlebars from side to side.

9 If it is possible to move the stem in relation to the fork, you should further tighten the clamp bolts in increments of 0.5Nm. Under no circumstances exceed the maximum torque specified by the fork or stem manufacturers. After riding your bike for 50 miles or so, check again whether the stem clamp bolts are still tight enough.

Replacing the classic headset

After removing the stem, tying the handlebar to the frame to support it, and removing the front brake from the fork, remove the upper bearing cup. Wipe the old grease and any dirt from the bearing cup using a cloth, and then check the cup for damage. If there are any obvious wear marks, indentations, damaged areas, or corrosion on its surface, the bearing cup should be renewed.

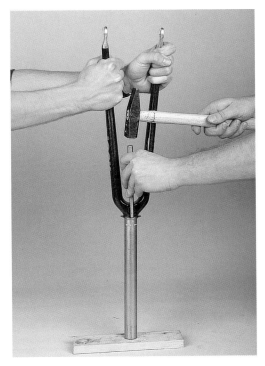

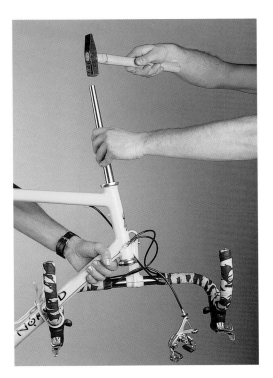

1 Invert the forks, and rest the steerer tube on a piece of wood with the head facing down. Ask an assistant to hold the forks. Knock the lower bearing cup off the seat at the bottom of the steerer tube, using a hammer and a suitable drift or a large screwdriver. Tap the cup evenly and alternately from the front and back in order to prevent the cup from tilting. Clean the steerer tube, and check the surface for wear and damage.

2 Remove the bearing cups from the frame tube, then clean and check the bearing surfaces. If the bearing cups are difficult to remove, you should ask an assistant to help support the front of the frame bottom tube so that neither the components nor the frame are damaged by the knocks when tapping out the bearings. If you attempt to support the bottom tube on a workbench, this may lead to ugly dents on thin-walled frames. Guide a tube – ideally with flat, rather than rounded, lower edges – into the frame's steerer tube from above and at an angle. Guide the tube so that it is resting on the edge of the lower bearing cup. Drive the bearing cup from the frame by applying light taps, alternately at the front and rear. While doing this, mind your feet, as sometimes the bearing cup can shoot out suddenly, falling to the floor, along with the tube!

Hint

- Carbon forks are very delicate components. You need to be careful when handling and fitting them. They are manufactured to tight tolerances, and need to match the bike and all surrounding components perfectly. This applies to the bearing cups as well as the stem.

Replacing the classic headset (continued)

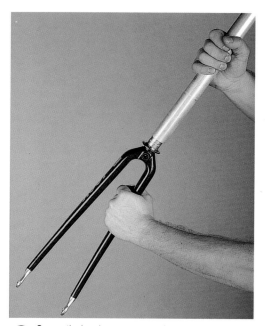

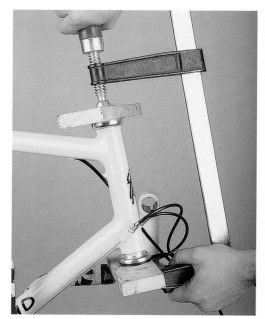

3 Grease the bearing cup seat on the steerer tube, and the bearing cup itself, before pushing it into position on the steerer tube. Tap the cup into position, using a tube which fits closely against the steerer tube. The tube must not rest on the bearing surfaces. A soft-aluminium tube will prevent damage to the bearing cup.

4 If no special tools are available, you can fit the bearing cups to the frame using a screw clamp. You should only do this if the contact surfaces are well greased. When using this method, fit one cup at a time – this will limit the risk of one cup being pulled at an angle, and also a ridge being produced. Place two wooden blocks on the cups or on the frame tube, and then fit the clamp making sure the jaws are centred on the frame tube. Tighten the clamp evenly and keep a careful eye on the movement of the cups. If a cup starts to tilt at an angle, you will need to adjust the clamp accordingly, to ensure that the cup is pulled squarely onto its seat.

Variations in handlbebar height using different stems

ANGLE LENGTH	-17	-8	0	+8	+17
70mm	-20.5	- 9.7	0	+ 9.7	+20.5
90mm	-26.3	-12.5	0	+12.5	+26.3
110mm	-32.6	-15.3	0	+15.3	+32.6
130mm	-38.0	-18.1	0	+18.1	+38.0

The table shows the difference in height that results from using a stem featuring different angles. For example, a stem that is 90mm long in combination with a –8-degree angle lowers the handlebar by 12.5mm. The height difference for a flip-flop stem is calculated by adding both figures together for the same angle. For instance, for a 130mm stem with a 17-degree angle, this results in a whopping 76mm height difference when the stem is flipped.

5 If you tend to replace your headset bearings frequently, you could make your own tools, relatively cheaply. You will need a threaded rod, three matching nuts, a hollow tube of suitable diameter, and several large-diameter washers of various different outer diameters to suit the different bearing dimensions. Screw a nut onto the rod, then slide on one large-diameter washer and secure this with a second nut. Tighten the nuts firmly against one another, ensuring that they cannot come loose when used at a later stage. The bearing cup can then be fitted using the tube and the various washers, and guided onto the steerer tube. Using a third nut, which is supported by a washer on the opposite side of the threaded rod, the bearing can then be pulled in.

6 Bearing cups that can be pushed into place by hand will be a nuisance while riding, as they are likely to produce creaking or rattling noises. Degrease the cups and the bearing seat in the frame and apply two-component adhesive to the contact surfaces (observe the adhesive instructions!). Leave the adhesive to dry properly before refitting the fork assembly.

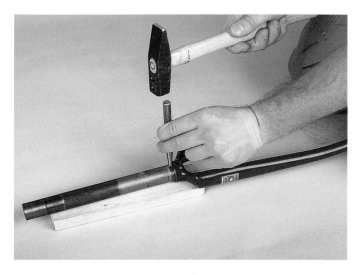

7 Should the bearing cup slide on to the seat without applying any force at all, this means that it does not fit tightly enough. This will also result in rattling noises in most cases. You can either glue the cup on so that it is fixed, or you can widen the seat a little. To do this, place the steerer tube on a wooden block, as shown in the picture. Apply a punch mark at the centre, or in the half of the bearing seat that faces away from the fork head and, using the hammer, knock evenly distributed shallow indentations into the material. Ridges will be produced around the edges of the indentations, thus increasing the seat's diameter.

Handlebar tape

Handlebar tape should not only be visually appealing, it also needs to provide a secure grip on the handlebars and protection for hands and joints. This chapter provides detailed information on the different types of tape that are worth considering, and also provides useful tips on how to wrap the tape correctly.

Although the consequences are far less serious, wear and tear does occur on handlebar tape, just as it does on tyres, chains and brake pads. Handlebar tape not only enhances the bike's looks, it also has a significant effect on the comfort of your ride.

Hence you should look for quality when buying tape. One criterion it must fulfil is providing good grip when it is raining, or when the rider's hands are sweaty. Another point to pay attention to is that the tape should create an evenly padded area on the handlebars, whose purpose is to soften the continuous blows and vibrations inflicted on the hands while riding. Hands will be less painful with adequate padding, and they will not become numb as easily, either. In terms of material, there are in effect only three options – tape made from fabric like cotton, synthetic material – called Pelton – or cork. Cotton tape is still available nowadays, and cheap, however it quickly becomes dirty and greasy and does not offer any padding. It is better suited as an anti-slip sub-layer under the actual handlebar tape. Tapes made from synthetic material can be slippery in wet conditions and therefore no longer recommended for competition riding in any conditions despite their low price.

By comparison, so-called cork tape provides the best qualities. However, the term "cork tape" is misleading, since very few of these products actually contain cork. Most "cork" tape is actually made from foam plastic, a material which has good shock-absorbing qualities due to its microscopic cushioning effect, and also provides a grippy surface.

Hints

- The lifespan of racing handlebars and stems is not unlimited. For this reason, after a fall you should always apply new tape for your own safety. Also check the handlebars thoroughly for potential damage from the crash. If in doubt, also replace the handlebars!
- Do not wrap the tape from the top of the handlebar outwards. This may look better at first glance, but experience has shown that the tape tends to slip around the top handlebar curvature.
- You need to leave plenty of time and be patient when wrapping the tape around the handlebars. Do not start on this job when your riding pals are already on their way. Do not despair if you need to unwrap a few centimetres of tape again – even experienced bike mechanics often need to correct the tape's position a few times before it fits perfectly.
- The adhesive strips to finish the ends of the bar tape that come as part of the handlebar package are often made from brittle adhesive tape that does not stick very well. You are better off using insulating tape or duct tape.
- On some handlebar types, the transition from the grip area to the handlebars themselves features a noticeable edge. This might result in pressure pain and numb fingers. Using soft plastic, for example silicone sealant, you can make precise inserts to fill the gaps. In an emergency, use a piece of tyre, or a few layers of handlebar tape will also do.

Tools and materials
Scissors, handlebar tape, insulating tape, rim tape, cleaning alcohol, cloth

Applying handlebar tape

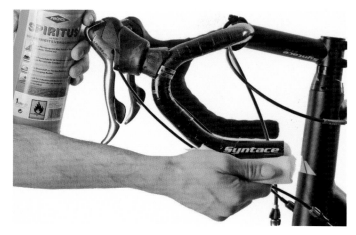

1 Fold the rubber sleeve on the brake lever away from the handlebar, and take off the old tape. Clean the handlebars using cleaning alcohol or solvent and let the substance evaporate completely. If the handlebars are discoloured, or are corroded in places, check with your dealer whether it is safe to continue using the part.

2 Apply a strip of rim tape or a leftover piece of carpet tape to the top tube. This serves as a non-slip base for the handlebar tape. Carefully remove the protective film from the adhesive strip on the back of the handlebar tape. Loosen the protective film a few centimetres away from where you intend to cut the tape, which will help to prevent the adhesive strip from coming away from the edge of the tape when you pull off the protective film from the cut area.

3 Start applying the tape at the inside of the handlebar ends and let it overlap the end of the bars by roughly half the tape's width. Hold on to the end and start wrapping it around the handlebars once, holding it almost at a right-angle. The tape needs to overlap by at least 5mm around the entire circumference of the bars. If this is not the case, you need to try again.

Applying handlebar tape (continued)

4 Hold the tape at an even tension and continue wrapping it at an angle on the bottom tube working towards the brake lever.

5 Lay the individual tape layers over each other in such a way that there is ideally an overlap of about a quarter to a third. This is usually determined by width of the adhesive strip. If the overlap is too large, the surface of the tape will become wavy.

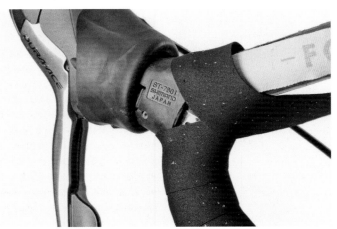

6 The trickiest part of the handlebar curve is the outer radius. Here, the tape needs to just overlap. On the inside, the tape overlaps slightly more because of the shorter distance. On the lower edge of the brake lever, the tape should cover the lever body slightly. On the Ergo Power grips offered by Campagnolo there is a gap between the brake lever and the handlebars through which the tape can be guided.

7 Wrap the tape over the brake-lever mounting bracket and have a look where you need to apply the short piece of tape (which was supplied in addition to the normal tape) in order to prevent any uncovered handlebar material from shining through. Then remove the tape again as far as the brake lever, stick the separate piece of tape on the area in question, and push the ends under the brake lever's folded-over rubber sleeve.

8 Pull the handlebar tape tightly upwards, and when wrapping it during the next rotation, take care to overlap the tape, wrapping it evenly around brake lever rubber sleeve, the top part of the handlebars and the brake lever. Wrap the tape (which needs to be held tight at all times) evenly around the top tube as far as the start of the thicker part of the handlebar tube.

9 Keep holding the tape tight, in the general wrapping direction and cut off the excess tape that overlaps the thicker part of the handlebar tube. Use scissors for this job. You need to hold the scissors vertically, at right-angles to the handlebars in order for the remaining end of the tape to be angled neatly at right-angles to the handlebar tube. Never try to cut the tape on the handlebars themselves using a knife, as any scratches or indentations you cause may result in the handlebars fracturing!

Applying handlebar tape (continued)

10 Lay the tapered end of the tape around the handlebars in such a way that a straight line is produced which runs vertically in relation to the direction of the top tube. With the end of the tape stuck to the bars, wrap two or three layers of insulating tape over the end of the tape.

11 Check how far the additional piece of tape at the brake lever and the rubber cover overlap. Shorten any tape ends that are too long, to prevent any unnecessary bulges in the rubber cover. It will provide a professional touch if you can trim the section of the tape thickened by the adhesive strip. Make sure that the tape does not prevent the rubber cover from sitting securely over the brake lever.

12 Working at the ends of the lower handlebar tubes, slide the protruding ends of the tape into the inside of the handlebar tubes and push in the end plugs. The plugs are held in place by the tape folded inside the tube. If the plug comes loose due to too little tape protruding into the tube, wrap an extra two to three layers of tape around it.

Double-Tap levers

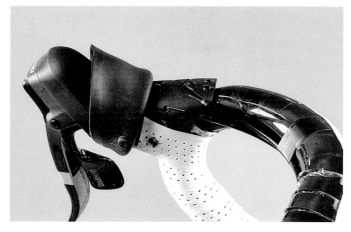

1 On some handlebar types, the transition from SRAM Double Tap brake levers to the handlebar curvature can be sudden and can provide an uncomfortable step. This might result in pressure pain and numb fingers.

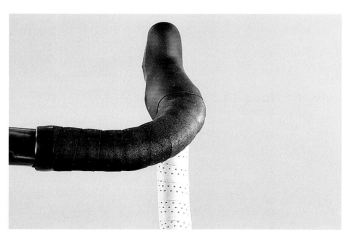

2 Using a suitable soft material, for example silicone sealant, make tailored inserts to provide a smooth transition between the lever assembly and the handlebars. As a temporary measure, a piece of old tyre, or a few layers of handlebar tape can be used.

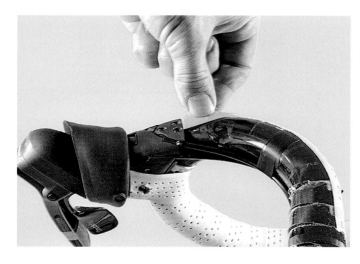

3 Secure your insert using tape, then wrap the handlebar tape over it as usual. This should achieve a soft and padded support for your hands.

Bike computers

Modern rim and fork shapes as well as exotic spokes can make mounting a cycle computer complicated. Using the following tips, however, you can set up computer sensors to provide accurate information.

Provided they work, cycle computers are an excellent investment, as they enable you to measure your performance. The latest electronic computers are able to display figures for instantaneous, average and maximum speed, distance and time. Regardless of the uses you have for the data you collect, being able to say "50 miles at an average of 20mph" is a lot more

meaningful than just saying that you rode your bike for three hours at a fast pace. Riders who invest in this sort of detailed display are after precise information. So it's particularly annoying if the displayed data is inaccurate or the computer fails to work altogether.

You can fix the most common faults yourself, as the devices are technically much less complicated than is often assumed. The sensors work as follows: a magnet attached to the spokes generates impulses in a sensor mounted on the fork. These impulses are then transmitted to the computer via a cable or wireless transmitter. The transmitter works in the same way as a light switch. A current can only flow when two wires are connected in the transmitter – this is the only way the computer receives information. This 'switch' is activated by the magnet, which passes the transmitter every time the wheel turns and causes the two thin wires to briefly make contact. Once the magnet has passed, the electric circuit is broken. In order for this system to work properly, it is important to fit the magnet and the transmitter exactly in accordance with the manufacturer's instructions. The manufacturer often provides alignment marks on the transmitter, showing the optimum position for the magnet. During each rotation of the wheel, the centre of the magnet should pass these marks exactly. The distance between the magnet and the sensor is also important – a 2–3mm gap is ideal. If the distance is greater than this, the sensor may not trigger, and if it is smaller, the magnet may touch the transmitter as the wheel rotates.

Despite the fact that the user manuals for cycle computers are normally quite detailed, problems are quite common. The most frequent issues are related to inconsistent data being displayed on different computer types – a problem that often crops up when riding with friends and comparing data. If there are variations in terms of the instantaneous speed or the distance, this is usually due to incorrectly programmed wheel circumferences. Differences in average speed at the end of a trip, however, are more likely to stem from the automatic 'start–stop' function featured on many current computers. This function causes the data recording to stop automatically when the bike comes to a halt for a period of time, for example when stopping at traffic lights. The exact moment that the computer stops recording varies from manufacturer to manufacturer, and it is not usually possible to make changes. The average speed displayed at the end of a trip is lower the longer the stopwatch keeps running. If

Hints

- If there are variations in terms of the instantaneous speed or the distance, this is usually due to incorrectly programmed wheel circumferences. The outer circumference of the actual tyre you use may differ significantly from the default figures given in the user manual.
- If the numbers on the display fade or some segments are not displayed at all, this is usually an indication that the battery needs to be replaced. If this has no effect, leave the computer without batteries for a few minutes and it will generally revert back to the factory settings.
- **Tuning tip:** The 'Pulsar' spoke magnet by Tune (see left of photograph) weighs less than half a gramme and is generally reliable. Use contact adhesive to glue it to the spoke.

you cannot read the numbers on the display properly, or some segments are not displayed at all, this is an indication that the battery is low. It is good practice to leave the computer without batteries for a few minutes before fitting new ones. This will ensure that any residual voltage has dissipated.

Tools and materials
Screwdrivers, small hex keys, small blocks of wood, double-sided tape, two-component glue or superglue, insulating tape, inner tube

Fitting the magnet

1 The magnet and sensor are a matched unit and must be exactly aligned. The magnet must align with the appropriate marks on the sensor.

2 The sensor must be fitted the correct way round. The position of the battery casing does not necessarily indicate which way round the sensor fits. Generally, a band logo of a product name appears on the outside face of the sensor. For wireless sensors, the signal to the computer is usually better the higher the sensor is placed on the fork.

3 For wireless computers, fit the sensor and the handlebar-mounted computer on the same side of the bike, as this improves the signal. Never fit the transmitter at the rear of the fork, as it may get caught in the spokes and lock the wheel!

4 The distance between the sensor and the magnet is of crucial importance for correct operation. A 2–3mm gap is ideal. Any less may cause the magnet to touch the sensor when riding out of the saddle. Move the sensor along the fork, and the magnet along the spoke until you have established the optimum position.

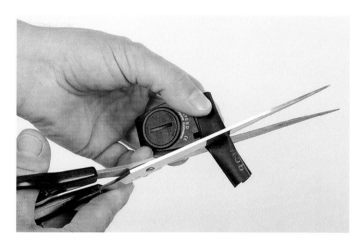

5 If you have difficulty aligning the sensor, you can use an additional rubber spacer which you can cut out of an old inner tube. Attach this using double-sided tape.

6 In addition, you can use a piece of inner tube to prevent the cable ties on the fork from slipping. This is particularly useful when mounting sensors on thin-edged fork blades.

Fitting the magnet (continued)

7 The type of magnet used is not important. Generally, most magnets will work with most sensors. If you have special rim or spoke shapes, the wheel manufacturer usually provide the magnets as part of the wheel package, often built into the wheel rims (see photo).

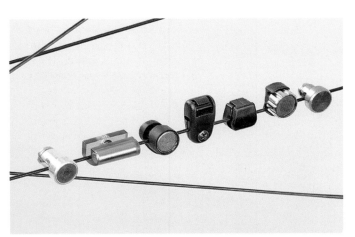

8 If you are dealing with a specially shaped spoke to which your magnet cannot be attached, try using a magnet from a different manufacturer.

9 Carbon wheels with fibre-reinforced spokes often make mounting impossible. With these spokes, never use magnets that require fitting via a clamp screw!

10 Fit the magnet to the carbon spoke, initially using insulating tape. Once you have established the final position, fix the magnet using two-component glue. In order to make sure that the magnet is securely attached, you could use an additional layer or two of insulating tape.

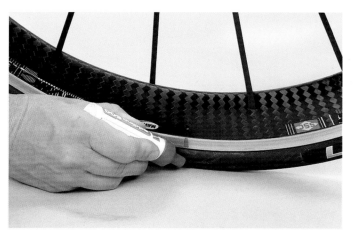

11 In order for the computer to display the correct speed and distance, you need to measure the exact rolling circumference of your tyre. To measure this, mark the tyre (fully inflated) and the point of contact with the ground by drawing a line, or using a piece of insulating tape.

12 Sit on the bike and let somebody push you forward by exactly one wheel rotation. Make a mark on the wheel rim or tyre, and a corresponding mark on the floor. Mark the floor again when the mark on the rim or tyre reaches its lowest point again. The distance between the two marks on the floor corresponds to one full revolution of the wheel. This can be used as the dimension (in millimetres) to input into the cycle computer.

Maintenance intervals

Using the correct lubricants and care products help keep the bike working smoothly and looking good. It also makes it easier to maintain the components.

Varnish, anodised finish, carbon

(Every six months, but more frequently when cycling in the rain)
Rub wax on all varnished, anodised and carbon surfaces, on aluminium and all metal parts, including screws, but with the exception of the brake contact surfaces. After allowing the polish to dry for a while, then polish the surfaces using a cotton cloth. Protect vulnerable areas such as hubs and cable guides using spray wax.

Brake body

(Every six months, but more frequently when cycling in the rain)
Wash the brake assembly and allow it to dry. Apply penetrating oil to pivots, cable mechanisms and the contact and friction points of external springs. Allow the oil to soak in, then wipe off any excess lubricant.

Derailleurs and gear shifters

(Every six months, but more frequently when cycling in the rain)
Clean all the components of the front and rear derailleurs and gear shifters, including the derailleur rollers. Apply penetrating oil to hinges and the contact and friction points of the springs. Allow the oil to soak in, then wipe off any excess lubricant.

Chain

(Every 100 to 200 miles, or after cycling in the rain)
Wipe the chain clean and evenly apply chain lubricant. Turn the cranks to move the chain through a full rotation, then allow the chain to absorb the oil for a while before wiping it off.

Seat post

(Once a year)
Remove the saddle, seat post and seat post clamp and apply assembly grease to all screws. Only use assembly grease on the seat post if the frame and post are made of metal. If there is a carbon component involved, you need to use special carbon assembly paste.

Cranks and inner bearings

(Once a year, but more frequently when cycling in the ra)
Remove and clean cranks and bottom bracket assembl. Apply assembly grease to the threads, the sides of the bottom bracket housing and the bearing cups. Apply bearing grease to non-sealed bearings. Unless recommended otherwise, also apply assembly grease t the cranks and their securing bolts.

Handlebars and stem

(Once a year)

Remove the handlebars and the stem and clean them. Where carbon components are fitted, apply carbon assembly paste to the steerer tube and its clamp and also to the handlebars and the handlebar clamp (in order to reduce the clamping torque). Apply assembly grease to screws.

Headset

(Once a year)

Remove the stem, clean the bearing assembly and bearing seats and refit the assembly after applying bearing grease.

Hubs

(Once a year, but more frequently when cycling in the rain)

Remove the cassette, remove the bearings and clean the bearing seats, bearing units and also the freewheel. Similarly, remove and clean the front hub bearings. Apply bearing grease to bearing units and bearing seats and where necessary apply special freewheel lubricant to the freewheel components. Apply assembly grease to the outside of the freehub or freewheel body.

Pedals

(Every six months, but more frequently when cycling in the rain or if pedals become noisy)

Grease exposed pedal springs using penetrating oil or spray wax. If you can hear squeaking or cracking noises coming from the cleats, apply grease to the contact points.

Tools and materials

Tools vary depending on the complexity of the assembly process. Carbon assembly paste, assembly grease, bearing grease, chain lubricant, penetrating oil, wax, spray wax, cloth.

Paint care

Scratches and chips due to stones and grit on your frame not only compromise the clean and unblemished look of your bike, but if damage is left unattended, corrosion can cause further damage. This chapter describes how to remove marks and flaws on varnished, anodised, chrome and powder-coated surfaces.

Your bike needs to shine, shimmer and gleam. A desirable road bike will be even more attractive the more squeaky clean and well maintained it is. Yet, however carefully and cautiously you treat your bike, over the years it is impossible to avoid getting scratches and marks on the frame surface that spoil the appearance. Dirt and stains are easy to wipe off. Damage to the paintwork, the powder-coated or anodised layer, however, is not. Yet this type of damage should be repaired as soon as possible. On metal components, once the protective layer has been penetrated, corrosion sets in immediately. If this is followed by sweat dripping on to the

vulnerable area, or liquid from the drinks bottle, or occasional rain, this will quickly become a problem area for corrosion.

If you manage to repair the damage straight away, little effort will be necessary to repair it. However, you will have to seek out a matching shade of paint before starting the repair work. Only a few bike manufacturers offer touch-up sticks in original colours. They are easier to find in shops selling car accessories. Car paint can be obtained in the form of touch-up sticks featuring a very fine paintbrush integrated into the stick cap. Considering the fact that there are more than 10,000 shades of car paint, your

- When carrying out cleaning work, do not apply wax to the clamping areas of carbon parts, the braking surfaces on the rims, or the brake pads.
- Do not use steam-cleaning devices or pressure washers to wash your bike (as some mechanics in the professional racing teams do). These devices not only remove dirt and salts, but also grease from areas which need to stay lubricated, for example between the chain links, the sprockets etc. Furthermore, the water jet may penetrate into the bearings, affect the lubrication and destroy them in the process.
- Steel and aluminium frames that have become unsightly can be sandblasted, or the varnish can be chemically removed, and then newly powder-coated. There are various companies experienced in carrying out these procedures.
- Carbon parts must not be powder-coated or lacquered, as the high temperatures used in the processes would cause structural damage. Sandblasting and the chemical removal of varnish/paint are also out of the question. You will only be able to remove the old varnish by slowly sanding it off by hand.

- Remove dirt and salts from aluminium parts using clear water and, when dry, protect them by applying wax polish. This way, the unvarnished surface will stay sealed for a long time and will therefore look good and stay protected. Don't try to seal the surface permanently using clear varnish, as the varnish will not adhere to the metal surface properly.
- When polishing with a power tool, protect your eyes using safety goggles. Also, wear work clothes. Working on metal can be dirty, as aluminium dust can be produced.
- If handlebars, stems or seat posts are scratched, they should be renewed for safety reasons. Whether it is possible to repair cranks and pedals depends on the extent to which they are damaged. If in doubt, ask your bike retailer.
- When using polishing pastes and discs, you need to adhere to the recommended sequence of discs, pastes and the recommended rotational speed specified by the product's manufacturer. The polishing process is a gradual one – the surface will become increasingly smooth with each step.

chances of finding a reasonable matching colour for your bike are relatively high. If your bike is powder-coated, it might be easier to obtain the correct colour, since the powder-coating shades correspond to the standardised and commonly used RAL colour chart.

Before starting any repair work on the paint, the bike needs to be thoroughly cleaned, ideally by hand. To remove oil and grease, use water diluted with a few squirts of washing-up liquid. It is possible that minute damage may only become visible after cleaning your bike! After washing, rinse your bike with clear water and let it dry off properly.

Most components are repairable. With a little effort, even this derailleur mechanism.

Tools and materials

Vice with aluminium block, power drill with stand, polishing set, files, keyhole files, tools for dismantling, triangular scraper, paint brush, screwdrivers, emery cloth, wax, spray wax, assembly grease, polish, thinners, varnish, touch-up stick, sandpaper, transparent adhesive foil, silicone spray, cloth.

Drying after rain or washing

1 Not every seat post is as open as this one, however water spray tends to run along the seat post and into the interior of the frame. Since the post and its frame tube hardly ever match precisely, water can penetrate into the frame via small slots and holes. Additionally, the openings for in-frame cable runs, and also the headset, can allow water to get in.

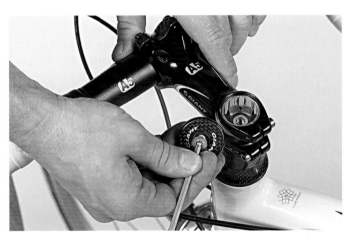

2 Remove the headset expander bolt and the end cap, and tilt it so that any water that may have got in will drain out. Put the bike in a well-ventilated spot so that the interior of the frame can dry before you refit the end cap and bolt.

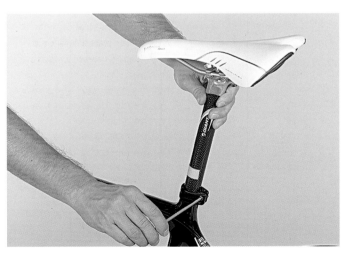

3 Mark the seat post's current position using adhesive tape, then remove the post. Stand the bike upside-down so that any water can drain out. Rock the frame slightly back and forth to help the water drain.

Cleaning and greasing properly

1 Washing is the best preventative measure to keep your bike in good condition. You should wash your bike at least once a month, using plenty of water, even if you have spent a lot of time riding in the rain! Water helps to remove corrosive salts from dried sweat and electrolyte drinks. Afterwards, let the bike dry thoroughly. Treat the frame with wax at least twice per season.

2 Remove the bottom bracket bearings, the headset, and the seat post once a year. Bearings and posts which have been fitted to the frame for years and not maintained may corrode and become stuck, which means you will only be able to remove them with great difficulty, or perhaps not at all.

3 Applying fresh grease to the bottom-bracket threads and housing, between the cups and bearings, and to the spindle and crank contact surfaces, helps avoid cracking noises and prevents corrosion from occurring. Remember that only special carbon assembly paste should be used for carbon seat posts and for posts in carbon frames!

Protection against scratches

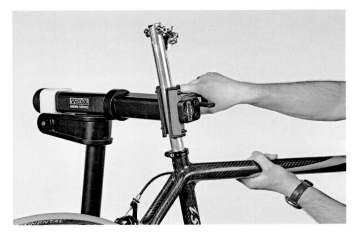

1 Never fit carbon frames directly on a workstand featuring a claw mechanism, as the clamping forces are easily capable of crushing a tube. Stands with a three-point or four-point linkage are more suitable for this job. Alternatively, you could have a cheap but robust metal seat post handy for jobs to be carried out on the stand, which you can then swap for the carbon post.

2 Transparent, thick adhesive tape will protect the frame from abrasion, and from damage due to stones hitting the chainstay, as well as scratches, without being visible. Transparent tape is ideal in areas where cables touch the frame.

3 In the area where the chainrings pass the chainstay on the frame, it's a good idea to protect the frame from damage due to jammed chains. For this, use multiple layers of transparent tape. Thin aluminium strip, for example taken from a drink can, can be used to increase protection. An aluminium strip fitted to the bottom bracket housing will provide good protection, should the chain drop off the chainrings.

4 Apply car wax to all treated surfaces, and to all metal parts such as brake levers, cranks etc. Allow the wax to dry, and then repolish. Treat complex-shaped parts, such as the hub body, including the spoke holes, using spray wax. This ensures that the wax reaches the inner recesses.

5 Carbon frames also have components that may corrode. These include bottle holder lugs, cable guides, derailleur hangers, seat post clamp and dropouts. There are often gaps where these components are joined to the rest of the frame. Spray wax will prevent salt and moisture from penetrating these areas.

6 Fibrous materials do not rust and require little care. However, carbon frames almost always feature aluminium parts which have been screwed on, bonded on, or riveted on. If the varnish in these areas is not perfect, or if gaps exist, the attachment points may corrode. For this reason you should seal the frame using wax before you first ride the bike, and then at regular intervals.

Care of anodised surfaces

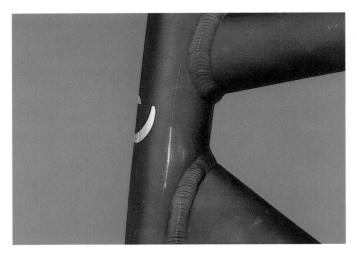

1 Scratch marks on the anodised surfaces of aluminium frames are often less dramatic than at first glance. Light-coloured marks often turn out to be abrasions on the tough protective layer caused by foreign bodies.

2 Use specialised care products for anodised surfaces, and apply to the appropriate areas. Using a cotton cloth, rub the polish thoroughly into the frame. This should remove dirt and abrasions from the surface and should seal any pores.

3 After the treatment, the entire surface should shine with a semi-gloss finish. If you do not succeed in removing the mark, you will have to degrease the area and seal it using protective paint.

Restoring powder-coated paint

1 Always polish minor scratches on a powder-coated surface using liquid polish (not wax). Deep scratches can be repaired using commonly available varnish. The polishing liquid contains added abrasive particles which remove a wafer-thin layer of paint, thus smoothing any uneven areas and renewing the shine. Paint restorers work even harder. They contain more aggressive abrasives and thus are also suitable for refurbishing very faded or dirty paints.

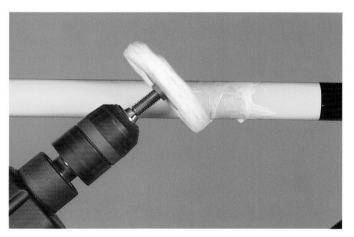

2 Apply some polish or paint restorer. Work over the affected area using a rotating buffing wheel mounted in an electric drill. Move the tool back and forth in order to achieve a smooth finish on all sides of the area. Not only does the polish need to be evenly distributed, it must be able to gently remove a thin layer of paint. Hence, you should moisten the area and/or the tool more than once during the process using fresh polish.

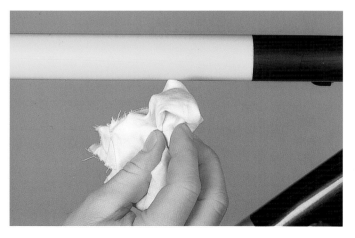

3 Once the polishing is finished, protect the new surface as soon as possible and, ideally, seal the whole frame, using liquid hard wax. Using a cloth, apply a thin layer of wax to the entire frame. Apply a little more polish around edges and corners, in order to prevent corrosion in the recesses. When the polish is dry, polish the dull wax finish using a clean, soft cloth. The paint should now shine like new.

Chrome parts

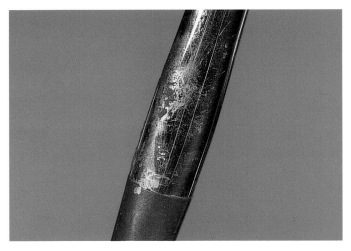

1 You may often find larger patches of rust on the surface of a chromed area which, though worrying, are due to a relatively minor problem. Rust which has spread across a chromed surface is easy to remove. If the chrome surface is seriously affected, however, even polishing will not help. In order to prevent further damage, you will need to remove the area of corrosion from the chrome, and seal the metal in a similar way to that described for the paint repair jobs.

2 Remove ingrained dirt and rust using steel wool. It is important to ensure that the steel wool's fibres run at right-angles to the polishing motion, otherwise the steel wool will not clean the material properly.

3 After this treatment you might have to polish vigorously – as described in the section on powder-coated paint. In any case, you will need to seal the surface with wax at the end of the chrome polishing process.

Repairing minor damage to the paintwork

1 If there is minor damage to the paintwork, you should repair this straight away in order to prevent bigger problems developing. You can pinpoint the area exactly, and prepare the frame, using a glassfibre abrasive pen. This will provide an ideal surface for the paint to stick, and will remove any corrosion.

2 Clean the affected area, and remove any dust and grease using a soft cloth which has been soaked in alcohol or paint thinner.

3 Carefully apply paint using a touch-up stick. Let the paint dry properly before treating the bike, or at least the repaired area, using wax. You can buy touch-up sticks from your bike dealer, or in shops selling car accessories.

Repairing major damage to the paintwork

1 Patches on which corrosion has set in are often larger than they at first seem. Therefore you need to completely expose the bare metal. Remove loose paint particles around the affected area using a screwdriver or small scraper. Only when no more paint flakes off is the area clean enough to provide a base for fresh paint and still sufficiently protected from further corrosion.

2 If the affected area has started to rust, you need to remove the corrosion using coarse emery paper until bare metal is exposed. You also need to remove all rust from any depressions or pores in the metal.

3 Finally, using finer emery paper, smooth out any grooves that have been produced by the initial sanding. The area that you need to paint should become as even as possible. Then clean the area using alcohol or thinner to free the base from grease.

4 Apply the paint in several thin layers – as thin as possible. This prevents the adjacent existing paint from being softened by the solvent in the paint. For the drying time and temperature, follow the manufacturer's recommendations.

5 An alternative method is to sand down the surface in between applying the individual paint layers, in order to produce a smooth surface. Again, use fine emery paper for this. Apply the final layer of paint as thinly as possible, using a paintbrush. When using metallic paint, the final layer needs to be clear varnish.

6 In order to obtain an even surface, you need to smooth the repaired area using very fine finishing paper. Use strips of wet abrasive paper (800- or 1000-grit) and carefully sand at right-angles to the direction of the tube run. As the final step, polish the repaired area, using varnish cleaner or paint polish, until it shines. On completion, seal the painted area using wax – or even better, wax the whole bike.

Polishing out scratches

1 Remove the scratched component, and dismantle as necessary so that you can clamp it in a vice. It should not move while you work on it, yet at the same time it must not be damaged. Note that while carrying out the subsequent jobs, chippings and fine aluminium dust will be produced. If these particles find their way into the component's mechanism, its operation might be compromised.

2 Dismantle the component further if necessary. Alternatively, cover sensitive areas with a clean cloth and seal any holes. Use a piece of cloth to protect the area which makes contact with the vice. The vice itself should be protected via soft jaw pads made of aluminium or plastic. Increase the clamping force carefully until the part you need to work on is secure.

3 File the surface of the damaged area, using a fine, flat-bladed file. File for as long as necessary to level out the biggest scratches and grooves. Work the file using long strokes, and try to cover the maximum area possible, thus making sure that you do not introduce edges and indentations into the area being worked on.

4 You can also use a flat file to work on convex curved areas. When working on curved surfaces, slide the file forwards while guiding the grip downwards at the same time. Concave surfaces are seldom damaged during a fall, however, if damage has occurred to a concave surface, it is best to work on them manually, using coarse emery paper.

5 Smooth over smaller areas of damage, inaccessible areas and small edges using a very fine keyhole file. These files come in round and half-round versions, which are useful for removing burrs from the inside of holes.

6 Cut a narrow strip from a piece of emery paper (roughly 180-grit). Hold the paper tightly, using both hands, and guide it over the area which you have previously prepared and smoothed using the file. Start at one end, and sand applying steady back-and-forth movements. Hold the paper at a slight angle in relation to the part. Keep moving, gradually working your way across the damaged area.

Polishing scratches (continued)

7 Once this has been done, turn the emery paper and rub again at right-angles to the previous working direction and repeat the process. This avoids introducing grooves to the surface. Work your way back to the starting point. Repeat the process until any rough file marks and surface damage have disappeared.

8 You can improve the finish using finer abrasive paper, for example 600-grit. This will mean that even the light sanding marks produced by the coarser paper will no longer be visible. Rub down twice, rubbing at right-angles to the first pass on the second, as before. Clean off any dust from the components, and blow off with compressed air if available.

9 Using a pillar drill, or a power drill mounted in a vertical bench-stand, fit a suitable polishing disc. Set the drill to a medium speed (unless otherwise specified) and lock the push button to switch the drill on continuously.

10 Apply the polishing paste to the disc. Hold the component carefully in your hands and guide it slowly towards the polishing disc. Gently increase the pressure against the disc. Pay attention at all times, making sure that the component is not snatched from your hands. In particular, watch out for areas featuring edges and holes!

11 It is more important to keep the part moving than to apply maximum pressure, to ensure that the whole area that needs to be polished moves over the disc. Every now and again, check the surface of the component, and also apply new polishing paste to the disc.

12 When you have finished polishing, wipe off the residues from the component and the disc. Finally, polish the component using hard wax. Allow the wax to dry to a matt finish, then polish off using a soft cloth. This will give the component its final shine.

Repairing varnished surfaces on carbon frames

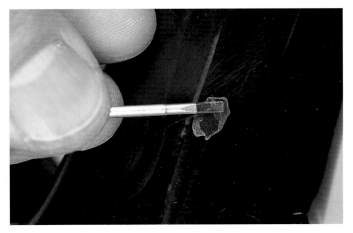

1 If you need to repair damage to the painted surface of a carbon frame, you should do this without delay. Using a small, flat-bladed screwdriver, completely remove any loose paint.

2 Using fine abrasive paper, sand the affected area very carefully, taking care to minimise damage to the surrounding area.

3 Most paints are compatible with the epoxy resin matrix used in carbon components. You can repair the damage using a commonly available touch-up stick. Matt patches or superficial scratches can be polished using a paint polish containing abrasive particles, although this is unsuitable for regular maintenance, since it will gradually wear down the surface.

Repairing varnished surfaces on plastic parts

1 Pedals and brake/gearshift levers made from injection-moulded plastic quickly suffer scratches due to their soft surface. You can smooth these out using rough abrasive paper.

2 Using fine abrasive paper, the surface can be sanded almost smooth again. On completion, apply silicone spray to the affected area in order to give a matt finish. If the surface of the plastic is discoloured, you may need to repaint it. Try applying a little varnish or paint to a hidden area of the component in order to check that the varnish/paint and the plastic are compatible – some paints may attack certain types of plastic.

3 Finish off by wiping off any dust, and then applying varnish/paint in several thin layers. Always allow the varnish/paint to dry and harden completely before applying the next coat.

Getting rid of noises

Generally, noises from the bike originate from tiny movements between two or more parts. This is nothing new, but since frames made up of large-diameter, thin-walled tubes tend to provide effective amplifier boxes, annoying noises often reach the rider's ear and can prove very annoying.

It is not easy to find solutions to creaking, as the source of this nuisance is often difficult to find. It is rarely a fault that causes the noise. Almost all components on the bike need to be considered when investigating the small movements that might cause a noise: frame, saddle, post, handlebars, stem, cranks and pedals. What they have in common is that they all suffer continuous minor deformation due to pedalling forces, pulling on the handlebars, and knocks from the road surface. Just a slight weight shift in the saddle can cause a noise – or sometimes remedy it. What makes finding the source of the problem more difficult is that the sound can carry over the entire frame, and the creaking sound does not necessarily originate where it appears to come from. Therefore, it is necessary to investigate systematically, carrying out a test ride on a quiet side road.

Here is a suggested procedure for your finding the source of the noise. Pedal at varying cadences, and let the bike roll for short distances in between pedalling. Increase and decrease the amount of weight you put on the different parts of the bike, such as the saddle and pedals. Gradually try to exclude one possible source of noise after another. Also, increase and decrease the amount of weight you put on the handlebars and stem while the bike is at rest.

For example, if you have established that the noise is coming from the bottom bracket area, you now need to home in on the problem. Work from the outside of the area to the inside. The first sensible action may seem obvious: spray some spray-wax on to the front derailleur area, the cranks and chainrings, as well as the bottom bracket housing. Once the wax has penetrated into all the gaps and has dried, check the tightness of all screws, using a torque wrench where possible. If you can still hear creaking, you will have to remove various components and investigate further.

If the creaking sound continues to be annoying, you will need to check the other components on the bike which are affected by pedalling.

The tips suggested previously for the seat post apply, but with one exception. If the post and/or the seat tube are made from carbon, do not apply grease to the clamping mechanism. If the components are greased, the clamp would only be effective after tightening the clamp bolt to an extremely high torque, which may damage carbon components. Instead, you are better off cleaning the carbon post and/or the interior of the carbon seat tube regularly using a cloth. This will prevent dirt or moisture from entering the components and possibly becoming the source of noises. All the other previous tips provided for seat posts apply equally to carbon components.

Once you have removed the seat post, you should also check whether it is long enough. Its lower end must reach at least to the bottom edge of the top tube, within the seat tube,

Finding noises

- **Rattling** – There is excessive free-play in a brake lever; tools are rattling in the saddle bag.
- **Knocking** – The headset is loose.
- **Cracking** – The bottom bracket, cranks, front derailleur, pedal spindle or dropout require grease and/or tightening to the correct torque; the wheel quick-release mechanism is not tight enough.
- **Creaking** – The pedal cleats need grease or are worn out; the seat post creaks.
- **Scratching** – The chain is rubbing against the front derailleur.
- **Squeaking** – The chain or the rear derailleur rollers are running dry (without lubricant).

otherwise it cannot provide sufficient support, since it will not be supported over a large enough area within the frame. If the post does not extend far enough into the seat tube, it will 'sway' inside the tube. Noises and a fractured frame are very likely consequences.

Once components settle, securing screws can loosen. For this reason, check all screws after approximately 100 miles of riding. Where possible, use a torque wrench to make the check. Make a habit of checking all screws on your road bike every 1,000 miles or so – or more frequently if you often ride on bad road surfaces.

Tools and materials

Bottom bracket tools, pin spanner and hex keys, torque wrench, sprocket tools, oil, carbon assembly paste, silicone spray, chain oil, assembly grease, adhesive, wax

Systematic investigation

1 Ride without your hands on the handlebars, and pedal, applying varying amounts of pressure. If the noise stops, the cause could be related to the handlebar and stem area. Stop the bike, hold the handlebars near the brake levers and push and pull alternately. If you cannot recreate the noise in this way, another possible source of the noise is the seat post (the load on the saddle is different when riding hands-free).

2 Pedal, applying varying amounts of pressure, and also stand up in order to ride out of the saddle. If the noise ceases, the origin is probably the saddle area. Stop the bike and hold the saddle at the front and back. Try to turn the saddle sideways in both directions away from the frame. Also push it upwards at the front and downwards at the back and vice versa.

3 Pedal, applying varying amounts of pressure, and each time let the bike freewheel for a short distance. If the noise occurs both while riding out of the saddle and while sitting down, but not when the pedals are at rest, the problem is likely to be caused by your shoes, or the pedals or cranks. Stop and push on the pedal from one side. Also push from the opposite side.

Handlebars

1 Remove the stem clamp bolts, and take off the faceplate. Take care while doing this – make sure that the handlebars do not drop down. Clean all parts. On aluminium handlebars and stems, grease the bolt heads and threads when refitting, and tighten them evenly. The gaps between the stem faceplate and the stem, at the top and bottom, should be equal.

2 On carbon handlebars, apply carbon assembly paste thinly and evenly to the clamping area of the handlebar as well as to the clamping surfaces of the stem and faceplate. Fit the handlebars using greased clamp bolts as described previously. Tighten the bolts, evenly and progressively, to the specified torque, where applicable. Take care not to overtighten the bolts.

3 Check that the brake levers are tightly secured and cannot move on the handlebars. Gently tighten the clamp bolts, but do not exceed the maximum torque. This is particularly important on carbon handlebars. To avoid the risk of annoying noises, it may be better to unwrap the handlebar tape and apply carbon assembly paste between the brake lever mountings and the handlebars.

Saddle and seat post

1 Apply silicone spray to the point where the top part of the saddle meets the saddle rails. Let the spray soak in, and then check for noise again.

2 Remove the saddle and dismantle the clamp at the top of the seat post. Clean the individual parts. Apply grease to the bolt heads and washers. Check whether the manufacturer recommends greasing the threads, as in some cases this is not an option due to the self-locking screw.

3 In all cases, tighten the saddle clamp screws in accordance with the manufacturer's recommendations using a torque wrench. Screws that have not been tightened properly are often the reason for sudden noise problems, particularly on posts that are secured with a single screw.

4 Mark and remove the seat post. Clean the post and the interior of the frame tube using a cloth. Check that the seat post is long enough. It should reach at least to the bottom of the top tube. If it is shorter than this, there is the risk that it may 'sway' in the seat tube – this will not only cause noise, but may also cause damage to the frame.

5 On bikes with metal frames and/ or aluminium seat posts, spread some assembly grease on the contact faces of the post and the frame tube in the clamping area, using a paintbrush. Also apply a thin layer of grease to the corresponding areas on the outside of the seat tube and on the inner face of the clamp itself, before refitting the components, and adjusting and securing them.

6 Do not apply grease to the clamping area for carbon components! Use special carbon assembly paste on the clamping surfaces inside the seat tube and on the post. Grease the seat-post clamp bolt, the clamping area on the outside of the seat tube, and the inner face of the clamp itself. After greasing, it will be possible to produce an effective clamping action with a much lower torque setting.

Derailleur hanger

1 Could a replaceable derailleur hanger be causing the noise? Check varnished or powder-coated hangers for signs of damage, or scuffs to the varnished or powder-coated areas. Clean any damaged areas found. Grease the contact surfaces, then refit the hanger and tighten the securing bolts.

2 If you can still hear creaking, you can also glue the hanger on. Carefully clean the areas where the glue is to be applied first, using cleaning alcohol or acetone to remove any grease. If necessary, you can use a recommended cleaning agent to finally remove grease and improve bonding – check the adhesive manufacturer's recommendations for details.

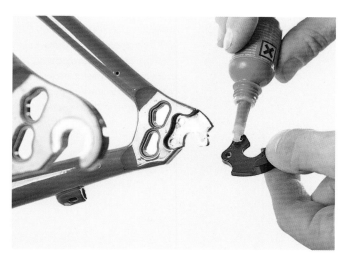

3 Apply the adhesive (two-part adhesive is ideal), then assemble the components and tighten the securing bolts. Fit the wheel and tighten the quick-release mechanism immediately to clamp the hanger to the frame. Wipe off any excess adhesive immediately.

Pedals

1 Are the pedals causing the noise? Remove them, using a long pedal key or a slightly offset open-ended spanner to prevent injuries from the chainring. To counterhold the crank, shift the gears to move the chain on to the largest chainring, then hold the crank, bracing it against the chain stay with one hand, while unscrewing the pedal with the other.

2 With the pedal removed, try moving the pedal spindle in various different directions. If the spindle tilts, if it does not run smoothly, or if there is a considerable degree of freeplay between the spindle and the pedal, you will need to dismantle the pedal and adjust it, or at least grease the components. There may be a chance that you need new pedal bearings.

3 Clean the threads in the crank and on the pedal spindle. Grease both threads with assembly grease, paying particular attention to the contact surfaces of the spindle – it should be well greased. On completion, refit the pedals.

Front derailleur clamp

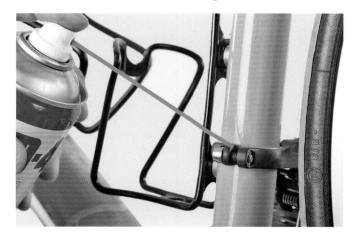

1 You need to work methodically around the bottom-bracket area in order to identify and prevent noises. To begin with, apply plenty of spray wax or penetrating oil to the front derailleur area, cranks and the chainrings.

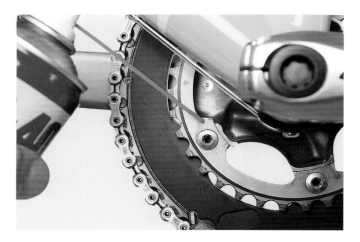

2 Once the wax or penetrating oil has worked its way into the components, check the tightness of all fixings in accordance with the manufacturer's recommendations.

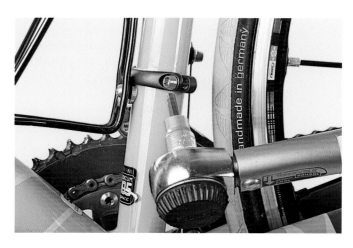

3 Retighten the bolts with the torque wrench. You will only be able to tighten the bolt effectively if you first slacken it by at least half a turn. If this does not help, you will need to remove the bolts and refit.

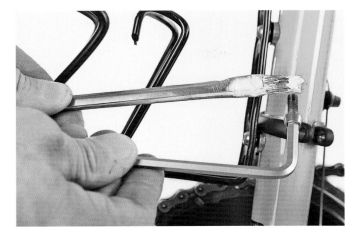

4 Noises may originate from the front derailleur clamp bolts, or between the clamp and the frame. Before removing the clamp, mark its position on the frame. Clean the seat tube and the clamp, then remove the front derailleur. Grease the parts and refit them again, aligning them carefully as noted before removal.

5 On anodised aluminium frames, apply grease to the inside surfaces of the clamp. On carbon frames, you should always use carbon assembly paste on the clamp. On varnished or powder-coated frames, you should fit the parts without applying any grease or lubricant.

Chainrings and cranks

1 Could the noise be due to the chainrings? Remove the chainring bolts. Special tools are available to prevent the sleeve nuts on the back of the bolts from turning as you slacken the bolts. Turn the bolts anti-clockwise using a long hex key. This will help to avoid injuries – chainring screws often slacken suddenly!

2 Remove the chainrings and use a cloth to wipe them clean. Grease the contact surfaces on the crank spider and the rings. When refitting the rings, the mark on the smaller ring (generally arrow-shaped) and the rivet on the larger chainring should be positioned behind the crank arm – ie, facing the frame.

3 Grease the inside and the sleeve nuts, and slide them into their holes. Grease the threads of the bolts, then refit the bolts, and screw them in as far as possible by hand. Check that all components are correctly positioned before tightening the bolts progressively in a diagonal sequence.

4 Could the problem be the bottom bracket? Slacken the crank clamp bolts by two or three turns (the clamp bolts are fitted tangentially to the spindle).

5 Unscrew the bolt from the end of the crank, and pull the crank from the end of the spindle. Pull the whole crank assembly, including the spindle where applicable, from the bottom bracket. Wipe both cranks and the spindle clean.

6 Remove the bottom-bracket bearings (using the appropriate specialist tools). On BSC threads (1.370in x 24tpi), the drive side is unscrewed clockwise! On BSC threads, the left-hand side is unscrewed anti-clockwise, and both sides are unscrewed anti-clockwise on Italian threads. Make sure that the tools do not slide off the components!

Chainrings and cranks (continued)

7 Clean the components and the bearing housing. Lightly grease the threads and the contact surfaces of the bearing cups, the threads in the frame, the spindle, and the cranks. Fit both bearing cups by hand, screwing them in two turns. Once they are engaged with the threads, tighten them to the manufacturer's specified torque.

8 Remove the clamp bolts from the cranks, and clean the bolts and the cranks. Liberally apply assembly grease to the bolt threads and the underside of the heads. Slide the cranks on to the spindle and lightly screw in both clamping screws by hand. Screw the bolts into the ends of the crank, but do not fully tighten them.

9 Tighten the crank clamp bolts using a torque wrench, initially to 8Nm, then to 12Nm. On Shimano cranks, tighten the bolts progressively to 15Nm. On completion, refit the bolts to the ends of the cranks, greasing the threads and the undersides of the heads before fitting.

Bottom bracket

1 If you can still hear noises, you need to tighten the cranks. On many modern cranksets, you can do this without additional tools, as there is an integrated crank puller. Slacken the bolt anti-clockwise with a long hex key. When the resistance increases, keep turning forcefully to push the crank from the spindle.

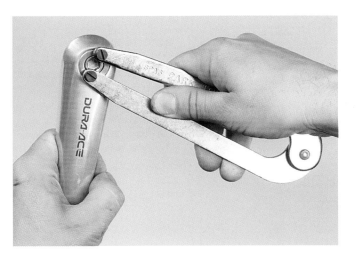

2 Unscrew the crank cover cap using a pin spanner. Make sure the correct tool is used, with pins of the correct size, otherwise the holes in the cover cap can be easily damaged. Remove the bolt and recover any washers. Clean all the components.

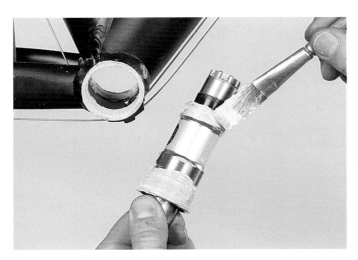

3 Use the appropriate special tools to remove the bottom-bracket bearings – normally a splined socket, which engages with the bearing cartridge. On BSC threads (1.370in x 24tpi), the drive side is unscrewed clockwise! On BSC threads, the left-hand side is unscrewed anti-clockwise, and both sides are unscrewed anti-clockwise on Italian threads. Make sure that the tools do not slide off the components! After cleaning, grease the threads on the cartridge and in the frame and also the contact surfaces between the cartridge (often made of steel) and the screw thread surface.

Bottom bracket (continued)

4 Screw in the bearing from the chainring side, by hand, by three to four turns. Also screw in the bearing cup on the opposite side a few turns, again by hand, before tightening the drive side to the specified torque. Similarly, tighten the remaining cup. Check the smooth running of the bearing and the fit of the cups in relation to the housing surfaces. If the bearing does not run smoothly or the cups do not fit squarely, the threads in the bearing housing need to be re-cut, and the surfaces must be milled in order to fit exactly parallel to each other.

5 On models with splined spindles, grease the splines on the spindle, as well as the contact surfaces on the inside of the cranks. The components need to fit smoothly together. Fit the greased crank bolt. You may need to twist the spindle and crank in relation to each other until the splines engage before the crank bolt can be fitted.

6 Only tighten the crank bolts once both cranks are accurately positioned on the spindle in accordance with the manufacturer's recommendations. Grease the crank bolt and the washer. Finally, refit and tighten the greased crank cover cap, again in accordance to the manufacturer's recommendations.

Miscellaneous causes of noises

1 Occasionally, the quick-release mechanism on the rear wheel hub develops a mind of its own. The tensioner is exposed to permanent load from the chain, which can result in noises. Remove the quick-release components and apply some (chain) oil to the inside of the hub and to the quick-release shaft and lever pivot. Move the quick-release lever back and forth so that the oil can reach the relevant areas. Note that silicone lubricant is not particularly well suited for lubricating steel parts. Wipe off any excess oil.

2 The cassette and freehub are also possible sources of noises. Remove the cassette and freehub, as described previously, clean and lubricate the components (using spray wax) and refit.

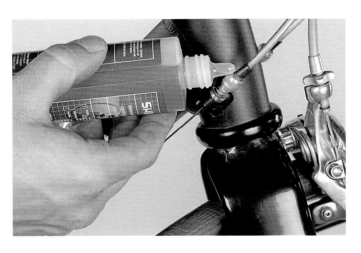

3 Noises may also originate from places where cables touch the frame or components, or where the cable outers move in cable guides. Work around the bike and lubricate all contact points and cable guides. Don't forget the cable guides below the bottom bracket. Leave the bike for a while for the lubricant to penetrate, then wipe off any excess lubricant.

Frames

Carbon frames last forever – provided you treat them well. We explain whether they can be repaired and by whom, how you can remedy faults such as broken water bottle mounts, and how to look after carbon and metal frames.

As a precaution, you already decided to take your precious carbon racer into the house to protect it from the risks of the garage, and then this happens: a thoughtless movement, a little push with your elbow and the bike falls over, with its top tube hitting the edge of a table. Now there's a small chip in the paint on the top tube, with small cracks spreading sideways. Is the frame broken now? The fact is that there is no general or easy answer to this. It is also hard to determine whether you can continue to use the frame, forks, handlebars, or other carbon parts after a crash on the road, or whether they need to be replaced. Checking and assessing

damaged carbon parts remains a considerable problem.

How do you identify the fault?

It is not good enough just to look closely. Even after being overloaded, carbon parts do not appear bent, as they maintain their original shape. Unlike aluminium and steel frames, measuring the frame will not produce any meaningful conclusions. Processes such as x-raying, or impulse thermography, sound promising in theory. On an x-ray image of a carbon part, for example, you can see the construction features, such as wall thickness

Before starting the repair, the carbon structure is carefully sanded down layer by layer.

and carbon/metal joints. Fibre layers that have delaminated, and small fissures, however, remain invisible. Computer tomography would provide useful information, but its costs are likely to be prohibitive.

To carry out impulse thermography, the component is heated up via flashes of light, and the heat emissions are recorded by a camera. With carbon parts, variations in heat emissions are caused by faulty areas in the laminate, resin deposits, foam inserts, metal components, paint layers varying in thickness, and even by stickers. A thermography picture can reveal all sorts of things. However, no expert is prepared to say for certain whether any problem areas identified are likely to have an effect on durability. It would only be possible to establish this if a thermography picture of the part in question had been taken when it was brand new, to compare with the possible damage. Comparing the images before and after a knock or a crash may indicate whether there have been changes to the material structure.

Stiffness tests provide a good method of checking the condition of carbon parts. The stiffness generally decreases when the fibre composite is weakened, or becomes loose,

damaged, or when the part is heavily worn. However, the same rule mentioned previously applies here: without comparing the used or damaged part's results to those of a new one, the measurement is pretty much meaningless. Mounting the part on a test stand will reveal more about a stressed part. Fissures, for example, which are not visible with the part in a relaxed state, become visible under load, or may cause noises when varying loads are applied. Both tests may indicate damage.

Who can repair what?

Carbon is in fact a material that can easily be repaired. Essentially, you only need epoxy resin and fibre matting. It depends on the expertise and experience of the person carrying out the work whether the repair is successful or not. It is common to apply simple bandages, although this can be unsightly. Additionally, transition areas between the bandage to the original part may result in abrupt changes in stiffness. This could potentially precipitate further damage. From a technical and aesthetic point of view, a better route is to grind down the damaged area layer by layer, although of course this is more labour intensive. This approach enables a gradual build-up of new laminate layers, providing a durable composite with uniform stiffness. If the affected area is professionally painted afterwards, the repair will not be noticeable.

Yet not everything can be repaired. With forks, handlebars and seat posts, the cost of putting them through the test processes and repairing them would be out of proportion to what they actually cost. Buying a new part is clearly the better choice. Examples of possible repairs are small holes and fissures in the top tube, or marks on the bottom bracket housing and chain stay caused by a dropped chain. If you are dealing with a frame that has broken into two parts, however, a repair is out of the question. You need to calculate the costs for each individual case, but be careful not to underestimate, depending on the repair and – above all – painting work involved. Whether the repair is worth it, and whether the work makes economic sense depends on your own personal judgement. One repair that you can do yourself in your own workshop involves the bottle cage mount on the frame. We will show you later in this chapter how to do it.

Other than that, we will limit our advice in terms of repair jobs to an easy-to-fix classic problem: the derailleur hanger. For example, if the hanger has become bent after a crash, this is no reason to dispose of the frame. If the hanger is heavily deformed, you need to check carefully whether the material has suffered damage. Fissures on a varnished or chrome surface do not necessarily reach as far as the frame material itself.

Spare derailleur hangers are invaluable if you suffer a problem, especially if you have a replacement part in your saddle bag when out and about. Due to the relatively thin nature of their material, they cannot normally be bent back to their original shape and must be renewed.

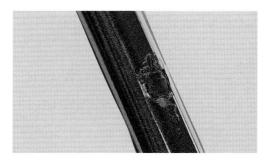

The damage. Two bikes leaning against each other fell over. The pedal of one damaged the upper section of the rear stays on the other.

The repair. Since the damage was relatively minor, only a small area needed to be repaired.

The finish. The challenge when painting and varnishing is matching the colour shade to the original paint. Even lettering can be reproduced.

Tools and materials
Hexagon key, ring spanner, pop-riveter, cordless screwdriver, thread tap, two-component adhesive, cutting oil, bottle holder

Derailleur hanger

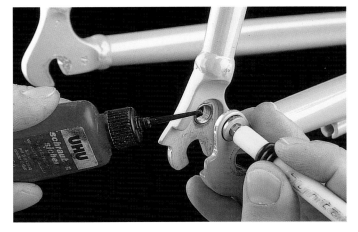

If you have a replaceable derailleur hanger, you should replace the entire part if it is damaged. First spray the securing screw with penetrating lubricant. If the faulty hanger was powder-coated along with the frame, in a single process, carve around edges of the hanger using a sharp knife. This will prevent varnish from chipping off when you remove the hanger. Before fitting the hanger again, clean and wax the contact surface on the frame. You should use medium-strength thread-locking compound when refitting the securing screw.

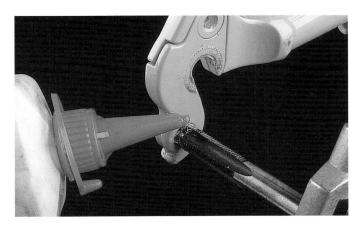

If the thread in the hanger was damaged, you could try re-cutting it. It's important to know that the hanger usually has a fine thread of M10x1! Apply oil to the tap and to the threads. Hold the tap vertically and turn it into the thread part. Turn the tap very slowly, and continue cutting the thread until the end of the tap emerges from the hanger.

Here's a tip for when you're out and about on a ride. You can use the back wheel of one of your fellow riders to fix a bent derailleur hanger. Using the hub spindle, engage the wheel with the derailleur hanger (with the derailleur removed), carefully, but as tightly as possible. The wheel itself serves as the reference plane for the adjustment. Ask somebody to help you hold the frame. Then take the 'spare' wheel in both hands and bend it in the direction of the most serious (largest) deformation until it is parallel in relation to the back wheel. If you have special tools available, the repair will of course be considerably faster and simpler.

Loose bottle-cage rivnut

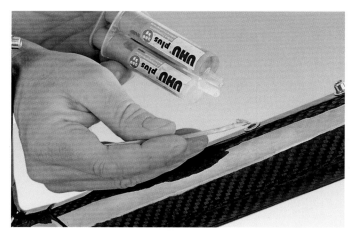

1 Place your fingers around the flange of the rivnut. If there is a gap between the flange and the frame tube, this may mean that the rivnut is loose in the frame. Mix two-component adhesive, then apply the adhesive between the rivnut flange and the frame tube as best as possible.

2 Take an M5 bolt with hexagonal head (the bolt must be at least 30mm long) and screw a nut on to it, almost as far as the bolt head. Place a washer on the nut – the washer's diameter should be at least as big as the outer diameter of the rivnut flange. Screw the bolt into the rivnut by at least 10mm.

3 Turn the nut, by hand, towards the frame, until the washer sits neatly on the top of the rivnut flange. Place a ring spanner on the nut and hold the bolt head tight with a second spanner, then gradually tighten the nut. As the end of the rivnut flange is squeezed against the frame tube, adhesive will spill out. If it is still possible to turn the bolt, the nut is not clamping tightly enough. Warning – applying too much force might damage carbon frames!

Damaged rivnut thread

1 Rivnut threads that have been damaged can be re-cut under certain circumstances. Align the tap (lubricated with cutting oil) with the hole in the insert, then carefully re-cut the thread. If the thread is damaged beyond repair or the rivnut is loose, it should be renewed.

2 Use two-component adhesive to glue a loose rivnut (as described previously), and allow the glue to harden according to the manufacturer's instructions. While the glue is hardening, remove the pedal cranks and the bottom-bracket bearing. Check whether there is a connecting hole between the down tube and the bottom bracket housing, to allow the swarf from the drilling, and the old rivnut to exit the frame. If there is no hole, you will need to remove the fork/steerer tube to provide an exit for the debris and the rivnut.

3 Drill out the rivnut gradually and with care – using an M6 drill first, then an M7 drill. It is important to align the drill with the hole in the rivnut. If necessary, drill alternately on the right and left side, but take great care not to drill through the frame tube.

Damaged rivnut thread (continued)

4 It is advisable to drill very slowly, and to break off the flange of the rivnut using pliers. Once the flange is off, you can push the body of the rivnut inside. Shake the rivnut remains out of the bottom-bracket housing or the steerer tube, or the debris will rattle later. Check the inside of the rivnut hole in the frame. It needs to be free from sharp edges and cracks.

5 If there are small cracks or tears, this does not have to be the end of the frame. Smaller tears in carbon, up to 1 or 2mm long, can be sealed with two-component adhesive. Where necessary, apply glue and allow it to dry before proceeding. For larger-scale damage, however, you should consult a carbon specialist.

6 If no damage is evident, slide the replacement mounting into the frame tube to check its fit. There needs to be plenty of space inside the tube to accommodate the replacement mounting. If necessary, you can file the hole in the frame tube slightly to enlarge it, using a round file and applying only slight pressure. Be careful when doing this. Also make sure that no rough edges remain. Under no circumstance use a drill to enlarge the hole! Seal the filed area using two-component adhesive.

7 Pre-assemble the bottle holder and the mounting. Fit the smaller washer below the screw head. The slightly curved and bigger washer is placed under the bottle holder. Make sure that the screw fits neatly into the hole in the frame. Place the sealing washer between the metal washer and the frame tube.

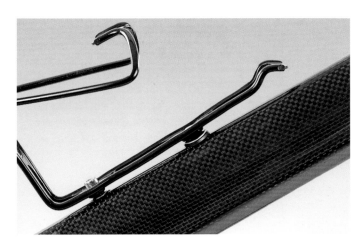

8 Unscrew the plastic expanding fixing by two to three turns and slide it into the hole in the tube until the expanding arms have been pushed completely into the tube. If you are only renewing one mounting, fix the bottle cage loosely on the existing mounting with the second screw. Make sure that you do not let go of the screw on the expanding fixing by accident, or the fixing will fall inside the frame and it will be difficult to remove again.

9 Hold the curved washer in position between your thumb and index finger, and at the same time pull the bottle cage away from the frame. This creates some tension in the system, and will prevent the expanding fixing from turning. Start tightening the bolt with a hex key. The tightening torque is only 1Nm. Take the key with you when going out for a ride.

Drain holes in the frame

1 If the bottom of the bottom-bracket housing features a drain hole, any water that has penetrated into the frame can be drained out. The frame will then dry by itself. These drain holes used to be a common feature, but nowadays many frame designers seem to have forgotten about this old trick that the steel frame manufacturers used to use.

2 If the hole is blocked, for example due to excessive grease, you will have to remove the cranks and the bottom-bracket bearing. Clean and dry the housing thoroughly. Open up the blocked hole, then refit the bearing assembly after applying fresh grease.

3 Remove the screw securing the gear-cable support and move the support to one side. If a drain hole is now exposed, and the cables pass close to it, you can drill a corresponding hole through the plastic support. Unfortunately, there is no such solution on carbon frames.

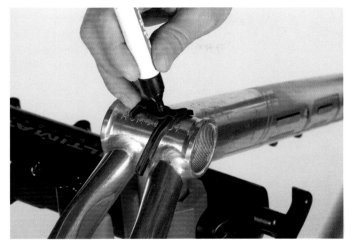

4 If you need to drill a drain hole, the bottom-bracket bearing must be left removed. Stand the bike on its wheels, and mark the lowest point on the bottom-bracket housing. Turn the bike upside-down, and make a final mark, which should not be covered by the cable support.

5 Place the frame into a work stand or clamp it on the seat post. Alternatively, you could ask an assistant to hold the frame for you. Centre-punch the frame at the marked position to prevent the drill from slipping.

6 Use a cloth to block the tube openings in the bottom-bracket housing. Additionally, place a piece of wood through the bottom-bracket housing, to support the drill bit after it has broken through the wall of the housing. This will protect the drill bit against breaking off. Drill a hole approximately 4mm in diameter.

Drain holes in the frame (continued)

7 Deburr the drill hole from the outside, using a countersink bit or a larger drill. On the inside, deburr the hole using a scraper or emery cloth. Clean the area thoroughly.

8 First, use primer to seal the grease-free drill hole, then use varnish in order to prevent corrosion from setting in to this area and spreading to the neighbouring surfaces. After the varnish has dried, fit the bottom-bracket bearing and the cranks, having first applied fresh assembly grease.

Hints

- Even if you only ride on dry roads, water can still get into the bike, for example when washing it or when transporting it on a roof carrier in the rain. Also, condensation builds up when you leave a cold bike in a warm room, and moisture from the air penetrates the bike.
- Good mudguards offer the best protection against water getting into the frame and fork while riding in the rain.

- Where possible, park your bike in a dry and well-aired room, so that it can dry off both externally and internally.
- On carbon frames there is no connection between the frame tubes and the bottom bracket housing. If there is no drain hole, then it does not make sense to make one. In this case, the only solution is to drain the frame regularly as previously described.

Drain holes in the wheels

1 It is not only the frame and forks that can start to feel heavier without you consciously noticing it. Wheels can also get heavier if spray water runs along the spokes and passes the nipples into the rim cavities. For this reason, high-profile rims require drain holes. Some manufacturers provide these. If this is the case, most of the water gets drained away while riding – or when the bike is parked – when the drain hole reaches the lowest point in the rim.

2 If no hole has been provided, you can drill one yourself. The best place is below the braking surface, just below where the tyre fits, where a hollow cavity can be found. Remove the tyre and the inner tube in order to locate the correct position. Punch-mark the location and then drill a 3mm hole. Deburr the area and seal it using varnish.

3 It is not advisable to use a drill on carbon rims. Not only is it difficult to target the hollow cavity on the rim, but the fibre structure may be damaged. Instead, pull off the tyre near a spoke hole and let any water drain out.

Travelling

Travelling with your bike entails a degree of learning – or at least good preparation. This chapter provides the most important tips for transporting your bike. It also deals with the most crucial emergency repair jobs – should anything go wrong.

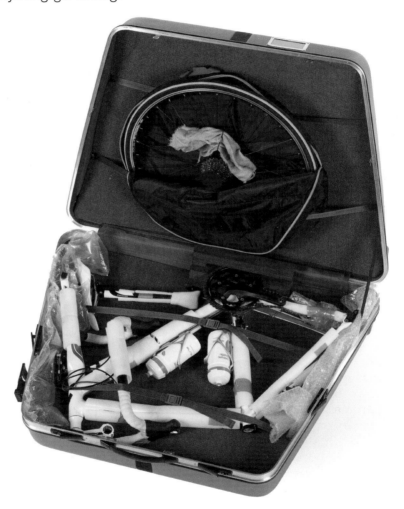

Even if there still is a trend towards hiring a bike for training-camp purposes, almost every cyclist gets into a situation where they want to take their own bike on a journey and therefore needs to package it safely. For air travel, there are certain regulations that must be observed. Unless a suitcase, or cardboard case, is compulsory anyway, many airlines stipulate that the handlebars need to be turned to the side and secured, the pedals taken off, and the entire bike wrapped in bubble-wrap or a similar protective material. However, if you want to protect your bike as much as possible during transport, you should opt for a special case.

FOR TRANSPORTING

- You can buy plastic foam tubes and spacers at a very low price, or perhaps even for free, at your bike dealer. Many manufacturers use items such as these to protect their bikes when transporting them to the retailer.
- Bike racks for cars which clamp onto the frame are not suitable for road bikes featuring thin-walled frames. The clamping forces may damage the tubes, even if the damage may sometimes not be visible.
- Coated copper wire from electric cables is more practical than cable ties. It can be removed more easily and reused in many ways.
- Lightweight clothes, wrapped up in plastic bags, are well suited for additional padding. Distributing your clothes cleverly in this way also ensures you will 'survive' at your destination in the event that one of your pieces of luggage is delayed or goes missing altogether!

FOR MINOR FAULTS

- After a breakdown, you should be cautious when riding on. Temporary repairs, like riveting a chain together after a breakage, might have an adverse effect on how the bike performs.
- If you discover bent components after a crash, such as a renewable derailleur hanger, you should renew them immediately, as they may have been weakened and could therefore break easily.
- The recipe for a trouble-free ride is careful initial assembly of the bike. Regular services, carried out by experts in a well-equipped workshop will guarantee that the bike will be less prone to trouble.
- In principle, you can join broken brake cables as described previously for gear cables. However, you should only perform this repair for the rear-wheel brake. If the front-wheel brake cable breaks, you are better off replacing it temporarily by using the rear-wheel cable, which is much safer and more effective!

All bike cases work on the same principle: two plastic halves fit around the dismantled bike. The wheels have separate protection, and they rest either behind foam-plastic inserts, in special compartments, or in separate bags that are part of the package (depending on the individual model). If you have to take your bike on frequent trips, investing in a good bike case will pay off. If you do not want to spend money on a bike case, you can enclose your bike in a cardboard transport case. In our experience, a cardboard case will survive several trips, unless it gets wet in the airport manoeuvring area, in which case it will quickly deteriorate. You can also hire bike travel cases/bags from some specialist companies.

A typical bike case weighs around 10kg. Your bike may weigh almost the same again, and this can quickly exceed the permissible 20kg upper weight limit for sports equipment stipulated by some airlines. In that case you will have to pay an expensive supplement for excess luggage. However, most airlines allow you to carry up to 30kg of sports equipment. You can only really exceed this limit if you put lots of clothes in your bike case as padding – which is not allowed by some airlines.

You should also make sure you register your bike for the flight as early as possible, ideally when booking. Otherwise, you might be successful at booking a seat for yourself, but not for your bike case!

Tools and materials

Hexagon sockets 4, 5, 6 and 8mm as required, flat-bladed screwdriver and chain riveting tool or mini tool, possibly spoke key, tyre lever and pump, torque wrench plus bit set, pedal spanner, pliers, repair kit, chain joining link, valve extension, electrical terminal strip, piece of tyre, cloth, coins, spacer, adhesive foil, foam-plastic tubes, chain oil, penetrating oil, cloth, assembly grease, possibly assembly paste for carbon parts. Packaging material: dropout spacers, insulating tubes, cardboard, copper wire, bubble wrap, plastic hub guards, securing straps

Parking – not like this...

1 Never rest the top tube of your bicycle on a lamp pot, a street sign or similar. The handlebars can turn round and the bike may roll off, damaging the top tube.

2 Do not lean the bike against a wall using the pedal as support. The crank can turn backwards, causing the bike to start rolling and fall over.

3 Do not wedge the pedal into the kerb, either. This could result not only in a scratched pedal and crank, but the bike can fall over very easily.

Parking – how to do it correctly

1 Lean the rear wheel against a post. The tyre's friction will prevent the bicycle from moving and falling over. Professional mechanics line up whole rows of bikes against the wall of a building when space is extremely tight.

2 Lean the saddle and the handlebars against a wall or a wide pillar. As before, the friction on the contact areas ensures that the bike stays in a stable position.

3 If you think the bike's position is not stable enough, there's a trick: clamp the brake on one wheel. Open the brake release lever and adjust the cable clamp screw so that the brake pads contact the wheel rim, then close the release lever.

Storing a bike

1 At home, place your bike in a suitable bicycle stand. The tripod stands that were common a while ago used to scratch some frame tubes. Stands that support the back wheel are more suitable. When parking the bike for longer periods, check the tyre pressures regularly.

2 The safest method of storage is to suspend the bike from a hook which is protected by a rubber or plastic coating. This takes the load off the tyres, so that they will not suffer even when the bike is parked long-term. However, not all aerodynamic rims are suitable for being suspended; carbon rims in particular may suffer damage.

3 Regardless of which method you decide on, if you want to be 100 per cent certain that your bike is protected, fit foam-plastic tubes around the frame, especially around the top tube.

Transporting and packing – in the car

1 Always insert fork spacers immediately when removing the wheels. This protects the dropouts from damage, the surface under the forks from being scratched, and the forks from accidentally being pushed together.

2 The bike should be protected with foam-plastic tubes, and should be transported standing as upright as possible, and where possible supported in a special mounting system. If this is not possible, secure the bike against sliding around with seatbelts or tie-down straps.

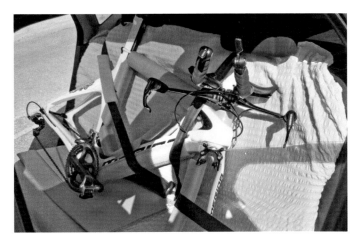

3 If you need to lay the bike down in order to transport it, do not place anything on top of the frame. Remove the quick releases from the hubs and place the removed wheels in wheel bags.

Using a bike case for transporting

1 Using a strip of adhesive tape, mark the seat-post position. This will simplify adjusting the seat height later on. Slacken the seat post's clamp bolt and pull out the post. Tighten the clamp just enough to secure it to the tube.

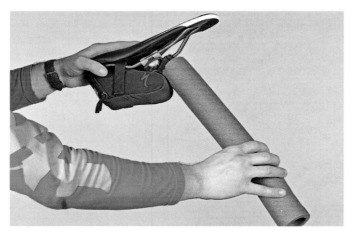

2 Clean the post and protect it using foam pipe insulation. Remove the pedals. The left-hand pedal features a left-hand thread, so is unscrewed clockwise. Be careful – pedals can come off suddenly with a jerk. To avoid the risk of injury, use an offset spanner and use the tool in such a way that your hand moves away from the chainring teeth when you slacken the pedal.

3 Operate the gearshift mechanism to move the chain to the largest chainring and the smallest sprocket. Open the brake release levers and remove the front and the rear wheels. Turn the drive-side crank parallel to the chain stay and, using wire, fix the pedal eye to the chain stay, which should be protected with pipe insulation. Also fix the chain to the chainring. This prevents scratches and covers the sharp edges of the chainring teeth a little.

4 Turn the rear derailleur slightly towards the rear and hold it with one hand. This will prevent it from falling off in an uncontrolled way due to the tension in the springs that occurs when you slacken the securing bolt. Package the removed derailleur and, using copper wire, tie it approximately in the middle of the protected chain stay.

5 Fit plastic spacers to the front and rear fork dropouts. Fix the spacers to the chain stays or dropouts, as applicable, using cable ties or copper wire.

6 Slacken and remove the stem expander bolt and end cap. Slacken the stem clamping screws by two to three turns. Now pull the stem, including the handlebars, off the steerer tube. Instead of the stem, slide on spacers, and secure them in place using the end cap and expander bolt – tighten the bolt just enough to hold the spacers in place. Leave the frame and forks assembled together – removing the handlebars and stem makes the package less awkward to handle.

Using a bike case for transporting (continued)

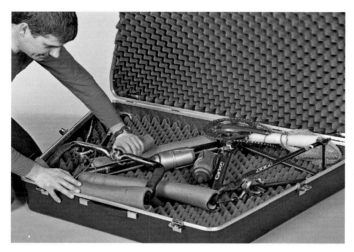

7 Insert the water bottles into their brackets. Protect the entire frame using either pipe insulation or bubble-wrap. Lift the frame into the case. The handlebar and stem unit should not touch with any frame tubes or the forks, and the cables must not be bent. Use foam-plastic to provide additional protection for critical areas.

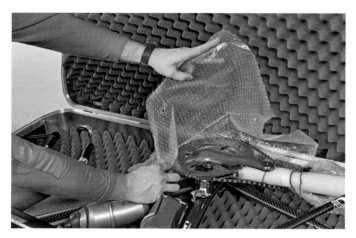

8 Wrap the entire crankset in bubblewrap. Ensure that the chain is always kept lightly lubricated, and is kept separated from the other components to avoid contamination and damage. Place the seat post in a convenient place.

9 Place a sturdy piece of cardboard between the case and the larger chainring. This protects the chainring and the bike case against damage.

10 Remove the quick-release skewers from the hubs, and package the wheels in bags, or wrap them in bubble-wrap. Hub protectors made from plastic are good at preventing the spindles from pushing through the packaging material. A cloth placed over the cassette will protect the packaging from getting dirty, and it will also be a useful item to have for bike maintenance at a later stage.

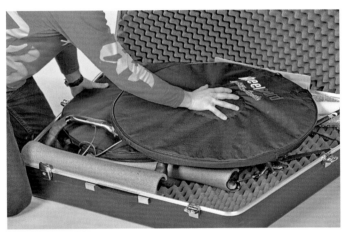

11 Place the packaged wheels in the case, with the cassette pointing inwards into the frame triangle area, where it cannot cause damage. Pack quick release skewers, pedals, the tools used, cloth, chain oil and penetrating oil for maintenance in a small cardboard box, unless your wheel bags feature special compartments for this. Do not forget your pump and saddle pouch.

12 Close the case while it is still lying flat, and check that nothing has got caught. Stand the case upright and wrap a belt around the entire case. Should the locks fail, the belt will still hold the package together.

Emergency repairs to gear cables

1 A cable failure on the front derailleur is not too disastrous, as the derailleur automatically switches over to the smaller chainring. Continuing to ride is not a problem. The rear derailleur, however, will swing outwards after a cable break, and the chain will engage with the smallest sprocket. On flat terrain or gentle inclines it might be sufficient to position the derailleur inwards as far as possible using the end stop screw, thus maintaining a single, lower gear for the rest of the ride.

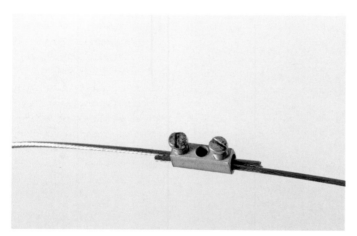

2 You could use an electrical terminal strip, from which you have removed the plastic insulation, to clamp broken cable ends. This only works if the broken cables are not too short, or the break is not inside the cable outer. Remove the cable clamp screw and pull the back part of the cable towards the front so that the ends overlap inside the terminal strip. Tighten the screws on the terminal strip and the derailleur, and engage the gear mechanism.

3 If it is impossible to join the broken cable again, slide the terminal strip on to the cable, from the front, right up against the front end of the cable guide on the chain stay. Push the derailleur towards the inside with your hand and pull the cable until a medium gear is selected. Secure the cable in this position by tightening both screws in the terminal strip. Readjust the tensioning screw on the derailleur to align the chain with the chosen sprocket.

Freeing stiff chain links

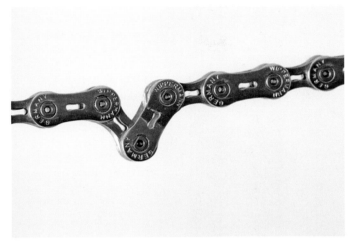

1 If the derailleur jumps when you are pedalling, or the chain suddenly jerks between the sprockets, this indicates a stiff chain link. If you experience this after roughly every second crank revolution, this is an even more certain sign. Get off your bike and turn the cranks slowly backwards. You can spot the stiff link because the derailleur will jerk, and the stiff link will look slightly bent when it leaves the chain roller.

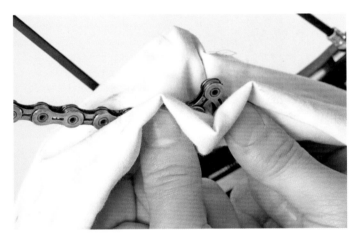

2 If the cause of this problem is bad lubrication or 'chain suck', it cannot be resolved. The consequences, however, can be remedied. Turn the chain until the stiff chain link has reached a position where you can grasp it with both hands. Place a cloth around the chain as shown in the photo, and bend the chain eiher side of the stiff link backwards and forwards – at right-angles to the direction of travel.

3 Carry out a safety check. Push the chain link together, and release the chain again. If the link is fully extended, the chain should operate properly again. To be on the safe side, turn the cranks backwards by a few turns. It is important to check the riveting in the affected area. The links must be undamaged, unbent and intact.

Mending broken chains

1 If the chain breaks or a rivet fails, you need to fix it. Temporary solutions using stones or nails will not work with modern 10- and 11-speed chains, as the chain links are too fine and the space between the sprockets is too narrow, meaning that nothing must protrude from the chain.

2 Using the riveting tool, completely push out the pin(s) from faulty chain links. Make sure that two pairs of adjacent internal links remain. If you remove only one pair of external links and connect the ends of the chain with a split-link, like those offered by KMC, SRAM or Wippermann, the correct chain length will be preserved.

3 It is easy to fit split-links by KMC and Wippermann and also to connect them. After connecting them, SRAM split-links need to be locked by applying pressure on the pedal.

Damage to the tyre

1 Occasionally, the tyre casing may be cut by stones or other sharp debris, or crushed due to a puncture. If you just insert a new inner tube, this will squeeze itself through the hole, form a blister and burst. You can use an old piece of tyre and put it between the damaged area on the tyre and the tube to remedy this.

2 Using scissors or pliers, cut out an approximately 50mm long piece from an old tyre, cutting the bead from the edges of the tyre. You should also remove the rubber tread to make the insert less bulky. You can do this using a cheese grater or, more easily, an electric belt sander and rough emery cloth. Warning: Fit the repaired tyre to the back wheel, in order to be safe (ie, if the front tyre is punctured, swap the good rear tyre to the front, and fit the repaired tyre to the rear wheel).

Spoke key

1 If a rear wheel spoke breaks on the drive side (cassette side), it cannot easily be removed while out on a ride. Instead, carefully wrap it around the adjacent spokes. Tighten the adjacent spokes on the drive side in order to at least prevent the rim from contacting the frame and the brake pads. Use the brake pads as a guide for positioning the rim accurately in the centre.

Pre-competition checks

During a competition ride, nothing is more annoying than ending up in the recovery vehicle due to a technical fault. In this chapter, we suggest the most important procedures to carry out before starting the race. This way you will avoid problems.

Never change a winning team! This saying not only applies to riders, but also to the bike components. In other words, do not change critical components on your bike just before taking part in a competition! Although some professional cyclists do this as a matter of course, you do not have to copy them, as using new, unfamiliar and untested equipment may simply result in losing out on a better end result.

Even if it's a great temptation to fit new aero wheels, for instance, as your upgrade highlight of the year, fitting a new set of wheels requires at least adjusting the brake pads and the gearchange mechanism. If you do not take this into account, you could end up being annoyed by a rattling gear mechanism for the entire ride. You may even risk your safety if the brake pads are not exactly aligned with the braking surfaces on the rims, which could result in a major tyre blowout!

Tools and materials
Floor pump with pressure gauge, mini pump, saddle bag with inner tube and on-board tool kit

Two rides before the competition

1 Fit your competition wheels. Check that they are positioned centrally by looking down the middle of the forks from the front over the top edge of the tyre. The distance between the two brake pads and the braking surfaces needs to be the same on each side of the wheel.

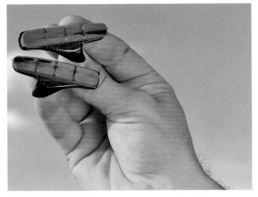

2 Check the brake pads, and replace them if they are seriously worn, or worn at an angle. It is important to note that just one marathon ride in the mountains during rain is enough to completely wear down even new brake pads. It is good practice to always fit new pads before a competition, in particular on carbon rims.

One week before the competition

4 Spin both wheels to check that they are true. Check the gap between each brake pad and the rim. If the gap changes dramatically, have the wheels trued. Also check the condition of the tyres – they need to be in good condition, and the treads must be free from damage and foreign objects. Replace the tyres if the sidewalls are worn down or damaged.

3 It is important that the entire surface of the each brake pad touches the rim simultaneously. Check for the correct position of the pads, and that the brake is centred. Also check the brake cables. If there is any sign of a cable being worn or split at the clamp bolt, it is high time to replace them.

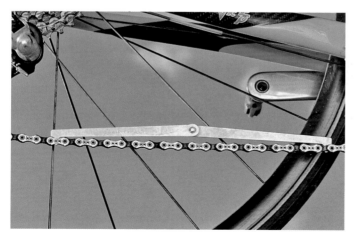

5 Check the wear on the chain, using a suitable gauge. Make the check in at least three places. If the chain is still in good condition, clean it with a cotton cloth, wiping off any dirt and encrusted oil. Apply fresh lubricant. Turn the chain several times and allow the lubricant to seep into the links overnight before wiping off any excess lubricant.

6 Have you swapped the wheels, or has your bike been knocked over in all the chaos before the start? In this case you need to check the gearshift mechanism at the very least! If you neglect this, you risk suffering damage to the rear derailleur, or damaged rear wheels during the race, if not before. Ask somebody to help you lift the bike, and carefully shift through all the gears. Pay attention – the rear derailleur should not get too close to the spokes when the chain moves to the larger sprockets. In first gear, press against the rear derailleur in order to ensure that the chain does not move any further than the largest sprocket.

7 Hold the fingers of one hand on the headset so that they encircle the steerer tube and stem. Pull the front-wheel brake using your other hand. Put weight on the saddle via your torso and try to push the bike forwards and backwards. If the headset bearing moves slightly against the frame, there is play in the bearings and the headset needs to be adjusted urgently.

8 Check your shoe cleats. Plastic cleats by Campa, Look, Shimano and others wear as time goes by. The small cleat nose is prone to breaking suddenly when exposed to heavy loads. If the wear indicators (generally small holes, indicated by the pen tip in the photo) are no longer visible, or the cleats become pointed at the contact points with the pedal, new cleats should be fitted to the shoe. Where applicable, clean and lubricate the cleat release mechanism.

Two training rides before the competition

9 A repair kit is an absolute must when entering a competition. Take at least a mini pump or a CO_2 cartridge, and take a small pouch containing basic tools, two tyre levers, an inner tube and a cloth.

10 Take a new inner tube with a valve length that matches the depth of the rim. The valve shaft without the knurled nut should protrude by at least 10 to 15mm, depending on the type of pump. This also applies to tubular tyres, but you may also need to take a valve extension.

11 Check the batteries for your bike computer. Where necessary, recharge the batteries or fit replacements.

Just before the start of the competition

1 Fit any wheels that you had removed for transport purposes back on the bike. Ensure that both wheels are centred within the frame or the fork. Spin both wheels to check whether they are rubbing against the brakes. Any quick-release levers which protrude to the side or the rear (see photo) are dangerous because another rider's wheel could get caught in them. Closed quick-releases should sit tightly against the fork or frame.

2 Be aware of the fact that quick releases which sit snugly on the tube when closed can be difficult to open, for example when your hands are cold. Check them for a tight fit by attempting to turn the lever and nut around the spindle axis.

3 Check the tyre pressure. Experienced cyclists can do this using their thumb. However, if you need to set the pressure correctly, this can only be done using a pump with a pressure gauge. The rule of thumb for a good compromise between comfort, protection against flat tyres and rolling resistance is: pressure in bar equals rider's weight in kg divided by 10. However, never exceed the maximum pressure specified by the tyre manufacturer.

Just before the start of the competition (continued)

4 Test the brakes while the bike is at rest. Pull the brake levers towards the handlebars, at first carefully and then forcefully. The pads should move against the rim equally, and there should be minimal, or no freeplay in the brake levers. When the brakes are applied hard, it should not be possible to pull the levers all the way to the handlebars! All four brake pads must touch the sides of the rims across their entire surface. They must not touch the tyres.

5 On Campagnolo brakes, the levers may not protrude evenly or the distance to the pressure point might vary. This could be due to the brake release pin being activated when the wheel was removed. Pull the brake lever slightly, and push the pin over to the other side. If this does not help, adjust the brake cable tension.

6 On Shimano and SRAM models, the brake release levers operate directly on to the brake body itself. If both levers to not operate evenly, adjust the brake cable tension adjuster on the brake body.

7 Stand in front of the bike and lean on the brake levers on the handlebars. While doing this, the handlebars must not turn in any direction. Note that the clamp screws cannot be properly tightened until the handlebars have been firmly attached. Tighten the clamp bolts to the manufacturer's recommended torque setting and look for possible causes if the handlebars do not clamp securely. Often grease in the clamping area can cause a problem.

8 Wedge the front wheel between your knees and attempt to turn the handlebars sideways, both to the right and the left. This will check whether the stem is firmly attached to the fork. If you need to tighten it further, take care not to overtighten, as this can crush delicate carbon steerer tubes.

9 Grab the saddle at the front and the rear and alternately put weight on each. Even when you apply maximum force, nothing on the clamping head must move. On posts featuring a clamp screw, a high tightening torque is necessary in most cases, which cannot be applied using tools from your on-board toolset. In order to check, use a torque wrench.

Winter training bike

During the winter, you can get your old third-best bike out from the shed and punish it so much that it becomes your fourth-best. Alternatively, you could pick your brain and think about how to prepare a really good winter bike. For example, a bike like the one shown below. With a bike like this, however, you will no longer be able to make excuses for not going out for a ride in the winter.

1 Components

Wet conditions, dirt on the road and salt can put a vast strain on the drive mechanism and moving parts. If you have relatively inexpensive components such as Shimano 105, which function very well, it does not hurt quite so much if you need to replace them slightly more often. In adverse conditions, mountain-bike pedals are easier to use than road-bike pedals – and, above all, you can use both sides of the pedal. Matching mountain-bike winter shoes make walking on slippery winter surfaces much safer.

● Shimano 105 group; Pedals: Shimano SPD-PDM 520

2 Disc brakes

The cable-operated disc brake offered by Shimano is a blessing in winter, since it responds much better in wet conditions, it does not wear down the rims, and it does not produce slimy aluminium abrasion dust which gets everywhere. The rear-mudgard stays, however, need to be manually bent around the brake calliper. Be consistent, and use stainless V2A screws to secure the components.

● Shimano BR-R505, SM-RT64 (160mm)

③ Frame

Titanium does not corrode – this is the secret of preserving the frame's immaculate appearance even when riding in the toughest winter weather. The components are also easy to replace should this become necessary in the future.

- Lynskey Cooper CX Disc, special order

④ Tyres

Having a flat tyre in winter is no fun at all. So a puncture-resistant tyre should be your first choice, despite weighing a few grammes more. When there is a threat of icy roads, these tyres can be replaced with studded tyres (eg Nordic Spike by Conti). An integrated reflective strip is useful for remaining visible when it is grey and foggy outside. At the present time, road-bike rims for disc brakes are still a rarity. Depending on availability, you may have to make do with normal rims and braking surfaces.

- Continental Cyclocross Plus Reflex

⑤ Lights

A wide range of bright lights is now available. Remember that when riding on unlit roads, your front light needs to be bright enough for you to see where you are going at speed, while being able to spot any pot holes or debris in the road, as well as to be seen! Modern LED lights provide a good spread of bright light, although with the brightest lights, battery life may be a concern on longer rides. Modern dynamo-powered lights may be an option, in which case battery life will not be a problem.

- Edelux with sensor and parking light
- Seculite Plus

⑥ Mudguards

Commercial 'road-bike' mudguards are far too short – normally for cosmetic reasons. Spray coming from the front tyre will splatter over your feet and also your bike. You can fix this by making a 'spray guard' from an old tyre, which you should cut to fit and attach using cable ties. This will prevent water from splashing upwards, and the flexible rubber guard will not be in the way even when riding over a kerb. Alternatively, fit full-length mudguards, where possible.

- SKS Bluemels B35

⑦ Dynamo

The SONdelux hub dynamo is very lightweight, durable and it fits into the overall look of the bike without standing out. We recommend a 32-spoke, three-cross lacing spoke-pattern wheel as an inexpensive and durable winter choice. With this option, the torsional rigidity will be less affected if you break a spoke, unlike light-weight road wheels. Thanks to the disc brakes it is almost always possible to continue riding. Repairing the spoke is simple and inexpensive.

- SONdelux disc (with Shimano centre-lock system)

The dedicated winter bike

1 With a few clever additions and alterations, you can prepare your racer – or a specially selected winter bike – for bad weather. The most important components here are mudguards. The guards chosen should fit the front fork and the rear end as closely as possible. Remove the brake and place the mudguard mounting bracket on the brake bolt at the front of the fork.

2 Slide the mudguard into position. First, bend the bracket lugs to leave sufficient clearance for the wheel, while allowing them to grip the mudguard. The front mudguard should be approximately 10cm above the ground at its rear edge, and should protrude forwards from the forks by around 15cm. Bend the bracket lugs to fully grip the mudguard when you are happy with the positioning.

3 Fit the mudguard stays using so-called mudguard catches which will release the guard in a dangerous situation. Only cut off the excess stay ends when everything has been properly fitted and aligned, then fully tighten all the fixings. On frames without eyelets, use clamps as shown in step 11.

4 If you want to add a mud flap, and your front mudguard does not already have one, you will need to make holes at the rear edge of the mudguard. You can melt them in using the heated blade of a screwdriver. This reinforces the edge of the hole at the same time and no sharp-edged burr will be produced. For cable ties, you can create an exactly matching hole of the appropriate size.

5 From a worn tyre, cut off a piece approximately 10cm long. Mark the desired position of the holes in the tyre. Fold the tyre exactly where you marked it. Fold it along its circumference and then cut off the corners at the marks using scissors. Now you have produced the mounting holes.

6 Fit the improvised mud flap, using either cable ties or a piece of coated copper wire. The latter can be twisted easily without tools, and can be repeatedly removed and refitted.

The dedicated winter bike (continued)

7 The mud flap should be positioned approximately 3cm above the road; this will provide protection for your feet. Pulling the mudguard down towards the road, instead of using this flap, is not recommended, as the mudguard might catch the kerb while riding over it and cause damage.

8 On modern frames there is not much room between the frame tubes and the tyre, and it is impossible to fit a whole mudguard in between. In this case, you need to cut the rear guard where it meets the brake mounting tube, and the front one behind the fork head. To do this, hold the guards alongside the tyre and mark the areas where you want to cut them, making sure you will have a neat fit. You can use a sharp hacksaw to cut the material.

9 You can obtain stainless-steel sheeting to make a bracket to fit over the brake mounting tube. Place the sheeting in a vice and bend it so that it fits around the tube and runs parallel to the tyre. Depending on the individual model, you may need to make a two-part bracket and join them together with a nut and bolt. You will also need to drill the bracket for the brake mounting bolt to pass through.

10 Fit the mudguard pieces to the front and the rear of the mounting bracket. Use stainless-steel screws and Nyloc nuts. Using large washers will protect the material. If you make an oblong, open-ended slot in the bracket for the brake bolt, with the opening facing downwards, you can remove the bracket quickly and easily by slackening the brake securing nut.

11 It is important that the brake securing nut can be screwed sufficiently on to the bolt to secure the brake properly. You might have to remove a washer from the brake bolt to guarantee this. If your road bike does not have eyelets on the frame, you will need brackets for the mudguard stays. You can obtain plastic-coated steel clamps from your bike dealer, as they are included with many luggage racks.

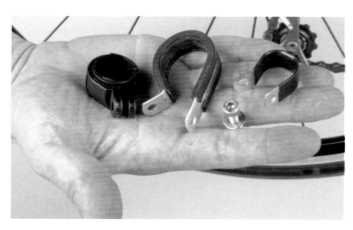

12 Plastic clamps from cycling computers may be useful, and suitable metal brackets with rubber inserts can be obtained from car accessory shops, or DIY shops.

The dedicated winter bike (continued)

13 Once you have fitted the rear mudguard, fit a rear reflector or rear light, depending on your set-up, so that the reflector is positioned vertically. A small mud flap, similar to that described for the front mudguard will win the approval of your fellow riders!

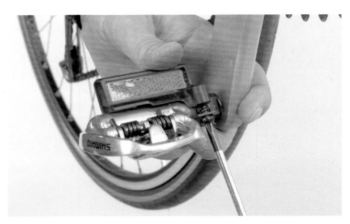

14 Some pedals only accept matching reflectors sold as accessories, for example for the SPD system by Shimano. They work very well, and will make you more visible, as light coming from car headlights is reflected back when pedalling and is also reflected back on to the road surface.

15 If your lights have cables, secure them carefully. Connect the lights' positive (+) and negative (–) terminals directly to the dynamo. The old method, whereby the frame was used as the earth will often lead to problems. Make sure that nothing can get caught in the cables.

Fitting a hub dynamo

1 A wheel equipped with a hub dynamo should be fitted into the front fork in the direction indicated on the side of the hub. Close the quick release as usual. The connection for the light should point to the rear at an angle, and should be positioned behind the fork.

2 Undo the brake securing nut and slide the light bracket on to the front of the brake bolt. Release the nut again and count the turns while doing this. The nut should screw on by at least eight turns before the brake, and therefore the lamp, is secured.

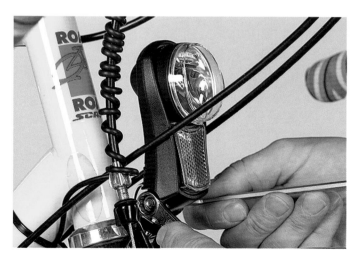

3 Depending on the type of light bracket, the sleeve nut might be too short for it. If this is the case, you will need to fit a longer sleeve nut. You can buy one at a bike shop. Fit the front light and guide the cable (which is usually already connected to the light) downwards in the direction of the dynamo.

Fitting a hub dynamo (continued)

4 Pull the plug off the dynamo's power supply. Slightly press into the plug's recess using a small screwdriver. Then take off the grey cap including the interior components.

5 Remove approximately 10mm of the insulation on both cables. Use a wire stripper for this or cut around the insulation using a sharp knife and then pull it off. Guide the cables through the holes, which – when new – are filled with grease and appear blocked.

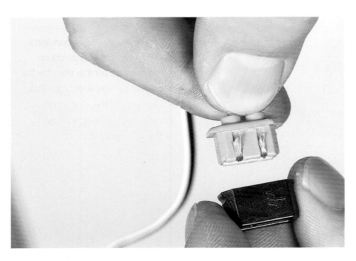

6 Pay attention to how you fit in the cables. The negative lead (usually two-coloured) is marked with an 'earth' symbol, which looks like an upside-down antenna. Bend over the small copper wires that protrude by roughly 5mm so that the wires are positioned neatly and do not touch each other.

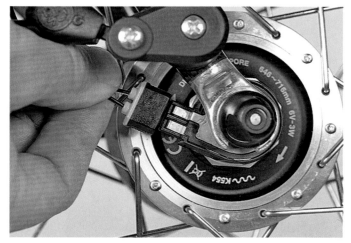

7 Slide the cable and the plug's cap into the plug and then fit the plug into the dynamo. It will only fit in one position. Run the cable down to the fork, leaving a curve in the cable at the plug end. The additional length ensures that the plug can be disconnected, for instance when the wheel needs to be removed. However, the cable should not be too long and it must not touch the hub or the spokes.

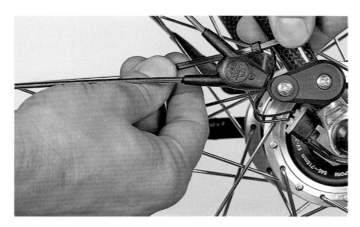

8 Additionally, make sure that there is enough slack to clear the brake and gear cables. The movement of these cables must not be restricted. Secure the cable on the inside of the fork using several cable ties.

9 Hub dynamos should be used in combination with special lights. Not only do these feature on and off switches, but they also offer the option of using just the rear light. Make sure you pay attention to the correct polarity of the cables, plus the colour coding of the wiring at the light.

The authors

Dirk Zedler (Dipl.-Ing.) is a vehicle construction engineer and a well-known personality on the cycling scene. He is a committed amateur triathlete and has completed several *TOUR* TransAlp challenges. Since 1994 he has worked regularly as a contributor to *TOUR* cycling magazine on the 'road maintenance' section. He is particularly interested in product safety, and has written many articles on this subject. He is an independent expert on bikes, and a sought-after consultant. His company produces instruction manuals and carries out testing for many well known manufacturers in the cycling industry. In addition, his company designs and produces testing equipment used by several bike magazines, including *BIKE*, *Freeride*, *TOUR* and *Trekkingbike*. More information is available at www.zedler.de

Thomas Musch is editor-in-chief of *TOUR* cycling magazine. He is one of the most experienced cycling all-rounders in Germany. His passion is for professional sport. For many years he has followed the international peloton during the Tour de France, and at classic bike competitions and world championships. He is a committed amateur racing cyclist who has written on many subjects, including travel, medicine, fitness, law and traffic. His numerous reports and articles have gained him a reputation as an independent specialist journalist. Since 1993 he has played a central role in the development of Europe's biggest touring and road-bike magazine.

鹿北
/著

You are
y dream

尔是我
遥不可及的
梦

新世界出版社
NEW WORLD PRESS

图书在版编目（CIP）数据

你是我遥不可及的梦 / 鹿鹿北著 . —北京：新世
界出版社，2014. 11

ISBN 978 – 7 – 5104 – 5203 – 1

Ⅰ . ①你… Ⅱ . ①鹿… Ⅲ . ①长篇小说—中国—当代

Ⅳ . ①I247. 5

中国版本图书馆 CIP 数据核字（2014）第 257714 号

你是我遥不可及的梦

作　　者：鹿鹿北

责任编辑：张　奇

责任印制：李一鸣　黄厚清

出版发行：新世界出版社有限责任公司

社　　址：北京西城区百万庄大街 24 号（100037）

发 行 部：(010) 6899 5968 (010) 6899 8733（传真）

总 编 室：(010) 6899 5424 (010) 6832 6679（传真）

http：//www. nwp. cn

http：//www. newworld-press. com

版 权 部：＋8610 6899 6306

版权部电子信箱：frank@ nwp. com. cn

印　　刷：北京中印联印务有限公司

经　　销：新华书店

开　　本：700mm × 1000mm 1/16

字　　数：160 千字

印　　张：17. 5

版　　次：2015 年 1 月第 1 版　2015 年 1 月第 1 次印刷

书　　号：ISBN 978 – 7 – 5104 – 5203 – 1

定　　价：32. 00 元

目录

{ 你 是 我 遥 不 可 及 的 梦 }

/ 楔子 /

"顾眄若，事到如今，你还想怎样？是你亲手毁了他的一切，也是你，亲手将他推入黑暗的深渊。"

"不是我，不是我，我爱他还来不及，怎么会害他？……"

"爱他爱到杀死他，这不就是你顾眄若一贯的'温柔'方式吗？"

"不是我，真的不是我……"

眼泪是冰冷的，站在地铁站台的边缘，顾眄若就像是失去灵魂的空躯壳，不停地自言自语："如果连你都抛弃这个世界了，那我也不需要再去尝试爱上它了。"

顾眄若闭上双眼，一步一步向前走去。

5秒。

0秒。

地铁列车呼啸而过。

黑暗的尽头，无数张脸一一浮现在她的眼前，有熟悉的，也有陌生的。最后一张，是属于他的。他绝望忧伤的表情，仍然令她心疼。他说："她是为我而死的，我亏欠她的永远都无法偿还了。眄若，我们再也无法回到过去了……"

疼痛溢满整个心脏，想要大喊出声，喉咙却像是被人生生遏制着，终是没有发出任何音节。

从噩梦中醒来，顾昉若的手心全是汗，凌乱的眼泪爬满整张脸。她抬头望着天花板，世界一片空白。

挣扎，争抢，逃亡，失去……

是梦境也是现实。

我没有你想象得那么勇敢

/01/

热闹的寂寞。

坐在教学楼顶层的天台上，边喝有氧汽水边遥望操场上来来往往的人群。路瑾言的脑子里突然就蹦出了这对相互矛盾的词组。

懊恼地拿起汽水罐，咕噜咕噜灌了一口，想填满空空的感觉，却在抬头的瞬间看到了距离自己一米外的顾晽若。是阳光有些晃眼吧，她用手遮住光芒，而后，透过双手的指缝瞥望阳光。

透过五指的细缝，路瑾言看到的是顾晽若斑驳的脸。

顾晽若安静地站立在天台边缘，夏末的微风吹过时，她的裙角就会微微上扬，像极了将要绽放的花骨朵儿。而她的整个身子也会随着风失去重心般往楼外倾斜，一点点，一点点地倾斜着，好像随时都会随风坠落。

路瑾言握着汽水罐的手不由得紧了紧。

“喂。”

没有回音。

“该不会是想跳楼吧?”

顾眆若有些气愤地转过脸，直愣愣地瞪着路瑾言，“我长得有那么像怨妇吗？干吗乱诅咒人……”

真是狗咬吕洞宾，路瑾言哭笑不得，只好伸出自己的手，说：“你先下来。”

“干吗呀，这地方又不是你的。今天报名的新生太多啦，等他们散了我就下去。去去，回到你原来的位置，刚才在干吗现在过去继续干吗吧。”

“你先下来，不安全。”

路瑾言这么一说，顾眆若才下意识地望了望自己所处的位置：七楼，天台边缘。

啊——摔下去的话，真的会“粉身碎骨”“满地开花”吧。顾眆若尴尬地傻笑两声，妥协地将自己的手放到路瑾言的手里。抬起头，想要看清楚这位“多管闲事”的先生时，触及的却是一道强烈的反射光——强烈的太阳光刚好照在路瑾言的眼镜片上，形成了一道反射光——顾眆若的眼睛被微微地刺痛了，一个趔趄，差点摔倒。

还好，路瑾言的手牢牢抓紧了她的手。

“谢谢你。”

是真心想要道谢。可是抬眼，终于能够将“多管闲事先生”仔细看清楚时，顾眆若却情不自禁地走到他面前，冒冒失失地将他的眼镜取了下来。路瑾言并没有被她吓到，他一边感到好奇，一边等待着顾眆若的下一步动作。

当顾眆若的目光接触到路瑾言的眼睛时，她的心突然就变得柔软了。

只因为，路瑾言眼底的温暖，直抵人心。

/02/

你相信眼缘吗？

当你的眼凝望我的眼，世界从此不再需要语言。

就是这样，第一眼看到的人，却会让你情不自禁地想要靠近他，想要更深一点地去了解他，甚至于，渐渐喜欢上他。当然，这并不属于一见钟情的范畴。因为从靠近了解到钟情喜欢，这其中还需要一个过程。

只是，大多数人，时常都会想要拥有第一眼看到的人或事物。

这也是巨蟹座的通病。不管第一眼看到的人最终会是怎样的，如果第一印象不错便会想着，嗯，先拥有了再说。好像最后是会受伤害或是会难过都没关系似的，只因为第一眼缘告诉了自己——他是温暖的。

顾晰若是典型的巨蟹座女生，自然也不例外。

/03/

就这样呆呆地看了路瑾言数十秒，顾晰若自己都觉得，这样的举动真的挺二的。

为了缓和尴尬的气氛，顾晰若摆出一副豁出去的样子，深吸一口气，说：

"嗯，果然，我的审美观是正确的，拿掉眼镜才是'人模人样先生'嘛。真的，挺好看的。"

"噗——"路瑾言戴好眼镜，被顾眄若的话逗得哈哈大笑起来。

笑点真低，冷笑话也能笑得乐呵呵的。

话虽然这么说，可顾眄若的心里也异常的高兴。不过，孙子兵法有云：三十六计，走为上计。面对眼前这尴尬的局面，对于顾眄若来说，逃才是最好的选择。

狼狈、失去、害怕、受伤，越是想要逃离的，就越是逃不开。顾眄若过往的人生，一直都是如此。

即便是现在，这样小小的逃离，她也逃离得狼狈不堪。顾眄若低着头死命地往前面跑，跑到楼梯口时，路瑾言的"小心点"还没喊出来，她就被放置在楼梯口前面的学生桌椅给绊倒了。是直愣愣地撞上去的，生疼生疼的。可是，顾眄若没有吭声。这点小伤痛，一点都不算什么。

路瑾言过来准备扶她时，她突然有一种想要冲上帝爆粗口的冲动，可是最终，她只是闷声地念叨了一句："真丢脸。"

她挣扎着想要自己站起来，脚下的疼痛却一阵阵地袭来。路瑾言蹲下身，想要背她去医疗室，却遭到了直接的拒绝。从来，只有自己可以依靠。别人的帮助，以前不需要，现在也不需要。顾眄若知道，一旦哪天依赖了谁，她就必须变得小心翼翼，因为她害怕自己变得脆弱，也害怕失去。

"应该是扭伤了脚。小时候我跟爸爸学过，按摩治疗跌打损伤，我会一点点，来，我帮你弄下。"

也没等顾眄若点头，路瑾言就将她的脚挪到了自己旁边，然后将自己的汽水罐递给她，"有点疼，忍一忍。"

咔，咔咔……像是快要散架了一般，很疼。有朦胧的水雾淹没了眼眶，一圈一圈。顾晡若下意识地咬紧嘴唇，深吸一口气，眼泪终究没掉下来，一颗一颗全部逼回了心里。

休息了片刻，脚部的疼痛一点点消失。接到南西的电话，顾晡若才懊恼地想起，是时候去报名了。第一天来到这所高中，还没来得及报名，就狼狈负伤了。这运气真够衰的，顾晡若在心里自嘲道。

她挣扎着站起来，挪着步子往前走。

路瑾言一直跟在她的后面。

到达教学楼后，顾晡若转过身，发现路瑾言还跟在身后，便有些纳闷了。她停住脚步，侧过身，做了一个请的动作，说："你先走。不许跟着我。"

路瑾言再次愣住，暗自感叹自己肯定是遇到了来自火星的小怪物，这脑子，这想法，完全是正常人无法理解的。可是，绕过顾晡若时，路瑾言还是好心地交代了一句："以后小心点。"然后才大步往前走去。这一幕，刚好被坐在教室窗边位置的南西看到了。

"我说小顾同学啊，刚走的那位小哥是谁呀？看着怎么不面熟啊？"

"你家许先生呢，你们不是都分到二班了吗？"

"他分到了六班，你分到了七班，而我，可怜兮兮地被分到了二班，每天都得仰望着楼上的你们而学习。小顾同学，拜托，长点记性。"

顾晡若傻笑两声，幸灾乐祸地说道："天意弄人啊。不就是'异楼恋'嘛，这种小打击，南西小姐你肯定能承受得住的。"

"别，你得好好帮我看着他。"

"不好说，万一许清木使出浑身解数来贿赂我的话，我可是很容易被腐败势力所诱惑的。你懂的，南西小姐。"

南西拿起桌上的书作势要朝顾晞若砸过去，下一秒，却又被她逗得哈哈大笑。望着捧腹大笑的南西，顾晞若也大笑起来。顾晞若突然想起一句话：陌生人认为我很安静，朋友们认为我很开朗，而我最好的朋友知道我就是个疯子。

南西就是顾晞若最好的朋友。

小时候，她们两个人会扎着一样的辫子，穿着一样的裙子，然后手挽手哼着不成调的歌，就像人和影子，走到哪里都是两个人一起。任何时候，任何快乐，任何忧伤，她们都一同分享，一同分担。即使是和许清木在一起后，南西也不会为了许清木而冷落顾晞若。

单身节的时候，南西会假装和许清木分手，在这一天里，他们彼此都不是对方的恋人。南西和许清木先生"分手"后，立马就会屁颠屁颠地跑到顾晞若身边，佯装成单身贵族陪她一起过单身节。被南西"抛弃"了的许清木则一脸可怜兮兮地跟过来，接着朝顾晞若哭诉他被"抛弃"的过程，博得了她的"同情"后，许清木先生终于成功地得到了和两位女士一起过单身节的许可。

情人节的时候，许清木先生也一点都不介意顾晞若这个会发光发亮的"大灯泡"；相反，他会很细心地准备两份礼物，一份送给南西，一份送给顾晞若。偶尔，许清木还会幽默地说：南西、顾晞若，我许清木可都要好好宠着，好好伺候着。

有南西小姐和许清木先生在，他们不会让顾晞若觉得自己是孤单的。因为，他们仨是从小一块长大的朋友。因为，这辈子，甚至是下辈子，他们都是彼此谁也不能取代的好朋友。

不过，这样的铁三角之间，却没有发生任何复杂纠结又破坏感情的三角恋故事。许清木的心从一开始就认定了南西，而南西也死心塌地地喜欢着许清木。至于顾晞若，她的心里一直都没有人。

一片空白。

报完名，来到教室时，顾晡若已经迟到了，她只好偷偷从后门溜进去。

同学们都已经到齐，只剩下最后的一个位置留给她。

也罢。

这样便可以更清楚地看到每个人的眼睛。

这个世界有太多双不同的眼睛，雾里看花，真假难辨。顾晡若从小就喜欢看他人的眼睛，她固执地认为通过眼睛就能洞悉一切。透过一个人的瞳孔，黑色或者白色，就会直接地被放大，变清晰。

就像现在正站在讲台上让每个同学介绍自己梦想的班主任，虽然眼角已经有了皱纹，明显是渐渐变衰老的痕迹，可是她的眼睛，却能带给人平静和温和的力量。顾晡若认定她是温柔善良的，所以，她已经开始乖乖地配合老师，思考着——我的梦想是什么。即使最初听到这个问题时，顾晡若的第一反应是：这样小儿科的问题貌似更适合小学生的开学问答吧。

目光扫过班级里的每一位同学，顾晡若意外地看到了坐在靠近讲台位置的路瑾言。他身上的蓝色 T 恤，像刚被雨水亲吻过的天空，澄清、湛蓝，柔软得好像一片蓝丝绒。顾晡若的嘴角扬起一个微笑，接下来的三年学习生涯，一定不会太无趣。

顾晡若想起小时候在幼儿园的时候，幼儿园的阿姨问自己，长大后的梦想是什么。关于梦想这个话题，其他小朋友都表现得很积极，有的小朋友长大后想要当科学家，有的小朋友长大后想做教育家，他们从小就怀着一个伟大的梦想。而顾晡若，她想了很久，最后得出的结论是：家，拥有一个完整温馨的家，一家三口开心快乐地在一起。

这样就够了。

只是，这样的梦想对于顾昐若来说，就像是奢侈品，可望而不可即。努力踮起脚想要碰触梦想的时候，总是还差那么一点。梦想于顾昐若，始终是需要高高仰望的。

现在，每一个陌生的同学，他们都有着一个陌生的梦想。

暴发户、幼儿园园长、炒房商人、贤妻良母等，他们在说着各种稀奇古怪、天马行空的梦想。

其实，顾昐若挺羡慕他们的。

有着将来想成为暴发户梦想的同学，结束了他的幻想。正专心转着笔的顾昐若听到了自己的名字。

"顾昐若。"

没有回答。

"顾昐若同学。"

还是没回答。

"顾昐若同学，有没有来？"

当路瑾言随着其他同学一样将寻找的眼光终于落到自己身上时，顾昐若才满意地站起来，大声地应了一声："老师，有。"

"好，顾昐若同学，请你来说说，你的梦想是什么。"

顾昐若想说，我从来都没有梦想。可是当她再一次接触到路瑾言的目光时，她突然看到了隐藏在他眼镜后的，那双温暖干净的眸子。

她说："我的梦想是，成为眼科医生。"

——这样，就可以矫正路瑾言的近视眼；这样，就可以看到他眼镜后的清澈。

对于顾盻若的回答，班主任很满意，她微笑着鼓励她："脚踏实地学知识，你的梦想一定会实现的。加油！"大抵是在众多鬼马的答案中终于听到了自己想要的靠谱的答案吧。对于班主任的鼓励，顾盻若也很感谢。

班主任让顾盻若坐下，然后念到下一个同学的名字："路瑾言。"

真好听。

顾盻若情不自禁地低声重复了一遍这个名字："路——瑾——言。"

也是从这个时候开始，顾盻若不再喊他"人模人样先生"，或者"多管闲事先生"，而是称呼他为路瑾言，或者瑾言。

正式开学后，顾盻若的座位被安排到了窗边。而这其中，其实是有着一段小插曲的。

最开始，顾盻若的座位是被安排在讲台底下的，跟班主任申请之后，才被换到窗户边上。班主任同意给她换位置后又语重心长地对顾盻若说："知识就是力量，梦想的实现需要知识作为其坚实的后盾。"

顾盻若知道，班主任是有心照顾自己的。

不过，顾盻若读书从来都不是走书呆子路线的，她不喜欢死记硬背，不会死脑筋地整堂课一字不漏地听老师讲课。她更喜欢劳逸结合的学习方式，疲了的时候，可以看看窗外，发发呆。当然，课堂笔记她是从来都不会落下的。加上她的记忆力真的很好，所以每次考试，成绩总是名列前茅，她不会让班主任失望的。

夏末初秋的季节，天干物燥，人心也更容易上火。

周末的午后，顾盻若怒火腾腾地跑到了杜胖子家开的服装店门口。玻璃橱窗里的女 Model 正摆着可爱的姿势朝顾盻若笑着，下一秒，气愤的顾盻若就抄起手上又长又厚的铁棍朝玻璃橱窗狠狠砸了下去。巨大的响声和着玻璃碎裂的声音惊醒了正在睡午觉的女主人——杜胖子他妈。

自家店铺被砸，杜胖子他妈立刻飞奔出来，并以迅雷不及掩耳之势打电话通知杜胖子抓人。不过，这速度再快也快不过顾眄若。此时的她，正站在大街的对面，满意地欣赏着自己的作品——满地的玻璃碎片，就像是冬日里的雪花。哈，挺美的。

杜胖子他妈眼睁睁地看着顾眄若得意地笑，也只能咬牙切齿地朝对街破口大骂。满街的车辆飞快地穿梭往来，杜胖子他妈想追也跨不过去。

"报复"得逞，顾眄若朝杜胖子他妈挥一挥手，便悠闲地离开了她的视线。好景不长，她还没走出去多远，杜胖子就带着他在社会上混的一群小喽啰追过来了。顾眄若边跑边兀自感叹道："到底是在道上混的，不仅消息灵通，追人的速度还不赖。"

"顾眄若，你别太猖狂，给我站住！"不用回头看，顾眄若一听就知道是杜胖子在鬼叫。

"放下你们手中的武器，我就停下。"顾眄若大声喊道。

"好，我们放下。"杜胖子回应道。

喊，明显的以少欺多，就算是放下武器又如何？顾眄若这样做只不过是为了降低杜胖子他们追人的速度——将手中的木棍、铁棍放在地上，等发现被骗后再拿起来，这段时间，足够顾眄若往前跑出老远老远了。从书店买完练习册的路瑾言，刚踏出书店的门口，撞到的就是这一幕。而未等路瑾言反应过来，他的手就被跑过来的顾眄若紧紧拉住，然后被迫跟着她一起往前跑。

路瑾言边跑边摆出一副"什么情况"的样子问顾眄若："拉我来当英雄的哦？"

"狗熊还差不多。"

"他们手上的棍子挺粗的。"

"你怎么知道？"

"我刚看到的，还没看清楚是铁棍还是木棍，就被你拉着跑了。"

"铁的木的都有。"

"啊！英雄不好当啊，更何况你也不是美女啊。"

"啊什么啊，废话怎么这么多？不想被打就快跑。"

顾昐若最后说的这句话似乎有魔力，因为，下一瞬间路瑾言就"反客为主"地跑到了她前面，然后拼命地拉着她往前跑。终于，将杜胖子那伙人甩到了后面，绕过好几个复杂的巷子口后，两个人气喘吁吁地坐在了稍隐蔽一点的巷子口。

呼吸平稳了一点后，路瑾言问："你哪儿得罪他们了，他们追着你打？"

"我把他们老大的服装店给砸了，就是那胖子。"

"为什么？"

"那胖子追我，跟他妈说我是他们家未来媳妇，结果他妈一见到我就媳妇媳妇地喊，喊得真烦人。今天上午我跑他妈店里想跟她说清楚，我跟她儿子是不可能在一起的。我也没多说啥，他妈就说我狗眼看人低，说我嫌弃她儿子是在社会上打溜的，说我一读书的也没什么了不起。"

"就这样，你就把她店给砸了？"

"不是，是因为她骂我妈。她骂我是畜生也好，是妖精也罢，可她不能骂我妈，不能冤枉我妈没教好我，也不能骂我'有其母必有其女'。我这辈子最恨的就是别人骂我妈。"

"顾昐若，你真像个小朋友。不过，小朋友，我们有危险了，他们追过来了。"

你 是 我 遥 不 可 及 的 梦

◆

　　顾昉若抬起头，便看到了从巷子两边追过来的两路人马，完全将路封死了。杜胖子一声令下，一帮人立刻做好了"迎战"的统一动作：右手拿着棍子，敲打左手，脸上换成得意扬扬的表情。路瑾言可不想当狗熊，他本能地将顾昉若护在自己身后，而后冲杜胖子喊道："你们想怎样？"

　　"还能怎样？当杜老大的媳妇呗。"其中一个小二哥说道。

　　"可是，我已经有男朋友了。"顾昉若伸出脑袋说。

　　"顾昉若，你别告诉我，你男朋友就是这手无缚鸡之力的小白脸！"杜胖子走到路瑾言旁边，将手搭在他肩膀上用力一压，路瑾言的右肩明显往一边倾斜了下去，"就他这柔弱的小身板，凭什么打赢我？"

　　"杜胖子，你真的喜欢我吗？"顾昉若问。

　　"喜欢啊。"

　　"可喜欢一个人是不会像你一样，带着兄弟操着铁棍、木棍满大街地追着她打，喜欢一个人不会强迫她也喜欢你，喜欢一个人至少会像这位手无缚鸡之力的小白脸一样将她护在自己身后，危险困难自己挡，给她安心的依靠。"

　　听着好像有道理。可杜胖子拉不下脸面，他生气地转过身，将跟在他后面的小太妹手中拿着的木棍抢过来，对那小太妹说："从今以后，你就是我女朋友，有困难有危险我会拿着这根木棍替你挡，我保护你！我们走！"

　　"杜老大，就这么算了？"

　　"走，我不想再看到她。"

　　"好，杜老大英明，杜老大威武。"

　　一场闹剧终于结束。

　　顾昉若轻轻地搭着路瑾言的肩，问他疼不疼，路瑾言却转了话题，"喜欢一个人，至少会像这位手无缚鸡之力的小白脸一样将她护在自己身后……顾昉若同学，你说的这位手无缚鸡之力的小白脸，该不会是我吧?!”

“呵呵……肯定不是啊，你又不是我男朋友，对不对？今天谢谢你啦，我还有事，先走一步，明天学校见。路瑾言，拜拜啊。”

之后，顾眒若将整件事说给了南西听。南西小姐的第一反应便是：“我说顾眒若同学，你该不会是一开始就对他一见钟情了吧?”

这时候，顾眒若当然是猛烈地，将头摇得跟拨浪鼓似的。她反驳道：“错。首先，第一回见到他时，虽然他很勉强地救了我一命，但除了感谢，我也只是感叹他的眼睛很好看而已，那可不是喜欢。那时候我还认定他是我的灾星来着，什么情啊爱的，都是浮云。其次呢，现在大狗熊救小朋友，也只能证明他这位同学勇于助人。而我现在呢，也只是对他有好感。请注意，是好感，不是喜欢也不是钟情。最后，我深刻地在考虑我到底要不要先主动喜欢上他。”

“你已经喜欢上他了，不是吗?”

第一眼的触碰，便感觉到了那无边无际的温暖，情不自禁想要靠近，情不自禁想要更深一点去了解；第二次的扭脚，感动之余，左心房的位置似乎有什么东西在悄悄启动，心脏从此便开始了以不规则频率跳动的旅程；第三回狗熊般的保护和不弃，越加使心动的痕迹变深刻了。

正解就是，顾眒若喜欢上了路瑾言。可是为什么要喜欢路瑾言呢？因为，喜欢一个人是不需要理由的。

南西，我肯定是疯了。顾眒若耷拉着头认真地说道：“太多的失去充斥着我过往的整个时光，而面对失去，我也从来都是无能为力的。我一直以为，只要不拥有，就不会有失去。可是，这一次，我居然很想彻彻底底地拥有。”

挽着顾眒若的手，南西的手用了用力，对她说：“每个人都拥有爱的权利，你也拥有。不要害怕失去和分离，至少还有我，会一直在你身边，和你一起，沿着时间的轨迹，往前走。"

南方的十月，恰巧是桂花开得正浓的时期。

校园里的金桂、银桂、丹桂争相绽放，乳白的、嫩黄的桂花，开得好不热闹。学校里的每一个角落都流淌着桂花香。秋风轻轻舞动的时候，顾昕若就会情不自禁地闭上眼睛，细嗅浓浓的花香。

顾昕若尤其喜欢这个味道。

小时候，母亲手中的糖果和糕点就是这个味道。她总是喜欢用糖果和糕点来哄顾昕若，然后顾昕若就会乖乖地跟着母亲去医院打针，或是努力背诵乘法表和课文。

和顾昕若成为同学后，路瑾言渐渐发现，其实顾昕若并没有自己想象中的那么活泼和开朗。偶尔看到她失神地望着窗外时，他甚至会觉得她的微笑和快乐都是假装的。

是的，她不快乐。可是，她又不希望别人看透她的不快乐。

尤其是陌生人。

开学已经好几个月了，她除了跟自己说话，其他人都是能不说话就不说话，好像他们都只是陌生人。路瑾言偶尔也会听到同学议论顾昕若，他们会说，顾昕若真自傲，顾昕若不喜欢说话；他们也会疑问，顾昕若是有自闭症吧？顾昕若是我们班同学吗？

路瑾言不知道，其实，在顾昕若的世界里，除了南西和许清木，其他人，她是能不接触就不接触。她害怕将自己的感情交出去，然后，被伤得遍体鳞伤。至于路瑾言，于顾昕若来说，是例外，一次勇敢的例外。不是因为听南西说了，"人生如果不是一场勇敢的冒险，便什么都不是"，而是打从心底里想要例外地勇敢一次。

路瑾言慢慢地发现，顾晛若只有和隔壁班的体育委员，以及楼下班级里一位漂亮的女生在一起时，才笑得放肆，笑得大声，笑得真实，就像卸下了所有的防备和害怕。他想，顾晛若对于这个世界，是带着抗拒力的。后来路瑾言才知道，隔壁班的体育委员被顾晛若称之为“许清木先生”，而楼下漂亮的女生则被称呼为“南西小姐”。

路瑾言终于发现自己对顾晛若多出一些关注的时候，时间已然转入冬天，而过去的整整一个秋天，顾晛若几乎都是缠着他的。

比如说，路瑾言去食堂时，顾晛若会突然蹿到他面前，对他说：“同学，真巧啊，帮我买一份吧。”末了，还自言自语地补上一句——缘分啊。比如说，路瑾言去操场踢球时，顾晛若则提着小水壶蹲坐在一旁看他踢球。路瑾言踢累了想喝水时，顾晛若就立马将水递过去。路瑾言说：“谢谢你。”顾晛若则牛头不对马嘴地说：“缘分啊。”甚至于每堂课的上课铃声一响起，顾晛若就会站在门口等着路瑾言，然后跟他说：“好巧，我也正准备进去，是缘分啊。”

每一次，路瑾言都只是笑笑，然后再一次暗自感叹：她究竟是把所有的男生都当成了单细胞动物呢，还是她自己才是不会用脑子思考的单细胞动物？

问题的答案，路瑾言没有去深究。

因为。

他已经有了喜欢的人。

这些，顾晛若都不知道，她依旧乐此不疲地继续着她的“缘分”计划。

南方的冬天时间特别长。还未来得及感受春天和秋天的气息，好像一年四季变成了冬夏两季的轮回。

南方的冬天格外冷。虽然不会像北方一样，让人沉浸在冰天雪地的视觉感里，但是它的冷空气却是直接蔓延到人心里的。

假若再遇上下雨天，整个天空就会像一幅泼墨画，墨黑色交织着墨绿色，蔓延，渲染，无限流淌……

将手撑在课桌上，顾晞若望着窗外，天阴沉沉的，像是一张大怪物的脸，好像下一秒就会张开它的大嘴巴，吞噬所有。

离晚自习下课还有十五分钟，提前去学校门口的便利店买把伞的话，来回刚好十分钟。可是，面对这样的大雨，前行的困难是顾晞若未估量到的。眼看就到便利店门口了，但她一路跑得匆忙，突然"哗"的一下，整个人摔倒在地，身上的白色棉衣很快就被泥水浸湿，变得脏兮兮的。

放弃吗？

不。

时间稍稍往之前调拨一点。

——你带伞了吗？发送至路瑾言。

——没有。发送至顾晞若。

因为收到了这样的短信回复，顾晞若才想要提前去便利店买伞的。

于是她从泥水中爬起来继续往便利店跑去。买好伞哼着小调跑回教学楼时，顾晞若才发现晚自习已经结束了，大家都纷纷跑向便利店买伞。这样的一场大雨来得太突然，许多同学都没有带伞，而便利店的雨伞数量也有限，不一会儿工夫，教学楼门口就挤满了人。等顾晞若穿过挤在门口的人群时，路瑾言早已经离开教室了。

找寻了好一会儿的顾晞若，最终还是从其他同学的口中得知，路瑾言已经走了，好像是和楼下班级的某位女生一起共伞的吧。

　　一厢情愿地去买伞，一厢情愿地等待，这样的感觉简直糟糕透了。和拥挤的人群站在教学楼门口，顾昤若进也不是退也不是，拿着伞傻呆呆地望着倾盆而下的雨。这样的进退两难，像极了现在自己对路瑾言的心情。

　　——我到便利店买了伞，你人在哪儿？

　　这样的短信，顾昤若发出去后便没有收到回复。懊恼地想要将伞扔掉，身边的一位男同学突然凑过身来，询问道："美女，要走吗？有幸跟你一起共个伞吗？"

　　噗——这话怎么听都不像是在询问是否可以共伞，而是更像在调侃顾昤若。她抬起头不由地打量起眼前的人来。阳光高大、儒雅帅气的模样，再搭配一个灿烂爽朗又让人百分百感觉无害的笑容，绝对绝对是能够祸害无数女生的雄性生物。

　　再往后稍稍一瞧，顾昤若就看到了站在他后面的女孩子，温柔似水的眸子，就像一汪清泉。顾昤若心想：明明是两个人，干吗还想要"处处留情"？男人啊。

　　"喏，伞给你们用吧。"顾昤若指指眼前的男同学以及男同学后面的"清泉"。

　　"她和我没关系。"男同学说。

　　"拿着吧。"

　　"我……嗯，谢谢。"

　　他撑开伞，大步往前走，身后的女生赶紧抓住他的衣袖，紧紧跟上他的步伐。没走多远，顾昤若就听到那汪"清泉"对着那个男同学大吼一声："呀！李嘉禾，你会不会打伞，我都淋湿了。"那位男同学显然被她温柔的小彪悍给吓到了，立马把伞挪到了她的头顶上。

大概和自己一样，是因为喜欢吧。

路瑾言还是没有回复顾旆若的短信。

一个人走在雨里，分不清脸上是雨水还是泪水，也分不清心里是难过还是不难过，顾旆若只是想起了母亲曾经喜欢的一首老歌：风中有朵雨做的云，一朵雨做的云。云的心里全都是雨，滴滴全是你。云在风里伤透了心，不知又将吹向哪儿去……

走着走着，顾旆若好像看到了路瑾言。可是路瑾言没有说话，他只是走到她的面前，将她湿透了的刘海拨到一边，露出了她的眼睛。

他知道，她难过了。

他的心，像是裂开了一条口子，感动，却也疼痛。

顾旆若，其实是讨人喜欢的吧。班级里同学那么多，却总能感觉到作为班主任的母亲对顾旆若的偏爱和特别关心。事实上，回到家的路瑾言，正好听到刚从顾旆若家做完家访回来的母亲在说：顾旆若这么晚了还没回家。打开手机准备找她时，才看到她的电话和短信，她的心意自然也明白了。所以他连伞都未来得及拿，就匆匆忙忙跑到大街小巷找寻顾旆若了。

可是，自己，已经有喜欢的人了。

这个傻瓜。

真的是路瑾言吗？顾旆若推开眼前的人，从口袋里拿出手机，两条未读短信，七个未接来电，都来自路瑾言：1. 你在哪儿？我手机没电了。2. 站在那儿别动，等我来找你。

这才相信，路瑾言是真的站在了自己面前。

没有责怪，没有抱怨，顾旆若只是冲他笑了笑，故作淡然地说：“伞借给一对小情侣了，你来晚了。”

摸摸她的头，路瑾言将自己的大衣脱下来给她穿上，顾昕若却固执地将他的衣服还给了他。最后，两个人一起将衣服罩在头顶才罢休。然后，顾昕若拉着路瑾言奔跑起来。这样，实在是像极了某部电影里的情节。顾昕若不难过了，心里被某种莫名的浪漫情愫充满着，感动着。

第二天，得知此事的南西心疼地在心里将路瑾言咒骂了无数遍，可是她没有当着顾昕若的面骂路瑾言。南西知道，那样只会让顾昕若更难受。所以，她只能忍着将路瑾言千刀万剐的冲动，给顾昕若买了一大堆的感冒药，叮嘱她下次不要犯傻了。

爱情始终不是一厢情愿。

许清木可不像南西那么心细，一听顾昕若受欺负了，他就找路瑾言打了一架。可是，看起来像个文弱书生的路瑾言，打起架来也不赖，最后结果是，许清木和路瑾言两个人都负伤了。

学校医务室内。

顾昕若和许清木大眼瞪小眼，路瑾言和许清木则是都不愿搭理对方的样子。南西实在忍不住，朝路瑾言吼起来："以后你再敢欺负顾昕若，我和你没完，你就是我南西这辈子的头号仇人。"

路瑾言不说话，拿着医生开的药往外走。顾昕若心慌地追出去，许清木和南西对视一眼，摇摇头，异口同声地感叹道："爱情，害人不浅。"

医务室外，顾昕若拉住路瑾言。

"对不起。他们也是因为担心我。"

"你有两个很好的朋友。"

"我不知道事情会闹成这样。"

"顾昕若，我们谈谈吧。"

"嗯?"

"我已经有喜欢的人了。"

顾晡若想说:那又怎么样?可碍于其口吻实在太不友好,脱口而出的话便换成了:"然后呢?"

"欸?"

"同班同学,还是同校校友?是御姐派的学姐呢,还是萝莉类的学妹?不然就是黏糊糊的青梅竹马,当然难得一遇的一见钟情也说不定。跟你喜欢的人,你们是哪一种?"

"顾晡若,我不是在跟你开玩笑。"

"我也没有时间跟你开玩笑。"

完全没有料到顾晡若会有如此反应的路瑾言,摆出一副"完全不知道要拿你怎么办"的表情重申道:"顾晡若,我说真的。"

"该不会是一见倾心,二见倾城,三见倾国吧?!"

"最后一种,青梅竹马。"

"路瑾言,你俗不俗啊?这都什么年代了,青梅竹马不流行了。"

"可是,我喜欢她。"

"不,你不喜欢她。"顾晡若忽然间无比认真地对路瑾言解释道,"在青梅竹马的相处中,两者之间更多的感情模式是依赖和习惯。见不到会想念,见到了会高兴,这些都只不过是正常的惯性现象。现在的你,正值青春年纪,久而久之,你就会错误地将这种想念和高兴理解为喜欢。事实上,你对她的喜欢不过是一种潜移默化所形成的思维定式,这不是喜欢,更不是爱。"

路瑾言不知道顾晡若这些莫名其妙的感情道理是从哪里听来的,总之现在的他感到非常的不安。顾晡若理智得有些过头,他反而有些担心起她来。

"路瑾言，你千万不要自欺欺人。"

"够了。谈话到此为止，我先回教室。"

"如果你非要自欺欺人，我拿你也没办法的。路先生，祝你好运。"

到底是谁在自欺欺人？

顾昕若太过刻意的情绪压抑，故意装作不在乎的语气，以及那些乱七八糟的感情道理，明明就是在自我安慰。

转身，逃跑，疼痛蔓延至心脏。

这件事终也被搁浅了。许是因为尴尬，再见面时，谁都没有主动提起。

/04/

1997 年，从幕后跃至台前，发行了首张专辑的陶喆，立即在乐坛掀起了一股 R&B 热潮。《爱很简单》《沙滩》《飞机场的十点半》，陶氏情歌受到了许多人的喜欢。2005 年的 1 月，《太平盛世》这张专辑开始发行，整个学校又掀起了一股陶喆音乐热。

路瑾言一直都很喜欢陶喆的歌。学校的新年庆典上，他抱着吉他自弹自唱了一首《爱很简单》。这段时间，晚自习的时候，学校点歌台每天都会有人拿着新买的 CD 去点陶喆的歌。每当这时候，路瑾言就会靠在走廊上欣赏着陶喆的音乐。上周末的时候，顾昕若拉着南西去西街买了这张专辑，只因为，她想要亲自为路瑾言点一首歌。

从教学楼到点歌台，要穿过另外两栋教学楼，然后绕过体育场，再上六楼，才能到达。顾昉若点了一首《就是爱你》，可是点歌台的同学听错了，《就是爱你》便变成了另外一首歌《爱我还是他》。

多荒谬的巧合。

跑回教学楼的时候，远远地，顾昉若就看到路瑾言的身边多了一个女生。她跑近的时候，那女生刚好离开，好像是走进了南西的教室里。

忘不了，逃不掉。躲起来，不面对，路瑾言喜欢的人也不会凭空消失的。

我喜欢你，从头到尾，都只是我自己的事。这样的心意，顾昉若终于想要宣泄出来。她拉着路瑾言逃掉晚自习，一路跑到学校的操场。

紧张的心稍稍安定，顾昉若开门见山地问路瑾言："你很爱我吗？"

一路跑，一路跑，路瑾言还没喘过气，就接到了顾昉若这个莫名其妙的问题。他条件反射地答道："我干吗爱你啊？"

"你得先告诉我，你爱不爱我。然后，我才能考虑接下来要考虑的事情。比如，我们要不要在一起，这毕竟是早恋啊。"

路瑾言大幅度咳嗽起来，一口气差点儿没喘过来。

"昉若，我说过的，我有喜欢的人。"

沉默了一会儿，顾昉若吐吐舌，说："哦，看来是我多想了。没关系，我刚才想清楚了，我也不喜欢你。所以，我们不能在一起。"

说完转身离开。

被路瑾言拒绝后，顾昉若失落地回到家。推开门，只见顾之淳还在看电视。顾昉若进来，他看了她一眼后又继续看电视。有时候，顾之淳一点儿都不像双鱼座男人，不煽情，不温暖。但他的确是彻头彻尾痴情的双鱼座男人，一旦你伤害了他爱的人，他将与你为敌。

关上房间门，靠着门板，顾昉若无力地瘫坐在冰冷的地上，她将头深深埋入自己双膝间，没有声音，但是身体却在颤抖。

顾晍若知道，顾之淳是恨着自己的。所以，她从来都不敢也不会奢望自己可以从他那里得到温暖。

记忆瞬间袭来。

蔓延，泛滥，直至淹没。

六岁时，顾晍若经历了生命中的第一次失去，那也是顾之淳生命中最难承受之痛。

和全天下每一个幸福的三口之家一样。暖意浓浓的早上，顾晍若的母亲会给她穿好衣服、鞋子，准备好营养的早餐。一旁的顾之淳也不闲着，他会将顾晍若的小书包亲自给她背上；会宠溺地亲亲她的额头，抱抱他的老婆；会温情地将顾晍若母女俩送到家门口，然后嘱咐她们一路小心。

左手牵着母亲的手，右手牢牢地拿着昨晚画完的画——

星光点点的夜晚，月光像清澈的流水温柔地倾泻在家的周围，房子里暖黄的小橘灯像是所有温暖的聚焦点，顾晍若和父母坐在一起，欢快地玩着成语接龙游戏。

这样温情的一幅画，顾晍若也赋予了它一个有爱的名字：小手拉大手。

她好像已经看到自己和母亲一同站上了学校的领奖台。绘画比赛第一名，非我顾晍若莫属嘛。站在人行道上等待红绿灯转换，闭着眼，顾晍若满足地幻想着，笑容满满。突然，一阵风将她手中的画带走了，她睁开眼，就见画正随着风在黑白斑马线上起舞，像是和着旋律一般。

顾晍若甩开母亲的手，匆忙地跑去拾画。眼看红色数字就要跳成绿色数字，母亲焦急地将跑远的顾晍若抱回来，然后对她说：“妈妈给你去捡，站在这里别动，等着妈妈。”

数字灯依旧是红色的。

可是——

嘀——吱——

刺耳的喇叭声、急促的刹车声，顿时响彻天际。顾眄若下意识地蹲下身，闭上眼睛，捂住双耳，然而绝望而刺耳的声音充斥着她的世界。

她知道，母亲离开了她的世界。

绮丽而绚烂的红像是一大朵一大朵的血莲花，迅速而糜烂地盛开在街道上，渐渐地淹没了顾眄若的画。还有，母亲的身体……

顾眄若没有哭，她像是一个外人被挤到了人群外。直到救护的医生将母亲抬上车，关上车门，车开走，她才跌跌撞撞地爬起来，拼命地往前跑，边哭边追着车子大喊："停车，停车！"

丧礼办得很简单，来往的亲人、朋友，都会安稳地亲亲或者摸摸顾眄若的头。

没有人责怪顾眄若。

警察将整个事故定性为酒驾事故。喝醉了酒的中年男子直闯红灯，把他驾驶的小轿车当成了飞机，在街道上飞奔起来。事故造成的人员伤亡是一死三伤。

顾之淳也没有责骂她。

他只是不理她。

只是，不和她说话。她哭，她难过，她害怕，好像都与他无关。

顾眄若知道，顾之淳是恨自己的。

事故后的一个月，为了防患未然，那条斑马线被油漆刷成了红色的爱心斑马线，它成为了全国唯一的一条爱心斑马线。

这样喜庆的红却成了顾眄若心中无法散开的血瘀……

一夜失眠。

顾昑若睁着眼睛数了一整晚天花板的小格子。

还好，都习惯了。

早上起床，她从抽屉里拿出眼部遮瑕膏将黑眼圈遮盖好，冲着镜子挤出一个笑脸，依旧是光鲜明亮的一天。不喜欢化妆的顾昑若，没有眼影，没有睫毛膏，甚至连隔离霜都没有，却从来都不缺眼部遮瑕膏。

她只是不喜欢陌生人看透她的忧伤。

上学，到达教室时，见路瑾言已经等在了门口。他知道隐藏在她微笑之后的难过，买早餐的时候便买了两人份的。

"给你的。趁热吃。"

连看都没看一眼，顾昑若漠然地走进了教室。路瑾言尴尬地站在门口，进也不是，退也不是。

如果不是一直在心里默念"顾昑若，出息点儿，长点儿志气啊"，她差一点儿就心软了。

学校附近有一家很特别的咖啡店，里面的咖啡饮品都是店主选用咖啡豆亲自煮的。顾昑若喜欢来这里喝卡布奇诺，然后要求店主做一个爱心形状的咖啡拉花。

享受其中，一个人也无妨。

南西打电话过来的时候，顾昑若看到路瑾言正焦急地从咖啡店门前跑过。南西在电话里说："昑若，来艺术大厅，我跟安眠闹翻了。"

安眠是南西的同班同学，也是她的死敌。南西嫌安眠太做作，安眠厌南西太泼辣。最近学校在办艺术节，要求各班文娱部长与艺术会长紧密合作。南西任艺术会长，安眠则是文娱部长，真是火星直接撞上地球了。

到达艺术大厅后，顾昕若看到了南西，看到了安眠，却也意外地看到了路瑾言。

他站在安眠的旁边。

顾昕若懂了，路瑾言是安眠搬来的救兵。而路瑾言的青梅竹马，就是安眠。

安眠，这个名字，她从南西口中已经听过不止十次。见面，却是第一次。顾昕若淡淡地看了安眠一眼，大眼睛，甜酒窝，应该是亲切温柔的吧。可是，接触到安眠蔑视的眼神后，顾昕若就知道了，这个人的内在，并不像她的长相那么温婉可人。讶异地见到路瑾言时，南西也明白了整个场面已经不受自己控制了。她也没料到，路瑾言就是安眠所说的男朋友。

在电话里，南西已经告诉了顾昕若她们吵架的缘由：南西正滔滔不绝地跟参与艺术节的成员分享自己的模特梦想，结果半路听到安眠幽幽的一句："身高不过161……呵，白日做梦。"南西也不是胆小怕事的人，她猛地抬手就将桌上的书朝安眠砸了过去。安眠也不示弱，反手将书砸回来，女人的"战争"便开始了。

顾昕若过来时，安眠已全然没了气焰，而是安静地像只受伤的小麋鹿一样依靠着路瑾言。像个小女生般，难过了受伤了，依靠着自己喜欢的男生，这是当然。可是，这个男生是路瑾言，顾昕若的心里就像被无数头刺猬扎着揪着扯着刺着，拧都拧不掉。

南西怕顾昕若为难，拉着她想走，顾昕若却甩开南西的手。反正以后都不会再见面，不会再有瓜葛了。顾昕若走到安眠面前，对她说："以后你敢欺负南西，我和你没完，你就是我顾昕若这辈子的头号仇人。"

类似的话，南西曾对欺负顾昕若的路瑾言讲过。

然后，转身，顾昑若拉着南西逃开了。

是的，逃开。

逃开那个碍眼的场面，逃开那个碍眼的安眠和她身边的路瑾言。随后，将南西送到许清木的身边，顾昑若这才放心。

一个人走在清冷的街上，失去了方向般，毫无目的地行走着。

这样，走着走着，就会忘记吧。

忘掉路瑾言望向安眠的坚定眼神，忘掉路瑾言安慰地拍着安眠的肩，忘掉路瑾言对安眠说的三个字——有我在，忘掉她转身离开时，路瑾言看向她的眼神。

同情。或者，可怜。

这样的一个眼神，隔了她倾其一生都无法消弭的距离，可她不想这么轻易地就向上帝投降。

痛了，累了，顾昑若蹲坐在路边的玉石板上。路瑾言送完安眠回到家时，就看到顾昑若蹲坐在自家门口冰冷的石板上。简单地和电话那头的安眠道了晚安，他匆匆挂断了电话。

"怎么来这儿了？"

"你刚才不需要挂断安眠的电话的，我爱待在这里，你让我待着就是，不要管我。"

"起来，石板凉。走，我送你回去。"

"不要你管。"

"起来，我送你回家。"路瑾言用命令的口吻说道。

"路瑾言，你是我什么人啊你？我走不走，我回不回去，要你管啊？走开，我讨厌你。"

"顾——昉——若。起来，跟我回去。"这一回，路瑾言将语气加重了许多，言语间透着一股不容拒绝的冷冽。

顾昉若整颗心都气酸了。

她气愤地跳起来，朝路瑾言大吼："如果你不喜欢我，讨厌我，我一点儿也不介意，我活着不是为了取悦你。可是，你凭什么凶我?! 我喜欢你，难道是我的错吗？是你先向我伸出手的，是你先让我体会到温暖的，是你让我这么喜欢你的。我从来都不敢奢望拥有，我知道那对我来说是虚幻的，不存在的。可是，我连努力尝试的机会都应该被剥夺吗？如果可以，我愿我从未遇见你。如果可以，我愿从今以后，忘记所有。"

忘记初见你时的惊鸿一瞥，忘记爱上你时的心心念念，忘记你的所有，你的全部，忘记我所为你做的一切，以及，我在你身上耗尽的所有勇气。

生生世世，再无纠缠。

"我们绝交吧。"顾昉若幼稚又毫无底气地说出这句话。

悲伤逆流，路瑾言的心溢满了忧伤。心疼她用尽力气来喜欢不完整的自己。想要抚平她的难过，想要给予她安慰，伸出手，触碰到的却只是空气。现在的他，什么都不能给她。看着顾昉若逃离的背影，路瑾言只能安静地站着。

突然，渐渐消失在夜色中的背影又重新回到了自己的视线中。

下一秒，冲过来的顾昉若紧紧抱住路瑾言，害怕他会消失一样，边摇头边喃喃地念道："路瑾言，我们不要绝交，好不好？我收回我刚才说过的话，好不好？我真的好喜欢你……请你允许我喜欢你，好不好……"这样的顾昉若，真是个不折不扣的小疯子。

待顾昉若情绪稳定后，路瑾言再次要求送她回家，她点头了。两人还没走到街道的转弯处，顾昉若的电话就响起来了。大概是太晚了，父母因担心才拨过来的电话吧。路瑾言也没在意，边数脚下的石子边等着顾昕若。

咚！

闻声路瑾言急忙转过头，只见顾昕若脸色苍白地晕倒在地，便赶忙过去抱起她往前奔去。

在顾昕若最后的意识里，她听到路瑾言对自己说："别怕，我带你回家。"

顾昕若想起了一首歌，来自 Michael Buble 的 *Home*。

May be surrounded by a million people

I still fell all alone

Just wanna go home

Oh, I miss you, you know

. . .

Let me go home

I've had my run

Baby I'm done

I gotta go home

Let me go home

It'll all be alright

. . .

Michael Buble 的声音能够瞬间就将人吸引住，充满了诱惑力。世间安宁，很温暖，镇定的旋律，浅吟低唱着——带我回家，一切都会好起来的。

{第二章}

我睁开双眼，你出现在我的世界里

/01/

顾昕若醒过来时，并不是在医院，而是在路瑾言的家里。

睁开眼，第一眼见到的人是班主任。看着她担心的眼神，顾昕若仿佛看到了自己的母亲，那些模糊却又清晰的幻象，不断地闪现在她的脑海里。她哽咽着小心翼翼地喊出许久未喊过的称呼："妈妈。"

听到"妈妈"两个字，班主任的眼里噙满了眼泪，于是，顾昕若又喊了一声："妈妈。"

对于顾昕若的身世，班主任一直都是知道的，所以，才会在平时给予这个女孩更多的爱和关心。路瑾言并不知道这些，后来，听身为班主任的母亲说起，他才知道。

原来，顾昕若的世界，并没有他想象中的美好。

她倔强的喜欢，又需要多少勇气。

她的生命中不能够再承受更多的失去了，路瑾言这样想着，一边将手中的纯净水递给她。

"多少喝一点儿吧。"

顾昉若点头，难得听话地喝了一小口水。路瑾言不忍心在她刚醒来的瞬间就要她面对残忍，转过身放下杯子，对母亲说："还是你跟她说吧。"

"晚上就会被运至殡仪馆。我和你爸先去那边，你在家，等她好点了再跟她说。"

残忍从未离开。

生离死别，在任何时候，都是一种痛。

可是，该面对的始终逃不掉。

不想让路瑾言一家为难，顾昉若做了一个深呼吸，对他们说："我接到幼儿园来的电话。他们说顾之淳在做义工的时候，为了救幼儿园的一个孩子而失去了自己的生命。我知道，他恨我，总有一天，他会抛弃我的。没关系，没关系的。"

"想哭就哭吧。我们不是外人。"路瑾言说。

"真的没关系。"

顾之淳的遗体直接被运到了殡仪馆，在那里摆上三天三夜后，再送去火化。

顾昉若打从心底里忌妒那个得到了父亲最后的保护和关怀的孩子。从来都不愿意给予自己爱的父亲，到最后，却把他的爱给予了其他小孩。

孤单地跪在顾之淳的灵柩前，来一个人，便要磕上一个头。南西和许清木则懂事地在一旁帮忙，和顾昉若一起穿着丧服，站在门口接待每一位前来吊唁的亲人朋友。

父亲工作所在的慈善幼儿园的小朋友都来了，在老师的领导下，他们排排坐，念诵着经诗。原本，小朋友的父母是不允许他们来的，可是小朋友每一个都主动要求要来。小小的他们知道，叔叔是好人，叔叔去了很远的地方，他们想念叔叔。

小朋友的眼睛都是红红的，他们都舍不得顾之淳。

顾眄若没有哭，她知道顾之淳不稀罕她的眼泪。她哭，或者不哭，难过，或者不难过，就像顾之淳在世时一样，他都毫不在乎。好像，她的生或者死，都与他无关。这样的凉薄，顾眄若一直是恨着的。

失去母亲的那一天，就已经连同父爱也失去了。

可是，心里，还是抑制不住地在疼。

不想被人看穿难过和忧伤，顾眄若一直逞强地仰着头，高高地仰着头，只有在磕拜的时候，才礼貌地低下头。很难过很难过的时候，就会一个人跑到角落待着，安静地望着属于殡仪馆的那片天空。

李嘉禾刚参加完一位亲属的火化仪式，就看到了曾借过伞给自己的笨笨女生。想要询问女生的名字，却听到她发出细微的声音，双手直捂着自己的肚子。

"痛……好痛……"

李嘉禾这才发现她的脸色已全然苍白，她白色的短裙上浮现出一小朵一小朵的血莲花。李嘉禾了然，立马将顾眄若横抱在怀里，拦了一辆的士，往医院方向驰去。一路上，顾眄若一直咬着自己的双唇，不愿意在陌生人面前失去神志，所以，咬到有了血痕，她还是固执地忍着。到达医院，对医生说出"痛经"两个字后，便晕过去了。

习惯性痛经。李嘉禾的眉毛整个都皱在一块儿了。

顾昑若醒来的时候，趴在她病床前睡了一小觉的李嘉禾也刚好醒来了。

"哦？醒了？"

"谢谢你送我来医院。"

"不痛了吧？给你买了当归红枣汤，趁热喝。"

"谢谢。"

"你……不记得我了？"

"我和你认识吗？"

"当真对我一点印象都没有了？"

"嗯……"

"你在说谎。"

"嗯？"

"你刚才对我说谎了。你的眼睛告诉我，你记得。"

"怎么说？"

"当我问你是否记得我的时候，你的眼球是向右上方转动的，也就是说你在说谎。当一个人在说谎的时候，眼球会向右上方转动。而当他们真的在回忆某事时，眼球则会向左上方转动。这种'眼动'是一种反射性动作，除非经过严格训练，否则是假装不来的。"

是的。当顾昑若看到将衣服盖在自己头上，蒙住自己双眼，并好心送自己到医院来的李嘉禾时，她就已经想起来，他是那个雨天向自己借伞的少年。他的笑容，很容易让人过目不忘。只是，这样光芒万丈的笑容向来都是顾昑若躲而避之的。心善、热心、阳光，诸多的美好，也都是她躲而避之的。所以，她说："我不记得你，不认识你。"甚至，还冷漠地反问他，"我记得你又如何？这里花了多少钱，我会还给你的。"

"不用。我不是这个意思。"

"我会还给你的。"

下床，收拾东西，办理出院手续。顾之淳，就算他狠心丢下了自己，最后的时光，她一定，一定要待在他身边。匆忙地解决着这一切，李嘉禾想帮忙，却被顾昹若拒绝了。无奈，他只好在顾昹若拦到的士前，强制性地将自己的 T 恤系在了她的腰部，正好将血色的小花朵挡住了。然后，又将自己的手机递给顾昹若。

"电话，你的电话。"

"以后都不需要再见了。"

"嗯？不想还钱了？"

李嘉禾自然得到了顾昹若的一记白眼。她输入自己的手机号码，面无表情地把手机递还给他。李嘉禾也不生气，自顾自地呵呵笑了两声，然后在存入名字的那一栏，输入了"顾昹若傻二妹"这样的字眼。这样的举动真的有悖于他平时在大家眼中儒雅、绅士的形象。可是在办理出院手续时，看到"顾昹若"三个字，李嘉禾立马就想到了"傻二妹"三个字。

另一边。

下一秒再找不到顾昹若就要报警的南西，在看到顾昹若完好地站在殡仪馆门口时，欣喜若狂地跑过去一把死命地抱住她，生怕一眨眼她又不见了。担心她做傻事，担心再也见不到她。就这样，抱紧她，再也不要放开……

不要离开我们，再也不要一个人消失不见。南西抽搐着，越加抱紧了顾昹若。许清木拉了拉南西，将她揽回自己的怀里，也给了顾昹若喘气的空隙。

"丫头，刚跑哪儿去了？南西担心死了。"许清木问。

"对不起。下次再也不会了。南西小姐，你哭起来真的很丑哦，不要哭了。"

"我就哭了，我就丑了，下次你再玩消失……不，没有下次。总之，你怕我丢丑就给我乖乖待着，好好的。"

"嗯。来，不哭了。"

许清木悬着的心也终于放下了，他伸出手摸摸顾昐若的头，说："丫头，下次不准再乱跑，玩消失了。"

"嗯……"

顾昐若点点头，心里溢满了感动。朋友，同样是她不敢奢望的美好，可是，这样的美好却对她不离不弃。

这个晚上，南西和许清木都没有回去睡觉，而是和顾昐若一起等待着天亮。天一亮，顾之淳就会被殡仪馆的工作人员推去火化。

路瑾言也没有离开。这些天，他一直都在。

第二天。

顾昐若就要与顾之淳道别了。

宣布结束的那一刻，顾昐若眼睁睁地看着工作人员将顾之淳推进焚烧的铁盒子里，眼睁睁看着大火弥漫，眼睁睁看着所有的一切灰飞烟灭。

难受，却拼命忍住眼泪。

站在一旁的路瑾言，看着这样的顾昐若，他是心疼的，他宁愿她放肆地、痛快地哭出来。他走到她身边，轻声地对她说："想哭，就哭出来吧。"

顾昐若倔强地说："我不会哭的。"

"哭出来心里会舒服点。"

而后，也不管顾昐若的反抗，路瑾言自顾自地用双手蒙住她的眼睛，对她说："现在，放肆地哭吧。谁都看不到你的脆弱，谁都看不到你的眼泪，只有我的双手能够感受到。哭吧……"

缓慢地将路瑾言的双手拿开，转过身，顾昐若挤出一个笑脸给路瑾言。距离很近，以至于连路瑾言镜片上满满的水蒸气，顾昐若都能够看得清清楚楚。她知道，因为自己，他难过了，虽然她是那么地不敢确信。轻轻地将他的眼镜取下，顾昐若询问他："是不是看不清了？"

"嗯。"

"这样，你就看不到我的难过了；这样，你就不会因为我而难过了。我流眼泪的话，你也看不到了，对不对？"可是，顾昐若并没有如此对路瑾言说，她只是用尽可能轻松的语气对路瑾言说："我不难过。谢谢你。"然后，她开始拉着路瑾言往前走。

"没有眼镜也没关系。以后，我就是你的眼睛。你只需要相信地跟着我走。"

此时此刻，路瑾言和顾昐若都被感动了。没有言语，却了然于心。

和路瑾言约好时间点的安眠，来到殡仪馆，刚刚好就看到了这一幕。想要假装看不见，心里的醋意却出卖了她。等顾昐若和路瑾言稍稍拉开距离之后，她迫不及待地走向他们。走到路瑾言的身边，安眠亲密地挽过路瑾言的手，像是宣告主权般地对顾昐若说："我是路瑾言的女朋友，你好，我叫安眠。"

"我们见过面的。"顾昐若淡淡地回应道。

"哦？"

"艺术大厅。"

"南西的朋友？"

"对。"

"你是路瑾言的同学？"

"对。"

"你叫什么名字？"

"顾昤若。"

"哦……是你啊。那瑾言，你在电话里说到的父亲去世了的顾同学该不会就是她吧？"

"对，是我。"顾昤若摆出一副"你还有多少问题想问，尽管问"的架势，抢过安眠询问路瑾言的问题回答道，火药味十足。

安眠的表情有一瞬间的错愕，但是很快她又礼貌地对顾昤若说："节哀顺变。"

"谢谢，没其他问题的话，我得过去领骨灰了。"

"好，小心点，看着路走。"路瑾言说。

顾昤若离开时和安眠擦身而过的瞬间，听到路瑾言问安眠："来很久了吗？"安眠回答："没有，我刚来。"可是，从安眠一瞬间的微动作反应中，顾昤若却读出了她说谎的信息。听到路瑾言问题的那一秒，安眠实际上已经下意识地做出了点头的微小动作，可是脱口而出的答案却是：没有。典型的说谎，顾昤若大胆猜想：她与路瑾言之间那个矫情的"接触"，安眠也一定全都收入眼底了。

在安眠的世界里，快乐是属于她的，路瑾言也是属于她的，她是不会允许任何人来破坏的。如此，对眼下不利的状况，她唯有选择视而不见。假装不曾看见，才是明智之举。

顾之淳离开后，顾昤若的收养权和监护人问题被摆在了首位。南西和许清木第一时间就跟家人下了通令：必须让顾昤若住进自己家。不过，考虑到各种因素，最后的结果是班主任成为了顾昤若的监护人，自然，也拥有对顾昤若的收养权。高中在读期间，顾昤若将住在班主任家里，而大学，住校或者继续住在班主任家里都可以。

这也意味着，从此，顾昀若就要和路瑾言处在同一屋檐下，敏感的她却在第一时间想到了安眠。

原本想着反正以后不会再有瓜葛，于是便和她闹翻了。可是，当顾昀若了解到安眠和路瑾言一家都关系甚好后，她知道，往后的时光里，她必须小心地处理和安眠之间的关系。因为她不希望路瑾言一家为难。

她亦心知，她和安眠都喜欢路瑾言。

这也是不被允许的。

和路瑾言住在一起后，顾昀若发现路瑾言每天早上都会在街角转弯的地方等候安眠，然后让她跳上自己的自行车后座。而她，依旧乘坐公交车上学，只是换了一条公交车路线而已。

南西有时候会开顾昀若的玩笑，她说："顾昀若同学，你难道就一点都不忌妒安眠比你先遇见路瑾言？"

顾昀若摇摇头，说："一点也不羡慕，不忌妒。"

羡慕忌妒恨，没有，都没有？

没有，都没有……爱情的世界里没有早与晚，只有适合与否。在对的时间遇见对的人，才算得上是一场欢喜。否则，都是空欢喜。

"不羡慕，不忌妒，不憎恨。不如，不喜欢吧。"

"南西，我做不到。"

"哎！每一个文艺女青年，都是伤不起的，伤不起的啊。"

"……"

南西知道，再说下去，只会是往顾昀若的伤口上撒盐，所以，她只能半疯半傻地大喊"伤不起，伤不起啊"，然后，将话题转移开。

　　而顾盰若，也是真的不羡慕不忌妒的。她羡慕忌妒的是，安眠比自己更早地融入到了路瑾言的家庭中。每一次安眠来路瑾言家玩，路瑾言的父母总是会笑脸盈盈地对她嘘寒问暖，然后热情积极地为她张罗一桌好菜。安眠也是极懂礼貌和处世之道的，一会儿跑到厨房里打打下手，一会儿又走回路瑾言身边，和他一起收拾碗筷。吃饭的时候，她不仅一个劲地夸奖路瑾言母亲的厨艺，偶尔，还会说几个冷笑话，逗得满桌子的人呵呵乐。吃过饭，闲下来，还会和路家人很自然地一起拉拉家常。

　　这些，全都是顾盰若望而却步的。

　　母亲离开后，她就渐渐习惯了吃饭的时候保持沉默，习惯了吃完饭将自己关在房间里。顾之淳就坐在客厅里看电视，偶尔抽根烟，偶尔起身走动下，倒杯水。

　　两人向来互不干涉。

　　之后，渐渐地，顾盰若还了解到，路瑾言一家与安眠一家认识已有多年。安眠的母亲是眼科医生，而路瑾言患有先天性弱视，从小就必须依靠眼镜，透过镜片来看整个世界。安眠的母亲就是路瑾言的主治医生。小时候误以为只是近视，因此便错过了最佳的治疗时间，为了防止眼疾恶化，路瑾言的眼睛需要做定期检查。

　　也因这样，路瑾言认识了安眠。

　　安眠的大气、聪慧，是路瑾言欣赏的；而路瑾言的优秀、温善，则是安眠所喜欢的。青梅竹马的关系，没有喜欢都会有习惯，安眠喜欢的心意托出后，两个人就顺其自然地在一起了。

　　甚至到现在，路瑾言的眼睛也需要做定期检查，而且，他也不得不依赖眼镜和药物。

可是，不清楚事实的顾昕若，之前的某一天居然还无比认真地对路瑾言说："如果有一天你爱上我了，可不可以为我取下眼镜？一天，哪怕是一天也好。让我看清楚你的笑，永远记在心里……"心里的后悔因子一个接一个地蹦出来，顾昕若懊恼极了。不过，这样的花痴语录，路瑾言大概也不记得了吧。

/02/

盛夏来临。

顾昕若想要买一些绿色植物放在房子里。可是，附近卖盆栽的老板总是睡到中午才开门。无奈，穿着暖黄小吊带、黑色小短裤的顾昕若只好在盛夏太阳最炙热的正午，行走一千米去盆栽小店。远远看去，她就像一只被烤熟了的橙子在马路上滚来滚去。脚上趿拉着的人字拖发出嗒嗒嗒的声音正宣泄着她的不满。

到达小店后，意外地碰到了安眠和路瑾言。他们正在给刚买好的盆栽取名字。顾昕若刚想转身离开，却已被安眠看到。

"昕若，你也来买盆栽吗？正好，我和瑾言想给这仙人球取个名字，你说叫什么好？"

"刺刺。"

"刺刺……取这个名字有什么内涵吗？"

"没有，单纯喜欢而已。"

"呵，呵。"对于顾昕若的直来直往，安眠还是有些不习惯的，只好尴尬地笑笑。

路瑾言站在一旁一直没说话。直到结完账要离开，经过顾昉若旁边的时候，他说："你自己挑选喜欢的盆栽吧，我已经付款了。"

意外地，顾昉若没有拒绝，而是简洁地回道："好。"

后来，路瑾言回到家，才知道顾昉若并没有买小盆栽放在自己卧室里，而是选择了一盆相对比较大的绿色盆栽，摆放在客厅里，大大方方，清清爽爽，路瑾言却觉得心里有些异样的滋味。

这段时间的顾昉若就像是没有灵魂的娃娃。

不哭，不笑，不闹，连表情都是不变的木讷。而南西，每天都毫无例外地会跑到路瑾言的家门口来看顾昉若。偶尔，两姐妹会说上几句话；可是更多的时候，彼此都不说话，就安静地靠坐在一起，听着时光流淌的温柔……

顾昉若有时候也会劝南西不要担心，可自己这样的状态的确难以让她信服，而南西也固执地要陪着她。许清木偶尔也会劝南西不要每天都来，可是，每一天，他也总是准时地和南西同时出现。这时候，南西就会反驳许清木："你自己还不是不放心她……"

"昉若，我就想知道你过得好不好……我担心路瑾言那浑蛋欺负你。"南西说。

一旁的许清木听到这话立马就跟着说："丫头，他要是敢欺负你，我给你讨回来。"

顾昉若摇摇头。

这些天，路瑾言不仅没有欺负顾昉若，他还会找各种办法逗她乐，她说什么他也会顺着她。顾昉若睡眠很浅，一点动静就会把她惊醒。所以，当路瑾言将交换日记放到她的床边时，她知道，他来过。清早醒来，翻开日记本，就看到了路瑾言大气而整洁的笔迹。

开心了就笑，不开心了就等开心了继续笑。

——早安。

上帝说，每一个喜欢微笑的女孩，运气往往都不会太差。

——午安。

我自横刀向天笑，笑完我就去睡觉。

——晚安。

开心也是过一天，不开心也是过一天。顾昕若同学，开心地度过今天吧。如果，你也有想要和我分享的心情，写在日记本里，月光爷爷会来收走的。

原来，路瑾言还有如此可爱的一面。顾昕若扯开嘴角，微微漾起一个弧度。

顾昕若自顾自地在想交换日记的事，撞到人才发现自己走神了。她礼貌地道歉，然后转身，却被对方拉住了。

"嗨，好久不见。"

顾昕若抬起头，是李嘉禾。

"不是吧！又不认识我了？"

沉默，无视之。

"顾昕若，女，五官端正，成绩优秀。联系方式：手机联系请拨 137 × × × × × × × ×，企鹅联系 275 × × × × × ×"

"你查我？"

"刚好我有朋友在移动，刚好你去移动做过兼职，刚好这个资料就被我拿到了。你说，我们是不是挺有缘的，啊？"

"麻烦让一让，我还有课，先走了。"

话说完，顾眆若当真就走了。望着她的背影，李嘉禾没有生气，反倒笑了，儒雅得一塌糊涂。好久好久没遇到这么好玩的了。不过，顾眆若同学，好戏在后头。

周末的早上，顾眆若想要睡一个懒觉，却被陌生的号码震醒。听到对方说：“你好，我是李嘉……”“禾”字还没蹦出来，顾眆若就将电话给挂断了。可是李嘉禾也不是吃素的，他铁了心要打进来，于是便一顿轰炸，一遍一遍地拨。

终于，顾眆若妥协地接通了电话。

“跟你很熟吗？闲着无聊玩手机游戏啊……你当是你家电视机在闹啊，一按就出人出声的。”

“哈哈哈……”明显，她的话起到了反作用，李嘉禾在电话的那头哈哈大笑。

“找我干吗？”

“还钱啊。还能找你干吗？”

“地点，时间，金额。”

“九点半。城西动物园。金额我还没算清。”

“赶紧算。回见。”

“成。回见。”

啪！顾眆若已经挂断了电话。

她伸了个大大的懒腰，起床。光着脚丫，拉开水蓝色的落地窗帘，有浅浅的光线透进房间。多亏了昨夜的一场大暴雨，清晨的空气感觉格外清新。而今天的温度似乎也不似昨天那么炎热，风过的时候，还夹着一点凉凉的清爽。这样的天气，不能睡懒觉，简直就是噩梦。

顾眆若拿起书桌上的水杯，咕噜咕噜一口气就将水全喝光了。然后，小心地迈着步子，走到阳台上，看到路瑾言房间的深蓝色窗帘还是遮下来的。

啊！还在睡懒觉。

路瑾言和顾晰若的房间实际上是并列的。而阳台，就在这两间卧室的前面。两间卧室靠着阳台的那面墙，其实是一道玻璃门，悬挂着不同颜色的落地窗帘。路瑾言的父母一直想要两个孩子，最理想的是龙凤胎，于是采用了两间孩子房的设计，而对阳台的设计，也是希望两个孩子可以将这块领域当成他们的私密城堡，彼此分享。

这样的美好，一直是顾晰若向往的。

她有些感伤地回到房间，换上 T 恤，短裤，背上小背包，气场十足地出门了。这个架势，倒更像是去收账的人。

到达动物园门口时，李嘉禾已经来了。顾晰若打开小钱包，开门见山地问李嘉禾："多少钱？"

"看完动物再说，走……"

"我是来还钱的。"

"这样，钱不用你还了，陪我玩一天，你欠的钱就一笔勾销，成吗？"

"我拒绝。"

"是你欠我钱！"

"那就还钱。"

"来都来了，不看看多遗憾。"

"我拒绝！"

"不可以。走。"

话说完，李嘉禾强势地拉着顾晰若往动物园里走去。顾晰若挣扎了一下，可她的力气怎么可能大得过李嘉禾，于是只好任由他拉着。见顾晰若不反抗了，李嘉禾心想：这对女孩子吧，必要的时候还是要使用一点"暴力"的，强势一点，霸道一点，这不，就变得乖乖的了。

不过，李嘉禾一直都清楚，顾眄若不是普通的女生。

大抵是天气很好的原因，来动物园的人特别多。李嘉禾拿出照相机想要拍照，顾眄若冷不丁地在旁边丢出一句："被动物围观，还要拍照留念。"

李嘉禾笑笑，说："错了，错了，是我们来观赏动物。"

"你看，那一群猴子正盯着你看，有没有？"

"你不看它，怎么知道它在看你？"李嘉禾反驳道。

"好吧，那我更改下措辞——互相围观，OK?!"

"顾眄若，我发现你很有讲冷笑话的天赋啊。"

"谢谢夸奖。"说这句话的时候顾眄若已经不自觉地有些得意，心情好像也变好了不少。

李嘉禾的兴致倒是一直极好，他无视顾眄若的臭脸，一会儿拉着她看狮子，一会儿拉着她看孔雀，一会儿又给她拍照，不管顾眄若是否愿意，总之，他要带着她好好玩，好好开心，抛开难过的事，彻底地放松一下。

——与其浪费时间摆臭脸，不如开心地玩一场。

游园的过程中，李嘉禾如是说。这话听起来挺有道理的。于是，顾眄若决定一点一点地将心绪释放开来，心甘情愿地被动物"围观"。

一路来到水族馆的区域，门口的老爷爷推着推车，卖着水果味饮料。动物园到处都是正规干净的饮料店，老爷爷的生意一点也不好。顾眄若掏出钱，问李嘉禾："喜欢喝什么口味的饮料？我请你。"

"柠檬。"

"老爷爷，麻烦你，两杯柠檬饮料。"

接过饮料，顾晞若一边喝，一边碎碎念着："大部分女生都喜欢喝甜蜜的草莓饮料，或者是浓香的香草味饮料。而我，只喜欢柠檬味。这样的味道，就像是生活，酸过之后总能尝到一些甜。我喜欢这样真实地生活着。"

李嘉禾没有接话。他知道，这些话，顾晞若只是在对她自己说，是不需要任何方式的回应的。只是，李嘉禾也想到了一句话：在陌生人面前沉默不语，在熟人面前是话痨。这样，是不是意味着，我们已经在慢慢变熟悉了？……

踏踏实实地玩了一整天，顾晞若整个人都累趴了，但是，是真的，感觉到了久违的快乐。所以，在回家前，她真诚地对李嘉禾说："谢谢你，今天玩得很开心。"

"我们是朋友了，对吧？"李嘉禾说。

"以后，还是不要见面了。"

"那你帮我一个忙，好吗？"

"你先说。"

拉起顾晞若的手，李嘉禾在她的掌心里比画着，边比画边对顾晞若说："你一定要帮我这个忙。李——嘉——禾。请你记住我的名字。"比画完自己的名字，他将顾晞若的手握成拳，继续说道，"握紧了，不要忘记。"

顾晞若失措地站在原地，手握着也不是，放开也不是。

她承认，这一瞬间，她被感动了。

许清木的摄影协会来动物园附近取景，远远地，他就看到顾晞若和一个陌生的男生在一起，于是加快了步伐，来到了她的旁边。

"丫头，怎么跑动物园来了？"

"一言难尽。"

"倒是你，怎么跑来动物园了？南西呢？"

"这不，摄影协会有活动，我带着学妹来这边取景。喏，给你介绍下，李沐禾，年纪虽小，摄影颇有自己的风格和想法。"

顾昕若点点头，朝两人笑笑。

南西从小就有两个梦想：成为模特以及摄影家。由于身高的原因，南西从小就固执地只穿高跟鞋。越是难以实现，越是要去实现，这才是南西。所以，模特这个梦想就成为了她的第一梦想。而摄影家的梦想，自然就被搁浅了。许清木学摄影，加入摄影协会，都只是为了将南西的另一个梦想延续着……

看到李沐禾的时候，顾昕若就已经想起那天雨夜中温柔的小彪悍了。那么，她和李嘉禾就是认识的。果然，下一秒，顾昕若就听到她对李嘉禾说："哥，你怎么也在？"

"我怎么就不能在？还有，李沐禾，我不是你哥。"

这一次，趁着温柔的小彪悍还没有爆发，李嘉禾拉着顾昕若就要走。无奈地与许清木交换了一个"下次解释"的眼神，顾昕若懊恼地被他拖着走了。

/03/

一直都在自己视线当中活动的人，突然间消失不见了。拨打手机，也只能听到客服不断地对你说："对不起，您拨的用户已关机。"如此情况下，担心、紧张，是不是再正常不过的心情，路瑾言不知道。这一天里他只是不时地走到阳台上，看回家的那条路上有没有熟悉的人影。

安眠是聪明的女孩，她知道什么事情应该计较，什么事情不应该计较。很多时候，她选择不争不抢不哭不闹，是因为她知道，一哭二闹三上吊这种伎俩其实都是男生最忌讳的。这样做，只会更快地失去他而已。安眠选择给路瑾言思考的空间，也是选择了给彼此的爱情一个考验。更何况，到现在为止，路瑾言的心在自己身上，对那小丫头顶多是同情和可怜而已。

天蝎座的安眠，是大气温婉的，也是知书达理的。但是，爱情，却是自私的，自我的，是宁为玉碎也不为瓦全的。

李嘉禾将顾昐若送到家门口，准确地说，是一路跟着顾昐若跟到了她家门口，抬头就看到了路瑾言和安眠。两人正凑在一起说着什么笑话，空气里都充满了欢声笑语。

四个人对视的时候，都愣住了。

安眠和路瑾言都是认识李嘉禾的，对此，顾昐若感到十分意外。而对李嘉禾和顾昐若认识，安眠和路瑾言也感到十分诧异。不过，眼下，大家谁也没有多问。李嘉禾挥手跟安眠和路瑾言打了个招呼，继而笑着说："小两口，下来吧。好久不见，一起去吃个饭。"

正好是吃晚饭的时间了。朝楼下回答了一个"好"字，安眠拉着路瑾言的手就下楼了。

对于这样的四人行，顾昐若是不自在的。她的朋友除了南西就是许清木，她不喜欢加入其他任何的圈子，更何况，这样的四人行，每个人都是怀着各自不同的情绪吧。吃饭的地方是安眠选的，是她经常和路瑾言来的小店。一路上安眠一直在给大家推荐里面的各种特色菜肴，而对每一道菜肴的解说安眠都选择了她与路瑾言的甜蜜故事。

也许，这样更有说服力和推荐力。也许，她是想让顾昐若知难而退。

这样的小心思，只有女生懂，或者，只有情敌懂。

吃饭的时候，顾眄若和路瑾言的话都很少。顾眄若几乎不说话，路瑾言偶尔会礼貌地搭上几句。而从安眠和李嘉禾的对话中，顾眄若则渐渐地了解到，李嘉禾和安眠是通过其父亲的关系认识的。李嘉禾的父亲是商业局局长，而安眠的父亲是一家上市公司的董事长。一来二往中，李家和安家两家也算是成了默契的伙伴。在一些商业派对和活动上，同龄的李嘉禾和安眠常常被长辈拿来开涮。在这个圈子里，诸如此类的政治婚姻、商业婚姻也有很多，长辈们是如此希冀着。不过，李嘉禾和安眠始终不来电，一直保持着极普通的朋友关系。

"眄若，你跟嘉禾怎么认识的呀？"安眠突然将话题转到顾眄若这边。顾眄若不想回答，便只是简单地点头说："嗯，就这样认识了。"

"呵呵，嘉禾可是个活靠山。"安眠继续说道。

"嗯。呵呵。"

顾眄若知道安眠话里的意思，便简单地回复她了。安眠不知道，对于李嘉禾的家庭背景，顾眄若现在才了解。而且，李嘉禾是富家子弟，但他从不炫富。与他显赫的家世相比，他平日里的为人处世，反倒算是低调的。李嘉禾的个性和品质，倒让顾眄若有些欣赏他了。

"来，多吃点。"路瑾言一边夹菜给安眠，一边将话题转移开，"吃完饭我们去江边走走，吹吹夏风吧。"

大家一致说好。

可是，众人准备离开，路瑾言去埋单的时候，一旁有个醉酒的男生过来戏弄安眠，当众将她的裙摆掀起。还好，安眠着了一条长裙，被掀起倒也不至于走光。不过出于防守，安眠下意识地反手就甩了那男生一个耳光。醉酒的男生倒也没太多意识，被甩了耳光还对着安眠呵呵地傻乐。倒是与他同行的两个男生见兄弟被欺负了，操起身边的啤酒瓶就朝安眠头上砸去。

你 是 我 遥 不 可 及 的 梦

眼看瓶子就要砸着头了，李嘉禾跑过去将安眠推开，同时将一个男生推倒在地。顾昕若默契地抢过另外一个男生的酒瓶。道上混的兄弟一般情况下是不打女生的，被顾昕若抢过酒瓶的男生扬起了拳头，又忍着放下了，他对顾昕若说："都是道上混的，老子也不想打女人的。让那个贱人给我兄弟道歉，这事就两清了。"

顾昕若点头，说："对不起。大家都在气头上，我代她道个歉。"

被人调戏在先，又被骂"贱人"，安眠也不甘心，冲过来将顾昕若推开，对着那男生大吼："你说谁贱人啊！是你兄弟手贱，先惹事的。"

"贱人，敬酒不吃吃罚酒。"甩手一巴掌挥向安眠，还好，被李嘉禾给挡回去了。李嘉禾以一敌二，还要同时保护安眠和顾昕若，显然是身处劣势的。这时候，顾昕若耍了个小聪明，大喊一声："停！我已经报警了，有怨气的跟警察说。"

"战争"立马就停下了，四周瞬间宁静。

啪！清脆的一记响声，是酒瓶碎裂的声音。

路瑾言结完账回来，看到的就是这样的一幕：躺在地上醉得不省人事的男生突然将啤酒瓶砸向了身边站着的女生，女生当时就感觉腿一软，低下头才发现自己的膝盖被酒瓶砸到了。

血和着玻璃碴儿从顾昕若的膝盖蔓延开来……她疼得蹲下身。李嘉禾从口袋里掏出一根烟，而后将烟纸全部撕开，把烟丝倒在顾昕若的膝盖上，再接过路瑾言递来的毛巾，一圈一圈将其裹起来。

闹事的三个男生早已经跑远了。李嘉禾将顾昕若交给路瑾言，然后拉过安眠，对她说："这事就交给你处理了。"

安眠默契地点头："替我跟昕若道个谢。"

“嗯，自己小心。”

事实上，安眠的父亲只是名义上的某上市公司的董事长，其隐藏在这个身份之下的真实身份则是一个帮派里的小头目。

当然，对于这些，路瑾言和顾昕若都是不知情的。

顾昕若膝盖处的伤口虽然已经停止流血了，可疼痛仍然令她无法走动。路瑾言蹲下身，让顾昕若趴在他的背上，再利索地背起她，往诊所的方向赶去。

趴在路瑾言的背上，顾昕若想起了顾之淳，想起了曾经遥远而宽阔的背部的温暖。路途并不遥远，可顾昕若也不是林黛玉的体重，背着顾昕若到达诊所的时候，路瑾言已然有些累了。经过简单的消毒止痛和伤口处理之后，便无大碍。医生又给顾昕若开了些药，并嘱咐她近期多注意休息，不要到处走动。

离开诊所的时候，路瑾言突然对顾昕若说：“昕若，我们像以前一样相处，好吗?”

像以前一样，该闹的闹，该缠的缠，该笑的笑。不要冷漠地拒绝他的早餐，拒绝他想关心她的这份心意。顾昕若知道，路瑾言是这个意思。

只是，回到过去，谈何容易。我们能够把握的仅仅只是现在。

“谢谢你。这段时间，谢谢你没有离开。”顾昕若笑着对路瑾言说。

顾昕若有一双笑眼，看起来任何时候她都是在微微笑着的，可是，隐藏在这双笑眼背后的却是无穷无尽的忧伤。这样的笑，有多久没看到了。路瑾言突然走到顾昕若的面前，抱着她，温柔地对她说：“不要忧伤，都会过去的。”

/04/

爱情是自私的，也是身不由己的。

站在 15 岁的尾巴上，顾昕若突然产生了一个自私的念头。以往每年的生日都是和南西、许清木一起度过的，这一次，她想要和路瑾言一起度过。虽然她知道这样的举动会伤害到安眠，可是，她只是单纯地希望在自己的记忆中，会有这样的一次美好。

哪怕，一次，就已足够。

爱情中是容得下这样无伤大雅的小城府的。

三天两夜的旅行，顾昕若并没有提前告诉路瑾言，而是在火车即将驶向那个城市前，将他拉上了火车。因为，顾昕若害怕，如果提前告诉路瑾言，他会拒绝。而安眠，则交由南西搞定，她简单地编了个蹩脚的理由。顾昕若和南西不知道，这样的大惊小怪，反而激起了安眠的怀疑和愤怒。但是，事已至此，她只能面不改色地说"好"，心里却早已风起云涌。

她，不动声色地，等着时机到来。

路瑾言这方，则是既来之，则安之。

更何况，他在来到火车站时，就已经猜到了缘由。同住一个屋檐下，顾昕若的生日，他没理由不记得。

一路向北，到凤凰。

开往吉首火车站的列车发出了轰隆隆的声响。当夜色渐渐暗淡，城市的喧嚣转为安宁，安静而古朴的湘西小镇，越来越靠近。

路瑾言和顾盷若的座位是相对的。隔着桌子，顾盷若对路瑾言说："对不起。"

路瑾言拿出音乐手机，递给顾盷若："喏，一起听。"

音乐和着月光温柔而宁静地流淌。*Valder Fields*，Tamas Wells 用吉他演绎得恰到好处。顾盷若知道，他是懂得的，所以，她不再说话。

时间转过零点的时候，火车停站。坐在顾盷若和路瑾言旁边的人换成了两个刚上车的小姑娘。火车行驶一刻钟后，其中一个小姑娘询问路瑾言："你会玩杀人游戏吗？"

路瑾言笑笑，然后摇头。

过了一会儿，另外一个小姑娘又问路瑾言："你会玩五子棋吗？"小姑娘将手绘的格子本都递过来了，路瑾言仍然微笑着摇摇头，继续闭着眼睡觉。

中途，路瑾言去厕所时，顾盷若听到两个小姑娘在议论他。

——他笑起来的样子真温暖，真美好。坐在路瑾言旁边的女孩说。

——是啊，是啊，等会儿我找他要联系方式。坐在顾盷若旁边的女孩说。

顾盷若笑而不语。路瑾言回来后，等坐在她旁边的女孩将手机递给他，并要求他输入手机号码时，顾盷若微笑着打断了她们。

"瑾言，我困了。"

路瑾言了然；而后对坐在他旁边的女孩说："可以跟你换个座位吗？"

女孩头点得跟捣蒜似的。

换好座位后，顾盷若将头靠在路瑾言的肩膀上，很安心地睡着了，羡煞旁人。

火车依旧向前，轰隆隆的声音回荡在深黑色的夜空里。醒来的时候，终于到达了这座安宁美好的城市。清澈浅绿的溪水，古色古香的吊脚楼，木板连接而成的小桥，火红喜气的大灯笼。一切都如人们所说般美好，这样的美好几乎不存在任何残缺。

因为，是顾眄若和路瑾言一起，看尽这美好，以及流年。

顾眄若十六岁生日当天，路瑾言带着她来到沱江边。大片大片的纸莲花，五彩缤纷，与沱江水相辉映，仿若花海。路瑾言挑选了一朵玫红色的纸莲花给顾眄若。

他说："送你的，生日礼物。"

在凤凰的沱江河畔放莲花灯，许个愿望，心诚则灵。顾眄若十六岁的生日，路瑾言送了她一个愿望。她双手合十，许下心愿，而后虔诚地点燃纸莲花，放入河中，看它一点点消失在夜色中……

我愿，我爱之人，健康快乐。

凤凰靠近沱江边的地方有许多家清吧和特色店铺。顾眄若在网上查询到一家叫作 "DO IT BY MYSELF" 的特色果饮吧。在这里，所有的饮料都是顾客自己亲手调制和冲泡的。顾眄若想要在这里为路瑾言亲自调一杯被称作 "绵绵暖年" 的果饮。

"绵绵暖年"，温暖如斯，就像黑夜里依然让人感觉到温暖和阳光的眼睛。

将调制好的果饮递给路瑾言，顾眄若说："可以让我再看看你的眼睛吗?"

路瑾言微笑着取下眼镜，说："那么，从现在开始，你要负责给我带路。"

顾眄若从他的语气里听到了调侃的味道，她笑着说："自己的路自己走。"

"最毒妇人心哪。"

"哈哈哈。"

…………

这样的气氛，这样的轻松，刚刚好。

"DO IT BY MYSELF"果饮店里唯一融入了柠檬味道的饮料被称作"心蚀"，顾昐若想调制一杯给自己。"心蚀"搭配柠檬，配合天衣无缝。美中不足的是，调制这款果饮的原料用的是柠檬味的奶茶粉末，而非新鲜柠檬。

奶茶粉末放置的位置有些高，顾昐若踮起脚够了够，还是没拿到。她转过身，想要去搬个椅子，却看到路瑾言已经起身。小店昏暗的灯光使得他眼前原本不清晰的一切成倍模糊。凭着感觉，路瑾言还是拿到了奶茶盒，可是一个趔趄，旁边的玻璃奶茶盒，瞬间一盒接着一盒，轰然倒塌。

奶茶粉末和着玻璃碎片倾泻而下。

顾昐若跑过去，将路瑾言的眼睛蒙住，慌乱地帮他吹眼睛。可是，已经来不及了。大量的粉末蒙住了路瑾言的眼睛，用大量清水清洗后依然感觉疼痛。路瑾言的眼睛因为患有先天性的弱视，一直都是重点保护对象，顾昐若焦急而担心地将他送往了医院。

从来不曾在外人面前暴露一丝脆弱、一滴眼泪、一次皱眉的顾昐若，这一次却哭得很大声。她不知道路瑾言的眼睛里到底是粉末多一点还是玻璃碎碴多一点，她害怕他的眼睛会因此而失明，她更害怕会这样失去他……

大颗大颗的眼泪滴落在刚才在果饮店里她亲自写给路瑾言的小卡片上，瞬间，就将卡片浸湿了。卡片上的字迹渐渐模糊，而后凝成一团黑，无穷无尽的黑。

I open my eyes（我睁开双眼）. I have you in my world（你出现在我的世界里）.

顾昐若 To 路瑾言，In 凤凰。

就这样，顾昐若一边愧疚地通知班主任，等候他们的处置，一边守在路瑾言的病床前，焦急地等待着医生的检查结果。

我不想再拥有，我不能再失去

/01/

有人说，忘记一个人只有靠两种方式——时间和新欢。

时间不够长，新欢不够好，心的位置就不会随之转移。那些想要忘记的人或事，依然可以轻而易举地触动你的心弦，无处可逃，无法可忘……

顾昕若从来都没有想过要忘记。

即便"失去"这个动词无时无刻不贯穿着她的生命。即便面对失去她只能选择接受，只有无能为力。

可是，当她意识到，她的拥有最终还是会变成失去的时候，她开始怀疑自己想要彻底拥有的念想。她害怕的不仅仅是自己的失去，而是失去的背后路瑾言所受到的任何伤害。

如果一开始就不拥有，是不是就不会失去？

　　十个小时之后，安眠到达医院的时候，在药物的帮助下路瑾言已经睡着了。双眼通红地来到路瑾言的床边，心疼地看了他一眼，安眠哭出声来。顾昐若将病房的门掩上，走到医院的走廊上。顷刻，就听到了安眠走出来的脚步声。顾昐若深呼吸，转身，停下，然后仰起头。

　　啪！安眠的巴掌朝她脸上挥过来。

　　顾昐若没有闪躲。

　　愤怒的，讨厌的，难过的，担心的……所有的情绪都集中在这一巴掌上。安眠用尽全身的力气，一巴掌下来，顾昐若的嘴边都能看到血迹。

　　打完顾昐若的右手被安眠紧紧地握成了拳。

　　"顾昐若，路瑾言是我的男朋友，请你下次想要找男生陪你过生日时，先看清楚事实，好吗？生日人人都有，年年都有，你用不着这么大张旗鼓吧。我麻烦你，拜托你，求你，请你，离他远一点，好让伤害也离他远一点。"

　　这样的安眠，真的是失控的。

　　哪知，顾昐若依然仰着高高的头，说："是他心甘情愿陪我来的，你管不着。他受伤了我也担心……"前一句是故意的，后一句才是真心话。安眠自是不懂的。她愤怒地抬起左手，一个巴掌又利落地落到了顾昐若的脸上。

　　这样的巴掌是没有控制力道的，打下来，就能感觉到疼。顾昐若想起一次和顾之淳吵架，当她朝着他大喊大闹的时候，顾之淳气愤地一个巴掌朝她挥过来，巴掌落下，顾昐若却一点也不觉得疼。因为，顾之淳在落掌的瞬间就已经控制好了自己手上的力度。

　　停好车，来到病房区的李嘉禾，看到的就是这一幕。事实上，李嘉禾和安眠是一同过来的。安眠的母亲接到路瑾言母亲打来的电话时，安家三口正和李家四口坐在一起边谈生意边吃晚饭。这边电话还未挂，那边安眠和李嘉禾已经往停车场跑去了。

李嘉禾知道，顾盺若是心甘情愿挨这两巴掌的，甚至于，她愧疚到自己送上门，任由安眠处置。

"都傻站在这儿干吗？安眠，去路瑾言身边待着吧，他醒过来最想见到的人一定是你。"李嘉禾人未见，声已闻。

安眠不甘地放下了握紧的手，走进了路瑾言的病房。

李嘉禾把顾盺若拉到走廊上的椅子旁坐下，还没来得及安慰她，就看到了大老远匆忙赶过来的路瑾言的父母。接到顾盺若的电话后，他们立马收拾了点日用品就跑到火车站买票，可怜天下父母心。李嘉禾站起身，将顾盺若护在自己身后，而后礼貌地同路瑾言的父母问好。

"对不起。"顾盺若推开李嘉禾，站到路瑾言父母面前。

"盺若，你没事吧？没受伤吧？"路瑾言的母亲关切地问道。

"对不起，路妈妈。对不起，路叔叔。都怪我，我不应该让路瑾言带我来这儿过生日的，我不应该带他去那家奶茶店……都是我的错，对不起……"

路妈妈抱着颤抖着的顾盺若，说："别担心，他会没事的。"路爸爸也拍着她的背说："傻丫头，不怪你的。"

"对不起，对不起……"

好像，只有不断地说着对不起，才能减少自己心里的愧疚感。

将顾盺若交给李嘉禾照顾，路瑾言的父母才放心地去了病房和检查报告室。

大概是因为顾之淳的关系，顾盺若会称呼路瑾言的母亲为路妈妈，却始终不肯喊路瑾言的父亲为路爸爸。在她的心里，"爸爸"和"父亲"这类词，是陌生的，也是遥远的。

这注定是个漫长的夜晚。

李嘉禾将顾晡若带到医院的花园区，坐在柔软的草地里，感受着清新的空气，但愿，她的内心也能够平和轻松一点。

“吃点东西吧。”李嘉禾说。

“我不想吃，谢谢。”

“那不如听我给你说个故事？”

“嗯。”

每个说故事的人都爱用“从前……”作为开头，李嘉禾也不例外。

“从前，有个小朋友撒谎，有一天，他死了。从前，有个小朋友很用功地念书，长大之后，发财了。从前有个小朋友不孝顺，有一天他扭伤了脚。从前有个小朋友早睡晚起，第二天，死了！”

“欸，这不是麦兜妈妈跟麦兜说的故事吗？”

“从前啊，有一个小朋友她不开心了，一个怪叔叔跑出来跟她说了一个故事，她就笑了。晡若，你还是笑起来好看。”

“谢谢。”

“傻孩子。”

“怪叔叔，我们聊聊天吧。我的心里好慌好乱，我不知道路瑾言现在到底是什么情况。”

“别担心，他会没事的，他那么善良。”

“嗯。”

“晡若，你想要聊些什么呢？”

“唔，聊聊你吧。”

“我？”

“对啊。都没有听你说过你的故事，或者说说你可爱的妹妹沐禾也不错啊。"从来都不曾了解，这个阳光、优秀、帅气，总是陪在自己身边的男生，顾昕若是真的想要了解他，是怎样的生活和过往让这个男生能够如此强大，如此有爱。而，这样的爱，仿若磐石般不会转移。

"……好吧，你想听我就说给你听。"

"嗯。从现在开始，你来说，我负责听。"

然而，李嘉禾的故事远远没有顾昕若想象之中的温馨、温暖、温情。相反，他的故事是微凉的，是忧伤的。

温柔且小彪悍的李沐禾是李嘉禾同父异母的妹妹。在李嘉禾两岁的时候，他的亲生母亲就离开了他，离开了整个家。母亲离开不到半年的时间，父亲就带着后母来到了自己的家。漂亮妖娆且清高得不可一世的女人，就像是战争中胜利的一方，得意扬扬地占领了整个家所有的范围。

这样的女人，死心塌地爱着的，一定是父亲的钱。

李嘉禾本能地讨厌她。

那些时光里，李嘉禾是沉默的，也是不会微笑的。直到李沐禾出生。最初，他是真的不喜欢，甚至排斥这个妹妹的。可是，这个妹妹和后母不同。她孝顺，父母生日、哥哥生日、母亲节、父亲节，她都会送上自己手绘的小卡片。她善良，她会收留流浪的小猫猫，无法收留的时候，她会将它们送到宠物管理所。她温暖，她真心地把李嘉禾当成亲哥哥，会拍好看的照片送给他，也会帮他准备贴心的小药箱……

甚至于，她会像天下所有的妹妹一样，和李嘉禾争吵打闹。偶尔她会宽容哥哥，偶尔她会跟他闹到底。但是，她所有的动机都是关心他，为他好。

这些好，李嘉禾都知道，可即便他能够接受他们俩的关系，最终却还是排斥与李沐禾太过亲密。

夜已深，天微凉。

故事到这儿，李嘉禾选择了完结。但是关于他的亲生母亲，他却只字未提。

顾昀若给了李嘉禾一个大大的拥抱，她在用行动告诉他："你难过的时候，我也会在身边陪着。"

离开她的怀抱，李嘉禾从口袋里拿出一个长方形的盒子递给顾昀若："喏，送给你的。"

打开盒子，只见一把精致的小乌木梳安静地躺在盒子里。深红的色泽像是沾染了灵气，微微闪着光亮。

突然，李嘉禾拿起小乌木梳，温柔地给顾昀若梳起头来。乌黑的长长的直发，李嘉禾尤其喜欢。这样的距离有些暧昧，顾昀若变得不自在起来。在与李嘉禾的相处中，她一直是有意地保持着距离的。于他于己，这都是最好的。

小心地挣脱开，顾昀若说："我又不是孩子，我自己来。"

李嘉禾却动情地说道："你是我的孩子。"

——可是。

——你是我的孩子啊。

暧昧的距离，有什么一触即发。这样的夜，越加漫长。

靠在李嘉禾的肩膀上，顾昀若，终于，微微地进入了浅睡眠。

顾昀若的睡眠状态一直以来都不好，睡眠浅，易惊醒，还多梦。外界一点点的风吹草动，她就能感觉到。醒来后，又需要很久才能睡着，甚至，整个晚上都会处于失眠状态。所以，口袋里的手机刚震动了一下，她就惊醒了。

是路妈妈的电话。

"昀若，检查报告出来了，你过……"

路妈妈的话还没落音，她就心急地将电话给挂断了，甚至忘了询问检查结果，忘了询问路瑾言是否已经醒来，就心急火燎地奔赴而去。她是用飞奔的姿态跑到病房区的，到达一楼后却停下了脚步："不会有事的，对不对？"

李嘉禾点头。

"我……相信你。"

窗外的天色微微发亮，恍惚间还以为天亮了，才发现一切如同昨日，担心依旧，害怕依旧。还好，上天是眷顾着路瑾言的：检查报告显示，眼部伤害并没有很严重，一个月内每周都坚持到医院进行"眼部清洗"就可以恢复。只不过，这样的意外事故，一定要尽可能地避免。

路瑾言醒来的时候，安眠靠在他的床边，已经睡着了，漂亮的脸蛋上有斑驳的眼泪的痕迹。他伸出手想要触碰她，小幅度地移动后，刚刚好看到了枕头底下的小卡片，是顾昁若的笔迹。

I open my eyes（我睁开双眼）. I have you in my world（你出现在我的世界里）.

顾昁若 To 路瑾言，In 凤凰。

可是，人呢？

打开手机，输入短信，发送至顾昁若。

——对不起，连一个完整的生日都无法给你。

已经站在病房门口的顾昁若收到了这条信息，汹涌的情绪涌向心脏，她真实地感觉到了心酸。已经握住了门把的手，迅速地抽回。回过头，压抑着所有的情绪对李嘉禾说："你先进去吧，我想一个人静静。谢谢。"

——谢谢。在这个时候，这两个字就等于"拜托！请你不要打扰我"，所以，李嘉禾选择尊重她的决定，也没有去找她。

一个人若是真的想逃，即便你耗尽所有力气，也是无处可寻的。

推开门，路瑾言微笑着和李嘉禾打招呼，眼睛却是望向了他的身后。直到李嘉禾将门关闭，他才收回自己的视线。嘘寒问暖地寒暄了几句后，路瑾言终于忍不住问李嘉禾："顾眄若没有跟你在一起吗？"

"她想一个人走走。"

"哦。"

/02/

顾眄若努力调整着自己的心情，几个小时后，终于说服自己去面对路瑾言，回到医院时却发现他已经出院了，所有的人都已经离开了。

空荡荡的病房里，没有一个人等她。

是哪里出错了吗？！

翻开手机，收件箱里的短信仍然是路瑾言发给自己的"对不起，连一个完整的生日都无法给你"，以及李嘉禾的短信："我在病房等你，平复好情绪就过来看看他吧。"发件箱里却只有一条回复短信，是她发送给安眠的，一个简短的"好"字。

顾眄若只好一个人坐火车回去。仓促地去买票，还算幸运，买到了车厢的站票。这是一趟不算拥挤的火车，找到一个无人的角落，顾眄若蹲坐在空地上，闭着眼，听着火车发出的轰隆声。

嗡——嗡嗡——

是手机震动的声音。

"喂?"

"眄若,我送你的梳子还在我这儿呢,回头我给你送过去。"是李嘉禾的电话,粗心大意的顾眄若居然忘了拿他送给自己的梳子。

"对不起,刚才跑得太着急。"

"没事。你们到了吗?"

"我们?"

"你没有和路瑾言他们一起回家?"

"嗯,没有。"

"你在哪儿?"

"火车上。"

"离下一站还有多久?"

"五分钟吧,火车行驶得很慢。"

"下车,在出站口等我。"

"嗯?"

"下车,在出站口等我。"

不容拒绝,因为,李嘉禾已经把电话挂断了。顾眄若只好在火车停站时下了车,而后坐在候车厅等李嘉禾。李嘉禾挂断电话后,就迅速将车掉头往回开。连续长时间地开车,李嘉禾已经很疲惫了,回去的路途中一路都开得小心翼翼,可现在他却倔强地踩紧了油门,加快了速度往回赶。

李嘉禾到达顾眄若所在的位置后,极绅士地帮她拉开了车的前门,却意外地遭到了拒绝。

顾眄若说:"女主人的位置还是留给值得的人吧。"

话说完,顾眄若绕过李嘉禾,拉开了车的后门。李嘉禾车子的后座,才是属于她的位置。李嘉禾的旁边，适合更美好的女孩子。虽然只是副驾驶座位和后座的距离，聪明的李嘉禾却明显感觉到了顾昉若刻意的疏离和客气，这样，一路下来，两人都没有先开口说话。

回到家，已是晚上，安眠还没离开。

安眠感到诧异，李嘉禾为什么会送顾昉若回来，她心里打的小算盘难道没有成功？不过，她也没有明显表现出自己的不痛快，调整好情绪，摆出笑脸询问李嘉禾道："嘉禾，来得正好，我们回家的方向相同，载我一程吧。"

没有回答安眠的问题，李嘉禾冷淡地问她："为什么顾昉若会是一个人回来？你说她会跟你们一起回来，我才开车先离开的。"

"哦，瑾言出院时，我打电话给昉若，她说还需要再静一静，我们才回来的。喏，她还给我回短信了。"安眠淡定地回答。

"她想再静一静，你就打电话给我啊。"

"这不，当时忙着担心路瑾言，忘记了嘛。我们走吧，嘉禾。"

顾昉若想要一个人静静，便选择了逃离，走着走着就走远了。求心静的顾昉若电话也不接，李嘉禾家里有事要先离开，便嘱咐安眠等顾昉若一起回去。而办理好路瑾言出院手续的安眠，在路瑾言和其父母都在找寻顾昉若的情况下，故意避开他们打电话给顾昉若，拨了好几次才接通她的电话，安眠气愤而夸张地对她说："我们马上就要走了，你赶快回来。"

"我想再走走，你让李嘉禾等我吧，我跟他一块儿回去。"

"那好，我让他在病房里等你。"

"……"

大概是因为顾昉若手机的信号不太稳定，她刚想说"好"的时候，安眠那边已经没了声音，于是只好挂断电话，给安眠回复了一条短信："好。"

李嘉禾在这通电话之前就已经离开了医院，安眠并没有告诉顾昕若，而是故意随了她的意思，说："我让他在病房里等你。"而当李嘉禾质问她的时候，她又只是轻描淡写地说："我有给她打电话，她也给我回复了短信。"模模糊糊地就将事情给揭过去了。

缺了明确的时间、地点、事情发展的来龙去脉，语句的含义自然就变得模糊了。

安眠不过是玩了一个简单的文字游戏，使用了一点小伎俩。而这个时候，对路瑾言一家满是愧疚的顾昕若自然是不会跟她深究到底的。至于其他人，个个都纯净得跟蒸馏水似的，一点小事而已，用不着打破砂锅问到底的。

顾昕若除了自认倒霉，还能怎样？所以，她只是冷笑着，没有说话，也没有揭穿安眠的小伎俩。就算是问清楚了，又能如何？！

何必去争去抢，去吵去闹。

是你的，终归是你的；不是你的，终究不属于你。

这时候，顾昕若也意识到了，她和安眠之间，这场没有硝烟的战争，已经点燃了战火。顾昕若从来都是勇敢的，所以，她不怕战斗。一路走来，她一直在与命运做抗争，虽然学会了妥协，学会了认命，可更多时候，她还是不服输，不认命的。

就像，明明知道会失去，她仍然想要彻底拥有路瑾言。

这一次，她却选择了放弃。

如果给不了路瑾言幸福，如果顾昕若的拥有就等同于路瑾言的受伤，如果连最基本的安全感都无法给予，那么，就像路妈妈和路叔叔所说的："我们家路瑾言以后就多了一个妹妹，两兄妹要好好相处。"

就心甘情愿地做"兄妹"吧。

窝在阳台的一角，想着想着，眼泪瞬间就爬上了睫毛，爬得满脸都是晶莹的小水珠。顾昉若脸上每一颗小水珠里倒映出来的都是路瑾言的脸。

"我想忘记你，所以不要出现在我的眼前。"

"不要哭。"

"为什么连梦里都是你？"

"傻瓜，这不是梦。"

时光的车轮驶向初秋，风很轻，云很淡，宛如初见。

岁月仿佛沾染了娴静的气息，所有人都相安无事地来往着，一派寂静欢喜。只不过，表象越是平静，暗流也越汹涌。

高二，分班。

在某种意义上分班就意味着重新洗牌。文科班、理科班，重点班、普通班，还有音乐特长生班、美术特长生班。正所谓，物以类聚，人以群分。

死对头南西和安眠终于被分到了不同的班级。许清木先生是脑袋里完全没有文科细胞的理科雄性动物，所以，主科目极其平衡的南西小姐只好选择弃文从理。她想要跟许清木那家伙在一起，就这么简单。还好她得以如愿，有情人终成眷属，南西和许清木分到了同一班。

安眠、路瑾言、顾昉若三人颇有默契地同时选择了文科。

当看到榜单上自己的名字细细密密地挨着路瑾言的时，安眠满心欢喜地摇着路瑾言的手："瑾言，快看，我们被分到了同一班啊。"而后，她又一本正经地弯下腰，朝路瑾言点头，故作模样地对他说，"你好，路瑾言同学，我叫安眠，以后我们就是同学喽。"

——溢于言表的开心和满足，是真的很爱很爱吧。

挤在人群里，顾昕若终于看到了自己的名字。虽然与路瑾言隔着远远的距离，可始终还是被圈在了一个班级里。

是有幸还是不幸，谁都不知道。

假如爱有天意，谁又会是被上帝真正眷顾喜欢的孩子？

分班后，顾昕若和南西、许清木不再是在同一栋教学楼学习了，而是隔了一个大操场的距离。

路妈妈也不再是顾昕若和路瑾言的班主任。由于路妈妈耐心足，负责任，有爱心，加之专业知识丰富，学校将她调往高三（二）班，仍然任班主任一职。她将带领那些孩子们全力以赴高考，李嘉禾就是高三（二）班的学生。

安眠和路瑾言成了班级里公认的最强匹配，男才女貌，羡煞旁人。

顾昕若的喜欢也不再那么高调，她将所有的喜欢一点一滴地沉淀在心底，如海般汹涌、广阔、纯净。有些人说不清哪里好，就是谁都取代不了。如若忘不了，那就远远地守护着。他微笑，你微笑；他幸福，你也幸福，此生足矣。

一切似乎都在变，唯独顾昕若和安眠的关系，依旧平淡、礼貌、客气。没有过分熟络，也没有过分排斥。在安眠的心里，住在路瑾言家里又喜欢着他的顾昕若简直就是一颗定时炸弹。生日旅游事件暂且抛开不计较，但是，当她偶然间知道顾昕若的胃不好，而路瑾言每天早上都会早起十分钟为她准备牛奶的时候，她便醋意大发，羡慕着忌妒着，也恨着。

终于，她耍起了小脾气，质问路瑾言，换来的却是一句不咸不淡的"昕若只是我的妹妹"。

"她又不是你的亲妹妹。"

"好了，小眠，不闹。"

一切又被迫回归平静。

只是，天意弄人，这句话，不经意地就入了顾眮若的耳中。

——原来，只是妹妹。

到底在期待什么？明明已经说好了，就这样远远地看着就好。可是，听到这样不痛不痒的回答，心还是不可避免地疼了。傻瓜，真是全天下最笨的大傻瓜。

/03/

暗战，一触即发。

国庆前夕，各大旅行社都在争先恐后地进行着各类促销活动，其诱惑力还是十分大的。安眠趴在床上，悠闲地浏览着各大旅行网站，即便是黄金周，她还是想要和路瑾言一起去旅行的。或许是某座闻名遐迩的文化古城，或许是某个未开发的荒凉小岛，或许是人潮汹涌的热门旅游区。哪里都好，最爱的人陪在身边，其他都不重要。

她满心欢喜地，打去电话，将这样的想法告诉路瑾言："瑾言，国庆我想和你一起去旅行。你想去哪儿？"

"你想去哪儿，我们就去哪儿，你决定。"

"那我们去野营吧，正好有一处新开发的山地很适合野营，我们去那儿吧，好不好？"平日大气的安眠在路瑾言面前始终是保持着小女人的姿态，凡事都会先询问他的意见，尊重他，在意他。

"不错的主意，就去那儿吧。"

🌢

"嗯，那我预订火车票啦。"

"好。预订四张，回头喊上李嘉禾和昕若一起，野营人多，好玩也安全。"

"可是……我已经预订好两张了。"

"那我给他们打个电话，让他们自己预订下。"

"哦。"

其实，票并没有预订好，她只是自私地想要拥有专属于两个人的旅游，于是撒了个小小的谎，却没有想到，撒谎后却无法拒绝路瑾言的四人行提议。安眠懊恼地将头压到枕头下，然后鬼喊鬼叫地以示不满。

——什么嘛，好好的甜蜜旅游变成了莫名其妙的四人游。

——非要喊上顾昕若吗？

——是去旅游，是去野营的，又不是去探险的，喊这么多人，壮胆啊？

这样碎碎念的安眠，像极了小心眼的怨妇，可是，这样的唠叨和抱怨却反而衬托出了她的小可爱，大抵，真实的东西往往会更容易打动人。

安眠好不容易说服了自己接受了四个人的野营旅行，却在出发前的十分钟，得知了此次野营旅行的人员增加到了七名——安眠、路瑾言、李嘉禾、顾昕若，还有死对头南西和她的小情人许清木，另外一名陌生的女生，最终确认是李嘉禾的妹妹李沐禾。

一眼扫过每一个人，安眠心里的战鼓已经敲响。眼前的形势实在是有些诡异，除了路瑾言，来参加此次野营旅行的其他人好像都是和顾昕若一国的——不是好像，而是肯定。不过，心理素质极好的安眠迅速地调整好了自己的情绪。

既来之则安之，走一步算一步吧。

其实，顾昕若的情况也好不到哪里去。因为李嘉禾的关系，也因为李沐禾讨人喜欢的原因，顾昕若和她之间已经慢慢熟络。平日里的李沐禾在和同学相处中，总是会被人误以为很清高，于是身边好朋友也不多，温柔动人的她对顾昐若有着莫名的信任感。遇到开心的事，她会找顾昐若分享；遇到难过的事，她也会找顾昐若倾诉。几乎，李沐禾把所有的心事都告诉了顾昐若。所以，李沐禾喜欢上了摄影社团里最最优秀和帅气，平日又对自己很关照的许清木学长，这事她也知道。当李沐禾指着许清木旁边的南西问顾昐若"那个女孩是谁"时，顾昐若只是简单地说："许清木的女朋友。"

没有渲染，没有加任何修饰词，因为顾昐若知道，如果她说的是"她是许清木爱到心坎里，爱到不能再爱的女朋友"，那么，李沐禾一定会很难过。当然，这样繁复的解说也不符合顾昐若的性格。她只是希望将伤害减少到最小。

"原来学长有女朋友啦。呀，真是太可惜啦。"

"他们感情很好。"所以放弃吧。后一句顾昐若没有说出口，压在了心里，因为她没有权力去要求李沐禾放弃。因为，从头到尾，顾昐若也没有放弃。

"那好吧。"李沐禾说。

以为她会说"那好吧，那就放弃吧"，可是，停顿了一会，她说出口的却是——"那好吧，那就公平竞争吧。"

到达野营山地时，时间已经接近傍晚。男生们负责搭帐篷，女生们则负责准备酒水食物，等天色暗了，他们就开始野营中的头等项目——篝火舞会。

一会儿工夫，计划中的三顶帐篷就已经搭好了。

左边的帐篷属于"老夫老妻"的南西和许清木，中间的帐篷属于安眠、顾昐若和李沐禾三人，右边的帐篷则属于李嘉禾、路瑾言。这样安排既甜蜜也符合安全性。可是，醋坛子打翻的李沐禾却提出了异议——左边的帐篷换成路瑾言和安眠，右边的帐篷则属于学长和我哥，我、昐若姐、南西就睡中间的帐篷。

这样的安排其实也不错，至少安眠的心里会是美滋滋的。可是，这样的安排南西却非常反对。南西不同意倒不是因为她不能和许清木共用一顶帐篷，而是，她不希望顾眄若不开心。而李沐禾刚说完自己的安排，李嘉禾就在一旁调侃起路瑾言来。

"兄弟，艳福不浅啊。"

一旁的安眠只是略显羞涩地说："嘉禾，别不正经。"

路瑾言没有说话，因为此时，李沐禾和南西意见不合，虽然没有吵起来，但是谁也不肯让步。顾眄若劝说李沐禾，许清木劝说南西，李嘉禾、路瑾言、安眠一脸无奈。最终，安眠和李沐禾，南西和顾眄若，李嘉禾、路瑾言和许清木分成了三组，各得到一顶帐篷。

虽然三个大男人挤一顶帐篷是有些委屈，但总算顾眄若提出的这个方案没有人反对。虽然少数人的心里还是会有些小遗憾和小疙瘩，但总好过尴尬僵持。

既来之则快乐之。不开心不玩乐，简直是浪费时间，浪费心情，折煞青春。所以，篝火晚会进行得还算顺利。舞的舞，唱的唱，趁着兴致好，喝了点小酒，大家都有了些醉意。

回到帐篷后，南西和顾眄若都睡不着，头并着头靠在一起，望着夜空里的星星。

"眄若，你不爱路瑾言了吗？"

"嗯？"

"他和安眠甜甜蜜蜜的，你就不难过不伤心吗？"

"喜欢，可是又能怎样？"

"我讨厌安眠，讨厌路瑾言，他们让你不快乐了……"

"南西，你醉了。"

"我没有。每一个让你不快乐的人，我都讨厌，我要代表月亮消灭他们……

消灭他们。"

"好好好，消灭他们。来，乖乖睡觉。"

"嗯……"

温柔地将南西哄睡了，顾晞若却仍然没有睡意。

隔壁李沐禾和安眠睡着的帐篷里也还亮着灯，她们也还没睡吧。回想方才的李沐禾喝得也不少，担心她酒后说胡话，顾晞若起身走出了帐篷。

然而，安眠和李沐禾两人压根儿就不在帐篷里。再拉开三个大男人的帐篷，里面也没有人。实在是令人匪夷所思，这天黑夜晚的，大家都去哪儿了呢？顾晞若回到帐篷里再次确定南西睡着了后，决定到附近走走，找找看他们。

绕过帐篷后，没走多远，顾晞若就看到了站在不远处的李沐禾和许清木。看李沐禾紧张担忧，许清木惆怅不忍的表情，顾晞若就已经猜个八九不离十了——李沐禾正趁着酒意勇敢地在告白。往深一点猜测，大概，李沐禾突然告白的举动，该是受到了安眠的怂恿吧。对于原本就讨厌南西的安眠，如此精彩的三角恋戏码，最佳观众又怎能缺了她呢？

许清木和李沐禾之间的这档子事，顾晞若是不打算掺合的。她深信许清木是只爱南西的，所以交由他自己处理会更好。让他们两个人解决是最简单不过的，这样，李沐禾的难过也会相对减少一点。而南西，不知者才会不难过不在意。

——还是不知道的好。

——安眠和路瑾言去了哪儿呢？李嘉禾在玩失踪吗？

——啊，夜色真美。顾晞若同学，你就安静地一个人走一走吧。

顾晞若小声地念叨道。

山地里的空气一定是透明的，深吸一口，心脏里都溢满了嫩绿的清新感。

空旷的山地，让人有种想要呐喊的冲动，宣泄所有的不痛快，释放所有的压力，然后整个人就轻飘飘的，只剩下快乐的重量了。或者，当你呐喊完，山的那边，某个陌生人还会出其不意地回应你。光这么想着，喉咙就痒痒的了。

喂！

顾昉若——你好吗——

我很好——顾昉若很好——

这样喊完，眼泪却掉下来了。顾昉若不好，一点也不好，不开心，不快乐，不幸福，顾昉若不喜欢路瑾言和安眠在一起，可是却又只能每天忍受着他们的甜言蜜语，忍受着他们绝配的男才女貌。顾昉若就是个傻子，猪头，大笨蛋。这样不能爱，也不能忘，真的好难受。

抬起头，泪眼依旧，却再次被跌入视线里的画面刺痛了眼。只见不远处，安眠和路瑾言十指紧扣，两人一脸甜蜜地往这边走过来。

是啊，这样静谧的夜晚是属于情侣的。

跌跌撞撞地，顾昉若不管自己是否已经被安眠和路瑾言看到，转身跑回了帐篷。害怕会吵醒南西，便躲进被子里，无声地流着眼泪。

一双手温柔地将她的脸扳过来，而后轻轻地帮她拭去眼泪。

她如此心碎，南西怎能感觉不到？

"不要哭，不要难过，还有我在。爱到痛了，爱到累了，就不爱了吧，不爱了吧……还有我，一直都在，一直在你身边。"

就这样，两姐妹抱着哭着，哭累了就睡了。

第二天的行程临时被安眠改了。

离山地不远的地方有一处村庄，属于半开发的旅游景区。小村庄坐落于山地中间，被山围绕，山清水秀，颇具特色。大清早的，安眠不仅租好了一辆拖拉机，还将所有人的住房都已经预订好了。

一行人都乐得轻松，欣然前往。

大自然的力量是无穷的。远离了城市的喧嚣，就这样简单地寄情于山水间，何乐而不为？脱了鞋子，踏入溪水间，一伙人欢快地打起水仗来。忘了死对头，忘了情敌，忘了尴尬，忘了疙瘩……只剩欢声笑语。

一整天，大家伙的兴致都很高。原本约好找一家农家吃晚饭的，结果临时改成了烧烤晚餐。正所谓自己动手，丰衣足食。男生们负责买肉杀鸡，提水搬运等粗活重活，女生们则负责择菜洗菜，调制烤汁。男女搭配，干活不累，大家伙配合得十分默契。

不料，烧烤晚餐刚结束，整理烧烤汁的安眠一个不小心把剩下的半碗烧烤汁全泼在了李沐禾的身上。酱色的烧烤汁瞬间就在李沐禾白色的棉质长裙上晕染开，一片连着一片，所有的好心情都被搅坏了。安眠连连道歉，可烧烤汁黏黏的，弄到身上实在是不舒服，所以李沐禾只好去招待所洗个澡，把衣服给换了。

安眠和李沐禾一同回招待所，可是没等李沐禾洗完澡换好衣服，安眠就小跑着过来了。安眠跑到许清木旁边的时候，许清木突然凑到她身旁小声地问："她没什么事吧？"安眠却故意装作听不懂地反问许清木："她，是指谁啊？"

许清木记得，昨晚李沐禾跟他告白时，明明就说了"是安眠姐给了我勇气，我才决定将心意全都告诉你的"。想来，安眠和南西的关系一直都很不好，许清木知道再问下去也不过是继续自讨没趣。

"没什么。"许清木对安眠说道。

安眠笑笑，凑近许清木耳边，小声地说道："许清木，你是说李沐禾吧，她没事，换好衣服就过来。倒是你自己，桃花运这么好，可要小心南西吃醋啊。"

语毕，只见南西和顾昒若正端着洗好的蔬菜往这边走过来，还好，安眠和许清木"聊天"这一幕，她们俩并没有看到。等南西走过来后，许清木有些心虚地又有些献殷勤地将烤好的烧烤递给南西，其实他明明只是因为昨晚拒绝了李沐禾的心意而想要多关心下她的，许清木当李沐禾只是学妹。

晚饭吃过后，顾昒若便提议大家散场，进行自由活动。看其他人也没什么异议，安眠便从口袋里拿出招待所的钥匙，说："喏，每个人一把钥匙，每个人一间房，自己选吧。"安眠摊开左手，大把钥匙安静地躺在她的手心里。

反正都是单人房，挑到哪间房都一样，不过是情侣间会想要靠得近一点。选好钥匙后，大家便开始了自由行动。安眠自然是和路瑾言一起行动的，南西和顾昒若还要将烧烤用具送还给烧烤区管理处，李嘉禾便和许清木一块先回招待所等她们。

一边是南西，一边是李沐禾，神经紧绷了一天，许清木有些累了。他用钥匙打开房门，看到床就立马躺上去了。

——啊！还是软软的床舒服啊。

闭上眼，想要好好感受这一切。可是，房间里却突然响起了淅沥沥的水声。难道下雨了？许清木站起来，拉开窗，只见夜空灿烂，点缀着星光点点。那，是哪里来的声音？这时候，从房间的浴室里突然传来一记女声。

——谁？

——外面有人吗？

许清木一个激灵，该不会是走错房间了吧？可是房间是安眠预订的，钥匙不可能是别人的啊。听这声音有点熟悉，难道？

"啊……"

果然，是李沐禾的房间。

"沐禾，是我，学长。你发生什么事了？"

"我滑倒了——脚，脚好痛……学长，怎么办？"

"能站起来吗？"

"好痛……"

"我知道了，你忍一忍，学长想办法。"

"嗯。"

做了一个深呼吸，许清木立马让自己镇定下来。

现在的情况是李沐禾洗澡摔倒在浴室，稍微推测便可猜到她是没穿衣服的，若是闯进去再将她送到附近的诊所，必然是行不通的。找顾眆若过来帮忙的话，她现在和南西在一块，单独喊她过来肯定不行，为了避免南西多想，还是都不喊了吧。

一个念头迅速地闪过许清木的脑海——嗯，只能这样了。

"沐禾，浴室里有浴巾吗？"

"没有，学长。"

"那你的衣服在哪里？"

"靠近床边的那个小矮柜的袋子里。"

"嗯，那现在我给你拿衣服，你先穿好，然后我带你去附近的诊所，好吗？"

"好。"

许清木从包包里翻出一条长袖的娃娃裙，又无比囧地勾出一条小内裤和粉色蕾丝花边的少女内衣，而后将它们递给李沐禾。因为摔到脚的原因，许清木不可避免地看到了李沐禾洁白无瑕的肌肤。有些尴尬地将浴室门关上，许清木的电话响起来了。

"喂。"

"我们忙完了，现在回招待所了。"

"哦。"

"你人在哪儿呢？哪间房啊？"

"我也不知道啊，没注意看呢。"

"……"

"喂？许清木？喂？"

"信号不太好。"

"嗯，开门吧，我和昤若已经到你房间门口了。"

"啊？你怎么知道是哪间？"

"这里隔音效果不好，已经听到你讲电话的声音啦。"

"你确定你没有走错房间？"

"许清木，你今天怎么这么婆妈啊？我对你的声音可谓是了如指掌。少废话啊，开门。"

——学长，衣服穿好了！

——咚咚咚！开门啊，许清木，搞什么鬼！

南西和李沐禾同时说话，许清木头都要大了，无奈只好硬着头皮打开门。南西大大咧咧地走进房间，舒舒服服地躺到床上。顾昤若则细心地发现浴室的灯光是亮着的。走过去推开门，便看到李沐禾坐倒在地上，脸色已然有些苍白，而手一直捂着脚。她很疼很疼，却也一直在忍着，等着，等学长将她带到附近的诊所，相信他，所以没有喊疼。

"怎么回事？"顾昤若询问李沐禾。

"摔倒了，好疼……学、学长呢？"

“马上，我来了。”许清木回答道。

“她摔倒了，我送她去医院，回来跟你解释。”许清木匆忙地对南西说完，便走到浴室将李沐禾抱起来，将她送往附近的诊所。

南西望着抱起李沐禾的许清木，一脸莫名其妙：“搞什么啊？”

大概碰得好不如碰得巧，死对头安眠和路瑾言散完步回来，看到的正是这一幕。路瑾言不想介入，便直接进了他的房间。安眠则一副幸灾乐祸的样子，对此南西讨厌至极。顾晽若看到了安眠的表情，不过她也不敢胡乱猜测。

安眠的房间在许清木房间的前面，经过南西身边时，安眠故意小声地念叨了一句：“李沐禾现在一定觉得幸福死了。”

“什么？”南西问。

“没什么。”

“李沐禾为什么觉得幸福？”

“都说了没什么。”

“你最好现在给我说清楚。”

“问你的好姐妹呀，李沐禾是李嘉禾的妹妹，她可比我清楚。”

“晽若？”

“嗯。”

“许清木喜欢她？”南西掉头问顾晽若。

“不是这样的，南西。”

“那到底是怎样？”

“好了，你们慢慢解释，我先回房间了。有什么事再找我吧。”

“是李沐禾单恋许清木，许清木一直都对她保持着距离，就当她是一个小妹妹。”

"许清木他全都知道？"

"嗯，是的。"

"许清木这家伙到底还有多少事瞒着我？他要是敢朝三暮四的，我跟他没完。昉若，你明明知道这一切，又为什么不告诉我呢？你不告诉我，李沐禾就不会喜欢许清木了吗？现在，他们两个在房间里当着我的面搂搂抱抱的，这到底又是怎么一回事，你实话告诉我。"

"南西，相信我，许清木对你绝无二心。李沐禾也是个善良的女孩子，不会做出出格的事情来。至于事情怎么会发展到现在这样，大概应该去问问安眠。你先睡会儿，许清木待会儿就回来了。"

打开门，顾昉若看到李嘉禾正急匆匆地往外跑，大概是去李沐禾那儿吧，他心里还是在乎这个妹妹的。

顾昉若来到安眠的房间，却找不到人，只好敲开路瑾言的房门，如她所料，他们俩在一块儿。顾昉若知道，所有的事情、所有的矛头其实都是冲着自己来的，李沐禾、许清木，甚至南西都只是刚好撞到了这支枪的枪口上。管不了路瑾言，顾昉若开门见山地问安眠。

"是你，对不对？"

"怎么了，昉若？"安眠故作亲切地询问。

"是你把李沐禾房间的钥匙给了许清木，是你害南西误会许清木，是你害李沐禾摔倒……你明明就知道李沐禾喜欢许清木。"

"那我问你，我为什么要这么做，就凭我讨厌南西？我想害她，不必等到今天。顾昉若，话不能乱说，你不要含血喷人。更何况，李沐禾和我无冤无仇，我干吗要害她？"

"因为，你真正想破坏的是我和南西的感情，我和李嘉禾的关系，甚至，是……”我和路瑾言。只是，后面的五个字顾晗若没有勇气当着路瑾言的面说出来。

“顾晗若，你就对你自己这么没信心？那么，你至少也应该对南西和李嘉禾有信心啊。再者，你污蔑我可以，但是证据呢？”

“钥匙是你负责分发的，李沐禾去房间里换衣服也是你跟过去的。”

“钥匙是你们自己亲自挑选的，至于李沐禾房间的钥匙为什么也在那一堆钥匙里，我想大概是我送李沐禾进房间后，忘了将钥匙拿给她吧。我只是不小心，并不是故意的，你这样说，好像我故意不给她。而且李沐禾摔倒完全是因为她个人的原因，这总不至于也栽赃到我头上吧？瑾言，你来评评理。”

一旁的路瑾言一直保持着沉默，听了顾晗若和安眠争吵的对话，说不上任何原因，路瑾言其实更愿意相信顾晗若的话，可是，安眠才是他的女朋友，他理所应当相信自己的恋人。所以他只好沉默着，谁也不帮，这样至少谁都不会伤害。可眼下，顾晗若解释不上来，安眠又求助于自己，局面僵持着，路瑾言只好开口说话。

“晗若，去陪南西吧。等许清木回来把事情解释清楚。”

路瑾言不评理也不分谁对谁错，理智地让顾晗若先去陪南西，想简单地将事情解决，结束争吵。不想，对于路瑾言这样的处理方式，顾晗若却误会了，她深吸一口气，喊出他的名字：“路瑾言……”却又将心里想要说的话，硬生生地吞回了肚里——路瑾言，我没有冤枉她，是她，一切都是她所为。

“安眠拿错了钥匙，我代她道个歉。晗若，回南西那儿陪着她。”

——路瑾言，为什么你要代她道歉？

——路瑾言，我不要你的道歉！

——路瑾言，你不相信我，对不对？

——你可以不爱我，但是你不可以不相信我。

走出门，顾昒若突然想起，当时大家在选择钥匙的时候，安眠双手都抓有钥匙，左手摊开任由大家选择，轮到许清木选择时，她则换成了右手，给了他右手握着的钥匙。

可是，路瑾言不会相信，顾昒若说什么他都不会相信。

对不对？

答案当然是否定的。只是，现在的顾昒若不愿去懂。

/04/

恋人之间，最重要的莫过于尊重和信任。所以，南西选择了相信许清木。

在顾昒若去找安眠后，南西就跑到了李沐禾所在的小诊所。许清木一见南西就着急地语无伦次地解释起整件事来。南西呢，不动不笑不说话，也不告诉许清木其实她已经不生气了。她双手交叉抱在胸前，好玩地看着许清木急得像是热锅上的蚂蚁。

是真的在意自己，真的害怕自己生气的吧。

想到这儿，南西狠狠地抱住了仍然在努力组织语言，想将事情解释得更清楚的许清木。

"许先生，我不生气了。"南西喃喃说道。

"真的不生气了？"

"傻瓜。"

"嗯，我是南西的傻瓜。"

终于放下了心里悬着的大石块，许清木用力回应了南西的拥抱。

许清木先生和南西小姐又回归到了甜蜜小情侣的状态。一直守在李沐禾身旁的李嘉禾也终于可以离开一会儿了。听南西说顾昐若去找安眠了以后，李嘉禾心里的担忧就变得越来越多。

顾昐若红红的双眼像是兔子眼睛，看到李嘉禾朝她走过来的时候，她赶紧挤出了一个笑脸，一个比哭还要难看的笑脸。

不希望他看到自己哭红的双眼，不希望他看到自己的难过，不希望他为了自己而担心……于是，挤出了一个笑脸，努力地告诉他：我很好。

可是，所有的"不希望"和"比哭还难看的笑脸"却刺痛了李嘉禾。他把这一系列的反应读成了顾昐若的"自我防备"。所以，他是生气的。在李嘉禾看来，开心了就笑，难过了就哭。他是可以和她一起分享快乐，也愿意和她一起分担忧伤的朋友。

对，现在的顾昐若和李嘉禾，只能是朋友。

——如果可以，顾昐若，请卸下你所有的防备，只需要安心地相信着我，我会是你坚定的依靠。

可是，最终，顾昐若和李嘉禾谁都没有说话。李嘉禾霸道地牵过她的手，说："跟我走，我带你离开。"直到将顾昐若安全送回家，他才不舍地松开她的手。这一路，顾昐若也没有反抗，而是任由他牵着自己的手逃离。

顾昐若发觉，这样的李嘉禾已经不再是那个阳光帅气的男生，而是值得依靠和托付的男人。他霸道里的温柔和温情，丝毫不输路瑾言。以至于，南西也常常问顾昐若："非要喜欢路瑾言吗？李嘉禾到底哪里比不上他？"

李嘉禾优秀、阳光、绅士、多情，他的魅力是女生难以招架的。霸道的眉目里，衬着一双温情的眸子。即便是在漆黑的夜里，有他在就像是有星星存在，闪耀夺目。而路瑾言，同样优秀，却内敛许多，他那邻家大哥哥的外表下隐藏着一颗如海般纯净宽容的心灵，安定温暖，令人向往。

这个世界上，每一种爱情的模样都是不同的。

李嘉禾的爱是充满行动力和霸道感的，若爱就会用力地去爱，自然也不缺乏各种甜蜜的攻势。他的爱，深情而甜蜜。与李嘉禾不同，路瑾言的爱则细小而隐匿，他不会深情地说"我爱你"，不那么懂得用浪漫感动喜欢的人，甚至连甜言蜜语都舍不得说给喜欢的人听。他只会低调地为你做许多许多事，你知道也好，不知道也罢，但凡对你好，他就会去做，但凡你喜欢的，他就会去做。所以，懂的人一定能够明白，他大妈般唠唠叨叨的牢骚里已经碎碎叨叨、清清楚楚地告诉了你——我爱你。

当然，这些都是后话。所以，对于"非要喜欢路瑾言吗"这样的问题，顾昳若总是选择用歌词来忽悠南西——有些人说不清哪里好，但就是谁都取代不了。

顾昳若正悠然地趴在窗台边望着夜空，但一看到路瑾言回来的身影，她立马就跑回了自己的卧室，却被路瑾言抓个正着："为什么要逃跑？"

"啊，困了，想睡觉了。"顾昳若回答。

"昨晚，在帐篷前，为什么要逃跑？"

安眠、路瑾言，十指紧扣，深情相拥，这样甜蜜这样令人刺痛的画面，不逃跑，难道应该虚伪地开心地祝贺和恭喜你们？路瑾言明知故问，顾昳若不想回答他的问题，走到门前，拉开门，朝路瑾言做了一个"请"的手势。

"为什么要逃跑？"路瑾言无视顾昳若请他出去的意思，锲而不舍地问道。

"不想打扰你和安眠。"

"只是这样？"

"只是这样。"

"那，为什么会哭？"

"我没有。"

"说谎。"

"我……没有。路瑾言，你到底想干吗?!"

"不要逃跑，不要哭，不要对我撒谎……"

"我真的要睡了。请——"

"睡吧。我在这儿看着你睡，等你睡着了我就离开。"

"路——瑾——言！"

"睡吧。"

其实，路瑾言也不知道自己到底是怎么了。此时此刻，他心乱如麻，好像只有看着她熟睡了才能够心安，心定。他知道，在她最需要他的时候，他没有给她安慰和信任；相反的，他伤害了她。他不知道，从什么时候开始，他已经越来越在意她的心情和感受了。

顾眄若将这段莫名其妙的小插曲告诉给了南西。南西大胆猜测，路瑾言正渐渐喜欢上顾眄若。可是，猜测终究只是猜测。所以，南西说：感情最忌讳拖拖拉拉，爱则爱，不爱则不爱，暧昧是不可取的。

顾眄若点头表示赞同。

"不如，我们试探一下路瑾言对你的感情吧。"南西提议道。

"可以吗？"顾眄若小心翼翼地问。

"嗯。"南西坚定地答复她。

爱情里的每一次赌注是需要倾尽真心和勇气的，爱或者不爱，顾眄若决定赌一次。

如若爱，即便是失去，是伤害，她也会一直爱到底；如若不爱，那就离开，永远地。

顾昐若曾听人说过："很多时候，一个人发现自己爱上了一个人，都是在跟那个人分别的时候，突然一下子见不到那个人了，才知道自己已经不知不觉地对那个人产生了很强的依恋。"

所以，顾昐若决定，在路瑾言的世界里消失一段时间。

就这样，顾昐若失踪了……

{第四章}

暧昧尽散，晚歌婉转

/01/

也许，爱的最初就是源于"习惯"。

习惯推开门就能看到她熟睡的脸，习惯走到阳台就能瞥见她的身影，习惯每天早起五分钟为她准备一杯热牛奶，习惯大清早就能看到她睡眼惺忪的模态，习惯她假装不在乎却时刻关注他的傻样，甚至，习惯她每次瞧见他与安眠在一起时那种隐忍又强装淡定的可爱。

这样的习惯，不同于青梅竹马的惯性定律。这样的习惯，真是甜蜜又变态。这样的习惯，直到路瑾言发现，他真的已经习惯了，他的身边不能没有顾昕若这个人。

偏偏，这段时间，路瑾言的父母也不在家。他的父母都是懂得经营生活和享受生活的人。为了庆祝结婚周年纪念日，他们"丢"下两个孩子，携手跑到韩国的济州岛，去度他们的周年"蜜月"了。

一瞬之间，记忆纵深，相思成灾。

其实，顾岾若的失踪只是小小的。甚至于，她都没有离开这座城市。她只是和路瑾言在玩她小时候常常会和小朋友一起玩的“躲猫猫”游戏。她躲得不远不偏不隐蔽，因为，她希望被找到。她甚至选择了她曾经告诉过他的，她最喜欢的地方——山顶大厦。

山顶大厦。

这座城市最高的建筑物。

乘电梯到达大厦的顶层，可将整座城市的美景尽收眼底。顶层的另一番美景则是飘扬在栏杆边缘的无数爱心小卡片。卡片上面写满了不同情侣的爱情誓言，证明着他们的爱，证明着他们曾一起来过这里，一起享受并拥有着这样的美景。

耷拉着脚靠坐在顶层边缘的栏杆边，顾岾若感觉整个世界都被瞬间放大了。抬头望天空，天空变得更高更远更清澈。世界就在脚下，没有什么不可以。这样想着，全身都充满了力量。说真的，顾岾若喜欢并享受这种变身大力水手的感觉。

以前，她和南西、许清木来过这里一次。遗憾的是，天生就有恐高症的南西一靠近栏杆立马就会感觉呼吸困难，好像下一秒就会窒息般。但即使是这般困难，她还是坚定地牵着许清木的手，将写满爱心的小卡片亲自贴到了栏杆的边缘。从那个时候起，顾岾若就希望有一天能够和自己心爱的男生来这里，然后也很俗很浪漫地在这里贴上爱的便利贴。

路瑾言去了很多地方寻找顾岾若。

山顶大厦他也来过，只是当他乘着左边的电梯来到山顶的时候，顾岾若正乘着右边的电梯下去买水喝——再试探，再玩失踪，也是要喝水的呀。于是，就这样，两个人好像是命中注定般，擦身而过。

南西、许清木和顾晒若是再好不过的知己，下一站，便是他们那儿。出乎意料地，对于顾晒若的消失，南西和许清木一点也不着急，也许，他们是知道答案的。

"南西，顾晒若不见了。"

"我知道。"

不是想象中的"顾晒若不见了？""她不是和你在一起吗？""你把她弄丢了？"诸如此类的追问，而是轻描淡写的三个字：我知道。路瑾言也因此断定，顾晒若在哪儿，南西和许清木一定是知情的。至少这样便确定了顾晒若的安全，路瑾言揪着的心也稍稍放松了些。

"她昨晚没回家，是和你睡在一起吗？"

"嗯。昨晚她是睡在我家的。"

"她没有给我打电话，也没有给我发短信。"

"放心，晒若现在很安全。"

"那……她现在在哪儿？"

"路瑾言，从现在开始，你可以诚实地回答我几个问题吗？也请你诚实地面对你自己的内心，可以吗？"

"嗯？"

"顾晒若消失，你很着急，你很担心，甚至你会害怕失去她，对吗？"

一整晚都辗转反侧；手机翻开关上无数次，打电话给顾晒若，查收短信箱、通信栏；听到一点儿声音就神经质地跑到阳台寻找熟悉的身影；最后，数了一晚上的喜羊羊、懒羊羊、美羊羊；从大清早开始就一直在找人……这样，是着急，是担心，也是害怕失去吧。

于是，路瑾言点头，回答南西："嗯。"

"为什么会着急？为什么会担心？为什么会害怕？"

"因为……每天都在你视线范围内的人，突然见不到了。"

"嗯？"

"她，在哪儿？"

"路瑾言，容我大胆猜测下，你已经喜欢上了顾昽若，是不是？"

爱或者不爱，这都是他和顾昽若两个人之间的事。所以，路瑾言选择了不回答这个问题，即便他的心里已经有了答案。

若不是顾昽若的试探和消失，路瑾言这个木头脑子、木头心也不会明了他对顾昽若的心意。现在的他已经完完全全地习惯了，他的身边不能没有顾昽若。可是顾昽若曾经不是说过，习惯不是喜欢，更不是爱吗？可是他和顾昽若又不是青梅竹马的关系。

女生的第六感是很玄妙的，大多时候，这种没有任何根据的第六感都是正确的。此时此刻，南西的第六感已经感应到了路瑾言的真心。所以，她对路瑾言说："山顶大厦，顶层。去吧，将你心里的答案告诉她。"

事实上，李嘉禾从昨晚开始也一直在寻找顾昽若。每个晚上，睡觉前，他都会给顾昽若发送"晚安"的短信，也会收到顾昽若回复的"晚安"短信。而昨天，发出去的消息却迟迟等不到回音。第二天来到路瑾言的家里，也寻不到任何人。打电话过去，手机里也只是冰冷地重复着同一句话："对不起，您拨打的电话暂时无法接通。"

顾昽若，到底去了哪儿？

有时候，缘分是不得不败于高科技的。

而"对不起，您拨打的电话暂时无法接通"总是要比"对不起，您拨打的用户已关机”有爱许多。通过手机全球跟踪定位系统，李嘉禾最终比路瑾言早一步找到了顾晞若。到达山顶大厦顶层时，李嘉禾远远地就看到了迎着风微笑着的顾晞若。

看来，这丫头心情还不错。

“嗨，顾晞若同学，真巧啊，你也在这里。”

“呀，学长，好巧哦。你怎么也在这里?”

果然，她心情是不错的，还懂得配合他的玩笑。不过听这丫头喊自己“学长”，这感觉吧还真奇怪，倒也不是说生疏，反而是亲切得过分。

“吃饭了吗?”

摇头。

“走，吃饭去。”

摇头。

“鸡腿、大骨汤，没有诱惑力?”

“呃……那好吧，人是铁，饭是钢，先吃饭，再吹风。”

“回头拎两罐啤酒上来，我陪你。”

顾晞若笑笑，没说好，也没说不好。

始终，顾晞若是要等待路瑾言的。而，李嘉禾，始终是要离开的。从头到尾，她就不需要他的陪伴，或者说，不愿意他舍弃一切来陪伴自己。虽然李嘉禾从来没有对顾晞若说过“我喜欢你”之类的话，但是他对顾晞若比朋友多一点的感情，顾晞若是明白的。所以，顾晞若打从心底里不愿意也不希望，有一天李嘉禾会因为她而难过受伤。那种爱而不得的心酸，不适合快乐幸福的李嘉禾。

而李嘉禾，虽然不知道此刻顾晞若到底为什么会出现在山顶大厦顶层，但是当他发现她的时候，她竟然是靠着栏杆边缘坐着的。风吹过的时候，他总是会产生一种错觉，顾晰若会随风而消逝，下一秒，他就会见不到她。这样的感觉是很糟糕的，所以，他必须陪着她，或者说，盯着她。

两人各自怀着不同的心思，走到电梯前。李嘉禾突然停住了自己的脚步："不如，我们走楼梯下去吧！"

李嘉禾果然是个不折不扣的怪叔叔。山顶大厦从地面到顶层可是有 63 层楼啊。从 63 楼走到 1 楼，要走多久啊?！这样的建议还真不可爱。顾晰若吐吐舌，满脸诧异和不可置信地对李嘉禾说："你是上帝派来整我的吧！"

"瞧把你吓得，我是开玩笑的啦。"李嘉禾说。

"那，我们下去吧。"

"嗯。"

事实上，李嘉禾一点都没有和顾晰若开玩笑。有这样的提议，全是因为李嘉禾患有轻微的幽闭空间恐惧症。在密闭的空间里会心跳加速，紧张冒汗，时间长了，甚至会产生窒息的感觉。之前，上楼时，他也是走走停停，一路顺着楼梯爬到山顶的。李嘉禾大概估量了下走 63 层楼电梯将会耗费的时间，当电梯门关上的那一刹那，李嘉禾闭上眼睛，紧紧拉住顾晰若的手，对她说："晰若，从现在开始，我需要你牢牢牵住我的手，不要放开。"

终于，顾晰若感觉到了事情的异常和严重性。她本能地放开李嘉禾的手去按电梯按钮，却被李嘉禾拉了回来，不偏不倚，撞个满怀。

"是哪里不舒服吗？嘉禾，你的样子好奇怪。"

是啊，现在的李嘉禾不再是那个潇洒倜傥、阳光灿烂的少年，而是满脸大汗，强装镇定的怪叔叔。可是，都已经这样了，怪叔叔还无比逞强地说："我没事，电梯很快就到达地面了。"

　　这样的李嘉禾是倔强的，也是勇敢的。明知道自己有幽闭空间恐惧症，可是他还是想要去尝试，看看究竟现在的自己是不是还是和以前一样会害怕。在他的人生里，每一次突破，每一次挑战，都是值得嘉奖的，所以，他从来都不惧怕挑战自己。

　　可偏偏，顾昐若也是执拗的。她左手拉着李嘉禾往前移动，右手则用力地去按电梯按钮。而电梯，也像是不听话的孩子，怎么按都没有动静，怎么按，电梯的门都没有开。然后，顾昐若和李嘉禾就听到了巨大的轰隆声。

　　电梯停住了。

　　门却没有开。

　　很倒霉的，他们被困在了电梯里。

　　原本三分钟就会降落到一楼的电梯，却停在了未知的时空里。李嘉禾的心理防线有一瞬间的崩落，他跌坐在地上，呼吸越来越困难。遇到这样的情况，换成其他女生可能会害怕会哭会闹。可是，顾昐若没有哭没有闹，而是来到李嘉禾的身边，用双手温柔地抱住了他，给予他力量。

　　也许，上天是不眷顾顾昐若的，她的生命里有着太多的死亡和失去。可也正是因为这样，她学会了坚强，学会了承受，这些坚强也渐渐变成了一种力量——温暖自己，也能够温暖他人。

　　顾昐若一边环抱着李嘉禾，一边和他说话，尝试将他的注意力一点一点转移开。慢慢地，李嘉禾的状态渐渐好起来，两个人靠着电梯，说起故事来。

　　顾昐若和李嘉禾说的故事是她自己的。

　　关于顾昐若，关于南西，关于许清木，这是迄今为止，顾昐若生命中，唯一一个快乐满足的故事，她将这个故事分享给李嘉禾。

　　李嘉禾和顾昐若说的故事也是他自己的。

关于他的幽闭空间恐惧症，关于他的亲生母亲。

李嘉禾说："她长得很美，不是妖娆而艳丽的美，而是仿若清水芙蓉，不沾染纤尘的淡雅。加之她的个性和脾气都很好，不温不火的，微微一笑，足以倾国倾城。若是我生在她那个年代，我也一定会被她的美所折服的。"

对这样的形容，顾晧若深信不疑。从李嘉禾身上便可看出她的美，以及她的好脾气、好性格。

"可是，看似柔弱的她，却有着倔强的、不可摧毁的力量。在没有遇到我父亲前，她就已经有了心仪的对象。然那时候婚姻是讲究门当户对、媒妁之言的。我外公外婆辈都是政治圈里的名士，她喜欢的人是连大学都没读过的穷小子。这样的爱情，注定不会被认可。"

"要不要休息一会儿?"顾晧若问。

"我没事。"

"后来，穷小子离开了她所在的城市，他许诺她，等他两年，等他出息了，有成就了，他就回来娶她。母亲同意了。接下来的两年里，她一直在等他。可是两年后，穷小子并没有回来。在我外公和外婆的压迫下，她嫁给了这座城市商业圈里'一把手'的儿子李启铭，也就是我父亲。

"我母亲和我父亲的婚姻就是建立在商业家和政治家利益联合的基础上的。日子就这样日复一日地过着。我父亲其实还是很爱她的，对她万般宠爱。可是，她的心里一直藏着一个人。直到，我两岁那年，他功成名就，来到她的身边，他要带她走。而母亲，为了她最初的爱情，她放弃了家庭，放弃了李启铭，甚至，连自己的孩子都放弃了。

"离开的那天，她和那个男人就是乘着电梯离开的。"

所以，准确地说，李嘉禾患的并不是轻微的幽闭空间恐惧症，而是电梯恐惧症。当他的母亲乘着电梯离开他时，小小的他只能眼巴巴地望着，电梯近在咫尺，可是，对于两岁的李嘉禾来说，这一切都是无能为力的。两岁的孩子能记得什么，知道什么，懂得什么？可是偏偏，他都记得。这巨大的悲伤，逃也逃不掉……

残忍，一直都在。

这是一个充满杀伤力的世界。

可是，嘉禾，我们不害怕。这样的成长固然疼痛，却也是最真实的过往。往后的日子里，我们会更加懂得珍惜和感恩。这是上天赐予我们的力量，我们依然要勇往直前，知道吗？勇往直前……

李嘉禾将头靠在顾昕若的肩上，说："昕若，你真像我妈妈。"

他从来都是顶天立地的，从来都是霸气十足的，从来都是不甘示弱的，亦从来都是不畏艰险的，这一刻，他却想要彻底地做个小孩子，赖着、依靠着像妈妈般温暖的顾昕若。这样的李嘉禾是最真实的，也是可爱的。

时针嘀嘀嗒嗒往前走着，电梯里的空气越来越稀薄，死亡的威胁越来越逼近……

李嘉禾挪了挪自己的身子，突然小心翼翼地捧起顾昕若的脸，对她说："昕若，如果我们逃出去了，我们就在一起吧。爱得痛了累了，就不要爱了。换我来爱，以后就爱我吧。将你的余生交给我，我会好好爱你。"

这样动人的情话，顾昕若听了怎会不感动？

在这段小小的时光里，李嘉禾已经渐渐变成了顾昕若蓝颜知己般的存在。任何时候只要顾昕若需要他，他都会在第一时间出现，可是，顾昕若也一直在心里算好了她和李嘉禾应该保持好的距离。她不愿伤害他，哪怕，一丝一毫，她也不愿意。

可是，她还没跟许清木、南西说再见，所以她不能离开，她一定一定不能离开。她握住李嘉禾的手，坚定地说："我们会逃出去的。"

"嗯。我们会逃出去的，逃出去后我们就在一起。"李嘉禾喃喃念道。

只是，李嘉禾的呼吸越来越困难，脸色也变得惨白，额头上的汗越来越多。是啊，他的电梯恐惧症是不会奇迹般地突然消失的，更何况，此刻电梯里的空气越来越稀薄，顾昤若都开始大口大口地呼吸了。感觉到李嘉禾渐渐失去了意识，她脑袋里突然蹦出了四个字——

人工呼吸。

不知道会不会有用。

她只是简单地觉得将自己的氧气传给李嘉禾的话，他就能坚持一会儿。

下一秒，顾昤若将她的脸靠近李嘉禾的脸，将她的唇贴上李嘉禾的唇，然后将氧气传递给了李嘉禾。

电梯门，却在这个时候，缓缓开了。

终于，有人来救他们了……

此时，站立在门前的路瑾言瞬间就石化了。电梯门打开的那一刻，他看到的正是两个人在"接吻"的画面。虽然，只需要稍微分析就可以知道顾昤若是在给李嘉禾做人工呼吸，可是，他心里还是像打翻了酸味瓶，一股心酸直涌上心头。

而现在的顾昤若像是压根就没看见路瑾言般，她着急地朝营救人员大声喊着："救他……快，快，送他去医院……要快！求求你们，快救救他……"听到呼喊，营救人员赶紧将李嘉禾抬起来，往医院送去。来不及顾及自己是不是有事，顾昤若一路小跑跟着营救人员，跟随着李嘉禾，前往医院。

路瑾言一直就站在电梯门口。

可是，他被顾昡若无视了。当顾昡若小跑着经过他的时候，他以为她会停下，哪怕只是看他一眼，可她没有。

她和他，再一次，擦肩而过。

路瑾言的真心，也被搁浅了。

然而顾昡若其实是看到了站在门口的路瑾言的。只是，当时的她，无法为他停下脚步……

/02/

大难不死必有后福。

俗语是这么说的。

可此时此刻，被堵在楼梯间的顾昡若一点儿也感觉不到福气，相反的，感觉到的满是"杀气"。当李嘉禾被从医院放出来，又恢复到生龙活虎的状态时，第一时间，第一件事，他就跑来找顾昡若了。当时正拎着东西准备上楼的顾昡若就这么无奈地被李嘉禾堵在了楼梯间。而当李嘉禾问她，还记不记得，困在电梯里，他对她说的"如果我们逃出去，我们就在一起"的话，顾昡若摇头说"不记得"时，她对面的杀气就变得越来越浓烈了。

看来，这丫头的记性还真是欠调教。李嘉禾玩味地靠近顾昡若，直到他的脸和她的脸近在咫尺，才慢悠悠地再一次问她："再仔细地、好好地想一想。"

原本就不大的楼梯间里，两个人还靠得这么近，顾昡若下意识地挪了挪自己的身子。这么一挪倒是不打紧，只是腹黑的李嘉禾这时候趁机迅速地用他的双手环住了顾晡若。就这样，顾晡若无奈地靠在墙上，而李嘉禾的双手环着她撑在了墙上。

仿佛，下一秒，他就会俯身吻下去。

还好，他只是轻轻地吐口气，问顾晡若："嗯？记不记得……"

心虚又气短的顾晡若只好点点头，说："记得。"

"记得什么？"

"如果我们逃出去，我们就在一起。"

"哈哈，哈哈哈。"

打开门，站在楼梯拐角处的路瑾言，刚好听到了这句话，心跳就这么漏了一拍。

如果我们逃出去，我们就在一起。现在的你们，都逃出来了。

路瑾言转过身，将门带上，假装一切都没听到，仿若一切都未曾发生过。只是，疼痛瞬间就溢满了心房。从来不曾有过的痛觉，心在很真实地塌陷、塌陷着。

然而，李嘉禾哈哈大笑几声后，却也不再逼迫顾晡若，而是笑着对她说："晡若，我们逃出来了，这样就好。至少我们已经拥有了这辈子都可以在一起的时间。所以，就算现在我们不在一起，也没关系。"

这句话，听起来异常矛盾也异常莫名其妙。可是顾晡若却听明白了，他是尊重她的心意和想法的。所以，她对他说："谢谢你，嘉禾。"李嘉禾也没有煽情地接下她的感谢，而是转身，边朝她挥手，边大声说："明天我来接你，准备好请我吃顿饭吧。"

"好。"

这一声，是顾晡若朝李嘉禾的背影大喊而出的。

李嘉禾和顾晰若最终也没有在一起。

离开后,李嘉禾边走边嘲笑自己的小气和幼稚。那些逼迫和那些故意说出的话,明明就是为了气一气站在楼梯转角处的某人,明明就是想要炫耀一下,想要吓一吓他,可是,这样做的意义又在哪儿?真是无比愚蠢和幼稚的李嘉禾啊。

回到卧室的顾晰若,推开门的瞬间就看到了站在自己房间窗前的路瑾言。见顾晰若进来,路瑾言一脸严肃地指指她面前的凳子,说:"坐。"

抽开凳子,顾晰若很听话地坐下来。

"李嘉禾已经出院了?身体都恢复了吧?"

明知故问,不知道他葫芦里卖的是什么药,顾晰若点点头,简单地回答:"嗯。"

"刚才,在楼梯间,你和他说的话,我都听到了。"

"偷听?"

"我在房间里听到你的声音了,就准备去开门的……"

"嗯。"

"听到你们说,如果逃出来了,你们就在一起。"

"然后呢?"

"现在你们也逃出来了……"

其实,顾晰若已经猜出来路瑾言大概想要说什么,想要问什么了。对于情商简直就是负数的路瑾言,她通常都抱着一点点等待惊喜,一点点好玩的心态在等待着他的下文。所以,她还是选择极为简单的方式回答他:"对啊。"

"晰若,早恋可不好。"路瑾言语重心长地说道。

"噗!"说真的,听到这句话的时候,顾晰若已经完全忍不住了,笑出了声。

明明就是想问"那你们在一起了没"，明明就是想说"那可千万不要跟他在一起"，偏偏说出口的却是"昕若，早恋可不好"。早恋不好，那你路瑾言和安眠就不属于早恋啊？平日里，顾昕若笑点不高的，这一刻却真的一点儿也忍不住了。大抵是因为，这一刻，她的心里满是欢喜。

"路瑾言，你是不是吃醋了？"鼓起勇气，顾昕若问出了她想知道答案的问题。

既然被抓个正着，干脆大大方方地承认，路瑾言说："是，我是吃醋了。"

"那你为什么吃醋？"

"我不知道。我……先出去了。"

第一次，顾昕若发现她深爱的这个男人，好像是一个大小孩，可爱的，羞涩的，傻傻呆呆的大小孩。整个晚上，顾昕若都没有睡着，翻来覆去地，脑海里都是傻小孩羞涩的模样。就这样，顾昕若一直躲在被子里偷偷乐着。

时光浅眠。

光阴的车轮沿着轨迹缓缓驶向未知的明天。

自从与南西分班后，安眠就离开了模特社团。当初她加入，也只不过是想用她天生就具有优越感的黄金比例的身材气一气南西。安眠是那种天生就有气场的女生，可以大气硬朗，也可以温婉可人，用"百变女王"四个字来形容她是不为过的。

喜欢她的男生，很多很多。

可她却独独偏爱路瑾言，甚至，第一次，也是最后一次，愿意放下她所有的气场和自尊去爱他。

路瑾言在心里已经确定了对顾昕若的心意后，他越来越不知道应该如何面对安眠。如此，索性不面对。可是，僵持了一段时间后，安眠又放下了她的小性子和自尊，主动示好。不过这一次安眠示好的对象却不是路瑾言，而是顾晌若。

“晌若，学校附近开了一家精品店，我们去逛逛吧？”

“我下午还有事，下次一起去逛吧。找我是有什么事吗？”

“就是好久没看见你了。”

“我们是同班同学，天天见面的。”

热脸贴冷屁股，这事安眠也实在应付不来。“成，我也就不拐弯抹角了。你知道你哥哥路瑾言最近下课都去哪儿了吗？一下课连个人影都见不着。”

恋爱中的安眠其实还是个小女生，她总是固执地认定路瑾言和顾晌若是“兄妹关系”。有时候，一大伙朋友去吃饭，在介绍顾晌若的时候，她也会刻意地告诉大家：“这是路瑾言的妹妹，晌若。”很直接又很亲切，连姓都给她省去了。

而一贯以“宁可我负天下人，不可天下人负我”为座右铭的安眠，霸气和自信从来都是满满的，这一次，却莫名心慌地感觉到了害怕。人都如此，越在乎便会越害怕失去。明知道安全感是必须自己给自己的，可是，在乎的时候就像是将自己弄丢了，让不安和害怕淹没了所有。

好学生、小宅男路瑾言下课后，又能去哪儿呢？自然是待在家。巧的是，顾晌若也是好学生，也是小宅女，刚刚好下课后也喜欢待在家。

这座城市迎来第一场大雪的那天，正好是路瑾言去医院进行眼睛定期检查的时间。

当路瑾言检查完眼睛正准备离开医院时，医院献血车正在做着的一个关于

“情侣献血”的活动吸引了他的注意力。这个活动的大概内容就是：有爱的情侣手拉手一起奉献爱心。如此，不仅可以得到一张由医院发出的情侣鉴定卡，还可以拥有抽取情侣礼物的机会。最重要的是，在这样特别的时刻，彼此在一起。

鬼使神差地，路瑾言将电话拨给了顾晞若。

飞速赶到医院的顾晞若在听到“献血”二字后，本能地想后退避开。可是当她看到“情侣”二字后，又勇敢地走向了献血车。对于顾晞若怕血、厌血的病症，路瑾言并不知情。等到开始抽血时，看到顾晞若由于紧张而瑟瑟发抖的模样，他才后悔莫及。

然后，为了将顾晞若的注意力转移开的路瑾言清了清嗓子，唱起歌来……

忘了是怎么开始

也许就是对你

有一种感觉

忽然间发现自己

已深深爱上你

真的很简单

爱得地暗天黑都已无所谓

是是非非无法抉择

没有后悔为爱日夜去跟随

那个疯狂的人是我

……

是陶喆的《爱很简单》。

不是那首顾晞若曾在电台为路瑾言点的《就是爱你》，也不是那首令人错愕的《你爱我还是他》，而是有着简单旋律，简单歌词的《爱很简单》。这一瞬间，顾昕若完完全全地沦陷到路瑾言的歌声里了。以至于后来，顾昕若所有的网络密码保护问题都一样。

问：你最喜欢的歌曲是什么。

答：《爱很简单》。

献完血，在抽取情侣礼品时，顾昕若和路瑾言抽到了适合夏天穿的情侣T恤。后来，盛夏来临时，顾昕若和路瑾言都有穿这件T恤，只是，他们从来都没有一起穿过。情侣T恤上那两个半颗心也从来都没有靠在一起合成过一颗心。

即便如此，每次回忆起这次献血的经历时，他们彼此的脑海里浮现的都是对方的模样。

美好至此，还有什么不满足？

路瑾言眼睛检查的结果，顾昕若从来都没有听他说起过，大概是，no news is good news。每次检查几乎都是稳定正常，自然大家也都不会每次都询问得清清楚楚。倒是献完血之后的路瑾言，行为举止，变得有些怪怪的。

比如，平安夜的晚上，路瑾言突然莫名其妙地问顾昕若："这样祥和的平安夜晚上，你愿意和我一起去流浪吗？"

多么文艺，多么煽情，多么狗血的台词啊！对于如此怪异的问题，顾昕若的心里七上八下的，忐忑极了。不过，最终她还是很配合他的，回答道："我愿意，就算流浪到世界尽头，我也愿意。"

听到这样的回答，路瑾言呆呆地笑了。

其实，这样的桥段路瑾言也是从韩剧里学来的。虽然他学艺不精，顾昕若总是忍着想笑的冲动。但是为了配合路瑾言，她还是会无条件地跟着他的"剧情"走。不过，路瑾言的韩剧剧情可没有这么快结束，他所谓的流浪就是将身上所有的钱用来买一堆好吃的，然后坐上两块钱的公交，在整个城市瞎转悠。

不过，当顾晞若端着哈根达斯的冰激凌，和路瑾言一起坐上公交，看着窗外夜景时，她切实地感觉到了浪漫。而这一次，天公也作起了美——路瑾言和顾晞若下车的那一刻，天空中下起了绵绵小雪。好像是顾晞若起了个头，随着雪欢快地跳跃起来，随后路瑾言也被带动了。

就这样，旋转，舞动，一点点地靠近彼此。然后，路瑾言就抱住了顾晞若，顾晞若像个小孩般哭了。

害怕下一秒，这个拥抱就不属于自己了。

所以，她哭了。

/03/

不知道是不是李嘉禾将顾晞若交给了他的妹妹李沐禾，在高考倒计时的这段时间里，李嘉禾越来越少地出现在她的视线里，可是，李沐禾却越来越多地出现在她的面前。不过，自从上次旅游事件闹出误会后，李沐禾已经很节制地对顾晞若提及她对许清木的喜欢，以及她曾那么倔强地想要不顾南西而去“争取”。

这段时间，李沐禾一直在学。

学会收敛自己的感情，学会不任性地宣泄这份喜欢，学会不让她的爱伤害到许清木，甚至学着开始遗忘。因为，她已经将南西和许清木的感情看得通通透透、清清楚楚了。她知道，那是她无法逾越的障碍，也是她无法去破坏的坚定。

可是，想忘却忘不了的感觉，好难受。

顾眄若就是在李沐禾感到无比难受的午后，被她喊到了家里。

这是顾眄若第一次来到李嘉禾和李沐禾的家里，也是她第一次完整地感受到了真正的富裕和奢侈——李嘉禾和李沐禾拥有的不仅仅是一栋楼房里的一层楼，而是每人一栋二层小别墅。如此想来，平时的李嘉禾和李沐禾两兄妹真的是无比低调的。

只不过，对于一个家而言，在这样的空旷里，温暖几乎无处可寻。也难怪李沐禾会和顾眄若说："我一个星期能够在家里见到我哥哥一次就已经很不错了。如果不是有规定，每周末吃饭的时候所有家人必须在同一张桌子上吃，大概一年半载一家人见不到面也很正常吧。"

靠坐在李沐禾房子里的游泳池边说了一会儿话，李沐禾的心情终于好了一些。在学校里有好几天没见到李嘉禾了，他的房子就靠着李沐禾的，顾眄若想要见见他，便问李沐禾："你哥在家吗？"

李沐禾摇头说："不在。"而后，她又神秘兮兮地靠近顾眄若的耳旁，补充了一句，"偷偷告诉你，他跟美女姐姐出去约会啦。"

"哦，约会啊。"

"吃醋啦？"

"哪有。李嘉禾那么阳光优秀，没有美女喜欢才奇怪呢。"

"骗你呢。马上就高三毕业了，他们同学聚餐去了。不过他们班里还真的有几个女生暗恋他，说不定会趁着聚餐这等好机会就自然而然地转明恋了。尤其是徐清婉，听我哥的同学说，她可足足喜欢了我哥六年，从初中喜欢到高中，那叫一个锲而不舍啊。"

🖋

"都没听他提过这个女孩呢。"

"那当然，他现在眼里心里就只有一个你。"

"别、别胡说。"

"害羞了吧，害羞了吧，哈哈。"

"呵呵。"

这样说着闹着笑着，连李沐禾的母亲——李嘉禾的后母——已经站到了两人背后都还没发觉。不过，李沐禾的母亲走路也还真的没声音，静悄悄的，连对声音很敏感的顾晒若都没听到一点儿响声。等看到她的时候，顾晒若连忙站起身，大方礼貌地喊了一声："阿姨好。"

对方却只是仰着头，用眼神将顾晒若从头到尾掠过一遍之后，略微地点了下头。

"沐禾，陪妈妈出去买点儿东西。"

"现、现在吗？"

"是的。"

"可是，家里有客呢。我要好好招待晒若。"

"改天来玩不是一样？"

这个女人的眼神里满是薄凉和清冷。顾晒若知道，她这是在下逐客令。自然，她也感觉到了，她是不受这个女人欢迎的。显然，在这个女人的眼里，她就已经认定了，像顾晒若这样穿着打扮的人想要和李沐禾交朋友，只不过是为了攀高枝，甚至是想沾染他们家的权贵。

真是，俗不可耐。

顾晒若也没有久留在这里，又或者是攀高枝、沾染权贵的想法。所以，离开前，她依旧大方礼貌地对这个女人说："我还有事，先走了。谢谢阿姨和沐禾的招待。"

对于这样的场面，顾昉若是不会感到难过的。这世间的薄凉和清冷，她早已见怪不怪。因为，顾昉若一直固执地觉得，顾之淳在看她的时候，眼神里流露出的所有，才是这世间最清冷的。所以，只有在遇到温暖，遇到美好时，她才会不顾一切地想要靠近，想要沾染。

比如，路瑾言。

/04/

隐匿在城市繁华的酒吧一条街里的"塔罗之恋"，是一家安静婉约的清吧。

清吧的老板叫倪斯，因其堂妹倪琴喜爱研究星座、命理，且懂塔罗之术，他便将自己所经营的这家清吧命名为"塔罗之恋"。另一方面，这家清吧每周的周一到周五，都会以普通的清吧模式营业，而周六日的晚上，倪琴就会来到清吧，从晚上九点开始到十二点结束，为有需求的顾客算塔罗牌。

光临过的顾客，都说倪琴算得很准，这家清吧也因此得以名声远扬。

一个暴风雨刚清洗过整座城市的夜晚，安眠来到路瑾言的家里，约他去这家清吧算塔罗牌。"不识趣"的路瑾言偏偏要拉上顾昉若，而"不识趣"的顾昉若则将电话打给了李嘉禾。如此，久违的四人聚会，再一次在多种"不识趣"的因素下展开。

周六日来算塔罗牌的人很多，按照客人的桌号大小来安排算塔罗牌的顺序，显然是最公平的方式。然而，一行四人点的酒水都还没送到，就轮到他们算塔罗牌了。可明明，安眠将座位号递给服务员还不到五分钟的时间。

事实上，清吧的老板倪斯和顾眂若是认识的，也算是朋友吧。倪斯的父亲和顾之淳是世交好友，因此，两位小朋友在很小的时候就认识了。但因为顾之淳的关系，顾眂若对这个常常为自己买巧克力和糖果的大哥哥冷酷极了。一直到现在，两个人也仍然像是萍水相逢的关系，不会深交，更不会经常见面和保持联系。

但是，倪斯于顾眂若，也算是特别的吧。通常，与顾眂若认识如此久的人，要么就是完全没联系，要么就是如南西、许清木般深交的，然南西和许清木已是唯一。像倪斯这种偶尔有联系，却也没深交的人，对顾眂若而言算是特别的，因为她愿意称他为自己的朋友——即便交往平淡如水，亦算是朋友。

前几日，顾眂若还收到倪斯发给自己的短信，说他找了个女朋友，让顾眂若有空来清吧玩。

怀着感激的心，安眠、路瑾言、李嘉禾去算塔罗牌时，顾眂若拿起清吧小舞台中央的吉他，自弹自唱为酒吧里的客人表演起来。上帝赐予了顾眂若一副好嗓子，她的嗓音里流淌着与她的经历完全不同的清澈和温暖。拨动琴弦，音律缓缓。

我知道他不爱我

他的眼神说出他的心

我看透了他的心还有别人逗留的背影

他的回忆清除得不够干净

我看到了他的心

演的全是他和她的电影

他不爱我

尽管如此

他还是赢走了我的心

一首哀伤而无怨无悔的《他不爱我》。

顾昉若的声音的确是适合唱莫文蔚的歌的，浅吟低唱，饱含感情，在清吧微暗的灯光的映衬下，她眼睛里晶莹剔透的光芒，一点点闪烁着。

清吧的另一端，已经轮到路瑾言算塔罗牌了。当他一边洗牌叠牌，一边在心里想着某个人或某件事时，顾昉若感觉到了他匆匆瞥过来的目光。

倪琴在给客人算塔罗牌前，会先问客人在今天想要算的内容，比如学习，比如爱情。然后她就会交给你一副塔罗牌，接着你要按照她所教的方式洗牌，同时心里一直默念自己想要询问的人或者事。最后洗完牌，抽出属于你的塔罗牌后，她就会给你解答。

接触到路瑾言的眼神，顾昉若的心咯噔一下，她想，路瑾言今天所询问的问题，一定是与她有关的。

待安眠、李嘉禾、路瑾言都将最终的结果牌抽好时，顾昉若正好唱完第二首歌，依然是莫文蔚的歌——《忽然之间》。

忽然之间，天昏地暗

世界可以突然什么都没有

我想起了你

再想到自己

我为什么总在非常脆弱的时候怀念你

我明白，太放不开你的爱，太熟悉你的关怀

分不开，想你算是安慰还是悲哀

而现在就算时针都停摆，就算生命像尘埃

分不开，我们也许反而更相信爱

如果这天地最终会消失

不想一路走来珍惜的回忆没有你

终于，轮到顾眄若了。她放下吉他，来到洗手间，将手洗干净。

这是"塔罗之恋"清吧算塔罗牌之前必须的步骤。虽然这样的塔罗牌每次所算的事情只不过是对未来三个月内所问之事的一个大概预测，但顾眄若仍保持了虔诚的态度。她相信，心诚则灵。和其他三个人一样，顾眄若也选择了算爱情塔罗牌，而在洗牌的过程中，她一直所想的人便是自己。

到此，四个人的牌都已经抽取完毕。仔细看了看不同的牌面和牌阵，倪琴开始解答。

"李嘉禾，天秤座。你的内心是不相信爱情的，或者说，你患上了轻度的无爱症，原因很有可能是你在上一段感情中爱得太刻骨铭心。现在的你那么努力地想要去爱，从某个方面来说，你只是为了证明自己依然还有爱的能力。但这只是你最初的想法，或者说只是你自我安慰的拙劣借口。现在的你，已经将新的关于爱的能力渐渐释放出来了。接下来的三个月，你依然心甘情愿。这份爱，渐渐会有转机。"

"哈哈，那可以问问有什么转机吗？"李嘉禾问。

"转机是未知的。下一个，路瑾言，水瓶座。你的牌面很复杂啊，障碍重重。这些障碍有来自你心里的，也有来自外界的，甚至是来自你身体的。你心里的障碍已经渐渐变得清晰，证明你在接下来的三个月里可以顺利清除心里的障碍，对于自己的内心会有一个更加明确的认识。不过，你所遇到的这些障碍很难去除，只有坚强面对，懂吗？"

“谢谢。”路瑾言说。

“安眠，天蝎座。很抱歉，你的牌面我算不出来。请三个月后再来算吧。”

“为什么?”

“当你心思混乱不已的时候，我的能力也就有限，塔罗牌的牌面跟你的内心是连接在一起的。抱歉。”

“好吧，我下次再来算。”

“顾晞若，巨蟹座。敏感、缺乏安全感是巨蟹座最明显的消极的特征。你的牌面很简单，未来三个月，能够给你带来安定的人，就是你所要选择的人。”

“嗯，我明白了，谢谢。”

“赠你一句话，你的安全感来源于你自己，你的选择也来源于你自己，尊重你内心最真实的想法。”

算是比较直白的解答吧，自然也是有人欢喜有人忧。

算完塔罗牌，刚回到座位，顾晞若便瞧见倪斯带着他的女朋友过来了。是该打个照面的。倪斯走过来，像是与顾晞若是老熟人了般，拍拍她的肩膀，笑着说：“嗨，晞若，好久不见。”顾晞若笑着将他的手推开，真诚地感谢他：“刚才，谢啦。”

“都十多年好朋友了，客气什么。对了，这是我女朋友，徐清雅。”

“嗨，大家好。”徐清雅大方地朝“四人行”打招呼，而后又补充了一句别有深意的话，“李嘉禾，好久不见啊。”

后来，李嘉禾告诉顾晞若，徐清雅是徐清婉的亲姐姐，难怪她第一次听到这名字就觉得耳熟。

后来的顾晞若常常会想，路瑾言到底是怎样的一个人。

◆

看起来木木讷讷的，却有着如海般透明宽广的内心。看起来沉默少语，却有着温暖如斯的内心。看起来是不懂浪漫，不懂甜言蜜语的，却总是在细节之处，用行动，用真心彰显着他的爱。

大抵，真的，只有懂得的人才能够明了。

而路瑾言，每次想起顾昐若在清吧里唱的那首《他不爱我》时，就会感到不知所措。这一段时间，他用尽心思带给她欢喜，带给她热泪，他希望，即便他不说，她也能够懂。可是，在这首饱含感情的歌里，他反而懂得了顾昐若所有的害怕和受宠若惊，以及，不确定。

路瑾言想起顾昐若曾经无比认真地对他说过的话。

——如果有一天你爱上我了，可不可以为我取下眼镜？一天，哪怕是一天也好。让我看清楚你的笑，永远记在心里……

于是，这个傻瓜加笨蛋的路瑾言，在某个清晨，偷偷地用隐形眼镜取代了他的黑框眼镜，勇敢地站在了顾昐若的面前，对她说："这一天，我会保持不戴眼镜的形象。"而后，这个傻瓜加笨蛋的路瑾言又在心里默念：一天，完全属于你的一天。请你看清楚我的笑，把它永远记在心里。

顾昐若受宠若惊，却也担心万分，在心里骂了路瑾言十遍傻瓜后，她才跑到他的房间，将眼镜拿出来，递给他，说："戴上。"

以为是被拒绝了，路瑾言条件反射地推开她的手，口气却有些可爱地说："我不要。"

想说"今天你到底是怎么了"，可是明明清楚他这样做的用意。然而，当这样的一份幸福真实地摆在面前时，她反而不敢靠近了。

"我知道，我都知道。可是，戴隐形眼镜不好，容易伤眼睛，快取下来吧。"顾昐若说。

"一天，哪怕一天也好。"路瑾言说。

——只是希望在我眼睛能够看清楚万物和你的时候，将这一切美好定格下来。

因为，在这座城市下第一场雪的那天，路瑾言去医院进行眼睛复诊时，医生告诉了他一个残酷的消息。由于上次的"粉末伤害"，使得他眼部内组织变得越来越脆弱，甚至在将来未知的某一天，双目失明也是有可能的。

所以，从那一刻开始，"失明"就像是一枚潜伏在路瑾言生命中的不定时炸弹，随时都有可能爆炸。还好，由于路瑾言先前就已经感觉到自己眼睛的不对劲，所以在这次复检时，他没有选择安眠母亲的医院，而是偷偷地在其他医院进行了检查。

这个消息，路瑾言对他身边的所有人一律隐瞒了下来。是真的需要很多很多的勇气，才能选择独自承受这一切的。

至于顾昕若，路瑾言以为，即便自己给不了她未来，至少能够在看得见的每一天里，带给她想要的欢喜和美好，想要给她的记忆中加入一份完整的爱，那就是——有我在。

"一天，哪怕一天也好。"路瑾言说。

说完这句话，路瑾言足足看了顾昕若有一分钟吧。顾昕若受不了他这么深情又肉麻兮兮的眼神，那深邃的眸子里藏着他太多的欢喜和爱，只好害羞地点点头，回应路瑾言。

"好吧，讨人厌的一天先生，我愿意。"

啊，"我愿意"三个字用在这里好像不适合吧？顾昕若说完才意识到，但是，有什么关系呢？讨人厌的一天先生现在可是笑得前仰后合，而顾昕若的内心也终于感受到了幸福。

完全属于彼此的一天，路瑾言和顾昤若来到了城市主题公园的蹦极处，这是顾昤若一直很想来挑战的极限项目，可每一次都因为害怕退缩了。这一次，当顾昤若和路瑾言紧紧拥抱在一起，绑带同时系上两个人的腰间时，她闭上眼，勇敢地跳下去了。

这是只属于我们的重生，对不对？

这一刻，顾昤若切切实实地感受到了来自路瑾言的爱。虽然他没有亲口对她说爱，但是他为她所做的每一件细小而让人感动的事，就是他能给她的最深刻的爱。能够拥有这些瞬间，已经足够。

很踏实、很彻底、很开心地在一起玩了一整天，回家的路上，两个人还在兴奋地讨论着蹦极的刺激感。快到家的时候，他们才发现站在门口的安眠。顾昤若倒是"识趣"，知道安眠不是来找自己的，简单明了地说了句"我先上去"，便逃离般地上了楼。

顾昤若刚走，安眠就开门见山地质问路瑾言："都去哪儿玩了？"

"城市主题公园。"

"手机为什么关机？"

"哦，没电了。"

"这么蹩脚的理由，你自己信不信？"

"我送你回家吧。"

"路瑾言，到底谁才是你的女朋友？顾昤若是你的妹妹，不是吗？能不能不要做这些让人误会的事情？你可不可以多考虑我的感受？路瑾言，你不要挑战我的极限。我告诉你，我才是你的女朋友，我有感受，我会生气，我也会难过。"

每一句，每一字，都是吼出来的，安眠真的生气了。

"我爸妈都睡了。去别的地方，我们谈谈吧。"

"前面的公园吧。"

"那座废弃的公园？"

"嗯。"

"那好，走吧。"

两年前，因为这座公园的建筑物倒塌造成了游客伤亡，从此便禁止游客入园了。而这座公园，曾经也是路瑾言和安眠热恋期常来的地方，如今满是回忆。长痛不如短痛的道理，人人都懂。如若不爱，将手放开是不是对对方最后的疼爱？路瑾言是想和安眠摊牌的，而在事实面前，安眠必然会受到伤害，她是那么骄傲的一个人。

聪明的安眠，怎么会感觉不到路瑾言的这些感受？只是，她不会放手，绝对不会放手。宁为玉碎，不为瓦全，这才是安眠的行事风格。

暮色降临，废弃的公园显得越加阴森，而周围连路人都几乎没有。已经如此晚了，考虑到安全因素，路瑾言对安眠说："我还是先送你回家吧，夜黑不安全。"

"那是我自己的事。说吧，你想谈什么？"

"安眠，对不起。我们……。"分手吧

可是"分手吧"三个字路瑾言还未说出口，就被安眠打断了。她说："瑾言，还记得去年的这个时候，我们一起在这里种过一棵小树苗吗？我们还给它取名叫'安静'，寓意我们能够平淡安静地走完一生。我们现在来找找它，好不好？"

"安眠……天这么黑，找不到了。"

"找不到，还是不愿意找？没尝试过怎么能轻易说放弃？路瑾言，你一直以来都是这么容易放弃的人吗？我们一起来找一找，可以吗？"

安眠话里有话，路瑾言长叹一口气，说："何必呢？"

是啊，何必呢？学校里喜欢安眠的人都可以排成好长好长的队伍了，干吗非要赖着抱着一棵木头脑袋不放呢？可是，怎么办？安眠就是喜欢这个木脑袋，不愿意也绝对不会放手。就算是放下她所有骄傲的自尊，也不会放开他。

所以，她对路瑾言说："我不同意。太晚了，我要回家。不需要你送，我要一个人静静。"而后，她骄傲地转过身，虽然眼泪早已爬满整张脸……路瑾言不放心，一路跟在她的后面。安眠走到红绿灯转弯处的时候，一个十六七岁的小混混突然横冲过来，抢过她手上的包包，还连带将她脖子上的金项链给扯掉了。她脖子被勒出血痕，链子才断掉。

"救命啊，抢劫！"

听到安眠的喊声，路瑾言急忙往前跑。在初中的时候得过全校长跑冠军的路瑾言跑起步来可不是盖的，抢劫安眠的小混混碰到了他，真的挺倒霉的。

当路瑾言追到小混混时，小混混就只有认命乖乖交出安眠的包包和金链子了。可是，夜深人静的，连个过路的人都没有。知道此时不会有人来帮忙，小混混便将包包和金链子全扔到地上，等路瑾言去捡时，他摸出插在裤后袋里的长刀，然后，趁路瑾言捡东西时不留神，将刀抵在了他的后背上。

"把东西留下，人滚开。"

"如果我不这样做呢？"

小混混将刀往路瑾言的后背又靠近了一点儿，说："刀不留人。"

被抢走的金链子是安眠的父亲在她十岁的时候送给她的生日礼物，对安眠来说尤为珍贵。路瑾言不能让小混混抢走她的金链子，然而刀尖已抵着背了，再近一点儿他就可能命丧黄泉，他必须尽快想出解决办法来。

"考虑得怎么样了?"小混混问。

"我们做个交换吧。我用我的手机和钱包跟你换那条金链子。我钱包里有张银行卡,我把密码告诉你,你可以买几条金链子了。怎么样?"

这边,路瑾言和小混混在"讨价还价"地商量着,那边,安眠已经气喘吁吁地追上来了。看到小混混的刀正抵着路瑾言的后背,刚好此时从安眠所站的角度可以斜着将小混混推开,她便一用力,想也没想,就这么做了,然后立马拉着路瑾言就要跑。

金链子就在路瑾言的眼前,手一伸就能拿到了,于是,他冒了个险,伸手从地上将金链子捡了起来。路瑾言站起身,准备跑时,小混混也已经速度地爬起来了。一旁的安眠眼疾手快,用脚将小混混的刀踢到了一边。可是,小混混到底也不是在道上白混的,没有刀,打起架来拳头也是不长眼睛的。和他打架,路瑾言明显不是对手。最后,当小混混操起地上的一块大砖头往路瑾言头上砸去时,安眠拿着刀,颤颤巍巍地将它刺向了小混混的胸膛。

啪!砖头落地,在安静的夜里听来格外响亮。

咚!将路瑾言打倒在地的小混混倒在了他的旁边。

安眠抱着路瑾言,撕心裂肺地哭喊着:"瑾言,我杀人了!我杀人了,怎么办?"

血液的腥味随着红色的液体爬满四周,整个世界都笼罩在这血红的腥味里……

{第五章}

时光小偷

/01/

时光是一个不折不扣的小偷。

偷走曾经的山盟海誓，偷走岁月中的细水长流。在时光面前，所有的感情都是平等的。如若不同，那便是人心的不同。抵得过岁月的摧残和磨炼的人心，时光自然会赠予其白头偕老；敌不过岁月的苦难和考验的人心，时光便也只能遗憾地予之叹息，无奈感叹，岁月匆匆。

然而，在时光交错的缝隙中，最伟大、最宝贵的莫过于生命。

很庆幸，被安眠用刀刺伤的小混混并没有因此而失去生命。由于事发后被及时送往医院，他的生命有幸被挽救了。不幸的却是，事发之后，安眠的心理压力急速膨胀，精神状态也很差。曾经她因为亲眼看到父亲与其他女人鬼混在一起的画面而患过严重的心理疾病。这一次，害怕和不安再一次冲击了她脆弱的心理防线，直至使其崩溃。

这样的安眠是脆弱的，也是令人心疼的。

虽然不至于疯癫卖傻，但她的情绪常常会莫名得剧烈起伏，需要用安定剂才能恢复平和。安眠的父母也因此向学校提出了休假的要求，让安眠能够充分地在医生的帮助下恢复健康。自然地，路瑾言每天都会去医院看望安眠，甚至于，每天放学吃过晚饭后，他都会在医院待到夜深了才回家。

顾眆若知道，路瑾言是在给安眠补习功课，对于高三的学生来说，除了生命，还有什么比学习更重要的？

可是，顾眆若还是会偷偷地羡慕安眠。

羡慕她能够得到"学习之神"路瑾言的补习，羡慕她能够得到路瑾言无微不至的关心，甚至会羡慕她能够为了保护路瑾言而不顾一切。而她顾眆若，只能在每天吃完晚饭后，装作毫不在意地坐在客厅的沙发上看电视。遥控器一直在手里，电视机里的频道转换未停。事实上，电视里播了什么，顾眆若压根儿就不感兴趣，她只是想尽可能自然地关注着路瑾言这段时间里的举动。比如他为了安眠收拾整理试卷，比如他拿好亲自为安眠抄写的读书笔记，比如直到最后他连看都没看她一眼便开门离开。

门关上后，顾眆若就像一只泄气的皮球，瞬间就塌陷了。

有时候，有着如此真实感受的顾眆若也会突然想到顾之淳。不知道从前的他，坐在沙发上冷眼看着她走走停停、进进出出的时候，有着怎样的情绪。会不会也和她一样，有着明明很在意却拼命假装无视的心情？

如果是这样，那该多好。

安眠待在医院的这些天，顾眆若一次都没有去看过她。她并不是不愿意去探望安眠，而是，她害怕看到对自己很好很好过的路瑾言，又开始只对安眠好。即便她明明懂，这时候的路瑾言只能对安眠好，可是，她还是会难过。但事情总归是躲不过的。

日光倾城的周末。

好久不见的李嘉禾霸道地将顾晱若整天的行程都安排得满满的，完全是一副要将之前错过的时间通通补回来的架势。而且对于李嘉禾的行程安排，顾晱若连修改和拒绝的权力都没有，她必须无条件服从。否则，李嘉禾今天就算扛都会扛着她配合和服从他的安排。

顾晱若无奈地耷拉着头，无法拒绝便只能暗自感叹："这才被高三折磨完，顺利升入本校大学部的李嘉禾，要么就是被高三生活给折腾傻了，要么就是因为顺利升入了大学，尤其是成功升入了本校大学部，而被高兴冲昏了头脑。还真的是完全颠覆了他的形象和性格啊。怪叔叔，绝对的。"

不过，对于刚进入高三生活的顾晱若来说，她倒是绝对愿意相信原因是后者的。因为，对于在这所学校读高中的同学来说，能够成功进入本校大学部才是最感到光荣和骄傲的。每一年，想要挤进这所名牌大学的学生，数不胜数。

啊，这样看来，其实怪叔叔李嘉禾也挺聪明的嘛。

"顾晱若，顾晱若，在想什么呢？喂，顾晱若，发什么呆呢？"

顾晱若自顾自地想着，居然进入了发呆状态。

"呵呵，没什么。"

"顾晱若同学，高三生活有这么黑暗吗？瞧把你折腾得，小傻丫头。"

这是什么默契呀，整一个不折不扣的傻瓜二人组。顾晱若微笑着，轻巧地将话题转开："来，汇报汇报你的行程单吧。"

"好吧。从现在开始，你，顾晱若小傻丫头，就必须按照我的行程单无条件地服从，懂了吗？"

"别贫嘴，快说吧你。"

"风和日丽、暖阳高照的上午，我们将来到城西的圣玛丽教堂，和教堂里的孩子们一同祷告，唱诗，远离所有哀伤，把哀伤化成一种动力，沉淀自己的心灵。"

"打住，理由。"

"不是说好无条件服从的吗？"

"好吧，继续。"

"中午，我们来到充满异域风情的西餐厅进行午餐。常言道，早餐吃得好，午餐吃得饱，晚餐吃得少。秉持着这个道理，我中午选择的餐厅其实是一家自助餐餐厅。尽情地发挥你吃的天性吧。不吃回本，不准走人。"

美食对于顾眆若，还是极具诱惑力的。

"饱饱的午餐过后，我们就去花店买一束美丽的鲜花。那么，买鲜花干什么呢？买鲜花当然是送人。那到底是送给谁呢？顾眆若，你猜会送给谁？"

"怪叔叔李嘉禾，请你直接揭晓谜底吧。"

"你这个人，一点儿都不懂幽默。好吧，答案就是——安眠。顾眆若，下午我们的行程就是去医院看望安眠。"

想都没想，顾眆若脱口而出："我不要。"

"小傻丫头，不要任性。从小的方面来说，安眠是你的同学，你理应去看看她。从大的方面来说，安眠现在始终还是你名义上的哥哥路瑾言的女朋友，等她恢复出院后，你们始终还是要碰面的。"

再一次将头耷拉下来。李嘉禾知道，这是她的妥协。还好，自己全心为了她好的心意，她是懂得并接受的。李嘉禾满足地敲了敲她的头，宠溺地对她说："走，先去甜品店吃一个你喜欢的巧克力蛋糕，然后我们再去教堂。"

在路上，顾眆若也知道了李嘉禾去教堂的理由。在李嘉禾上初中的时候，

你 是 我 遥 不 可 及 的 梦

他被家人送到了英国留学。家长以为这样做是给了他最好的学习条件，然而对于仅仅十二岁的李嘉禾来说，却是不得不习惯一个人的生活。甚至，他常常会因为孤单而感到害怕。那段时间的李嘉禾就和当地的学生一起，学会了祷告，学会了去教堂寻求一份心灵的安稳。不过，最终，叛逆的小嘉禾还是逃回来了。

原来，我们都很孤单，努力在别人面前假装得很勇敢，在自恋、自卑之间寻找一种平衡感。

坚强又脆弱的李嘉禾，霸道又可爱的李嘉禾，优秀又勇敢的李嘉禾。

这个怪叔叔真的很棒。

上午的行程进行得很顺利，顾晰若感受到了来自诗歌的力量——平和，沉静。可是，下午的行程却糟糕得可以，几乎是完全撞在了枪口上。

当李嘉禾和顾晰若有说有笑，俨然一副小情侣的模样推开安眠的病房门时，顾晰若看到了三张完全陌生的脸，和一张路瑾言的脸，以及一张李嘉禾后妈的脸。后来通过介绍，她才懵懂地弄清楚了状况。

在一场小商业聚会后，李嘉禾的父母同安眠的父母一同来看望安眠，而不知情的李嘉禾和顾晰若则不合时宜地出现在了安眠的病房里。礼貌地给各位长辈打完招呼后，顾晰若便找了个凳子坐在了角落里。

可是，即便是找了个角落安静地躲起来了，顾晰若还是不可幸免地中枪了。李嘉禾的后母不喜欢她，顾晰若是知道的，不知所措地撞入这样的场面也是她极度不愿的。不过，李嘉禾的后母也应该是铁了心地要找顾晰若的碴儿。

一分钟前，她已经明知故问外加扭曲事实地询问了顾晰若——你就是上次来我们家找嘉禾的那个女孩吧？如此，话题便成功地转向了顾晰若。不过，庆幸的是，其他的长辈们正在聊着一些他们感兴趣的事，因此，也并没有因为这个小问题就将目光转向顾眄若身上。顾眄若想要澄清事实，说"那天是李沐禾约的我"。但是她既认识李嘉禾又认识李沐禾，势必会越解释就越说不清，于是，她只是轻微地朝李嘉禾的后母微笑着点了点头。

显然，这完全不是李嘉禾后母想要的结果。

一分钟后，见长辈们将话题转移到了李嘉禾身上，自然地，李嘉禾的后母不会放过这样的好机会，她执着地想将话题嫁接到顾眄若的身上。当安眠的母亲微笑着询问李嘉禾，"在学校一定有很多女生喜欢你"的时候，李嘉禾的后母立马就将眼光瞟向了坐在角落里的顾眄若，一边还阴阳怪气地说："那是当然，我们家嘉禾条件好，家境富裕，加之家教又严格，所以……"

所以，喜欢他的女生很多。这样的"所以"应该才算是正常的，顶多再补充一句：虽然升入大学了，但还是应该以学业为重的。但李嘉禾的后母说的却是："所以，我们家对李嘉禾女朋友的要求也挺高的，相貌倒是其次，但家教总归要有，门当户对也是很重要的。"末了，还意味深长地询问了顾眄若一句，"小姑娘，你觉得我说得对不对？"

顾眄若仍然只是微笑着，点头，不说话。

挺执拗的一小姑娘啊，李嘉禾的后母心想道。

"小姑娘，你和我们家李嘉禾是好朋友，对吧！那你父母都是从事什么样的工作？跟我们家产业有没有关系？有需要的话尽管提啊，我和李嘉禾的父亲可以帮助你。反正你和我们家李嘉禾交朋友也是为了必要的时候能够依靠，能够利用吧?!"

明知故问，真够恶毒！顾眄若轻声地回答道："抱歉，我……父母双亡……"

终于，李嘉禾的后母把大家的眼光成功地都转移到了顾眄若的身上，就连李嘉禾的父亲也开始打量起这个女孩来。而李嘉禾的后母立即换上了一副等着看好戏的模样，那稍稍上扬的眉毛则暴露出了，对于顾眄若父母的这个问题，她是在明知故问。人物微表情心理学研究指出过：当一个人的眉毛微微上扬时，证明他并不是在征求问题的答案，而是明知故问。显然，李嘉禾的后母调查过自己。

这一点，顾眄若想到的同时，李嘉禾就已经想到了。所以，他像个勇敢的骑士般，立马"站"到了顾眄若的前面，将接下来会发生的任何"中伤语言""伤害事件"都一一拦截了。

他说："既然安眠已经睡着了，那下次我们再来看她吧。"

而后，他拉着顾眄若就要离开。可就在顾眄若离开的瞬间，她刚好就听到了李嘉禾后母尖酸刻薄的小声嘀咕。她说："没爸没妈的，还想学人家麻雀变凤凰攀高枝，哼，没门。"这句话里缺失的主语显然是"顾眄若"三个字，而这句话也显然是说给顾眄若听的。

顾眄若全身僵硬，停住脚步，而后客客气气，礼礼貌貌地回过头对李嘉禾的后母说："阿姨，请你收回刚才那句话。"可是，对方却敬酒不吃吃罚酒，一脸无辜地说："什么？莫名其妙！小姑娘，你到底在说什么啊？"

终于，顾眄若忍无可忍了。

"认识李沐禾的第一天，我就在想，如此可爱灵巧的女孩有着怎样的父母。对，我父母双亡，所以我自然地便会想到她的父母有着怎样的模样。我甚至羡慕李沐禾，因为从她的身上我已经能感觉到她父母的万般好。可是，今天，您让我失望了。不是因为您调查我的身世，不是因为您一而再再而三地想要贬低我，挖苦我，也不是因为您一秒钟前说过的话一秒钟后就不敢承认了。而是，在您的身上，我找不到李沐禾所拥有的那些优点。最后，请您大人有大量，不要介意我现在对您说的这些话。"顾眄若深吸一口气，然后说出了她离开医院前的最后一句话，"我无父无母，家教便只有这般，但是，对我而言，他们是全天下最好的父母。"

顾眄若语毕，李嘉禾聪明地顺着接话："安叔叔、安阿姨、爸、瑾言，我们先走了。"

逃离了是非之地，任凭病房里的人如何"战乱"，皆已与己无关。

病房里。

顾眄若离开后，李嘉禾的后母气得肺都要爆炸了，但碍于面子便也不好大肆发作，只能气得牙痒痒地骂道："太没家教了！"安眠的父母也不好多说，只是简单地附和几句："以后嘉禾交朋友还是要看清楚，回头你们多跟他说说。"以此来安慰老朋友的情绪。

一旁的路瑾言却忍不住没心没肺得低声笑起来，笑顾眄若的勇敢和大胆，笑李嘉禾后母的愚蠢和幼稚。那些哭着求着男主角后母的女主角，事实上只有在韩剧中才会出现。更何况，这些大人们也不过是一厢情愿地将李嘉禾放在了男主角的位置上。而顾眄若也不是韩剧女主角，顾眄若只是顾眄若，独一无二的顾眄若。

而安眠，因为吵闹，早就已经醒过来了。她虽然不想参与，但又想更清楚地了解一切，便选择了假装熟睡以置身事外。自然，发生的一切她都听到了，也听懂了。而这一切中也包括了路瑾言所发出来的低低的笑声，以及他发送手机短信，输入文字，删字，再输入文字时细小的按键声音。

李嘉禾将顾眄若安全送到家。顾眄若上楼梯的时候，便收到了这条来自路瑾言删删打打，几经锤炼而最终出炉的短信——不要哭。

不过三个字。

却是安眠出事以来，他对她说的第一句话。哪怕每天晚上，顾昐若都会很努力地复习功课，直到路瑾言从医院回来，他都未曾跟她说过一句："以后早点儿睡，复习功课不要这么拼命。"又或者是一句，"以后这么晚，不用等我。"

"不要哭"，只不过是三个字。

顾昐若的眼泪，瞬间汹涌而出。

/02/

湖水先生。

是顾昐若给路瑾言取的外号，也是在顾昐若给路瑾言取的众多外号中，她最喜欢的一个。就连她的手机里，路瑾言一栏的姓名也被替换成了"湖水先生"。

不过，顾昐若从来都没有告诉过路瑾言。

她怕太矫情。

汹涌的湖水终会回归平静。而在顾昐若心里，路瑾言就像湖水般的存在。大抵幸福的意义也是如此吧，无论爱得多么汹涌，多么轰轰烈烈，结局终会趋向于平和宁静。真实而平淡，细小而绵长，这也是顾昐若想要的幸福。

而，其实，这也是路瑾言想要给顾昐若的幸福。只不过，理想很丰满，现实却充满骨感。

经过一段时间的调养和休息之后，安眠回到了学校。

那天，是路瑾言亲自去接她，然后两人一起来到学校的。安眠在班级里的人缘很好，迎接她、关心她的人也很多。大家一起簇拥着她，在她身边嘘寒问暖。远远看去，就像是公主随着王子归来。

幸福洋溢，羡煞旁人。

这样的场面对于顾昄若来说早已习以为常。

以为习惯了就不痛了，却忘了心的流浪，从来都是自由的，流动的，且它从来都不是受控制的。眼不见为净，顾昄若同学当即决定——逃课。

其实，顾昄若最近常常会逃课。大抵是高三的生活太过压抑和磨人，成堆的考试试卷和练习试题绕着地球都可以转好几圈了。自然，这段时间学生的叛逆心和玩乐心都要比平时重许多。庆幸的是，这所学校带高三班的班主任和其他任课老师都很懂得劳逸结合的学习方法。对于偶尔的"脱离轨道"，他们也不会对学生太苛刻。学习，最重要的还是靠自觉。

生活处处充满压力，老师有老师的解压方法，自然也要体谅学生的解压方式。

逃课后到处闲逛的顾昄若有时候也会想，她到底是因为高三而压力"山大"呢，还是因为路瑾言和安眠而感觉到压力"山大"，不过，直到高三结束，她也一直没有想到这个问题的答案。

这段时间的路瑾言实在是太"变幻莫测"了。

在学校里，他是属于安眠的，即便是不得已，他也确确实实站在了她那一边。

回到家里，他是属于他自己的，埋头复习功课，他完完整整地将自己关入了学习的天地。

只有在学习完毕，夜幕降临，准备睡觉前，路瑾言走到阳台上放松的那一小段时间，他才是属于顾昄若的。每一次，只要看到路瑾言走到了阳台上，无论顾昄若在看书还是在做英语听力，又或者她正准备去洗澡，她都会放下手上的一切事情，来到阳台上。

你 是 我 遥 不 可 及 的 梦

🌢

　　这时候的路瑾言，会和顾昞若谈心，会和顾昞若打闹，会给顾昞若说笑话来放松学习压力，会给肚子咕咕叫的顾昞若去买夜宵，偶尔，他还会很煽情很突然地对顾昞若说："我们一起上大学，我们要一直快乐，直到我们一同老去。"

　　喜欢？不喜欢？沿着校园里的行道树又或者沿着公园附近的花坛，一直数一直数，顾昞若也没数出一个最终答案来。

　　相反，数着数着顾昞若就数出了一个怪叔叔李嘉禾。

　　如此凑巧的"缘分"，顾昞若都忍不住小小地自恋一下："啊，怪叔叔，你是不是看我逃课，故意跑出来和我'火星撞地球'的呀？"

　　这时候的李嘉禾就会故作神秘地反问顾昞若："你说呢？"

　　男生的心思你不要猜，猜来猜去都是自作多情。顾昞若不理睬，自娱自乐地继续她的逃课旅程。

　　后来，李嘉禾与顾昞若如此凑巧的"缘分"发生的次数变得越来越多了以后，李嘉禾就会用他那一套李式理论来忽悠顾昞若，什么进入大学一定要做的三件事——逃课，谈恋爱，通宵；什么我李嘉禾天赋异禀，大学课程都是在高中所学课程的基础上延伸的，我一学就会，一点就通；什么时间一多，自然而然地就想到了逃课，这样的想法压都压不下去，心烦啊……

　　什么乱七八糟的李式理论嘛。

　　流光容易把人抛，红了樱桃，绿了芭蕉。

　　黑板上用粉笔涂鸦的高考倒计时，上面的数字一天天在变小，教室外的气温却在一天天升高，人心里的燥热也越加难耐。高老头的数学强化训练课越听越没意思，顾昞若用手支撑着自己的头，舒服地靠在课桌上，昏昏欲睡。

　　叮——

终于熬到了下课时间，高老头却站在讲台上迟迟未走。顾晰若打起精神准备听下一堂她最喜欢的英语课时，只听见高老头笑呵呵地对大家说："同学们，下一堂课还是上数学，我将给大家讲解去年和前年的数学高考试题，上课前，请大家将试卷准备好。"

这……还真的是有点伤神呢！

一边转笔，一边思考着接下来该怎么处理的顾晰若，在高老头走出教室门的一瞬间，立马果断地选择了逃课。说逃就逃，顾晰若迅速地收拾起东西来，然后拎着自己的东西就从教室后门溜走了。想要去看一看南西和许清木，便来到了他们的教室门口。可是，找来找去，也没看到他们。

顾晰若心领神会地一笑。

哈，原来，就连逃课我们都这么有默契。死党什么的，果然是最有爱的。

和往常逃课时一样，顾晰若选择了毫无目的地闲逛和溜达。到达"城市猎人"游戏城时，顾晰若停下了自己的脚步。里面传来的真实而干脆的枪声，吸引了她的注意力。走进游戏城之后她才发现，其实那不过是一档从国外引进的3D版枪击游戏，围在周围的大多都是男生。顾晰若站在旁边看别人玩了几轮。这款游戏所具备的画面真实感和音响效果真的很棒，光听声音还以为是发生了什么枪杀案呢！可是，若是真的发生了枪杀案，自己也不敢闯入枪杀现场吧。有些矛盾的顾晰若自言自语道："无聊的顾晰若呀，还是走吧！"

想走？谈何容易。

事实上，从顾晰若踏入"城市猎人"游戏城的大门时，她就已经被盯上了，准确点来说，是被一群人盯上了。为首的男生应该是认识顾晰若的，自打她进来后，他的视线就一直没离开过她，只不过他眼神里透露出来的不是爱，而是恨。对于这些，顾晰若倒是一点觉悟都没有，仍旧自在开心地看着别人玩游戏，直到打算离开游戏厅，而被一大群人堵在门口时，她才意识到出事了。

仔细将眼前的一群人打量了一番，顾吤若一个都不认识。有几张面孔倒是有些面熟，好像在学校里见过。“城市猎人”游戏厅是离学校最近的娱乐城，有校友在很正常。不过，据顾吤若观察，眼前的这些人就算不是街头混混，也应该是成天打架斗殴的学生。

怎么会惹上他们的?!

现在，大概也不是寻求“怎么了”的时候，而是应该先好好处理“怎么办”。不过，一群人围堵一个人，顾吤若还是有些心慌的。她记得路瑾言曾经教过自己：在遇到危难的时候，如果不知道怎么办，那就先拖延时间，然后飞快地运转脑子，思考解决方案。如果事情已经到了你无法控制的地步，那就顺其自然，走一步看一步，命随天意。

顾吤若选择了拖延时间的方法。所以，她站在人群中，选择了沉默，正所谓“敌不动，我不动”嘛。

“顾吤若?”为首的男生问。

“是我。”

“想不想离开这里?”

“想。”

“好！爽快！芊芊，准备笔、纸、数码相机。”为首的男生转过头对站在他旁边的女生说。而这个被称为芊芊的女生，长得眉清目秀，温婉可人，与这男生，还真是不相搭啊。顾吤若能肯定自己在哪里见过她，只是到底在哪里见过，她已经完全没了印象。

“给，纸笔，写保证书。写完以后，再录制一段视频，将你所写的保证书内容对着镜头原原本本地读一遍。”

"内容。"

"什么?"

"保证书,写什么?"

"离开路瑾言,永远不做第三者。"

"路瑾言?第三者?什么跟什么啊?"顾昕若气愤地将纸揉成了一团,说,"如果我不呢?"

"你没得选择。"

顾昕若沉默了一会儿,说:"那好,你重新拿张纸给我,这张纸已经被我揉成了一团。"

"给。"

"不过……我可不可以先去趟洗手间?我肚子好痛。"

"不可以。"

"那我写不了,我肚子真的很痛。你找人守在 WC 门口就是时立。这么多人,你们还能让我跑了不成?!"

"去吧。"言简意赅。

蹲厕所的时候,顾昕若突然想起来了,那个叫芊芊的女生,她曾经在安眠的生日聚会上看到过。而为首的那个男生,应该就是芊芊的男朋友。仔细想想,安眠生日那天,他也在场,而且和安眠还挺熟络的。那么,推断下现在所发生的一切,大概就是他们在替好朋友安眠抱不平吧。得到这样的结论,顾昕若心里对未知的恐慌立马消除了。

解铃还须系铃人。

还好,顾昕若的手机一直是放在口袋里的。她将同样的一条短信同时发给了三个人。接下来,她只需要负责继续拖延时间就好。

——城市猎人，SOS。

“喂！该不会是掉马桶了吧?”是芊芊的声音。

“马上出来!”顾吥若回答。

收信人：李嘉禾。

收到顾吥若短信时的李嘉禾正在实验室做化学实验。看到这条短信时，他差一点就将手中的化学品全倒在了地上，那后果简直不堪设想，还好，与他同桌的同学接住了。看完这条短信后，他果断地将化学器材移交给同学，火速从实验室后门溜了出来，刻不容缓地前往了“城市猎人”。

一路上，他已经将各路能够帮到忙的兄弟都通知到了。

收信人：路瑾言。

自习课，在老师的安排下，路瑾言站在讲台上为同学们讲解数学练习题。习题讲解到一半，他便感觉到了口袋里手机的震动。像是感知到了顾吥若的SOS，他非常“不负责任”地停止了讲解，拿出手机，浏览短信，而后，满脸焦急地跑出了教室……

讲台下的同学面面相觑。

收信人：安眠。

由于网络和顾吥若发送先后的原因，实际上安眠才是第一个收到这条短信的人。瞥了一眼顾吥若发送过来的短信，明明是“触目惊心”的求救，在她眼里却不过如此。将手机放回口袋，安眠继续欢喜地听着路瑾言讲解习题，却在抬头的瞬间，发现路瑾言满脸担心地跑出了教室，手里紧握着手机。

这时候，安眠才着急地跟随着路瑾言向目的地跑去。

自然，李嘉禾是三个人当中最先到达"城市猎人"的。不过，顾晰若手机里的第一条回复短信却是来自路瑾言的，再简单不过的三个字"有我在"，给顾晰若带来了满满的心安和力量。

到达"城市猎人"的李嘉禾并没有直接冲动地闯入"包围圈"，在观察了周围的形势，以及确定了顾晰若的安全后，他选择了站在人群的一旁，先以旁观者的角度了解整个事情。安眠和路瑾言赶过来的时候，李嘉禾已经大概了解了事情的始末。所以，当他看到安眠时，便直接走到她身边，对她说："这件事，你来解决。"而这个时候，安眠已经看到了顾晰若，以及站在她面前的自己的好兄弟——张鹏。张鹏和安眠的关系，偏偏路瑾言也是知情的。

似乎有千万张嘴都无法解释清楚了，可是安眠还是转过头想要解释给路瑾言听，这一切与自己是无关的。

"瑾言……我、我不知道……"

"走吧，先看看到底发生了什么事。"路瑾言说。

此时此刻，整件事情与安眠有没有关系，事实上对路瑾言而言是不重要的。他只是想带顾晰若离开这里，哪怕顾晰若现在是安全的，没有受伤害的。

"张鹏，你到底想干什么?"来到"包围圈"里，安眠的第一句话是询问她的好兄弟张鹏，现在是在干吗。这样的明知故问只是为了证明她自己与整件事情毫无关系。如此着急地证明自己的清白，也显露了顾晰若有没有事之类的，她安眠是不在乎的。

一旁的李嘉禾，也终于走到顾晰若的身边，不停地问她："他们有没有欺负你？有没有伤到哪里？有没有不好？"而其实，无论顾昐若是点头还是摇头，他都是担心的，难过的。路瑾言则保持了他一贯的沉默作风，他安静地听着安眠和张鹏的对话，始终未插一句话，只不过，在走到顾昐若身边的第一时间，他就已经用力握紧了顾昐若的手，他在用他自己的方式告诉着顾昐若——

有我在。

"安，我这不是为你抱不平嘛。"张鹏解释道。

"张鹏，我想你大概误会了。我过得很好，很开心，很幸福，不需要你为我抱不平。"

"你哪里高兴，哪里幸福快乐了？你拿个镜子照照，你照照你这笑，简直笑得我心酸。安，你知不知道，为了你的快乐，兄弟我上刀山下油锅也在所不辞。更何况，就这么一个姓顾的娘们儿。"

"我说了，我过得很好。"

"好好好，你过得好，是我多管闲事。那，路瑾言，你告诉我，这个姓顾的娘们儿到底是你什么人！"

"顾昐若是瑾言的妹妹。"

"不，安，我不要听你说。路瑾言，你倒是说说看，这个女人到底跟你有没有关系！如果今天是我多想了，误会了，我给她道歉。"张鹏用手恶狠狠地指着顾昐若说。

路瑾言将张鹏指着顾昐若的手拿开，说："她是我什么人，跟你没有关系。"

"这话是什么意思啊？她不是你妹妹？那她就是第三者啊！"

"嘴巴给我放干净点儿。"李嘉禾突然朝张鹏吼道。

"呦呦呦！这第四者都出来了啊？我说路瑾言啊，你女朋友安眠还在呢，你就已经等不及要'英雄救美'了吗？"

"我说过，这事跟你没关系。"路瑾言强调道。

"总该跟安眠有关系吧，安眠的事就是我的事。路瑾言，痛快点儿，给个选择，以后是要好好跟安眠过，还是随了小三的意，忘恩负义？"

一瞬间，整个场面和时间都静止了，所有的人都在屏息等待着结果。

顾昑若明明是希望路瑾言选择她的，可是她的手在路瑾言的手心里却开始挣扎起来，她突然觉得她自己好像真的是他们口中的小三，卑鄙无耻地抢了属于安眠的路瑾言，以后，也不会有好下场的吧。然而，路瑾言却始终没有让顾昑若的手挣脱开来。

这样的双手紧握，安眠自然是看到了的。她清楚地知道，如果事情任由张鹏来操控的话，她就会被迫失去路瑾言。可是，她不能失去路瑾言也不会失去路瑾言。所以，她再一次自欺欺人地对张鹏说："顾昑若只是路瑾言的妹妹。听清楚了吗?! 走。"

"安，这样的男人不值得你付出，不值得你爱。"张鹏说。

"够了！这事我自己解决，走吧。"安眠忍无可忍，声音提高了好几度。张鹏知道这样的安眠是不好惹的，便说："那行，总之，无论是姓顾的那娘们儿，还是这姓路的浑蛋，谁欺负了你，就是跟我张鹏过不去。姓路的，对她好点儿，否则，你的下场一定不会好！"

"走吧，兄弟。"安眠说。

张鹏转身走进了游戏厅。安眠这才走到顾昑若的身边询问她："有没有哪里受伤？"顾昑若立马甩开了路瑾言的手，说："我没事。"而后转过身，对李嘉禾说，"嘉禾，送我回家吧。"

很喜欢很喜欢路瑾言，顾昑若的心是不受控制的。可是，顾昑若并不希望以伤害安眠的方式来成全她自己的心意。最初将这样的一条求救短信发给了李嘉禾，也是希望他可以在尴尬的境地中带她离开。解铃还须系铃人，其他事情的解决自然是交给安眠和路瑾言来处理。

想要和路瑾言在一起的心意和不能伤害安眠的心意好像是矛盾的。可是，对顾昤若来说，这样矛盾的想法却也真实地存在于她心里。

一场闹剧，剧终人散，却在即将落幕的时候，出现了意外的插曲。

转身走进游戏厅的张鹏，等他的女友芊芊从游戏厅老板娘的房间里拿完东西出来。两人搂在一起准备离开游戏厅时，芊芊却在擦身而过的瞬间看到了李嘉禾，而李嘉禾也看到了芊芊。芊芊立马拿开了张鹏搂着她的手，而跟在顾昤若旁边的李嘉禾也停止了脚步。

"芊芊？"李嘉禾喊出她的名字。

"嘉禾……"

如此深情的语调，一旁摸不着头脑的张鹏总算在芊芊口中喊出的名字里听出点状况来了，于是，他问李嘉禾："姓李，名嘉禾？"

不理会张鹏的询问，李嘉禾继续追问芊芊："你怎么在这里？和他在一起？"

"嗯。一言难尽。"

李嘉禾心中全世界最乖最可爱的芊芊公主，怎么会和街头巷口的流氓张鹏混在一起？李嘉禾的脑袋里产生了无数疑问，同时也产生了对她的关心和怜爱。

顾昤若从李嘉禾看芊芊的眼神里看到了不一样的关心，她知道，芊芊对于李嘉禾来说是重要的，或者，他们之前还曾有过一段轰轰烈烈的故事也说不定。因为，在确定嘉禾就是李嘉禾后，张鹏一拳就朝李嘉禾挥了过来。

"好啊！原来你就是李嘉禾，你就是那个抛弃芊芊的负心汉李嘉禾啊，看我今天不揍死你。"

——并且，听到了这样的话语。

一场闹剧好像演变成了两场闹剧。五分钟后，终于，打闹和争吵停止了。顾晞若也终于想起，她到底是在哪里见过芊芊。

不是学校，不是商场，而是李沐禾的相册里。

李沐禾曾经将她所有的相册都翻出来跟顾晞若分享过。照片上与李沐禾留着一样齐刘海的芊芊，吸引了顾晞若的注意。在李沐禾所有的相册里，她和芊芊的合照就占据了满满的一本。两个人站在一起的模样，俨然一对亲姐妹。而在这本相册的最后，是芊芊和李嘉禾的合照，也是他们唯一的一张合照。

当时看到这张合照的一瞬间，顾晞若只想到了四个字：天生一对。

安眠、路瑾言，李嘉禾、芊芊。

这里好像已经没有自己存在的必要了。顾晞若转过身，朝大街上走去。

孤单地，仿若失去了灵魂般地，飘荡着。

迎面而来的大卡车，一点减速的想法都没有，直冲冲地往顾晞若的方向开过来。耳边，好像传来了刺耳的鸣笛声，就像是母亲离开时那般令人讨厌憎恶的声音，顾晞若下意识地捂住了双耳，双腿好像是失去了知觉般，一动不动，忘了奔跑。

车子仍然在前进。

耀眼的车灯晃过顾晞若的眼睛，而后，一切停止。

/03/

呲——！

一个急刹车，大卡车停在了顾晞若的面前。

恍惚中，睁开眼，发现大卡车并没有碾过她的身体，顾昕若笑着的眼里都噙满了眼泪。这一幕的发生，不过五秒钟，对路瑾言来说，却仿若熬过了五个世纪。而李嘉禾也紧张得整颗心都要跳出来了。两人同时想往顾昕若的方向跑去，却被牵绊住了。

才迈开步子的路瑾言，手就被安眠拉住了。而李嘉禾，甚至还未动，就已经被芊芊拉住了。

身不由己。无须等待。

站在大卡车前回过神来的顾昕若，一个人勇敢地往前走去……

将脑袋放空，什么都不去想。

悲伤总会远去。

回到家，顾昕若翻开手机，将路瑾言发给她的那条短信反反复复地看了又看。

——有我在。

这样的三个字是不是意味着，路瑾言已经给了顾昕若想要的答案和幸福？可是，顾昕若不敢确定。

"嘟嘟！主人，您有新的短信，请注意查收。"

我会给你想要的答案和幸福。

发信人：路瑾言

这样的默契，会不会太巧了？这样的宠爱，会不会太美好？这样的短信，好像，看千遍万遍都不够。顾昕若趴在床上，翻来覆去地折腾着。呀！该不会是做梦吧。跑到镜子前，顾昕若死命地捏了捏自己的脸，会疼会变形，好像是真的。

啊，这一切是真的。

于是，一整个晚上，顾晞若同学都像个小疯子般，自导自演地——微笑着？傻笑着？疯笑着？总之一定是偷偷地呵呵乐着。

然而，直到中午，路瑾言也没回家。倒是李嘉禾一大清早就跑过来了，见到顾晞若，劈头盖脑就是一句："晞若，芊芊是我前女友……"

"唉，其实我已经猜到了。"

"你不吃醋？"

"干吗要吃醋？"

"我很有可能会回到她的身边哦。"

"你试试看。"

——你试试看。

说完这句充满威胁意味的话，顾晞若和李嘉禾同时僵住了。明明是想要说"关我什么事"，说出口的却是"你试试看"。这样一来，气氛好像不可避免地变得尴尬了呢。顾晞若吐吐舌，说："怪叔叔，自己欠下的感情债，一定要勇敢地去还。只有还清了感情债，才能更好地走向未来嘛。正所谓，有借有还，再借不难嘛。"

"有借有还，再借不难，这句话，不适合用在感情上吧？"

"呼——感情什么的，最伤神啦。"

"顾晞若。"

"嗯？"

"没什么……"

"怪叔叔，不许调戏良家小同学！"

其实，李嘉禾是想问：顾晞若，路瑾言还没回来吗？其实，李嘉禾是想说：

顾晰若，感情什么的，不伤神的，我可以给你甜甜蜜蜜的感情。其实，李嘉禾想告诉顾晰若：曾经，他真的真的很喜欢很喜欢芊芊，他也真的很有可能很有可能会回到她的身边。

然而最终，他都没有说。现在的顾晰若是开心的，无论她是因为什么而开心，他李嘉禾都不愿意去破坏这样的开心。

路瑾言回来的时候已经是下午了。

推开门，房间里的窗帘是拉起来的，无边的黑暗映入眼帘。排斥黑暗，厌恶黑暗，路瑾言有些烦躁和反感地打开了客厅里的水晶吊灯。正在看恐怖电影的顾晰若扔掉了手中的零食，吓得"哇"的一声大喊起来，整张脸都藏进了李嘉禾的怀抱中。

一片狼藉。

一片刺眼。

"爸妈去哪儿了？"路瑾言问道，口气里满是气愤。

"路妈妈和路叔叔去亲戚家了，说是你国外的表弟一家回来了，要去聚聚。"顾晰若小声地回答道。

"你们在干吗呢？"

"看……恐怖电影。"

"那，零食怎么满地都是？"

"刚不是你进门，那个女尸正好坐起来，我一吓，零食就飞出去了！"

"哦。"

好像一切都符合逻辑，也没什么可找碴儿的，明明就是他路瑾言吃醋了。有些心虚的他只好对顾晰若和李嘉禾说："那你们先看电影吧，我累了，休息一下。"而后，走进了他的卧室。这之后的顾晰若哪里还有什么心思看电影，一心都想着路瑾言昨天发给她的短信。李嘉禾也不挑明，只是在一旁不断地喂东西给顾晢若吃，塞不满她的心，至少先塞满她的胃吧。

恐怖片里的画面和音效，好像都没有之前那么吓人了，倒是路瑾言的房间里总是有奇怪的声音不断传出来。

砰！

滴沥沥沥……滴沥沥沥……像是打碎了什么东西。

顾晢若站起身，敲了敲路瑾言的门。

“门没关，进来吧。”

原来是打翻了跳棋，满盒的玻璃珠子满房间乱跑。一盒跳棋大概有六十多颗玻璃棋子，路瑾言蹲下身不停地将玻璃珠子捡回棋盘里。准确点说，他不是在捡，而是在抓，用手一抓，就能抓起好几颗。他抬起头，见顾晢若进来了，便对她说：“你来帮我捡吧。”

“嗯，好啊。”

“你先扶我到床边，休息休息。”

“伤到哪里了吗？”

“没有没有，累了，头昏眼花的，没力气。”

头昏眼花和走到床边有着什么必然联系吗？顾晢若也没细想，将路瑾言扶到床边，不消一会儿工夫，就听到了路瑾言发出的小声的鼾声。

是昨晚发生了什么事情吗？还是，他和安眠之间的事情已经到了无法解决的地步？

“如果很累很累的话，不给我答案，也没关系的。”

坐在路瑾言的床边，顾晢若一个人自言自语道。

再回到客厅时，李嘉禾已经走了。地板上大堆的零食中间，压着一张纸条，上面写着：芊芊找我，先走了。

——因为是芊芊找，所以连"再见"都来不及说吗？

——啊！应该是这样吧。

顾昐若蜷着腿坐在沙发上，大口大口地吃着零食。李嘉禾真的买了很多零食给她吃啊，以至于，最后顾昐若喊来了南西和许清木才将这些零食干掉。这样的"零食聚会"还真应该多多举行才对，而零食的提供者，当然必须得是李嘉禾，谁让他中途莫名其妙地跑掉了呢？

他这样不明不白地离开，顾昐若对李嘉禾还是充满怨念的。

最近的顾昐若同学也真像是一位充满魔力的怨念小姐。不仅仅是对李嘉禾充满怨念，就连路瑾言也无法幸免。不过，若是有人说顾昐若是怨念小姐的话，她就会站出来理直气壮地反驳对方：你怨念，你姐怨念，你妹怨念，你全家都怨念。明明就是李嘉禾不辞而别啊，明明就是路瑾言的脑袋搭错了线啊。

不过，路瑾言最近也还真是乱糟糟的。

不是打掉了棋盘就是打碎了餐盘，甚至于，放在客厅里的花瓶也差点被他撞碎。棋盘、餐盘、花瓶，打碎撞碎了都是小事，人没被玻璃弄伤就是万幸。然而，最近的路瑾言好像格外地跟玻璃过不去，这不，一大清早的，就听到客厅里的小鱼缸发出了清脆的碎裂声。

水和鱼，满地蔓延。

玻璃碎片在阳光的照耀下闪闪发光。

路瑾言不顾满地的碎片，挣扎着想要站起来。顾昐若走过去想要扶他，却被他直接甩开。而下一秒，路瑾言一个趔趄，一片玻璃片便硬生生地扎入了他的脚掌心，鲜红的液体立马就染红了整片玻璃片。

路妈妈急忙跑到房间里拿来医药箱，又是消毒又是包扎的，一边还训斥着路瑾言："怎么这么不小心?"换作平时的路瑾言，顶多说一句："我也不想啊。"更多时候，他会笑着说："年轻人，流点儿血算什么。"可是，现在，他有些烦躁地反驳道："它非要跟我过不去，我有什么办法，我难道还想扎一下啊。"

对这样的一句话，全家人都不知道要怎么往下接。片刻之后，路妈妈才说："那就在家休息下吧，今天我去学校给你请假。"

仔细回想近来的路瑾言，不仅总是跌跌撞撞，而且脾气也变得很古怪。幽默风趣少了些，生气怨念多了点。无论是路妈妈、路叔叔，还是安眠和顾昕若，在他的怒气面前都无一幸免。真是，简直连"好好先生"的美名都要被他自己给毁掉了。

因此，顾昕若也一直都不敢询问短信的事情。至于路瑾言那天为何一夜未归，他与安眠之间又到底如何了，顾昕若也不敢问。也许还因为，这些天的路瑾言一直都在刻意地疏远着她。

实际上，也没有具体的事情显示路瑾言在疏远顾昕若，可是敏感的顾昕若就是感觉到了他的远离。只因为路瑾言不再来阳台和她小聚，不再和她打闹沟通，甚至于，大半个月下来，两个人说话的次数都能用五个手指头数清楚。偶尔，顾昕若想要找他聊聊天，也会被他用各种理由推托或是直接拒绝。

她以为是路瑾言和安眠和好了才会变成这样，可是，路瑾言脚受伤，安眠来看望他时，他也是摆出一副臭脸给人家看，冷冷的酷酷的，一点儿都不像是两个人已经和好的样子。

顾昕若拿出手机，将路瑾言发给自己的短信又再一次看了看。

——我会给你想要的答案和幸福。

这完全就是一个不同的路瑾言所发送的短信嘛。真是见鬼啦!

事实上，顾昢若的感受是没有偏差的。

路瑾言的确在刻意地远离她。

上课，吃饭，学习，睡觉，路瑾言每天的生活就这样按部就班地度过着。而在他的生活里，他也在刻意地抹掉有关顾昢若的痕迹。

这样的冷淡和距离，让一切好像又回到了从前。

周四的晚上，忍无可忍，实在憋不住的顾昢若，趁着路妈妈和路叔叔晚饭后去散步的时候，直接冲到路瑾言的房间里，然后拿出手机，翻出那条短信，开门见山地质问路瑾言。

"这短信是不是你发的?"

"是。"

"那么，答案呢? 幸福呢?"

"昢若，这件事情等高考之后再说好吗?"路瑾言说。

"可是，我不想再等了。瑾言，爱或者不爱，我都能承受。"

"好吧。"

"嗯?"

"如果放手也是一种疼爱的话，昢若，我愿意给你最后的疼爱。"

"疼爱，可是又必须放手，这样的逻辑是不是连你自己都不能说服? 你又怎么能说服我?"顾昢若说。

——昢若，我想要给你幸福，可是我给不了你幸福，我没有能力给你幸福。

想要这样彻底地清晰地告诉顾昢若，可是路瑾言知道执着的顾昢若在知道真相后一定不会选择放弃，相反会更加死命地坚持，可是，这样的他已经无法给予她想要的幸福。既然给不了她想要的幸福，那就彻底地放弃，让值得的人，让真心喜欢她的人来给她真正的幸福。

狠了狠心，路瑾言对顾昕若说："昕若，我不喜欢你。"

顾昕若没有马上回应路瑾言的话，而是在沉默了一会儿后，安静地对他说："瑾言，我也可以不喜欢你的。"

"以后，我们就做兄妹吧。"

"以后，我们就做朋友吧。"

不过是一词之差，顾昕若和路瑾言却是在同一时间将这句话出了口。然后，两个人却又在同一时间里想到了一个词——

说谎。

转过身，顾昕若回到她的卧室。

在不同的空间里，顾昕若和路瑾言靠坐在各自卧室里的落地窗帘旁，无声地流着眼泪。两间卧室中间隔着的那堵墙，就像是一段永远都无法跨越的距离，死死地，冷冰冰地，横在了他们中间。

那是，生生世世，都无法逾越的距离。

/04/

情绪低落的时候，顾昕若是一定会逃课的。

刚从大教室上完课出来的李嘉禾，远远地就看到顾昕若提着两罐菠萝啤往天台走去。自然，下面的课，李嘉禾也选择了逃课。尾随顾昕若来到天台后，他发现她正站立在天台边，风吹过她的白裙子，摇摇晃晃的。

"喂——"

没有回音。

"顾昕若小同学，你该不会是想跳楼吧？"

顾昕若突然觉得这一幕好熟悉，像昨天和今天同时在放映。过往的记忆像是放电影般在顾昕若的脑海里不断重放。一路走来，无数心酸，无数傻傻的坚持，无数懵懂的不顾一切，无数倔强的勇敢……顾昕若又不是铁人，顾昕若也不是没心没肺的。

啊——喜欢路瑾言真的好累好累。可是，如果不喜欢路瑾言的话，好像是会很痛很痛的，而且比很累很累要难受很多很多。

心痛到无法呼吸。

眼泪顺着脸颊流下。

这样脆弱的顾昕若李嘉禾还是第一次见到，他有点儿不知所措地愣在一旁。直到顾昕若像个孩子般地大哭出声，他才来到她的身边，像抱孩子一样抱住她，而后像哄孩子一般哄着她。等到顾昕若哭累了，宣泄完毕后，李嘉禾就照例带着她去寻找美食。

美食当前，谁都无法抵挡诱惑。

自然，也包括安眠和路瑾言。

李嘉禾和顾昕若也没想到，会在午饭的时间遇到路瑾言和安眠，尤其是这家餐厅还是李嘉禾选择的"私人会所"。事后想想，他才回想起，这家餐厅本就是父亲的朋友所开的店，安眠知道也不为奇。餐厅的餐位基本上都是以独立的小包厢为主，所以，即便是遇到了也可免于尴尬。双方大方地打过招呼后，便你点你的重庆火锅，我吃我的湖南特色菜。

真正令人尴尬和难过的却是，吃过饭后，当李嘉禾和顾昕若路过路瑾言和安眠的包厢时，透过门帘，顾昕若看到了抱在一起哭的路瑾言和安眠。

顾昑若瞬间就明白了，原来，他们一直深爱着彼此。

自己这是在瞎凑什么热闹?!

真够犯贱的。

一厢情愿，孔雀开屏，活该遭受此下场的第三者……好吧，如果还委屈地当众大哭一场的话，实在是有点儿作戏的成分。在大众眼里，这大概就是自作孽不可活吧。顾昑若深吸一口气，吸吸鼻子，努力不让眼泪掉下来。反正逞强什么的，不就是顾昑若最擅长的吗？可是，心还是疼了。

顾昑若转过身对一直跟在自己身后的李嘉禾说："让我一个人静一静，我会安全地回到学校的。"

"我送你回学校吧。"

"嘉禾，相信我，好吗？我会没事的。"

李嘉禾沉默了一会儿，然后说："那好，你自己小心，到学校后给我发个短信。"

"好的。"

离开餐厅后，顾昑若仍然没有哭。她只是一个人走在人来人往的大街上，心里空空荡荡的。

逃离，一次又一次地逃离路瑾言和安眠在一起的画面。勇敢，一次又一次地勇敢面对路瑾言不喜欢自己的心意。坚强，一次又一次地坚强应对各种悲催的局面。偶尔，顾昑若也会问自己，到底值不值得，那些最初的温暖和她最坚信的平和，最终会不会属于自己。然而，每一次的询问，得到的答案都是一样的——

爱就是不问值不值得。

目送顾때若离开的李嘉禾并没有马上离开餐厅，而是来到了路瑾言和安眠所在的包厢。这两个人已经没了之前的拥抱和亲密，这一切不得不让李嘉禾心生怀疑，这两人刚才该不会是演戏给顾昕若看的吧?！但是，个中原因，李嘉禾思来想去却也没想明白。

解铃还须系铃人。

李嘉禾礼貌地走进包厢，客气地对安眠说："我有点儿事情想单独和路瑾言谈谈，方便离开一会儿吗?"

"嗯，好。"

难得安眠这么乖地同意了。等到安眠离开后，李嘉禾一拳就朝路瑾言挥了过去。路瑾言已经猜到李嘉禾朝自己挥拳头的原因，所以他选择了不躲不闪。李嘉禾看路瑾言不躲不闪的，自己一个人闹也没意思，干脆坐下来，准备与他冷静地谈一谈。

"路瑾言，我今天只要你一句话，你到底喜欢谁?"李嘉禾开门见山地问。

"李嘉禾，你是真心喜欢顾昕若的吗?"

李嘉禾点点头，继续追问："顾昕若和安眠，你到底喜欢谁?"

"真心的，那就好。李嘉禾，替我照顾好顾昕若，好吗？她的生命需要温暖，需要真心的纯净的爱。从此以后用心地守护她，可以吗?"

"不用你说我也会好好照顾顾昕若的。"可是，事情完全没有按照李嘉禾预想的轨迹发展。路瑾言这样的托付，就好像他有什么难言之隐般。所以，李嘉禾又追问了路瑾言一句，"是发生了什么事情吗？需要我帮忙吗?"

"没有，谢谢。真心想要帮我的话，就请守护好顾昕若。"

"可是，你知道的，她喜欢的人是你。"

"我有安眠。"

"不喜欢……顾眄若?"

"嗯。"

"路瑾言，我会好好守护顾眄若的。从此以后，她不会再爱你，我会让她爱上我的。"

"好……"

路瑾言一直微笑着看着李嘉禾离开，直到确定他真的走开后，他的情绪才全然崩溃。一杯一杯的白酒下肚，男儿之泪也顺着杯沿滴入酒里。顾眄若的世界已经不能再承受任何失去了，如果可以，即便自己不能给予她最大的幸福，也一定要尽全力替她寻找到幸福。只有确定她是幸福的，自己才能够放心与黑暗相伴。路瑾言从来都不曾为顾眄若做许多许多，但是他真的愿意为她做更多更多。

真心地，愿意。

坐在餐厅一角的安眠，将这一切都收入了眼底。等到路瑾言的情绪稍稍好转后，她才走进包厢里。她轻轻地拥抱着路瑾言，一遍一遍地低声重复着："何必呢，瑾言?"而后，又坚定地对路瑾言说，"瑾言，我爱你，我会一直陪在你身边的。"

"谢谢你，小眠。"

倒带重放，时光倒流。

张鹏闹事的那天，顾眄若离开后，在街角的转弯处，路瑾言选择了向左走，安眠选择了向右走。碍于张鹏在现场的李嘉禾和芊芊也只是像老朋友一样，留下彼此的电话号码后就各回各家了。路瑾言一夜未归，并不是和安眠在一起，而是他一个人，在酒店住了一晚。

◆

——我会给你想要的答案和幸福。

向左走以后，路瑾言发送给顾昤若这条短信。他满怀欣喜地想要马上赶回家，给她惊喜的答案。可是，上天给他开了一个黑暗的玩笑。就在路瑾言一只脚已经踏上回家的巴士时，他发现他眼前的人物和事物都被模糊化了。

眼前的一切。

偶尔很亮，偶尔很暗。

却不似夜空中美丽的星星。

站在路边，路瑾言小心翼翼地抬起左手遮住自己的左眼，一切仍然清晰。而后，又小心翼翼地抬起右手遮住自己的右眼，模糊仍未散去。甚至，所有的事物都在一点一点地被黑暗吞噬着。路瑾言知道，他最害怕的事情发生了。

——我不怕看不见世界，我就怕看不见你，顾昤若。

——你的世界不能再承受失去了。如果可以，我想把整个世界的温暖都带给你。可是，当我无法亲自给予你时，那么，请允许我自作主张地寻找天使替我来爱你。

路瑾言的心里如是想。

所以，这一切，他需要对顾昤若保密。

聪明敏感如顾昤若，一点儿风吹草动，她都能感觉到。如此，也意味着，路瑾言必须对所有的人都保密。

那一个住在酒店的晚上对路瑾言来说犹如死后重生。原本打算彻底和安眠摊牌后与顾昤若在一起的路瑾言不得不逼迫自己做出新的决定——疏远，甚至远离顾昤若；彻底地拒绝，将顾昤若推离开自己的身边；找一个真心喜欢顾昤若的人来守护她。

也许，当路瑾言真正明白顾昤若想要的幸福只有他能够给，其他任何人都不行时，他会感到遗憾，感到后悔，可是，现在的他，能想到给予顾眄若最美好的最温暖的，便是如此决定。所以，顾眄若的感受和李嘉禾的猜测从某种意义上来说都是对的。不过，在餐厅，顾眄若撞见路瑾言和安眠抱在一起大哭的那一幕，并不是路瑾言导演的一场戏。

只是，路瑾言一个人独自承受着这一切，无处发泄，无人发泄，是很难受很难受的。

一方面，路瑾言必须坚强地面对眼睛在任何时候都有可能失明的问题。另一方面，他还必须努力地不着痕迹地隐瞒着顾眄若和其他所有人，不让人怀疑。与此同时，他还得小心翼翼地控制好和忍受着这一切给他带来的所有的负面情绪。而刚好因为脚伤来看望他的安眠，给予了路瑾言很大的安慰。

和安眠认识这么多年，路瑾言对安眠，就算没有刻骨铭心的深爱，喜欢也一定是有的。而路瑾言对于安眠的信任也是超乎他人想象的。

他相信她，就像相信自己般。这样的相信，是路瑾言给予安眠的最珍贵的朋友般无条件的信任。

所以，他选择了将这一切真相告知安眠。

所以，当路瑾言和安眠抱在一起大哭时，只不过是情绪的自然流露。

也是在那一瞬间，安眠明白了自己对路瑾言的深爱，所以她决定无论如何都会留在路瑾言的身边。

她爱路瑾言，是谁都无法比的，所以，她也害怕，害怕当路瑾言的眼睛失明时，满世界的黑暗无边无际地朝他袭来，而她却不在他的身边……

如此深爱。

固然心是不甘的，嘴却选择了妥协。

{第六章}

我不怕看不见世界，我就怕看不见你

/01/

这么近，那么远。

有时候，顾晞若会感觉路瑾言离她很近很近，即使他不在她的身边，她也能够感觉到他的那份关心和爱护。有时候，顾晞若又会感觉路瑾言离她很远很远，即便他就坐在旁边，也仿佛隔着千山万水。

近在咫尺，却无法触及彼此的真心。

路瑾言前天晚上对顾晞若说过的话此刻正在她的脑袋里一遍遍地重放着。

——原来是不喜欢我的啊。

——可是，为什么又给了我喜欢的错觉呢？

在没有开灯的卧室里，顾晞若靠窗坐着。在黑暗中思考，思路也许会更清晰。然而最终，顾晞若还是没有得出最准确的结论。大抵爱情本身就是一件复杂无比的事情，犹如心有千千结。这无数的结若瞬间解开了，自然会少了一番趣味和神秘；解不开，如此才能细水长流，慢慢来解。

爱亦如此，悟透彻了，就没意思了吧。

躲在黑暗中思考的顾昤若突然看到一个熟悉的人影走向了阳台。

是路瑾言。

顾昤若的心脏里突然迸发出一股力量，迫使她向他奔去。就这样，顾昤若站到了路瑾言的身后。

"还没睡？"

"嗯。"

"昤若，你喜欢星星吗？这夜空中的星星，多少人喜欢它们啊……"

"啊？星星啊……不喜欢。"

"不喜欢？是因为星星忽明忽暗，闪烁不清吗？"

"嗯……不是。"

"那是？"路瑾言的头自然地向右边侧了侧。

"因为……全世界最闪耀的星星此刻就站在我的面前。"

这句话是她在看韩国综艺节目时学到的……可说完这句话，连顾昤若自己都被吓到了。这样的告白也太羞人了吧，好像是会让人掉下无数鸡皮疙瘩的话欤。可是，十秒钟后，顾昤若见路瑾言沉默着，便又凑近他耳旁，将这句话重复了一遍："因为全世界最闪耀的星星此刻就站在我的面前。"

沉默。

依然，沉默。

不知道哪里来的勇气，顾昤若突然从后面紧紧地抱住了路瑾言。

恍惚间，似乎也不过一日光景，那个前一秒还在逞强地说着"瑾言，我也不喜欢你"的顾昤若，下一秒就妥协地委屈地死命地抱紧了路瑾言。

因为是真心喜欢。

能够逞强地说出违心的话，却终究骗不过自己的内心。

"是不是发生了什么事情，是不是你无法摊开你的真心，是不是我无法承接你的真心……可是，我真的感受到了，你是喜欢我的。"顾昕若的声音已然有些沙哑。

路瑾言的身体微微颤抖着。

感觉到路瑾言的身体在微微颤抖着，顾昕若下意识地再一次抱紧了他。路瑾言闭上眼感受着顾昕若的勇气和真心，他的心脏也在不规律地剧烈地跳动着……然而，睁开眼睛的刹那，黑暗不可阻挡地袭来，现实摆在眼前，忽明忽暗的景象，残酷地将路瑾言拉回现实，他瞬间被柔软化的心再一次被迫冰封。

挣脱开顾昕若的怀抱，路瑾言冷冷地对她说："够了！昕若，放手吧。"

言罢转身离开，毫不拖沓。

黑暗中，只剩下顾昕若悲伤地站在原地，一动不动。

/02/

——嘉禾，顾昕若感冒发烧。

第二天的清晨，因为收到了这样一条来自路瑾言的短信，还在睡梦中的李嘉禾立马被惊醒，来不及漱口洗脸，套上简单的 T 恤，就匆匆跑到车库。

路过大厅时，听到里面依旧传来尖锐的吵闹声和沉重的叹气声，李嘉禾知道，父亲又与后母吵架了。这样的戏码几乎每天都会上演，每一个安宁静好的清晨若是听不到他们的吵架声，一切反倒会显得不对劲。十多年了，父亲和后母的争吵，一直是为了一个相同的问题，便是父亲每日的早餐，无论多饿，无论多忙，他始终只喝一杯热牛奶。

渐渐地，连他的肠胃都已经完全适应了这样的早餐模式。而这样的早餐模式，最初是李嘉禾的亲生母亲所喜欢的。父亲如此，也不过是在延续母亲的早餐方式而已。

他用自己的方式，想念着曾经属于他的女人。

李嘉禾不得不承认，父亲也是感性的，在他的内心深处，他还是一个重情重义的人。有其父必有其子，李嘉禾也完整地继承了父亲的这一个性。

天生的情种。

爱上了，即便万劫不复，也不后悔。

将车速调至尽可能快，李嘉禾不顾生命安全地向前驰骋着。手机不断重复地拨打着顾昐若的电话，电话那头却一直没人接听。

事实上，昨天晚上李嘉禾也无数次拨打了顾昐若的电话，电话那头也是无人接听。因为担心所以深夜飙车来到了路瑾言家，却在靠近的那一瞬间，远远地却无比清晰地看到了阳台上从后面紧紧抱住路瑾言的顾昐若。

李嘉禾不是傻子，更不会傻到连顾昐若到底有多喜欢路瑾言他都不知道。在靠近的那一刻，李嘉禾选择了将车灯熄灭，安静地坐在车里，点了一根许久都没抽过的烟……所以，顾昐若被路瑾言推开的过程，他也清清楚楚地看到了。

李嘉禾心想：是真的决定远离她吗？那就彻底地远离吧，以后，换我来守护。

到达目的地后，给李嘉禾来开门的是路瑾言，路伯父和路伯母似乎都不在家。李嘉禾想问路瑾言，顾昕若现在的状况如何，回想起昨天的那个推离的画面和今早明知顾昕若感冒发烧却将自己喊来的短信，李嘉禾欲言又止，直奔顾昕若房间。

烧糊涂了的顾昕若一直在喃喃地骂着："路瑾言，大坏蛋、傻子、二百五、猪头。"路瑾言站在一旁，尴尬地解释道："我不是好哥哥，一天到晚欺负妹妹。"

李嘉禾尴尬地回应给他一个生硬的微笑。

在心爱的女生面前，男生都是有好胜心的。李嘉禾不甘地抱起顾昕若，一边温柔地摸着她的头，一边暗示性地对她说："昕若，醒醒。是我，李嘉禾。你感冒了，我带你去医院。"

顾昕若恍惚地睁开眼，看了一眼眼前的人，而后很乖很乖地将头耷拉到李嘉禾的胸前，低低地说："怪叔叔，你来了，就好了。"

很低很低，很轻很轻，却像是无数根刺，刺入了路瑾言的身体里，瞬间，遍体鳞伤。

安眠就是在这个时候过来找路瑾言的，却是在顾昕若的房间里找到了他。

先前上楼的时候，安眠就刚好碰到了送顾昕若去医院的李嘉禾，大概了解了下情况后便匆匆跑上了楼。沉浸在自己情绪里的路瑾言对于安眠的到来却是没有一点儿感觉的。所以，从路瑾言安静地站着到他透过指尖轻轻抚摸属于顾昕若的每一样东西，甚至于他大口呼吸和感受顾昕若房间里气息的小举动，安眠都尽收眼底。

想要逃离。

也想要冲上去狠狠地质问路瑾言。

可，最终，她只是轻声地对路瑾言说："瑾言，我来了。"

　　到达医院的李嘉禾把顾昉若交给医生后，坐在病床旁陪她输液，却越想越觉得不对劲。安眠早上看顾昉若的眼神，怎么看都是带着恨意的。明明是关心地询问顾昉若的病情，却连看她一眼都不愿意；相反，在安眠的眼神里李嘉禾感觉到了嫌弃和憎恨。

　　李嘉禾的心里咯噔一下，像是感应到有事要发生。

　　此时的顾昉若在药物的帮助下已经安然入睡，安静的侧脸透着一股倔强和不甘。李嘉禾所认识的顾昉若是倔强的，也是不容易屈服的。所以，她的内心总是更容易被柔软温暖的情感所触动，而强硬冰冷的情感，只会让她变得更加冷漠和淡薄。

　　庆幸，你遇到了我。李嘉禾这样想着时，手机里收到了一条新的短信。

　　嘉禾，我和张鹏分手了。

发信人：芊芊

　　李嘉禾拿起手机迅速地将电话拨过去，一边匆匆地来到了医院走廊处。电话那头的芊芊一直哭个不停，李嘉禾握着电话来到顾昉若的病房，确认她暂时不会醒来后，对芊芊说："在原地等我，哪儿也不要去，我来找你。"

　　"嗯。"

　　芊芊和张鹏分手是因为李嘉禾，这一点李嘉禾事先已经想到了。可是当面对面地亲口听到芊芊这样说出来时，李嘉禾情不自禁地心疼地抱住了芊芊。

　　"对不起，芊芊。我无法给你美好的将来，连回忆都要变成你幸福的羁绊。"

　　"呜呜，呜呜……"

　　"乖，不哭。"

　　安心地靠在李嘉禾的怀里，芊芊的情绪很快好转起来。

　　李嘉禾和芊芊所待的这座摩天大厦的顶层是一座露天餐厅，餐厅里的甜品盛名远播，其中的榴莲蛋糕则是芊芊的最爱。从医学角度来说，吃甜品会使一个人的心情变得愉悦、快乐，于是李嘉禾带着芊芊来到了这里。

面对面地享用美食，躲不开的是回忆。

在熟悉而又遥远的画面里，李嘉禾因为讨厌臭臭的榴莲味，总是离餐厅远远的；却因为芊芊对榴莲的无限喜欢，渐渐地靠近餐桌，靠近芊芊，渐渐地开始接受榴莲的气味，甚至于，也开始享受水果之王——榴莲。

爱情中潜移默化的影响，是真的会渐渐改变一个人的。

不可避免的话题，亦是回忆往事。

李嘉禾和芊芊一边享用美食，一边回忆往事。聊的大多都是美好的事情，关于那一场悲伤逆流的分手和离别，两人都颇有默契地只字不提。在芊芊的世界里，是李嘉禾抛弃了她，放弃了那段感情。而在李嘉禾的世界里，却以为是芊芊无故失踪，他只不过是被迫接受了分手的现实。

误会如果不被解开，便会一直存在。只是，这样一场误会，谁也不知道到底会牵扯多少人和事。也许，现在的李嘉禾和芊芊选择只字不提，反倒是正确的。如此，也算是对过去的感情的一种祭奠吧。爱了那么久，恨了那么久，最终说服了倔强的自己，安静地选择了淡然。

借口看一看芊芊新买的手机，李嘉禾实则是在给张鹏发送短信。从芊芊难过的情绪中，李嘉禾看出了芊芊对张鹏的喜欢。就算不是因为他的原因而导致两人分手的，李嘉禾也会想办法帮助芊芊和张鹏和好。他只是希望芊芊可以幸福，被人爱着，被人疼着，被人放在掌心好好呵护着。

这样的举动，李嘉禾也不打算瞒着芊芊。放下手机，他对芊芊说："我给张鹏发送了短信，他马上就会过来。"

"嗯？"

李嘉禾拿起芊芊的手机，在半空中晃了晃："喏，偷偷用你的手机发的。"

"不怕我生气？"

"怕。"

"怕你还偷偷发短信给那个浑蛋？"

"我更怕你不幸福，不快乐。"

"嘉禾……"

"好啦。男主角即将到来，打酱油的我还是提前退场好了。"

一个玩笑刚刚好缓和了紧张又煽情的气氛。

"谢谢你，嘉禾。谢谢你让我知道，我从未失去过你。"

"嗯，从未。那，我先走了。"

"嗯，一起下楼吧，我到大门口等他。"

"好。"

李嘉禾开车离开后，分针完整地走过四分之一圈时，张鹏闪亮登场。而事实上，在芊芊等待的这十五分钟里，李嘉禾一直都没有离开。他把车开到离大门有一段距离却又能清楚地看到芊芊活动的树荫下，直到确定张鹏来到了芊芊的身边，才开着车子回到医院。

/03/

医院里。

月光已经偷偷爬上了窗台，窗台边绿色植物的影子倒映在病房白色的墙壁上，像极了张牙舞爪的妖魔鬼怪。值班的护士小姐给顾昢若的房间打开灯的刹那，顾昢若从梦中惊醒过来。白炽灯发出强烈的亮光，顾昢若厌恶地缩回被子里。几分钟后，她才慢慢地将头一点点地露出被子。

浓重的药水味扑鼻而来。

顾昢若环顾四周，四面都是惨白惨白的墙壁，由此可以确定她此刻是身在医院了。往回想想，好像是她感冒发烧，李嘉禾送她来医院的吧，可是，怪叔叔人呢，该不会是被医院的妖怪给吃掉了吧？

吓！

等待了大概十分钟，依旧不见怪叔叔的人影。极度讨厌在医院过夜的顾昢若，倔强地坐起身，然后神不知鬼不觉地拔掉了手上的针头。大多数女生在输液的时候都会表现出柔弱无助的样子，顾昢若却是十分熟练地就把针头抽出，然后死命地摁住还在冒血的针口，其实，还是能感觉到细密的疼痛的。

这样的举动对顾昢若来说已经不是第一次了，所以拔针头时她已经没有了畏惧感。她所畏惧的是医院，这个充满死亡，充满离别的地方。

离开病房的时候，顾昢若像个小朋友般，故意挺直了腰板，神气十足地走了出来——心里还是害怕被护士小姐抓回去的啊。她一路"神气昂昂"地走到下楼的地方，却意外地听到了熟悉的声音。

"芊芊，晚安。"

无女声回复。

"嗯，我一直都在。"

仍然无女声回复。

忍不住好奇，顾昢若探出头瞧了瞧。啊！原来是在打电话啊，对象好像还是那个叫芊芊的姑娘。那么，他这次的突然失踪也是为了芊芊吧。似乎，每一次李嘉禾抛下顾昕若都是因为芊芊。顾昕若缩回她的头，现在真的是非常不想看见李嘉禾啊。她转身就要跑，却被李嘉禾从后面拉住了手。

"液输完了？医生跟你说可以出院了？办好出院手续了？"

"先放开我，我再一个个回答你。"顾昕若心虚地说道。

"该不会是你自己跑出来的吧？"

"又不是进了精神病院，干吗要跑啊……"声音越来越小，底气越来越不足。

"手，伸过来给我看看。"

"你不是正抓着吗……"

"输液的那只手。"

"李嘉禾，你真奇怪啊。就允许你半路跑掉，却不允许我半路跑掉啊？这医院的味道我闻不习惯，到处都是药水味，到处都是死人味。我连医生护士都没麻烦，自己给拔掉了针头，这样还不行吗？医药费我也会补上的，我不会欠钱的。我只是不喜欢这里……"

顾昕若的情绪是有些乱的，所以才乱七八糟地朝李嘉禾喊了一堆话。

"昕若，你真像个任性的小朋友。"

"对，我就是任性的小朋友。你不要管我，管好你的芊芊就行了。放开我的手。"

听到"芊芊"两个字，李嘉禾声调突然上升地说："哦，顾昕若小同学，你偷听我讲电话。"

被抓个正着的顾昕若，硬着头皮扯高嗓子，以增加底气："明明就是你自己好大声好大声地在讲电话，整个医院都能听到，我凑巧听到了而已。"

"真的只是凑巧听到了？"

"嗯，是的。"

"哈哈，可是你吃醋了喔！"

"什么跟什么啊。我要走了，这医院我待不下去了。"

顾昕若的精神倒是明显好了很多，输了液感冒应该也会慢慢好起来。李嘉禾突然将手放到她的额头上，不那么烫了，看来也已经不发烧了。顾昕若啊顾昕若，你这身体还真的是坚不可催啊，早上还病快快的状态，晚上就立马恢复到了刚强的模样。

这样想着，李嘉禾的心里也不可避免地心疼了。他将顾昕若的手放开，再拿起，温柔地问她："疼不疼？"

有什么好疼的？

原本应该和往常一样这样回答的，却在接触到李嘉禾心疼的眼神时，放下了坚强的心理防备，顾昕若真心地点点头说："疼。"

"疼，下次就不要这么任性，这么不爱惜自己了。"

"嗯。"

这样的一个"嗯"字，是赞同也是允诺——答应你会好好爱惜身体，至少，会努力这么去做。

"不想待在医院，就不要待在医院。我现在送你回家。"

回家。

听到这两个字顾昕若下意识地往后退了几步。

"怎么了，昕若？"

"不，不要回家。"

"不回家的话，路伯父路伯母会担心的。不回家的话，路瑾言会担心的。"

"路瑾言？不要，不要回家。"

顾昤若之所以会如此排斥回到路瑾言的家，李嘉禾知道，路瑾言那个略带坚决的推离和拒绝，是真的伤到了她。可是不回家的话，该送她去哪里呢？想来想去，李嘉禾最终决定提前公开他给顾昤若准备的生日惊喜。

盛夏还未来临，生日礼物早已准备好。

李嘉禾还真是有心。

对于顾昤若的身世和成长经历，李嘉禾一直了然。想要给她一个真正意义上温暖的家，对于现在的他们来说似乎不太现实。可是要她长久地居住在路瑾言家，李嘉禾终是不放心的。当父亲投资经营的酒店公寓正式落成时，李嘉禾通过自己的努力向父亲要了一间，所以，这间房无论是设计还是装修，都是由李嘉禾亲自指导完成的。

从某种意义上来说，房子就是安全感和归宿的象征。也许现在的李嘉禾无法给予顾昤若真正意义上的家，但是他愿意为她准备一间小房子，一间真正只属于顾昤若的小房子，一间对她来说有着家般意义的小房子。

而此时的顾昤若为了不回家，言语间已经开始"威胁"起李嘉禾来。

"好吧，怪叔叔。既然我们无法达成共识，那么，我们在这里好聚好散。从此，你走你的阳关道，我过我的独木桥。保重！"

李嘉禾摆出一副真拿你没办法的样子，妥协地冲顾昤若说："走吧。"

"去哪儿？"

"开房……"

"唔，开房啊！那还是你走你的我走我的吧，虽说大家都是成年人，可是被误会什么的，总归不太好的。"

"顾昤若同学，拔掉针头的时候怎么那么勇敢啊，开个房就把你吓成这样？"

"具体事情具体分析。马克思没告诉你？"

🌢

"走吧，给你变魔法。"

"怪叔叔，能不用'魔法'这个词吗？听起来真够俗的，一点儿都不潮。"

"……"

一路上，李嘉禾和顾晰若贫嘴不断，抬杠不断，吵着吵着，闹着闹着，忧伤分子也渐渐从顾晰若的心里飞出，融入了无边无际的空气中。

到达酒店公寓后，为了使整个惊喜计划更加完美，李嘉禾甚至细心地事先嘱咐了前台人员，在房间里喷洒了柠檬味的空气清新剂，如此，房子新装修所留下来的油漆味道也全然消失了。小心翼翼地打开房门，透过细小的门缝确认一切 OK 之后，李嘉禾才做了一个"请"的手势将顾晰若请进公寓。

这个房间就像是为她量身定做的。

映入眼帘的窗帘是顾晰若最喜欢的水蓝色的，而且还是颇具文艺感的落地窗帘。床边的床头柜也是顾晰若喜欢的收纳柜的式样，烦琐却无比精致。最令顾晰若惊讶的是，床前的那片墙壁上用一根根的彩色丝线串联起了无数张的照片，而每一张照片的主角都是她。甚至于，整间房的墙壁颜色，也被刷成了顾晰若所喜欢的深蓝色。

这是一间不够女生、不够粉嫩的房间，却是独一无二适合顾晰若性格的房间。自然地，顾晰若忍不住惊呼出声，同样是那么不淑女的三个字："老天爷。"

"怪叔叔，这个魔法什么时候会消失？在消失前，我可以多享受一会儿吗？"

李嘉禾微笑着向顾晰若走去。恍惚间，顾晰若以为自己是遇见了天使。

"晰若，这是一个不会消失的魔法。以后这里就是属于你的，你可以把它当成你的秘密空间，也可以把它当成你的水蓝城堡，或者，把它当成你的家。这是房间的钥匙。不想回去那就不回去吧，睡在自己的家里，谁都管不着。"

真心被打碎，决绝地被推离。

温暖的惊喜，暖暖地被感动。

这些天的顾眄若是真的有些累了。伪装的坚强，轰然倒塌，顾眄若很感动很感动。

"谢谢你，嘉禾。"

"傻瓜，不哭了。"

墙壁上的时针指向晚上八点。李嘉禾突然想起，一直忙于"争吵"的两人，连晚饭都没来得及吃。通过手机搜索，李嘉禾搜到附近有家饺子馆，里面的热炒鸭锁骨和云吞面口碑十分不错，无奈这家店不提供外卖服务，他只好亲自前往。

"眄若，我去买点儿吃的回来，你先休息一会儿。"

"不提供外卖吗？"顾眄若问。

"没有外卖。"

"呵呵，那小心点儿。我等你回来。"

"嗯。"

毕竟还是感冒着的，李嘉禾离开后，顾眄若立马就像只泄气的皮球，躺在了床上，闭上眼，脑海中一片模糊。

顾眄若想起了和李嘉禾一起做过的许多许多事情。比如，一起去图书馆看书；比如，一起沿着操场跑圈圈；比如，一起去滑冰场滑冰。以及，高三那个凉风习习的早上，李嘉禾端着一碗山楂陈皮营养粥等在顾眄若的教室门口，因为老师拖堂导致他足足等了一节课的时间外加十分钟的课间休息。那段时间的顾眄若患上了轻微的厌食症，吃什么都没胃口，李嘉禾询问过后为她买来这碗山楂陈皮营养粥。最后，等顾眄若下课后，李嘉禾将粥递给她，只说了一句"给，趁热喝，我还有课"，便匆匆地跑回了大学部。而她手中的粥还是温热的。

顾昕若的眼角有温热的泪在流淌。

啪嗒！啪嗒！

窗外突然下起了雨，雨点打在玻璃窗上，发出"啪嗒啪嗒"声。顾昕若从床上爬起来，往窗外看去，只见李嘉禾正提着两只塑料袋躲在大树下避雨。因为路途比较近，李嘉禾便没有开车过去。猝不及防的一场大雨早已经把他淋湿。

从烦琐的抽屉里一个一个找，终于找到了一把伞，顾昕若迅速地往楼下冲去。电梯门打开的瞬间，却见李嘉禾已经站在了她的面前。

"怎么这么快？刚才还在树下的……"

"看到你探出小脑袋了，所以我跑过来了。"

来不及说什么，顾昕若急匆匆地回去打开门，冲进浴室，拿了浴巾和毛巾，一块罩在李嘉禾的头上，一块披在他的身上，而后接过他手中的食物放到了桌上。转过身又来到李嘉禾的旁边，用浴巾帮他擦头发。李嘉禾也顺从地将头低下，任由顾昕若一遍一遍地为他擦拭。

两个人之间的距离此时是很近很近的。甚至于，李嘉禾可以闻到顾昕若身上淡淡的气息。突然，他抢过顾昕若手中的浴巾，抬起头，直直地望着她，她也望着他。而后，一点一点地，靠近，靠近，在李嘉禾的唇几乎快要碰上顾昕若的唇时，顾昕若的电话响起来了。

是路瑾言。

"喂。昕若，还在医院吗？"

"没有，我今晚不回去了。"

"哦……是和嘉禾在一起吗？"

"嗯。"

"好，那我就放心了。"

"……"

什么叫"和嘉禾在一起，那我就放心了"啊？顾昕若生气地挂断电话。电话那头的路瑾言挂断电话后，强装镇定地对父母说："昕若和朋友在一起，今天就不回来了，放心吧，她很安全。"路伯母和路伯父安心地回到他们的房间后，安眠才问路瑾言："昕若，是和嘉禾在一起吗？"

"嗯。"

"哦，不会发生什么事情吧？孤男寡女的……"

"不会的。我们不也是孤男寡女吗？"

"瑾言。"

"嗯？"

"不如我们发生点儿什么吧。"

"嗯？"

"哈哈，我开玩笑的。"

心理书上说，每一句开玩笑的话中多少都包含了一些真实的想法。

安眠和路瑾言谈恋爱以来，两人似乎除了牵手便是牵手，青涩得好像初中生的恋爱。有时候安眠会主动地亲吻路瑾言，可每一次路瑾言也只是像蜻蜓点水般地轻轻回吻安眠的脸。其实安眠也不是多主动的人，她也有女生的矜持和保守。只是，现在的她，是那么迫切地想要将路瑾言纳为己有。

所以，离开路瑾言的家之后，安眠打了一通电话给李嘉禾的后母。她说："你看到的人的确是李嘉禾和顾昕若，顾昕若今天不会回家了。"

电话那头立马爆发出来的笑实在是有些狂妄，以至于安眠都忍不住将电话拿到了离她耳朵相对远一点儿的位置。

"小眠，好戏即将上演，等着看好戏吧。"

"好。"

"顾昤若，好自为之。"挂断电话后，安眠喃喃自语道。

无疑安眠是爱着路瑾言的，所以在听到他因为信任而倾诉的所有"真相"之后，她选择了嘴上妥协，也选择了帮他保守秘密。可是，另一方面，路瑾言对顾昤若的守护和关爱已经超出了她所能够容忍的限度，她可是"宁可我负天下人，也不可天下人负我"的安眠，她怎会甘心选择妥协？

公寓内。

路瑾言的电话之后，李嘉禾和顾昤若之间出现了短暂的尴尬和沉默。

李嘉禾心想，如果刚才吻下去，顾昤若会不会拒绝？不过既然已经被打断，也只好作罢。拿起浴巾，李嘉禾冲顾昤若傻笑："不介意我在这里洗个澡吧？"

看着满身湿透了的李嘉禾，顾昤若早就想让他去洗个澡了。衣服交给服务员烘干的话，也不过十多分钟。

"不介意的话，那我现在先去洗澡，回头再喊服务员来热东西，我们一起吃。"

"嗯，快去吧。"

大概是有些饿过了头，顾昤若已经全然没了吃东西的胃口。倒是头好像又开始痛起来了。李嘉禾洗完澡出来的时候发现顾昤若已经躺在床上睡着了，走到她的身边，用手摸了摸她的额头，果然，又开始发烫了。

"昤若，醒醒，我们去医院。"

"啊？不，不去。"

"乖啊，你又发烧了，我带你去医院。"

"不要，不要去医院。"

顾昤若现在是无比排斥医院的，李嘉禾知道再劝她也是没用的，只好用洗脸盆接了冷水，然后用冷毛巾帮她敷额头。这一晚，李嘉禾都得陪在顾昉若身边了，只有这样他才能够放心。所以，当李沐禾打电话给他询问他什么时候回家时，李嘉禾说："今天我不回去了。"

就这样，敷额头，洗毛巾，换水，敷额头，洗毛巾，换水……循环了多次后，顾昉若的烧终于退了。吃了感冒药的顾昉若此刻也已经睡得很熟，累趴了的李嘉禾也终于可以放心地睡一会儿了。

一觉到天亮。

直到细细碎碎的敲门声一直不休不止的传来，李嘉禾和顾昉若才醒过来。醒来后的李嘉禾发现他竟然是睡在顾昉若身边的，而他身上只裹了一条浴巾。李嘉禾有些尴尬地冲顾昉若解释道："昨晚睡觉的时候都忘了去服务员那儿拿衣服了。"

知道李嘉禾是因为自己而"忘乎所以"，如果不是一直在帮发烧的她换水换毛巾，他怎么会累到直接倒头就睡？顾昉若感激地冲李嘉禾微笑。

"嘉禾，谢谢你。快去开门吧。"

没有想太多，以为是早上过来送衣服的服务员，李嘉禾便直接地开了门。打开门后，发现是学校的领导人，李嘉禾当下就懵了。眼下，只见一个裹着浴巾的男人和一个正躺在床上裹着被子衣衫不整的女人，好像再多的解释也是无用的。

学校校规虽然没有明令禁止学生谈恋爱，但是对于在校学生公然在酒店开房、在学校外租房同居的现象，学校一旦知道，那是一定会给予惩罚的。学校曾经因为学生开房和租房同居现象受到过教育部门的公开批评。所以，这一点，是校长乃至校董事会都特别反感和反对的，以至于后来学校还制定了相关条例，明令禁止此现象的发生。这一条例，高中部和大学部都适用。

你 是 我 遥 不 可 及 的 梦

🌢

两位校领导站在门口连门都没进，直接对李嘉禾和顾昕若下通知："两位同学，回学校，等待处分。"

这个时候，怎么会有学校的领导人过来？感觉到事情有蹊跷，李嘉禾立马打电话给家里的管家，吩咐他查清楚整件事情的来龙去脉。

顾昕若坐在床上无奈地对李嘉禾说："我们学校的校规还真是有趣。不过，怪叔叔，我好像连累你了。对不起。"

"清者自清，浊者自浊。你没事吧，顾昕若小同学？"

"我可是见过大风大浪的人，这点儿小风小浪算什么？这又不是旧社会，他们还能给我定个什么不矜持的罪不成？"

"昕若，保持这样的乐观情绪。不要怕，天塌下来还有怪叔叔顶着。"

"天若真的塌下来，我就踩在高凳上和你一块顶着。"

"走吧，去学校。"

"嗯。"

说真的，顾昕若的乐观是真的有些过头了。以至于她来到学校，看到到处都贴满了她和李嘉禾昨晚一起进入酒店的照片时，立马就感觉到头嗡嗡嗡嗡地作响，像是被人当头给了一棒。再仔细看一看上面的文字，什么"顾昕若身世凄惨""顾昕若麻雀变凤凰，搭上富二代李嘉禾""优雅王子李嘉禾玩弄杂草傻瓜女顾昕若""屡次开房×公开同居！不要脸"等等，简直无奇不有。

如此，不仅顾昕若的身世被公诸于世，李嘉禾显赫的家世也被曝光了。

顾昕若原本并不想哭的，这点儿侮辱，其实真的不算什么。可是，当顾昕若远远地看到许清木拼命地扯着墙上粘贴的纸，南西撒泼地轰开围观的学生时，她的鼻子酸酸的，只好选择了与南西和许清木相反的方向绕到学校管理处。她害怕在南西和许清木面前，她的眼泪会忍不住。

在学校师生面前公开道歉或者自动退学——这样的惩罚似乎不算太狠。大多数学生都会选择公开道歉，而后息事宁人。可是，在莫须有的罪名面前，顾昀若的自尊心就像是牛皮糖，粘得她紧紧的，所以，她宁愿选择离开，也不要向别人道歉。可是对于高三的顾昀若来说，自动退学就意味着放弃高考，放弃升入大学。

李嘉禾是不会允许这样的事情发生的，所以，他选择了追随顾昀若的决定。

这下，该轮到校领导为难了。

拥有学校股份的李嘉禾的父亲若是知道了自己儿子退学一事，撤股不说，事情追究起来，更是麻烦。因为他们都清清楚楚地知道，这一事件的幕后操纵人就是李嘉禾的后母。校领导为难地叹气，心里抱怨道：这家事干吗要扯上校事呢？为难啊为难。

"鉴于李嘉禾同学情况特殊，这样吧，你们先写一份检讨书吧。"校领导最终说道。

"眼见并不属实。检讨书我们不会写，因为我们没有错。"李嘉禾说道。

"人证物证都有了，还会有什么错？"

"那不如，给我们三天的时间，我们自己来查出真相，如何？"李嘉禾步步紧逼。

"……好吧。"校领导无奈地答应道。

接下来的几天，李嘉禾便全力以赴调查这件事。无奈，管家那边查来查去都查不到任何消息。所有有利的信息好像都被人刻意地隐藏起来了，而显然，这个人的能力是凌驾于李嘉禾之上的。顾昀若这边也开始发动南西和许清木一同去寻找能够证明自己清白的证据。

三天的时间眼看就要到了。这时候，学校的"大字报"又惹出了一些事端。当第三天进入到二十四小时倒计时时，学校的各个地方都贴满了"顾昕若证明清白的方法"。大概意思就是让校方带着顾昕若去医院验明其清白之身，简直是侮辱之极的方法。

愤怒而又着急地踢打着路边的垃圾桶时，顾昕若收到了一条新的短信。

你是骄傲的顾昕若，是不允许被任何事物打倒的顾昕若。笑一笑，事情马上就会解决的。

发信人：路瑾言

大概路瑾言说的话是带着魔法的吧，刚刚读完短信的顾昕若，就接到了李嘉禾汇报事情已经解决的电话。在操场会合后，李嘉禾告诉了顾昕若整件事情的始末。

李嘉禾和顾昕若进入酒店的那一刻，事实上就已经被人跟踪了。对方倒也不是刻意跟踪他们，而是发现熟悉的身影后不由自主地就跟踪了。渐渐地，对方就衍生了邪恶的想法，拍了照，当晚便和学校取得了联系，在第二天又雇了一些学生到处散发和张贴诋毁两人的"手写报"。

这个人就是李嘉禾的后母。与其串通一气的，知晓事件整个过程和真相的人便是安眠。

"有证据吗？"

"喏……手机录音。"

"谁给你的？"

"我的一个同学，叫徐清婉。她出身政治家庭，她母亲和我后母关系一直不错。她们聊天的时候刚好被徐清婉听到了，于是她便将她们的对话用手机录下来了。虽然她不方便出面作证，但是……有这段手机录音也足够证明我们的清白了。"

"嘉禾，这事我们低调处理吧。"

"我不会放过她的。"

"嘉禾，想想你的父亲。"

"是她让你受尽侮辱的，就这样原谅她吗？还有安眠，你打算一直瞒着路瑾言吗？"

"我难过，我受伤，甚至于我抱怨为什么上天要让我遭受这些侮辱。也正因为这样，我不愿意看到我在乎的人再因为我而受伤……有时候，隐瞒和欺骗也是一种关心。"

"……我……好吧，晞若，按你说的做。"

因为，一方是父亲心爱和信任的妻子，一方是路瑾言相信和爱护的女朋友，即便他们应该受到惩罚，可是顾晞若和李嘉禾也真的不愿再多伤一个他们自己在乎的人的心了。

校方也不愿意将事情越闹越大，自然同意了顾晞若的低调处理法。

这件事情就这样告一段落。

/04/

真相被还原。

南西却消失了。

结束高三生活的那天，大家聚在一起庆祝所有人都顺利地升入了本校大学部。南西却在庆祝的途中将安眠喊出去了，然而直到安眠回来好几个小时后，南西仍然不见踪影。

庆祝会被迫中断。

许清木这时候才将所有的真相说出来。

阴差阳错地，南西在学校废弃的教堂里听到了安眠对顾盺若的忏悔。虽然校方已经证实了顾盺若的清白，可是从顾盺若的陈述中，南西只知道李嘉禾的后母是主犯，而安眠是共犯这回事她一点儿都不知情。知晓之后，南西气得当时就想扇安眠几巴掌，再扯着她的头发往墙上撞。然而该死的系主任却在这个时候杀出来，将南西给派去当免费劳务工了。

爱情，可以拯救一个人，也可以毁灭一个人。

不可避免地，路瑾言也知道了整件事情背后更完整的真相。朝顾盺若的方向望过去，只见她了然气愤的眼神。原来她是知情的。那么，大概也是因为他的原因，所以她隐瞒了这一点吧。

被怀疑、被质问、被揭穿的安眠早已开始烦躁和不安，对于他人的询问，也一律直接给予了"我不知道"这样的回答。这样的态度实在令人愤怒。顾盺若走到安眠的面前，抬起手一个巴掌就朝她脸挥过去了。

"如果南西有事，我不会放过你。"顾盺若对安眠说。

下意识地，被打之后的安眠反手就朝顾盺若甩去，手却在半空中被李嘉禾给牢牢握紧了，任她怎么挣扎也甩不开。

这时候，路瑾言走到安眠的旁边，轻而易举地就将安眠的手从李嘉禾的手中抽离出来。

"现在最重要的事情是寻找南西。"路瑾言说。

对，现在最重要的事情是找南西，路瑾言说得一点儿都没有错。只是，现在的路瑾言是在维护和帮助安眠吗？顾盺若的心里瞬时像打翻了五味瓶，不理解也不想去理解。这样轻轻柔柔的一句话，却像是一把利剑毫不留情地刺入了顾昕若的心脏。

是伤。

可，再勇敢的人也会有自己难以愈合的伤。

"路瑾言，你一点儿都不害怕我会离开你吗？"顾昕若凑近他的耳边轻声询问。

答案，已无须等待。

语毕，顾昕若转身消失在了夜色中。

我只是难过不能陪你一起老

/01/

爱是多么无奈的一件事，眼穿肠断也枉然。

明明彼此喜欢，却又无法厮守。

夜色中，许清木、李嘉禾和顾眄若分头去找南西。

路瑾言和安眠留在原地。

安眠低着头，静静地等候着路瑾言的惩罚。不堪的真相如此赤裸裸地袒露在心爱的人面前，安眠的骄傲已全然消失。然而，路瑾言并没有凶她，骂她，连一句重话都没有对她说，他只是低声地求她："不要伤害眄若。"

安眠不可思议地抬起头："你说什么？"

"她是无辜的。"

"是我，是我联合阿姨害的顾眄若，是我故意的。你不骂我，居然还求我。

你凭什么求我？你凭什么求我不要再伤害顾昤若，啊？"

"小眠……"

"路瑾言，你浑蛋！"

路瑾言也不说话，任由安眠一个人骂着喊着，张牙舞爪地朝他捶打着。可路瑾言越是不出声，安眠就越是气愤。安眠抓起路瑾言的手就朝上面咬去，想要用尽全力去咬疼这个男人，让他也尝一尝心疼的冰凉。可是，牙齿刚碰到路瑾言的手臂，安眠的眼泪就落到了他的手心里。

"路瑾言，我是不是犯贱啊？你告诉我，我是不是犯贱啊？你路瑾言喜欢顾昤若，让你去喜欢就是啊，咱们好聚好散就是，我怎么就这么拿得起放不下啊？我怎么就这么不要脸，一天到晚还想着要去害顾昤若啊？我安眠不是黑心的巫婆，我安眠也不是没人要，我何苦这么作践我自己啊？……啊？路瑾言……"

安眠冰冷的眼泪，一滴一滴滑入手心。

路瑾言又不是冷血动物，怎会感觉不到心疼？

他伸手将颤抖的安眠拥入怀中。

"傻丫头，我都已经是半瞎之人了，你为何还要喜欢我？你那么优秀，那么美丽，有那么多完整的人可以给你更幸福的未来。我不值得你这样付出。"

"傻子，你不会瞎的。就算你哪天真的瞎了，我也会让我妈找全世界最好的医生给你治疗的。"

"小眠，不值得的。"

"我说值得就值得。"

"傻丫头……"

"我爸妈想送我去美国学习两年，他们已经在给我办手续了。我不想走的。瑾言，我可以留下的，如果你挽留我。嗯？"

"好的学习机会不是任何时候都有的。"

"我知道该怎么做了。"

"对不起，安眠。"

"那么，答应我吧，在那之前，如果我不说放弃，你也不能放弃。除非是我甩你，懂吗？"

"好。"

有些爱，只给到这儿。

无论是仍然爱着的一方，还是已经放手的一方，是真的，都会痛。

/02/

失去，离散。

对于从来就没有真正拥有过什么的顾昕若来说，这一切就像是家常便饭，时常发生。

难过，悲伤。

太过频繁的情绪，以至于现在的顾昕若，心脏的承压能力已经远远超过了她的同龄人。

李嘉禾通知顾昕若，许清木已经找到南西的时候，顾昕若正站在地铁口。

顾昕若的方向感不太强，常常会分不清地铁的行驶方向，所以，几乎每一次她搭乘地铁的时候，都有南西在她的身旁。顾昕若一直记得，南西第一次带她来这里坐地铁时的情景，那是顾昈若第一次坐对方向。

记忆中的南西左手牵着顾昈若，右手拿着相机，然后对着列车即将驶来的方向一顿乱拍，直到列车稳稳地停在了两人的面前，她才放下相机。走进车厢坐好后，她便翻出相机里的照片给顾昈若看。顾昈若记得，有一张照片是这样的——无边的黑暗深处，因列车的来临而出现了一小股微弱的光。而这张照片的下一张照片上，便是微光冲破黑暗，光亮直抵人心。

而后，顾昈若就听到了南西对她说的话。

她说："顾昈若同学，如果这个世界没有黑暗，我们就不会知道这个世界还有光明。肉眼看去，黑暗是无边无际的，实际上，光明就在转角的地方，它只是调皮地想要跟你玩一会儿躲猫猫游戏。耐心地等等它，光明很快就会来到你的身边。"

南西说这些话的时候，她的手一直紧紧地牵着顾昈若。

如果有一天，如此温暖的存在，将永远地消失在顾昈若的世界里，顾昈若想要随她一块消失的心情也是能够被理解的吧。

站在地铁站台的边缘，眼泪只剩冰冷的温度，残留在脸上。

地铁口的风声听起来就好像是李嘉禾的声音，他一遍一遍在顾昈若的耳边说："许清木找到南西了，因为车祸……她，暂时，离开我们了……"

下一秒，顾昈若闭上了双眼，一步一步向前迈去。

——南西小姐，如果连你都抛弃这个世界了，那我也不再需要去尝试爱上这个世界了。没关系，不怕的，跳下去。列车呼啸而过的瞬间，我就可以看见你了。

20 秒。

10 秒。

0 秒。

一切静止。

大概，上帝现在还不想要顾昉若的命。所以，当她一只脚几乎已经踏入半空中时，她整个人突然就朝后面晕倒过去了。悲伤溢满了身体里的每个细胞，苍白到连死亡的力气都没有。只能眼睁睁地，身体完全不受控制地，直直地向后倒去。

咚！

站在站台边等地铁的人们也终于发现了顾昉若的存在。

想要装作没看见似乎不太可能了。而真正行动起来，打电话给附近医院急救中心的人，却是一位已经年过花甲的老奶奶。还好，在她的帮助下，顾昉若被顺利地送往医院，生命安全得已保证。

李嘉禾得知南西车祸死亡的消息后，最担心的便是顾昉若，所以在已经快要赶到她所在的位置时，才告诉了她真相。而当他赶到她所在的地铁口时，却看到一辆医院急救车从他面前呼啸而过，他的心瞬时咯噔一下，心跳漏了一拍。他立马掏出手机打电话给顾昉若，接电话的却不是她。对方只是告诉他，手机的主人现在正被送往医院……

"至少在你遇到危难的时候，我们是心灵相通的。可是，如果可以，我愿在你遇到危难的时候，守护在你身边。如果可以，我愿我可以抵挡所有的危难，而危难也永远不再找上你。"李嘉禾心里想着，坐在顾昉若的病床旁。这样的场景，太过熟悉，也太过让人心疼。

时间一分一秒地过去，李嘉禾一直默默地守着顾昉若。时针转过零点，他才趴在顾昉若的病床旁打起盹来。顾昉若就是在这个时候醒过来的。了解李嘉禾睡觉时深眠的习惯，醒来后，她再一次偷偷地将针头拔掉，然后连鞋子都没来得及穿，就往外逃。

可是，在万分担心的情况下，李嘉禾如何深眠？

在顾昕若刚跑出病房门口时他就已经清醒，随后立马往前追去。看到李嘉禾在后面追，顾昕若加大了步伐，拼命地朝前奔，奔到医院门口时，跳上了一辆刚送急诊病人来医院的出租车。还好，李嘉禾的车就停在医院大门口，他立马发动车子，朝出租车追去。

两辆车子间便展开了一场追逐战。

李嘉禾自小对赛车就有着浓厚的兴趣，平时有机会的话，也会练练手。自然，追上一辆出租车对他来说并不算太难的事，尤其在开车的司机车龄也不是那么长的情况下。所以，当李嘉禾的车子横到出租车前面时，顾昕若知道，她已无处可逃。可是，她顾昕若不能就这么妥协了，连挣扎的机会都放弃。在李嘉禾下车的瞬间，顾昕若抢先一步下车，然后继续往前跑。

好歹，脚短的跑不过脚长的，更何况是在这条漫长无边际的公路上。

李嘉禾在抓住顾昕若的瞬间就将她拉到了自己面前，然后拽着她就往自己车子的方向走去。

"放开我。"

"李嘉禾，放开我。"

"喂，你拽疼我了。"

"……"

"上车。"李嘉禾说。

"你别管我。"

"上车。"

"不上。"

李嘉禾也不想跟顾昕若啰唆，现在说再多也无法减轻她的难过，索性便将顾昕若打横抱起，丢到了车内，然后锁上了车门。而后他系好安全带，只简单地朝后面的顾昕若说了一句："坐好，我带你去找南西。"之后，便加快了车速。为了在加快车速的情况下全力保证两人的安全，到达南西家门前，李嘉禾一句话都没有再说，一路只专心地开着车。

凌晨一点整，顾昕若终于见到了微笑着的南西。

摆在灵柩前的那幅照片还是许清木帮南西拍的。因为当时的许清木和顾昕若都一致表态，南西笑得真是全世界最最最好看的，于是南西便没头没脑地说："那以后这照片我得放我灵柩上，你们看到了可不许哭，要和我一样笑得最最最好看。"

这句话还未说完，南西就遭到了顾昕若和许清木同时给予的白眼和鄙视："真是，有这么诅咒自己的人吗。"

所以，到达灵堂后，顾昕若并没有失声大哭。她苍白着脸走到角落，抱住在角落里哭得像个孩子的许清木。她什么也没说，只是紧紧地抱着他。待了几分钟后，顾昕若才看到南西的母亲，那个和南西一样倔强刚烈的女人一夜就苍老了许多。

顾昕若走过去，轻轻地拥抱住她，抱着抱着就忍不住哭了。

南西的母亲抱着顾昕若说的每一句话都像是一根细密的针，然后一针一针扎入她的心脏，细细密密的疼，细细密密的都是伤。

她说："他们找到我的小西时，她就已经被车撞得面目全非了……到处都是血，到处都是碎裂的骨肉，脸都变形了……都看不出来她还是我的小西了。如果不是我的小西该多好，可是医生……医生说是。昕若，你是小西最好的朋友，你陪陪她……告诉她，一定要去天堂，沿着去天堂的路往前走。告诉她，等着我和她爸，我们很快就会过去陪她的，她不会孤单的……"

白发人送黑发人，悲恸万分。

南西的整个身体都被白布盖起来了。一想起南西母亲说的话，顾昕若就会难过得连呼吸都困难。得知消息后赶过来的路瑾言一直紧跟在顾昐若身后。这样的顾昐若让他想起了他第一次见到她时，她站在天台的边缘，好像随时都会随风而逝。

他的心就紧张地缩在一起，感到窒息。

两天两夜，顾昐若不吃不喝不睡，就这样一直坐在南西的水晶棺材旁，呆呆地看着，偶尔自言自语两句，也许她是在和南西说话。最后去往殡仪馆的途中，顾昐若临时从车上跑下来，决定不去殡仪馆送南西了，她害怕再一次看到自己深爱的人在她的眼前灰飞烟灭。

因为，还有许清木。

南西和顾昐若同时担心的人，还有许清木。

顾昐若下车的时候，路瑾言和李嘉禾也同时想要下车，然而，李嘉禾却被路瑾言挡在了车门口。

"我会带她回家，放心。"

"好。"

车子继续往前行去，南西却离自己越来越近，在顾昐若的心里，她是永不消失的天使。路瑾言走到顾昐若身旁，牵起她的手，说："我带你回家。"

"家？"

"嗯，家。昐若，我们回家。"

"好，回家。"

连南西的最后一面都没有见到。

顾昐若回到房间后，匆匆忙忙地打开电脑，进入南西的博客。喜欢拍照的南西总是会将最近新拍的照片放到她的博客里。好像只能通过这样的途径见到南西了。

然而，博客里最新显示的一张照片却是许清木和顾旆若的侧面照——吃着南西买的爆米花，喝着南西买的鲜榨果汁，顾旆若和许清木脸上的表情欢快而明媚。

滑动鼠标将页面一直往下拉，顾旆若就看到了图片下面南西留下的文字。

明明知道照相机很难真的拍出直接进入眼睛的一切，

我还是忍不住拿起相机胡乱地拍了一阵，

因为很喜欢。

顾旆若，许清木，你们不知道，我有多喜欢看到你们笑。

南西的离开使得路瑾言内心的矛盾极度爆发，是继续自己的“守护计划”，还是选择留在她的身边给予她爱，给予她安慰，谁也没有答案。

此时的路瑾言，站在阳台的一角，望着房间里的顾旆若。好像现在的他只能够选择这样不靠近的方式感受着她的悲伤，感受着她的难过，感受着她的遗憾。

路瑾言害怕自己一旦靠近，便不愿再离开。

之后很长一段时间，顾旆若不是彻夜失眠，就是反反复复地梦见南西，梦见她们在一起时的所有美好。路妈妈因为担心顾旆若，便陪着她睡了好几晚。很神奇的是，那几个晚上，顾旆若真的睡得比较安心，无梦无牵挂无伤心。然而懂事地强装出一副没事的模样，将路妈妈劝回到自己的房间睡后，她又回到了之前的睡眠状态。

她只是不希望路妈妈、路叔叔为她担心，而她也真的用尽了全力去微笑，可是只要那么一碰一触，心里绷着的那根弦立马就会断。

这一切，路瑾言都是懂的。

所以，他最近的睡眠也很浅，耳朵恨不得贴在墙上，这样顾旆若的一举一动他就都能听见。所以，最近的几次，每当顾旆若因为做梦而惊醒时，路瑾言都会穿着拖鞋立马站到她的卧室门口。而顾旆若睡着睡着就能感觉到有人透过门缝悄悄确认她的睡眠状态。所以，他会坚定地告诉顾昉若，失眠就失眠呗，做梦就做梦呗，不怕的，我随时待命陪着你。

随时待命，陪着你，不离也不弃。

这样的小情话，听起来真让人心欢喜。

可是，能够让人欢喜多久？

小众电影《80后》里有一个问题，顾昉若和电影里弹钢琴的小女孩一样，找寻了四面的白墙，蕾丝边的白色窗帘，钢琴的白键，可仍然找不到答案。

问题是："这个世界上有没有一样东西永远是白色的，永远不会由白色变成黄色或者其他颜色？"

答案是："没有。"

就像是在询问"永远有多远"一样，谁都不知道"永远"到底有多远。

——那么，路瑾言，会不会有那么一天，你也会离开我，永远地离开我？如果结果会是这样，那不如不拥有吧，反正拥有了也会失去。其实，我是害怕失去的，害怕得要命，却还在拼命假装，拼命习惯。以为伪装好了，以为渐渐已习惯，可我发现，我仍然害怕失去。

所以，对路瑾言这一次的陪伴，顾昉若选择了沉默。

/03/

南西离开后，许清木的状态似乎比顾昉若更加糟糕。

酗酒，抽烟，泡吧，打架，每一样他都不放过。

有好几次许清木因为酗酒过度，胡言乱语，而在酒吧与别人打架，最后还是倪斯出面，才避免了事故的发生。不过，许清木好像就是冲着被人打而去闹事的。每一次，当拳头狠狠地落在他身上时，那一刻，他才觉得爽，那一刻，他真的恨不得就被人这么活活打死。

倪斯将这一情况告诉顾眄若后，顾眄若便来到了酒吧。那时候的许清木正端着一杯酒走到一对情侣的桌旁，暧昧地将酒递给其中的女生，还趁机伸出了他的咸猪手，朝对方的小裙上拉了拉。自然，一杯酒直接朝许清木的身上泼去，随后，一个耳光清脆地打在他的脸上。许清木也不还手，反而继续傻笑，十足的街痞流氓样。

顾眄若本想要淡定地走到许清木的身边，然后温暖地给予他拥抱。可是，走到许清木的身边后，她却是强硬地抢过他手上的杯子，然后"啪"的一声摔碎在地。许清木抬头看了一眼顾眄若后，蹲下身捡起地上的玻璃碎片来，边捡边用手握紧了手心里的碎片。直到鲜红色的血液随着他手心的纹路往下流，顾眄若才蹲下身，摊开了许清木的手心，然后一片一片将碎碴儿挑出来，扔到桌子旁的垃圾桶里，再接过路瑾言递过来的消毒毛巾，温柔地擦拭他手心的血迹。

"看到你这样，南西会难过的。"

"嗯。"

"以后不要这样了，你还有我，你不是孤单的。"

"嗯。"

"许清木，我们逃课去海边吧。"

"嗯。"

事实上，逃课去海边散散心这个建议是路瑾言提出来的。不过，最初顾眄若是拒绝了的。站在顾眄若的背后，听到她对许清木说的话，转过身，路瑾言便立即嘱咐倪斯帮忙预订车票和酒店。乘着海风，阴霾也会渐渐消失在海与天交接的未知处吧。

生离死别，在任何时候都是一种痛。

明明是带着想要释怀的心情奔赴这场旅途的，可是，一路上，所有的人都保持着沉默。路瑾言想要说几个冷笑话逗乐顾昕若和许清木，可是话刚到嘴边，他又咽回自己肚子里去了。许清木和顾昕若沉重的表情，让路瑾言的心也变得沉重起来。其实，南西的离开，对路瑾言来说，也是难过的。那个大大咧咧，毫无心机，重情又仗义，总是没形象哈哈大笑的女孩，路瑾言也常常会怀念她，即便他们之间的交情真的很浅很浅。

这样的一趟旅行，李嘉禾其实是知情的，他之所以没有像往常一样跟着顾昕若跑过来，是因为，他知道，对于顾昕若来说，有路瑾言在已然足够。所以，他选择了待在家里睡觉，不分昼夜地睡觉。得知哥哥李嘉禾完全麻痹在家不出门的李沐禾立马跑去超市，买了肉松，买了黄瓜火腿，还买了做寿司要用到的材料，给李嘉禾做了一盒美味的李沐禾樱花招牌寿司。

饱饱得将所有寿司都消灭地一干二净的李嘉禾，不但没有感谢的话语，反而装起大小孩的模样，语重心长地对李沐禾说："强扭的瓜不甜。"

李沐禾自然知道哥哥话里的意思。

"哥，我不后悔。"

"嗯？"

"爱上了，如果连努力都不努力一下就放弃，这不是我李沐禾的个性。即便会被伤得遍体鳞伤，我也不后悔。我爱，所以我愿意。不是每一个人都有不顾一切去爱一个人的勇气。呀，李嘉禾，我很勇敢的，不是吗？你可别小看我，许清木现在真的很需要很需要我的安慰。"

"他不会稀罕的。"

"哥……"拖长了尾音，李沐禾不满地撒娇地喊道。

"这是路瑾言的电话号码。许清木和顾昕若现在正处于难过的情绪中，给你指路，给你方向不太可能，你找他吧。有任何事情，打电话给我。照顾好自己，保护好自己，安慰好自己。"

"错了错了，是安慰好许清木。"

"不要害怕他的拒绝，不要害怕他的推离，安抚好他的情绪，也安慰好自己，不要让他的冷漠和难过伤到自己。你很勇敢的，李沐禾，对吗？"

"呀！李嘉禾，你从来都不关心我，对我好的，突然这样，我还真有点儿受宠若惊……哥，我会好好的。"

"我的傻妹妹。"

奔赴一场冒险，勇气和信心，李沐禾准备得满满的。得知"逃课去海边"的计划之后，她当即决定也要跟随许清木一起去。可是，当她看到许清木苍白的脸色和毫无生气的模样时，她全身上下每个毛孔顿时就溢满了心疼。即便很想要立马冲到他的身边告诉他："还有我，还有我李沐禾会一直陪着你，你不要难过。"即便真的很想要很想要这么做，但李沐禾最终还是选择了"跟踪"。

还好，有路瑾言帮她，不时地提供地点和情况给她。

对于顾昕若、路瑾言、李嘉禾三人之间的情感纠葛，李沐禾多少还是有所耳闻的。从路瑾言短短的几条短信中，李沐禾就已感觉到此情敌来势汹汹啊。革命尚未成功，李嘉禾同志仍需努力。

此时此刻，李沐禾能够保持这样轻松的心态，是很不错的。因为，她知道，如果她自己都不能保持好的状态和情绪，她又如何能做许清木最坚强的后盾？

另一边，三人行的散心团队已经扎好帐篷，铺好坐垫，"阴阴沉沉"地来到了海边。

时间已经接近黄昏，秋日的海风吹过来已然夹杂着丝丝的凉意。这样的温度，似乎刚刚好适合清醒。顾昕若抱着自己的双腿蹲坐在沙滩上，远远望去，大海和天空的交界处，正在一点一点地融入黑夜。可是，她知道，黑夜过后，那片无尽的黑暗处又会出现光亮。

是南西这样告诉她的。

顾昕若的情绪已经在渐渐恢复中。死者已逝，生者当应好好生存，而微笑，是南西对顾昕若和许清木最大的要求。顾昕若此刻似乎已经在尝试慢慢去满足南西的要求。许清木那家伙呢，仍然是不吃不喝，不吵不闹，安静地站着或者坐着，偶尔才会走动几步，就像已经失去灵魂的人。

海风微凉，海浪汹涌地翻滚着。

顾昕若坐在离海比较近的地方。担心她会感冒，一直站在她身后不远处的路瑾言，走进帐篷里拿了一条毛绒毯递给她。

感觉到毛绒毯的暖意，顾昕若转过头，对路瑾言说："谢谢。"

"嗯。"

对话便不再延续。

顾昕若再次回到她自己的情绪中。路瑾言则神神怪怪地绕着顾昕若的四周走了两圈，确认海风刮得最强烈的风口方向后，挡在那个方向坐在了顾昕若的旁边。这样，也算是帮顾昕若"遮风挡雨"了吧。路瑾言坐下来以后，没有安慰，也没有讲冷笑话，他只是很安静地陪着顾昕若，只是很安静地用他的小身板为她挡着风。

时间仿若静止。

顾昕若的头就这么轻轻地靠在了路瑾言的肩膀上。

幸福的姿态似乎只维持了几分钟，熟悉的女声就传入了两人的耳朵里。不远处，李沐禾正急匆匆地跑过来，边跑边上气不接下气地朝这边大喊："不好了……许清木、许清木崩溃了……"

"崩溃了？"路瑾言站起身朝李沐禾喊过去。

"快……快跟我过去……出、出事了……"

意识到事情的严重性，顾昕若拉着路瑾言就跑。跑到李沐禾旁边时，顾昕若问她："崩溃了是什么意思？"

"他……死命地往海里走，拉都拉不住……"

"自杀？"路瑾言补充道。

"应该……是……"

"许清木，你真没出息！"顾昕若忍不住低吼道。

到达许清木所在的位置后，顾昕若突然停下了脚步。路瑾言和李沐禾不懂顾昕若停下的原因，面面相觑。

"你们在这里等我。"顾昕若说。

"我跟你一起去。"路瑾言说。

"我有办法的。"

"昕若姐……"

"没事的，沐禾。"

其实，顾昕若也不知道她的办法到底可行不可行。不过，没关系，此刻她已经做好了和许清木一起消失的准备。所以，在踏入海水中之前，她劝阻了路瑾言和李沐禾继续前进。

"前面的许清木，你给我站住！"

顾昕若踏入海水中，边往前走边朝前面的许清木大喊道。冰凉的触感侵袭而来，顾眏若的声音中都有着微微的颤音。听到顾眏若的声音，许清木稍稍地停下了脚步。只不过，很快地，他又不管不顾地继续往前走去。

“喂——许清木，你给我站住，停止前进。否则，绝交！”

仍然，没有反应。

眼见海水已经漫过许清木的上身，顾眏若焦急、担心的情绪交织在一起，以至于她突然迎着海浪拼命地朝前跑去，边跑边喊：“许清木，许清木，你不要我了吗，和南西一样不要我了吗?!”

终于，许清木停住了脚步。

“你别过来。”许清木说。

“许清木先生，我不怕死的。等我走到你身边的时候，海水应该就会漫过我的。”

“你别过来。”

这一次轮到顾眏若不听话了，眼见海水一点一点地漫过顾眏若，许清木终于忍不住往回走。站在沙滩边的路瑾言早已踏入了海水中，他需要的是随时待命，保证顾眏若的生命安全，所以，他也不听话地一点一点朝前走着。自然，李沐禾也不会乖乖地待在一旁，她跟在路瑾言的后面，任由海水一点一点漫上来……

“眏若，停，停止！”

“许清木，你浑蛋。你以为就你爱南西，我就不爱她吗？我告诉你，我不怕死的。你想死？好啊，我们一起死，死了就可以见到南西了，死了我们三个人又可以在一起了。”

“死了你们就对不起南西了。顾眏若，你不记得南西博客里的文字了吗?”路瑾言终于忍不住，朝她大喊道。

"南西写了什么?"许清木问。

"明明知道照相机很难真的拍出直接进入眼睛的一切,我还是忍不住拿起相机胡乱地拍了一阵,因为很喜欢。顾眆若,许清木,你们不知道,我有多喜欢看到你们笑。"

一字一句像是已经刻在了顾眆若的心里,喊完这段话,她已经泣不成声。此时的许清木也走到了她面前,将她拥入自己的怀里,疼惜地拍着她的后背。

"许清木先生,看到这样的我们,南西小姐会难过的。"

"是,顾眆若同学。"

"我们好好活着,一起去完成南西的梦想,不行吗?"

"眆若……"

"不行吗?"

"好。"

"我们上岸吧。"

"嗯。"

一场惊慌,终旧安宁。

收拾好帐篷里的东西,四人一起来到了酒店,一个单间一个标准间,因为李沐禾的到来,被换成了两个标准间。按照路瑾言和李沐禾之前商量好的,路瑾言照顾顾眆若,李沐禾照顾许清木,刚刚好,两个标准间。

一间房里。

终于清醒的许清木和刚从海水里出来连衣服都没得换冷得全身发抖的李沐禾。

"不能让我为你擦干眼泪吗?不能让我暂时陪在你身边,替你抚平伤口吗?"李沐禾颤抖着问许清木。

许清木也不回答，站起身从浴室里拿出浴巾递给李沐禾："擦擦吧，别感冒了。"

"是，不可以吗？"

"空调好像坏了，我去找人来弄下。"

好像许清木这么一走，又会跑到哪里想要结束他的生命似的，李沐禾条件反射地从后面拉住他："我不问你就是了，你不要走，也不要赶我走。明早天一亮，我会自己走。如果我在这里你不方便的话，我现在走也可以。"

"沐禾，我不值得你这样付出。"

"爱不就是不问值不值得吗？"

"……"

另一间房内。

顾昉若喷嚏连连，全身发烫。路瑾言将手伸到她的额头处，果然发烧了。他想要带顾昉若去医院，却被拒绝了，想要下楼给她买个药，顾昉若却死拽着他的手不放。无奈，路瑾言只好坐在她的床边，问她："你要怎么样？"

"用被子把自己蒙起来睡觉。"

"胡说八道，病了就要去医院，病了就要乖乖吃药。"

"路瑾言，我不去好不好？"

破天荒地，顾昉若向路瑾言撒起娇来，而路瑾言也完全败下阵来。

路瑾言只好端了一盆凉水，洗好了帕子给她自己先擦拭全身。而后，找了两条毛巾，轮流沾湿，折叠好，放在顾昉若的额头上给她降温。这样的一幕，多么熟悉，李嘉禾也曾这般呵护她，守着她，替她敷额头降温。然而顾昉若此刻却完全沉浸在路瑾言悉心的照顾中，脑海中只是闪过那么些片断，感动而非心动。所以，从一开始，顾昉若就选择了远离和推开李嘉禾。然，李嘉禾和顾昕若一样，都是彻头彻尾的傻瓜，不顾一切爱到伤了自己的笨蛋。

对于执着于爱的人来说，不爱才是真正残忍的事。

好在，路瑾言是爱着顾昕若的。

只不过，明明彼此相爱，明明近在咫尺的两个人，却无法选择厮守，甚至于连一句“我爱你”都无法说出口。害怕，一旦说出口，所有的坚持都会破碎。

在路瑾言的贴心照顾下，顾昕若终于渐渐睡着了。

也是在这一瞬间，路瑾言纠结的问题突然有了答案——他决定留在顾昕若的身边，即便只是暂时的，即便只能以哥哥的身份去完成这一切。

/04/

时节转入冬日。

安眠决定离开。

也许暂时的消失和冷静，对于她和路瑾言都是最好的选择。

冬天的冷风刮过的时候，安眠能够感觉到沁骨的寒冷。

离别的时候，安眠没有丝毫的拖拉，即便是有，她也一并隐藏起来了。怕好不容易下的决定顷刻间就会崩落，怕和母亲做好的约定无法遵守，怕连最后的安宁都无法带给路瑾言。安眠决定听从父母的安排去美国留学一段时间，一方面是因为安眠想给她和路瑾言一段时间和距离，感情经受一些考验，也许结果会不一样；另一方面则是因为安眠的母亲以路瑾言眼睛的病情相逼，也就是说，去美国留学这件事，安眠完全没有决定权。

好歹，安眠的母亲也是眼科界赫赫有名的医生，路瑾言多数找借口逃避检查，她已有所察觉。仔细一打听，便了解了路瑾言眼疾恶化的情况。他选择隐瞒必然是有原因的，却也不能因此让病情恶化。

当安眠的母亲询问安眠关于路瑾言所隐瞒的真相时，安眠只是说："他是孝顺懂事的孩子，在眼疾并未恶化和完全失明的情况下，不愿让父母担忧和难过。"

"请您帮他保守秘密，好吗？"安眠向母亲祈求道。

"孩子，他值得你为他这样付出吗？"

"值得，值得的。"

"好。在他病情不持续恶化的情况下，我答应你。但是，一旦恶化，我就会带他出国治疗，那么，他的父母肯定就会知道所有的情况了。"

"嗯。"

孩子的感情事，做长辈的通常都是任由其发展，不会去多加干涉的。可是，毕竟是自己的孩子，她变化的情绪，执着的眼神，做母亲的又怎会看不懂？选择将安眠送出国也完完全全是为了她好。若是真的相爱，必然能够经得起时间和距离的考验。更何况，安眠的父母并没有限定其归来的时间。

安眠要离开，路瑾言还是不舍的。想要跟安眠说对不起，可话刚到嘴边，安眠就制止了他。最终，路瑾言只是一脸抱歉地嘱咐安眠："在外要好好照顾自己。"

"我会的。"

"不会想我吧？"路瑾言开玩笑道。

"不会想你的。"

"呵呵。"

"呵呵。"

气氛颇尴尬，点单的服务员都忍不住好奇地多看了两人几眼，无聊地揣测了一下两人的关系，好朋友？情人？恋人？兄妹？好像都不是，该不会是仇人吧？点完单，服务员收好菜谱迅速地逃离了这个"冷库"区域。

吃饭的时候，和往常一样，路瑾言会不停地给安眠夹她喜欢的菜，而安眠也会突然夹起一块肉塞到路瑾言的嘴巴里。这样的一幕，在他人眼里是十足的情侣范，然而两个人脸上的表情却是无比暗淡悲伤的。不愿最后的时刻变得毫无意义，安眠便尝试着打开了话匣子。

"有坚持去做眼部检查和护理治疗吗？"

"嗯，有。"

"医生怎么说？"

"没事的，别担心。"

"医生怎么说？"

"重点保护对象吧，还是可能会失明，就像一枚潜伏的炸弹。"

"那么，视力呢？"

"一天天下降中。"

"通过调整眼镜的度数来纠正视力呢？"

"在尝试中。"

"那我妈给你制定的眼部针对性的护理和治疗，有没有作用？"

"坚持的话，会有作用。"

"瑾言，留学几年后，我会回来的。你答应我，一定要爱惜自己的眼睛，我不要你失明。"

——瑾言，我不要你失明。

顾昽若一大清早就被李嘉禾的初恋女友芊芊莫名其妙地喊出来逛街，经过一家土菜馆餐厅的时候，一眼就看到了屏风里背向着她坐着的路瑾言和安眠。让芊芊等在外面，她一个人进去，想要恶作剧地打个招呼，看看路瑾言的表情。却不想，靠近屏风的那一刻，听到的话便是这一句："瑾言，我不要你失明。"

"失明？"

脑海里突然闪现出许许多多的片段，一幕幕就像是放电影般在她的脑海里重放。

我会给你想要的答案……

推离拒绝……

哭泣中拥抱着安眠……

南西离开后又温暖地陪伴自己……

一切的一切，与路瑾言的失明扯上联系的话……顾昽若在这一瞬间也开始有些明白路瑾言这段时间里所有的情绪转变了。

水汽弥漫双眼，顾昽若将隔在她和安眠、路瑾言之间的屏风拉开。

"安眠刚才说的都是真的吗？"

"昽若，你怎么在这儿？"

顾昽若不回答他的问题，她蹲下身，靠近他的眼睛，想要找寻不可能。坐在路瑾言旁边的安眠，完全被顾昽若当成了空气。有些不甘心，有些妒忌，在顾昽若泪光闪烁地问路瑾言"是不是还能看到我，是不是没有失明"时，安眠站起身将顾昽若推开，一个吻狠狠地就落到了路瑾言的嘴唇上。

"看清楚了，顾昽若，他是我的男人。"末了，还是放软口气加了一句，"虽然我马上就要去美国留学了，但此时此刻他仍然是我的男人。"

她仍然是那个骄傲的安眠。

"让我确定一件事，确定完我就走，可以吗，安眠？"几乎是乞求的语气，顾眄若也搞不懂自己为什么要乞求安眠，好像路瑾言真的是属于她的，至少，如她所说，此时此刻是属于她的。

"好。"安眠回答道。

顾眄若伸出右手，然后清晰地用手指在路瑾言的面前比画"1、3、1、4"给他看。

"说出我刚才比画的数字吧。"

"眄若，我能看见。是1314，对不对？"

"对……可，刚才安眠说，她不要你失明，她为什么要这样说？"

"我眼睛是出了一点儿小问题，你也知道的，我眼睛患有先天性的弱视，最近视力又有些下降，身为我主治医生的安眠的母亲大人自然就十分担心，自然就夸张性地吓吓我，吓吓安眠嘛。"

"顾眄若，你应该相信路瑾言，他是你哥。"安眠附和道。

"好，我知道了，那不打扰你们了。"

以往的每一次，路瑾言都是留在了安眠的身边。而这一次，在顾眄若转身的瞬间，路瑾言将她拉回了自己身边。

"我们一起回家。"路瑾言对顾眄若说。

顾眄若不敢相信地望着路瑾言，路瑾言也没有再说话，只是坚定地朝她点了点头。"从今以后，我会以哥哥的身份，陪在你的身边，直到我的世界变得完全黑暗。"路瑾言在他的心里对顾眄若说。

一切就像是一枚不定时炸弹，谁都不知道它爆发的时间，谁也不知道未来会怎样，一切都是未知的。

{第八章}

我很庆幸，与你相逢

/01/

我试着恨你，却想起你的笑容。

我们已经认识了很久很久，久到我可以慢慢开始忘记你了。

再见，路瑾言。

离开这座城市，奔赴新的国度。

坐在飞机的头等舱里，安眠的眼泪毫无征兆地往下掉。坐在她旁边的某国际知名女影星，用余光飞快地瞥了安眠一眼，而后，从容而优雅地从她昂贵的手包里拿出笔，扯过飞机桌上的空白垃圾袋，接着龙飞凤舞地在上面留下了她的亲笔签名。

"给。"是骄傲而清冷的语气。

接过知名女影星递过来的亲笔签名，安眠看着看着，突然就哈哈大笑起来。

你是我遥不可及的梦

这位知名女影星还真的是超级自以为是啊。敢情我安眠在这儿哭哭啼啼地就是为了演一出苦情戏给您看，然后得到这一"珍贵"的亲笔签名吗？

面对这样的自大，安眠连搭理她的心情都没有。放下签名，安眠同样从容而淡定地对女影星说："生活不是演戏，你也没有那么多的观众，谢谢你的签名。"

"狗咬吕洞宾，不识好人心。"女影星气愤地露出了她的本性，转过头对安眠说，"飞机就要起飞了，别哭了，明天我还要通宵拍戏，安静点儿让我睡会儿。"

呵，原来是这般德行。

飞机已经滑到跑道上，美丽可人的空姐提示大家关掉手机、电脑等一切通讯设备。安眠打开手机，输入打了无数次草稿的手机短信，然而选择短信发送。

在飞机冲上云海的刹那，安眠关掉了手机，而后取出手机卡，扔在了垃圾桶里。

之后，再也没拾起。

短信发送至：路瑾言

我试着恨你，却想起你的笑容。

我们已经认识了很久很久，久到我可以慢慢开始忘记你了。

再见，路瑾言。

路瑾言站在机场大厅，看着飞机呼啸而过，轰隆隆的声音通过耳膜灌入他的心里，左心房的位置，突然就产生了空荡荡的冰凉感。

对不起，安眠。

十三个小时的飞行时间，不长也不短。

安眠乘坐的飞机还未抵达美洲大陆，从父亲那儿得知安眠离开这一消息的李嘉禾就沉不住气地跑到路瑾言家以求证实。不过，李嘉禾想要求证的并非是安眠是否真的已经离开这座城市了，他想要求证的是顾昤若和路瑾言，在安眠离开之后会不会在一起。

所以，当他跑到路瑾言家，发现顾昤若和路瑾言同时都不在家后，心立马就拧成了一团麻花。偏偏顾昤若和路瑾言的电话还好巧不巧地同时处于"无法接通"的状态。无奈，着急得足以跟热锅上的蚂蚁媲美的李嘉禾只好回到车里，继续锲而不舍地拨打顾昤若的电话。

终于，在一刻钟后，顾昤若的电话接通了。电话刚接通，李嘉禾劈头盖脑就是一句："路瑾言在不在？"

"李嘉禾，敢情您是打错电话了吧？找路瑾言得打路瑾言的电话呀。"

李嘉禾奸计得逞，大笑两声后，十分满足地问："那，顾小朋友，你现在在哪儿呀？"

"翠园路上。"

"左拐，星巴克。一杯浓缩康宝蓝，十分钟后见。哈哈。"

"怪叔叔，你从火星来的吧，这都什么跟什么啊？"顾昤若不满地说道。

"你懂的……好啦，我开车，回见。"

左拐有个星巴克，帮我点一杯浓缩康宝蓝，十分钟后见面，不见不散。跟着火星人怪叔叔混久了，顾昤若也差不多成了半个不折不扣的小火星妹，不懂才怪了。挂断电话后，顾昤若到星巴克，给李嘉禾点了一杯浓缩康宝蓝，又给自己点了一杯整个店里最便宜的饮品——白开水。翻开钱包，顾昤若发现这个月的开销似乎有点儿大，兼职打工的工资还得过一段时间才会打到她的卡上，她不由得在心里告诫自己：得节约了。

李嘉禾停车的时候，透过玻璃窗看到了顾昤若桌上的白开水，了然于心。

所以，停好车后，李嘉禾推开星巴克的门，便直接到点单处给顾昉若点了一杯卡布奇诺。不过李嘉禾却没有在点完单后就立即来到她的旁边，他知道这样做的话会伤到顾昉若的自尊。

李嘉禾选择一直等在点单处，等到服务员端着卡布奇诺出来，他接过服务员的咖啡和托盘后，才优雅地扮演着服务员的角色踱着步子来到顾昉若的位置。

"这位冰雪聪明、美丽动人的顾小姐，您要的卡布奇诺咖啡。"人未到，声先至。李嘉禾站在顾昉若的后面就开始"吆喝"起来。

"卡布奇诺？我没点呀……不对呀，你怎么知道我姓顾啊？"

转过身，就看到了一脸腹黑、笑意盈盈的李嘉禾，顾昉若很配合地"扑哧"笑出声来。

这样的方式刚刚好。顾昉若对李嘉禾说："谢谢你，怪叔叔。"

"嗯。"

"你找路瑾言有什么事吗？"

"啊！这个，没事，找你也行。"李嘉禾心虚地说道。

"是发生了什么事情吗？"

"听说安眠去美国了，你知道吗？"

"嗯，听路妈妈说了。"

"哦。顾昉若小同学，那……你不会像一条小狼一样扑到路瑾言身边去的，对吧？"

"路瑾言又不是喜洋洋，我干吗扑他啊？而且，我不要当灰太狼。"

"哈哈，那你想当谁？"再一次得逞的李嘉禾得意地大笑道。

"喜羊羊，每天都开开心心，喜感十足。"

"哈哈，嗯。"

"问这些干吗呢，怪叔叔？"

"这不就是随便问问嘛。"

"哦。"

"其实灰太狼也不错的。不过，顾晰若小朋友，你是狼也好，羊也好，你怎么样我都挺喜欢的。"

"哦？"

"哈，我开玩笑的。"

顾晰若低着头，不说话，拿过咖啡勺子一小勺一小勺地舀着杯子里一圈圈浮着的泡沫。其实李嘉禾的心思，顾晰若都已猜到，他这般沉不住气地来找自己，全是因为他害怕，在安眠离开后，她会不顾一切地奔赴到路瑾言的身边。

然而，李嘉禾却想错了。现在的顾晰若早已丢失了当年那份不顾一切的勇气。

现在的她，小心翼翼，患得患失，害怕失去，也害怕在拥有之后仍然还是要失去；现在的她，前进也不行，后退也不行，前进会伤害她在乎的人，后退又会伤害她深爱着的人。所以，她只能安静地待在原地，听天由命。现在的顾晰若需要的是一个出口，一个能够与命运对抗的爆发点。

喝完咖啡，走出星巴克的大门，李嘉禾搭着顾晰若的肩，俨然一副好兄弟的模样，然而他眼神里那些宠爱又心疼的情绪马上就将他出卖了。

有时候，顾晰若也会自私地希望李嘉禾会是自己一辈子的好兄弟好朋友，她喜欢待在他身边，被他霸道地安排着一切，被他细心地呵护着的感觉。可有的时候，顾晰若又希望李嘉禾能够远离自己。他给了她太多美好和温暖，而她除了感动，除了珍惜，除了懂得之外，其他的，她都无法给他。

感动并非心动。

感情的两端，若是不平衡的，伤害必不可免。

/02/

原本拥挤而喧嚣的小世界，因为南西的消逝和安眠的离开，变得空寂而安宁。时光终于收起了它所有尖锐的刺，这些孩子们的世界一点点地趋于安好。

路瑾言的眼疾，也开始慢慢有了好转的迹象。在安眠母亲悉心的照料下，路瑾言眼镜的度数不再升高，眼睛的视力也不再降低。

只是偶尔，在他盯住某个事物看久了的时候，眼前的一切便会由清晰转入模糊。好在安眠离开前和她母亲之间有着约定，如此，路瑾言便不再需要担惊受怕地去其他医院进行检查和护理，也不需要时时刻刻担心着他的父母知道这件事情后会难过和担忧。少了一些心理包袱和压力，这样的情绪状态对于他的眼疾康复有着极大的积极作用。

触目可及的光亮存在，希望便存在。

现在的路瑾言只需要全心相信、全力配合安眠的母亲便好。

那么，与路瑾言朝夕相处的顾昑若同学呢？

从"餐厅失明事件"之后的第二个清晨开始，她就有模有样地当起了路瑾言的家庭小医生。每个清晨起床后的第一件事，不是刷牙，不是洗脸，也不是去厕所蹲大大，而是揉揉眼睛，然后迅速地跑到路瑾言的房间里，在他的眼前比画1、2、3、4等数字让他来猜。等路瑾言全都答对了，她才呵呵呵地拖着她那双吧嗒吧嗒的人字拖满足地去刷牙洗脸。后来，时间久了，路瑾言连看都不用仔细看顾昫若在他面前比画的数字，就能猜到她比画的是什么，因为，顾昫若小同学比画来比画去都逃不开"5、2、0、1、3、1、4"这样的数字排列。

呵，顾昫若小同学还是挺有浪漫情怀的嘛。

有时候，腹黑的路瑾言也会玩心大起地逗逗顾昫若，比如他明明就清楚地看到了她在他面前比画的数字是"3"，却偏偏要吓唬吓唬她，说自己看到的数字是"2"。顾昫若又重复比画了好几遍，路瑾言看着她慢慢浮起水汽的眼睛，才低着头心虚地小声地坚持说："我看到的是2哦。"然后，顾昫若的眼泪就掉下来了。

路瑾言立马就慌了。

"是3是3，我看到的是数字3。"

沉默。

"昫若，我跟你闹着玩的，我看得清清楚楚，是数字3。"

"真的？"

"嗯。"

"那你干吗骗我？"

"就是想看看你为我担心的样子。"

"坏蛋，有病。路瑾言，别以为我哭就是担心你，我刚才是在演戏，我演技不赖吧，你被我骗了。"

"嗯嗯，小影后。"想要宠溺地刮刮她的鼻子，手却停在了半空中。

顾昫若假装没有看到路瑾言的尴尬，笑着对他说："好吧，以后就允许你膜拜影后顾昫若吧。"

可是，嘴上在逞强，笑容浮上脸颊，眼泪却仍然止不住地往下掉。

"路瑾言，以后不要再欺骗我了，好不好？"

"遵命，小影后。"

这样的顾昐若就像是一个患了多疑症的孩子，每天都神经兮兮的。不过，原本顾昐若就是典型的巨蟹座女生，敏感多疑自她出生以来就伴随着她。所以，顾昐若始终都觉得安眠对路瑾言说的那句话——"瑾言，我不要你失明"里藏着许多的秘密，而路瑾言之后的解释，也是模棱两可、含混不清的。虽然此刻路瑾言的眼睛依然清晰明亮，可顾昐若也相信安眠所说的话里有着她自己的理由。

真相远没有这么简单。

所以，"餐厅失明事件"后，顾昐若也开始顺藤摸瓜，寻找起这一切的真相来。当然，这一切都是瞒着路瑾言进行的。

自然，想要知道真相就必须联系身在国外的安眠。然而，等顾昐若和安眠联系上了之后，安眠对于顾昐若想要知道的关于路瑾言的所有事情都一律给予了"我和他已经结束了，请不要再来打扰我"的回复，硬生生地回绝了她。即便顾昐若很坚持很坚持地"缠着"安眠，安眠也只是淡定地劝说顾昐若："别太在乎，也别太挣扎，路瑾言永远都不可能属于你。"

"为什么他永远都不会属于我？"顾昐若问安眠。

"命中注定。认命吧，顾昐若。"安眠回答。

之后，顾昐若再也没有主动联系过安眠，而真相也和顾昐若玩起了捉迷藏的游戏。

2008 年的 7 月，奥运前夕。

一场举国欢庆的盛会即将举行，整个城市变得热闹而喜庆。在这欢天喜地的气氛中，顾昐若也迎来了她十九岁的生日。

路叔叔再次提议一家四口一起去照相馆拍套家庭艺术写真留作纪念。事实上，这个提议，在顾眄若十八岁生日的当天，路叔叔也曾提出来过。只不过，去年的顾眄若因为南西的离开整个人都变得支离破碎的，整颗心都处于揪着的状态，哪里还有什么心思庆祝生日。顾眄若记得，十八岁成人礼的晚上，她和许清木一起在海边哭喊着，宣泄着，也缅怀着南西。也正是在那个晚上，路瑾言决定以哥哥的身份留在顾眄若的身边。大抵，这也是顾眄若在成人礼时，所收到的最完整最宝贵的生日礼物吧。

和上次一样，路叔叔的提议迅速地得到了路妈妈和路瑾言的支持，不同的是，这一次顾眄若点点头，也投了赞同票。

"路叔叔，谢谢。路妈妈，谢谢。路瑾言，谢谢。"

"老婆，瞧这傻孩子，这么客气干吗。快，打电话给照相馆预约拍照时间去。"路叔叔高兴地说。

"好好好。"路妈妈开怀地附和道。

拍照时间预约得十分顺利，去拍照那天的天气却不那么给力。推开门，抬头望天空，十足的一幅水墨画。浅绿色的水墨用淡淡的线条勾勒，一点点沿着天空的轮廓蔓延；墨绿色的浓墨则是大片大片地铺满整个视野，连同无边的远方，一同无止境地蔓延着。

倾盆大雨，蓄势待发。

好在，这一场大雨是在这一家四口到达照相馆之后才落下的。不过，这一场大雨，却也导致了照相馆里的人异常的多。为了避免麻烦和重新预约时间，大多数客人都临时将外景拍摄改成了室内拍摄，如此一来，更衣室和化妆间里就变得拥挤许多。所以，当路叔叔和路妈妈已经换好衣服准备进行拍摄时，顾眄若还等在更衣室门口。

🌢

摄影棚内，在摄影师的建议下，路家夫妇两人先拍了夫妇系列的照片，而顾昕若那边则交给路瑾言去催促催促。路瑾言快步走到女生更衣室门口，却不见排队的人，心里突然担心地一紧，立马走到帘布前，紧张地朝里面喊了一声："顾昕若！"

更衣室里的女生傻傻地回答道："有。"路瑾言笑笑，悬着的心放松了。

"衣服换好了吗？得开始拍了呢。"

"很快了，很快了，这个衣服的拉链有点儿麻烦，等我一下，很快了啊。"

"拉链怎么了？"

"好像卡住了。"

"那，我来帮你吧。"

"可是……你是男生我是女生啊。我自己弄就好啦。"

"没关系，我是你哥哥。"路瑾言说这句话的时候，已经拉开门帘，走到了顾昕若的身后。顾昕若不自然地移动了下步子，路瑾言却不管不顾地将手移到她裙子背部的拉链上，而后将卡在拉链里的布料扯出来，再顺利地将拉链拉好。

"好了，我们走吧。"

"谢谢。"

毕竟不是亲哥哥，毕竟是喜欢着的人，顾昕若转身欲走的时候，因为着急和害羞，路瑾言还没走，她就先移动了步子，而结果就是，她的头直接撞到了路瑾言的前胸。她仓促地抬起头想要逃跑，却又直直地对上了路瑾言的眼睛。

就这样，彼此静静地凝视着对方。

他温暖如斯的眼底藏着许多的宠溺和温情，此刻的眼神，却是炙热的，进攻的。

她笑眼弯弯的眼角藏着许多的喜爱和信任，此刻的眼神，却是娇羞的，期待的。

然而，就在顾晞若欲闭上眼的瞬间，路瑾言向她伸出了双手："晞若，你真美。走吧，爸妈还在等我们。"

这一幕，仿若最初，他将手伸向了她。这一幕，又不同于最初，路瑾言说"爸妈还在等我们"时的口气，多像是儿子带着小媳妇去见公婆的口气。所以，当一家四口拍全家福，摄影师说老夫妻和小夫妻都很相配时，顾晞若忍不住附到路妈妈的耳边，小声地对她说："路妈妈，我真希望在我长大嫁人，穿上真正意义上的婚纱时，能亲口喊你一声妈妈。"是真正意义上的妈妈。

之后收到的相册里，全家福上的一家四口好比真正有着血缘关系的亲人，温馨至极。而顾晞若与路瑾言两个人的合照，也如摄影师所说，"不像兄妹，而像是一对甜蜜的小夫妻"。这一幕，很久很久以后，顾晞若想起来，都会感伤。

始终是不被上天眷顾的孩子，那么勇敢，那么努力，仍然无法得到这一份温暖而完整的爱。

八月九日，奥运会开幕式之后的第一天，随着奥运会比赛的开始，这个城市的温度空前高涨，高温天气席卷全城。路瑾言的父母决定搬到乡下去避避暑，休养一段时间，一封重要的信件也是时候公开了。

四个人的家庭会议，气氛显得有些沉重。路瑾言的父亲想要缓和一下气氛，便给每个人倒了一杯白开水，倒完水之后他咳了几声，清清嗓，而后，拿起面前的信交给顾晞若。

"晞若，这是你父亲顾之淳同志留给你的信。其他的，我们也不多说，你自己看，自己体会。你父亲顾之淳同志还是很爱你的。为人父的心情，我很清楚。"路叔叔说道。

"嗯，谢谢路叔叔。"

“那个，对了，旆若啊，你称呼路瑾言的母亲为路妈妈，称呼我为路叔叔，这样其实是不对的。”

“哎呦，老公，旆若也是因为她父亲的原因才这样的嘛，你理解下啊。”路妈妈解释道。

“我也是希望听到旆若喊我一声路爸爸嘛，我和你一直都想要一个女儿，旆若现在就是我们的女儿。”

“路叔叔，我……”

“想喊的时候再喊吧，回房间看信吧。”路妈妈通情达理地说道。

“嗯。”

拧开床头的小台灯，暖黄的光亮洒满整个房间。顾旆若靠坐在床边看着父亲写给自己的信，整整十多页。这是顾旆若第一次仔细看顾之淳写的字，大大方方，真是一笔好字。而这也是第一次，顾之淳那么直接地将真实而充满感情的自己袒露在顾旆若面前。

顾旆若母亲的离开，对重感情的双鱼座的顾之淳来说，整个世界都在那一瞬间完全崩溃了。因为失去了最心爱的女人，悲恸万分，自然对孩子便无暇顾及。所以，那段时间，顾之淳对待顾旆若是无心的，冷淡的，以及不知所措的。与其说顾之淳是恨着顾旆若的，倒不如说他是不知道该怎样面对孩子，面对未来，而顾旆若一开始就误会了顾之淳。

后来，顾之淳的情绪和生活慢慢回归正轨，他努力与顾旆若靠近，却遭到了顾旆若的排斥。她小小的心灵受到了伤害，所以她拒绝和顾之淳靠近，甚至连顾之淳抱她一下她都会躲开。久而久之，父女两个的距离也被拉开了，而顾之淳也越来越不知道应该如何处理他和自己孩子之间的关系。男人本就要粗心一些，而那时候的顾旆若又那么小，父女之间谁都不懂要如何去经营这一份感情，只能任由其恶化。

不可否认的唯有爱，一直存在着的爱。

顾昐若爱着顾之淳，而顾之淳也爱着顾昐若。

每一次顾昐若晚上外出，顾之淳其实都是十分担心的。时间晚一点儿，顾之淳就会站在小区大门外的马路边等着顾昐若，等到顾昐若进入小区大门后，他才放心地回到家里，打开电视，安静地看着搞笑的娱乐综艺节目。然而这些，在顾昐若的眼里，却成为了不管不顾，不闻不问。而其实，多年独身的顾之淳只是不知该如何表达。

到后来，顾之淳失去了稳定的工作，为了顾昐若的学费，他不得不同时兼几份职，以至于有一次还晕倒在路边。可是为了不让顾昐若担心，顾之淳在医院扯掉了吊着药水的针管，按时回到了家。而这些，顾昐若从来都不知道。

"有其父必有其女，原来扯针管这事在我们家是有先例的。"顾昐若在心里默念道。

信好长好长，夜好深好深。

顾昐若闭上眼将头靠在床边的墙壁上，这一次，她没有哭，因为，她知道顾之淳不希望看到她哭。所以，她将眼泪全部流入了心里。信件中顾之淳终于说出了自己所有真实的情感，顾昐若第一次感觉到父爱如山，深沉而伟岸。顾之淳信尾那一句"女儿，我爱你"，从此也深深地刻入了顾昐若的心里。

然时光不可倒流，唯有珍惜当下。

墙壁上的时针已经指向十一点半，顾昐若也不管现在到底有多晚，甚至于她连拖鞋都没穿就跑到路瑾言父母的房间里，只为对他们说一句："路爸爸，路妈妈，晚安。"

🌢

/03/

从今以后，无论是顺境或逆境，富足或贫穷，健康或疾病，忧伤或喜乐，我都将爱护顾昉若、珍惜顾昉若、保护顾昉若。守护在她的身边，终此一生。

宣誓人：李嘉禾

见证人：路瑾言

生效日期：_____

这样一份矫情的书面保证书，是在李嘉禾和路瑾言之间签订的。

时间大约还得追溯到李嘉禾和顾昉若在餐厅碰到安眠和路瑾言之后，李嘉禾单独找路瑾言谈话那会儿。整份保证书的中心内容就是路瑾言将顾昉若交给了李嘉禾照顾，李嘉禾必须在未来的日子里守护好顾昉若。可是，这样的一份书面保证书事实上是不具备法律效力的。这一纸协议，不过是李嘉禾和路瑾言两人之间的口头约定而已。

顾昉若不是东西，也不是专属于路瑾言的私人物品？凭什么交给他来自由处置，凭什么由他决定李嘉禾应该守护顾昉若？可是，对于这样一份保证书，李嘉禾又舍不得将其撕掉，又或者揉成团扔掉。从另一个方面来说，这最起码也是路瑾言不跟自己争抢顾昉若的一个证明吧。

李嘉禾从来都不是自卑的人，平日里的他虽行事做人都颇为低调，但实际上他的自负也是天生具备的，可到了顾昉若这儿，就什么都变了。

比如以前的李嘉禾只会喜欢像芊芊那般温婉可人、眉清目秀、公主般的女孩子；比如他以前绅士优雅，对每个女生都好，现在除了顾昕若几乎完全"不近女色"；再比如之前的他绝对不会为了一个女人而跟其他男人争风吃醋；总而言之，言而总之，以前的李嘉禾是女孩眼中的"万人迷""大众情人"，现在却好似已经成为了顾昕若的"专属情人"。

顾昕若打电话给李嘉禾的时候，他正拿着这份文件左看右看，文件的生效日期一直都是空白的，李嘉禾心想："路瑾言这家伙，什么时候把这日期给填上啊，这一直空白着，不会是搞这么一份文件忽悠我吧。"

"李嘉禾，干吗呢？这么久才接电话。"

"顾昕若小同学，是不是想我了呀？"

"是是是，想你了。"

"看吧，这招就叫欲擒故纵，我要是立马接了你的电话，你就不会发现你想我了吧。"

"唉，怪叔叔，最近又去火星修炼了一段时间才回来吧？"

"哈哈，找我有什么事吗？"

"嗯，见面说吧。"

"成，我开车来接你，你在哪儿呢？"

家里。

顾昕若整理好东西准备出门的时候，路瑾言正在客厅张贴幸福的家庭艺术照。顾昕若路过客厅的时候，路瑾言举起手中的照片给她看。

"昕若，你穿婚纱裙真好看。"

"你已经说过一次啦，路先生。"

"你结婚的时候一定会是最美丽的新娘。"

"我可还是未婚单身女青年的，不要污蔑我哦。"

"我看楼下那等你的小同志挺不错的。"

顾昕若的语气突然变得冰冷起来："你真希望我和李嘉禾在一起？"

"嗯。哥不会看错的。"

"那行，我现在就去告诉他，我要跟他在一起，我们会很幸福的。"

"昕若，祝你幸福。"

"谢谢。"

"莫名其妙，神经搭错线！"顾昕若边下楼边气愤地碎碎念着。

李嘉禾刚想开心地跟顾昕若打招呼，就看到她摆着一张苦瓜脸，可是，走到他旁边的时候她却又亲密地挽住了他的手，只不过脸上的表情仍然没有转换过来。

还真是诚实的孩子呢。

李嘉禾很配合地将顾昕若的手牵住，两人立马十指紧扣。路瑾言站在阳台上，将这一切全部收入眼底，嘴角微笑的弧度渐渐凝固成悲伤。

车内，已经松开手的两人，默契地选择了沉默。车子行驶五分钟之后，李嘉禾终于忍不住开口打破沉默。

"刚才电话里说有事找我，是什么事呢？"

"帮我调查一件事，找一个人。"

"嗯。说说看事情的来龙去脉。"

事实上，顾之淳留给顾昕若的不仅仅是一封信件，还有一本顾之淳的日记本。

日记本里不仅表露了顾之淳对女儿隐藏至深的爱，同时也将十多年前妻子所遭遇的那一场车祸的真实面目原原本本地呈现在了顾昕若的面前。

当年六岁的孩子只知道车子撞过来，母亲便离开了世界，哪里知道这一场车祸实际上是人为的酒后驾驶所造成的。其实，事情的来龙去脉说来也就这么几句话，最终肇事司机受到了法律的制裁，而受到伤害的家庭也得到了一大笔的赔偿金，这些内容当年的新闻都有报道。然而，藏在这些"官方处理"背后的却是一再的"宽容大度"。当年这一场酒后驾驶撞人事件在伤亡程度上是非常严重的，并且肇事司机在撞到人后，最初选择的是逃逸，而非承担责任。可法律处理上，肇事司机却得到了一再的从轻处理，甚至是不断地减刑。

车祸的真相，顾之淳是不希望顾昑若知道的，他不愿顾昑若在知道真相后去怨去恨。所以，这么多年，即便顾之淳知道真相，可是为了给女儿平淡安宁的生活，他选择了隐忍。这样的一本私人日记原本也并不是顾之淳留给顾昑若的，而是慈善幼儿园的负责人在整理顾之淳遗物时找到的，便将其一并交给了路瑾言的母亲，于是，阴差阳错地，又一并交给了顾昑若。

"昑若，也许顾叔叔并不希望你查清楚整件事。"

"可是我已经知道了。"

"那行，我现在就给管家打电话，他人脉广，查起来快。"

"谢谢。"

顾之淳的想法，顾昑若是懂的。所以她不会去恨去抱怨，但是，她会查清楚整个事件，也会找到当年的肇事司机。顾昑若想要的，其实很简单，一个真心的道歉，一个诚心的祈祷，仅此而已。若得不到，她心里的那道坎，也是无法逾越的……

城市的另一端。

上一秒还嘱咐顾昑若让她好好和李嘉禾在一起，下一秒站在蒂芙尼巨幅海报前，又忍不住将顾昑若约到这家首饰店里来的路瑾言，真的是不怎么懂得诚实面对自己内心的人。

明明说好放手，可实际操作起来，却好像比登天还要难。

美国珠宝和银饰公司蒂芙尼在 2005 年的时候曾经推出过一款名为"Paloma's Tenderness Heart"的情侣半心戒指，该公司对这对戒指的推广做出了"不能相聚的遥望也成为一种爱恋语言"的解释，并同时赋予了这对戒指很美的寓意。

我很庆幸，与你相逢。无法企及的永恒的爱。

顾昑若尤其喜欢"我很庆幸，与你相逢"这八个字。她曾经送过一个刺绣给路瑾言，上面的图案和字样都是顾昑若一针一线亲自绣的，而整块刺绣的字样就是这八个字。

2008 年的 7 月 6 日，世界亲吻日。城市北端的蒂芙尼专卖店正打着情侣的主意如火如荼地进行着各种优惠活动。路瑾言给顾昑若打电话的时候，就正好站在蒂芙尼专卖店门口"SWEET&KISS"的巨幅海报前。十分钟后，路瑾言就瞧见顾昑若气喘吁吁地赶过来了。

奔赴所爱之人的"约会"，顾昑若毫不掩饰她的开心和急不可待。

"伸出手，闭上眼。"路瑾言下命令道。

"嘿，是不是要送礼物给我呀？"

"乖乖闭眼。"

"唔，好吧。"

下一瞬，一枚闪闪发着银光的戒指套上了顾昑若的无名指，指间的皮肤立马感受到了微凉的触感，内心却是无比雀跃的。

"呀，这个戒指真好看，谢谢。"末了，顾昑若又贼笑着问路瑾言，"这戒指该不会是一对情侣对戒吧？"

被猜中心思的路瑾言心虚地将话题转移开："这鬼天气，阴沉沉的，怕是要下大雨了。"然后不等顾昁若反应过来，就撇下她，大摇大摆地往大街上走去。

夏日的天气，真像是一个情绪多变的孩子，顷刻之间，骤雨倾盆。路瑾言拉起顾昁若的手跑到街边小店铺的走廊下躲雨。长长的狭窄的走廊里挤满了躲雨的人，路瑾言和顾昁若只好一前一后地往前挪着步子，偶尔，顾昁若会调皮地将手伸到走廊外，屋檐上的雨水就滴到了她的掌心上。

到达街尾转角的地方时，路瑾言突然停下脚步，想确认一下，调皮的顾昁若是否还跟在他的身后，转身的瞬间，却忽略了仍在前行中的顾昁若，于是，她的头撞到了他的胸口。两个人的距离异常的靠近，差一点儿就碰到了彼此的嘴唇。

时间戛然停止。

连路瑾言的心跳几乎都要停止。

而后，顾昁若踮起脚尖，闭上双眼，将她的唇贴上了路瑾言的唇。路瑾言下意识地揽住顾昁若的腰，才发现她的身体一直在微微地颤抖着。像是得到了一颗珍贵的糖果，路瑾言轻轻地吸吮起来。

原来这就是接吻的感觉。

凉凉的，甜甜的。

这一瞬间，顾昁若却哭了，路瑾言心疼地将她的每一颗眼泪都吻进了自己心里。

在美好的时候戛然停止，也算是对于爱情的一种最美的定格吧。

所以，亲吻之后，顾昁若和路瑾言谁都没有再提起这个亲吻，也没有开口说"我爱你"或是"我们在一起"。后来，顾昁若才知道，这样的一枚银戒指耗费了路瑾言在整个暑假兼职赚到的所有钱。那时的路瑾言只是希望，有生之年，他能够努力满足顾昉若的所有愿望，将所有她喜欢的东西都买给她。

一切，好像只能是这样。

可是，人的欲望却是无止境的，尤其是在爱情面前。

明明最开始只是想要一个拥抱，得到的却是亲吻，于是想要的也变得越来越多。顾昉若不是贪心的人，却是无比缺乏安全感的人。这种说不清道不明的暧昧关系，她从来都不喜欢。那么，再赌一次吧。

倾注所有真心和勇气地赌一次。

街角的音像店里，范晓萱真真切切地在唱着："我要我们在一起，不像现在只能这样遥远地唱着你……"

——我要我们在一起。

自从这样的想法从顾昉若的脑袋里蹦出来之后，她在第一时间想到的人居然是李嘉禾而非路瑾言。顾昉若想要与之在一起的人当然还是路瑾言，可是对于一直守护在她身边，一直默默为她付出的李嘉禾，她又该怎样去面对？

顾昉若想要和李嘉禾继续保持友好关系，甚至是亲密的好朋友关系，可这样做未免又太自私。单方面地选择远离和淡出他的视线，这样做对李嘉禾似乎又不太公平。其实，无论顾昉若怎么做，对李嘉禾的伤害都是不可避免的。

然而，就在顾昉若内心十分矛盾，完全无法做出决定的时候，一直处于调查中的酒驾事件，终于有了一些眉目，而这些眉目所呈现出来的部分真相，则直接逼迫顾昉若做出了她这辈子最难做的一个决定。

那就是，抛弃李嘉禾。

冬至日，冷空气席卷而来。

顾昉若将李嘉禾约到学校附近的奶茶店，她知道直接无理由地让李嘉禾停止参与酒驾事件的调查是不可能的。他聪明，洞察力超强，不打破砂锅问到底才怪。说不定，触到了李嘉禾那反叛的心理，酒驾事件的真相反而会更快地呈现在他面前。

这是万万不能的。

无数次的挣扎和思考后，顾昑若最终选择了最极端也是最偏执的方式——欺骗。

"因为我已经不再需要真相，因为我已经拥有了路瑾言。拥有了他，我就等于拥有了全世界，其他的东西，都不再重要。嘉禾，我们停止调查吧，我不再需要它了。"

最初，顾昑若是不愿靠近阳光而帅气的李嘉禾的，却也是在最初，轻而易举地就被他可爱而明媚的个性所吸引。这样的温度和感情是刚刚好适合做知己的，却也是无法逾越的。比友情多一点，比爱情少一点的暧昧注定不会甜蜜，只会伤人。

如若不爱，就拒绝，就放手，不再牵绊，彻彻底底地结束吧。

"因为有了路瑾言，所以一切都可以变得不重要。顾昑若，你还真是冷漠啊。"李嘉禾回应道。

"我和路瑾言，好不容易才走到一起，当然要好好珍惜当下所拥有的一切。"

"连你交朋友的权利路瑾言都剥夺了吗？"

"嘉禾，如果你愿意，我们仍然可以是朋友。"

"呵！"李嘉禾冷笑道，"朋友？顾昑若，我和你之间的关系，就一直都只是朋友吗？"

"是的，只是朋友。"控制住情绪，顾昑若故作淡定地回答。

"那依我看，从今以后，我们也不需要再维持这份所谓的朋友关系了。你有路瑾言，全世界都可以抛弃的，不是吗？"

"那么，从今以后，我的生活你也不需要再介入了。"

"还真是决绝啊。这样的你，我还真的是第一次认识到。顾晡若，隐藏不浅啊。"李嘉禾气愤地说道。

"嘉禾，我很感谢你，陪我走了一段很长的路。"

"可是，现在你只需要路瑾言，不是吗？晡若，我最后问你，是不是就算我下一秒立刻就与芊芊和好如初，你也不会在乎，也不会感到一丝丝的遗憾？"

简言之，李嘉禾这句话的意思就是——你有没有一点点地爱过我。顾晡若深吸一口气，冷淡地说："那很好，祝你和芊芊幸福。"

"老板，结账。"

李嘉禾拿钱，起身，离开，一点儿都不拖沓。

有人曾说过，分手后还能做朋友的两个人，要么是没爱过，要么就是没忘过。虽然李嘉禾和顾晡若不曾是情侣关系，但对他们来说这个道理却是适用的。霸道自负的李嘉禾，怎么会在顾晡若说出如此狠心的话之后，还苦苦地哀求她两人要做朋友？

既然是结束，那当然就是最彻底最决绝的结束。顾晡若早已猜到会是这个结局。

而其实，关于顾晡若母亲的酒驾事件，随着时间的推移也已经查出了许多的内幕，肇事司机也已经被找到。然而，这件事却像是一个不断在翻滚着的雪球，越是查到后面，牵扯的人和事也越多。令人无法接受的是，这则案件中，也牵扯到了李嘉禾的父亲。

一旦多年前的这桩酒驾事件再次被公开，李嘉禾的父亲包庇罪犯的罪证也会被一同公开。

顾昀若知道，只有彻底离开，一切真相才可以被雪藏起来。所以，她被迫选择了这个极度偏激的方式——与李嘉禾绝交。彻彻底底地让他淡出她的生活，顾昀若也彻底地用她的方式保护着这个很爱很爱过她的男人。

——怪叔叔，谢谢你，曾经带给我许多的美好。

推开奶茶店的大门，顾昀若跌坐在路过，不顾形象地大哭起来……

/04/

时针依旧在向前转动。

农历新年的前夕，大红灯笼高高挂，每家每户都洋溢着喜庆。

顾昀若原本不是迷信之人，这个时刻，却想要趁着这股喜庆之气，赌一赌，告个白。于是她便去市集上买来了灯笼、春联、录音娃娃，来到公寓里精心地布置了一番。等一切准备就绪，才打电话给路瑾言，邀约男主角。

"在哪儿呢?"

"倪斯的清吧。"

"在那儿干吗?"

"和倪斯聊天。"

"哦。聊什么呀?"

"聊你。"

"怎么突然会聊到我呀?"

"因为我想要多了解你一点儿。倪斯和你一起长大的，我想从他这里多知道一些你的事。"

电话这头的顾眄若，脸立刻羞红一片，心里突然就有了预感：今天的告白会成功吧！她趴倒在床上，捂着被子呵呵地唱着："我要我们在一起……"

顾眄若拿着亲自给路瑾言织的围巾，来到了倪斯的清吧。推开门，映入她眼帘的人却是李嘉禾和芊芊，看他们气势汹汹的表情，好像是在质问着倪斯的女朋友徐清雅什么。

"怎么回事呀？"顾眄若问道。

路瑾言摇摇头："他们刚来，听听看。"

原来，李嘉禾当初和芊芊之所以会分手全是源于一场阴谋，而策划整个阴谋的人就是徐清雅。徐清雅的妹妹徐清婉一直都喜欢着李嘉禾，却因为个性文静胆小，就将这份喜欢一直深埋在自己的心里了。在姐姐徐清雅的鼓励下，她好不容易鼓起勇气向李嘉禾告白，得到的结果却是李嘉禾冰冷冷的拒绝和芊芊指桑骂槐的侮辱和警告，徐清婉十多年纯真的心意在瞬间破灭。

争强好胜的徐清雅自然是咽不下这口气的，于是编了一个谎言，玩了一场文字游戏，演了一出好戏。哪知芊芊和李嘉禾信以为真，真的分了手。

"说到底，还是你们的感情不牢固。如果当时你们对彼此多一点儿信任的话，事情也不会如我所愿。"徐清雅辩解道。

"如果不是你，我就不会和李嘉禾分手，不和李嘉禾分手，我就不会伤害张鹏，不会到现在才明白我忘不掉李嘉禾。到现在了，你还是一点儿都不知错吗？"

"芊芊，你可别血口喷人。如果当初不是你在我妹妹告白后，瞒着李嘉禾将她当众羞辱了一番，事情也不至于闹到那步田地。现在李嘉禾在这里，你就装好人，装可怜，你可真虚伪。说到这儿，李嘉禾啊，你还真要感谢我，这女人可不值得你爱。"

"那你说，谁才值得我爱，你温柔的妹妹徐清婉，还是热情大胆的你？你写给我的情书，里面的内容我还记得。"李嘉禾说。

心底的秘密被突然揭发，被赤裸裸地羞辱，徐清雅拿起桌上的一杯水朝着李嘉禾泼去："你无耻！"

站在一旁的倪斯再也看不下去了："各位，抱歉了。倪某没有调教好自家老婆，今天献丑了。大家都是朋友，望不计较。今天我请客，大家尽情地吃。"

"倪斯，你这话什么意思呀？"徐清雅不满地问倪斯。

"别闹了，你还嫌丢脸丢得不够？"

"丢脸？倪斯，你老婆我被人欺负，你不帮忙就算了，你胳膊肘还往外拐。是不是因为今天顾昕若在这儿？你不是怕我给你丢脸，是怕扫了她的兴吧。姓倪的，我告诉你，我早看出来你跟这小妖精有一腿了，什么从小一块儿长大，明明就是从小一块儿勾搭！装什么纯啊，我呸，老娘不吃这一套！"

啪！

倪斯一个耳光利索地朝徐清雅扇去。

"道歉，给昕若道歉。"

徐清雅怒视倪斯，抄起酒桌上的瓶子就往他的头上砸："道歉？你等下辈子吧！"

都说如今无论是酒吧还是清吧里的保安个个都是有背景的，出来喝的混的才是凡人，有背景的保安哪里是他们得罪得起的？所以，当老板倪斯冲着他店里的保安大喊"保安，保安，把这个疯女人给我拉走"的时候，徐清雅只是冰冷地朝他笑着说："倪斯，你别忘了，这里所有的保安都是跟我爸混的。"

眼下，谁也不肯示弱，徐清雅更是恨不得将李嘉禾和倪斯这些臭男人通通碎尸万段。柔弱的芊芊跟张鹏待久了，难免也沾染了一些江湖气息，她拿起酒瓶，参与到了这场乱战中。坐在一旁的顾昐若和路瑾言出于帮助朋友的目的，也被迫加入了进去。

扭打，嘶喊，拳头飞舞，无数酒瓶被砸碎……

混乱中，保安一个个身手敏捷；混乱中，芊芊喊着李嘉禾的名字；混乱中，路瑾言保护着顾昐若；混乱中，顾昐若将原本砸向保安的酒瓶砸到了路瑾言脸上，架在他鼻梁上的眼镜镜片瞬间碎裂……

"对不起，你有没有伤到哪里？疼不疼？"顾昐若紧张地询问道。

"我没事。"

"瑾言，你转过脸，让我看看有没有伤到。"

"都说了我没事。"

"是不是伤到了哪里？对不起啊，我不是故意的。"

"你跟李嘉禾先回去，我脚崴到了，晚点儿再回去。"

"我不要回去，我要跟你一起回去。"

"你烦不烦啊。"

"脚崴到了对不对？那让我看看，疼不疼啊？"顾昐若说着就走向路瑾言。

"走开啊，还嫌不够灾星啊。"

"我……对不起，我真的不是故意的。"

"走啊。"路瑾言凶狠地将顾昐若推开。

"瑾言，对不起。"

"走啊，顾昐若。每一次都是不小心，每一次都是意外，每一次都是因为你我灾难重重，你这辈子肯定是我的灾星。走吧，我再也不想见到你。"闭上眼，路瑾言说出了这辈子他最违心最心痛的谎话，"离开我，好让灾难也远离我，求你了。”

顾晞若忍住汹涌而出的眼泪，跌跌撞撞冲到了大街上，过往车辆的喇叭像是失去了控制，刺耳的声音充斥着世界。

清吧里，李嘉禾挣脱开芊芊的手，抱歉地对她说：“我不能丢下她不管。”之后，便追了出来。

顾晞若跑到路瑾言熟悉的地方“躲”起来，路瑾言却没有追出来。李嘉禾找到顾晞若时，她正蹲坐在地上，反复地念叨着：“我害怕你不会来找我，害怕你会找不到我。所以，我找了一个你能够找到我的地方‘躲’起来，可是最终你还是没有来。”

李嘉禾将难过的顾晞若带到公寓，却在开门的瞬间，将顾晞若精心准备的“告白惊喜”的开关打开了。录音娃娃里立刻传来了顾晞若亲自录给路瑾言的语音告白。

多讽刺的一幕。

顾晞若的眼泪汹涌而出。哭累了，好不容易睡着，却在半夜又突然惊醒，央求李嘉禾送她回家。回家后发现家里空无一人，又央求李嘉禾带着她去找路瑾言。

凌晨两点，二十四小时营业的便利店里，一遍一遍地循环播放着：“我在过马路，你人在哪里……”

顾晞若也一遍一遍地在这样深黑的夜色里寻找着路瑾言……

我曾拥有你，想到就心酸

/01/

最终，顾晰若还是没有找到路瑾言。

天微微亮的时候，李嘉禾的电话响了。电话那头的父亲质问他为何一夜未归，同时告知了他所有出国的手续都已经办好。而实际上，去往日本这个决定也是李嘉禾主动向父亲提出来的，就在顾晰若彻底和李嘉禾摊牌，决心结束所有的那一天。

寂静的清晨，电话两头的对话，顾晰若听得清清楚楚。

李嘉禾要离开这里，离开自己。

这座城市，终究会沦为一座空城。

最终，顾晰若决定搬离路瑾言家，暂时去公寓住一段时间。

来拿行李的那天，路瑾言仍然不在家，路瑾言的父母也只是说："安眠回来了，他在安眠那儿。"好像只一瞬间，顾昉若便完全醒悟过来。从一开始，路瑾言就是安眠的，最终，也还是要还给她的。这段时间的美好和心伤，终究不过是一场梦。

顾昉若简单地和路爸爸路妈妈拥抱了一下，相互道了个别，然后就离开了路瑾言家。以后还是会来看他们的，对于路爸爸和路妈妈，顾昉若有着尽孝道的责任。

顾昉若离开后的那个晚上，她做了一个梦，梦里她和路瑾言结婚了。婚礼上到处都是她和路瑾言上次一起拍下的合照，梦里，所有来参加婚礼的来宾都称赞他们：真般配的一对。

明明是美好的梦，顾昉若醒来时却感到莫名的心慌。

/02/

眼科医院里。

安眠问她的母亲："我们是不是做错了？"

"不是你的错，这一切都是顾昉若造成的。"

"可是，你知道，就算没有顾昉若，按照我们的原计划发展，路瑾言的眼睛也会失明的。"

"眠眠，现在是顾昉若误将酒瓶砸到了路瑾言的头上，玻璃碎片跌入眼睛里，才导致了他的失明，不是你的错。"

"从一开始我们就隐瞒了路瑾言视力一直下降的事实，不是吗？妈妈，我现在好害怕，害怕路瑾言会知道这一切，害怕他会再次离开我。"

"冷静点儿，眠眠。这不是你的错。如果非要说是什么错了的话，那就是爱情错了，都是因为爱。换个角度，我问你，现在路瑾言已经失明了，并且很有可能永远都好不了了，这样的话，你还是爱着他的吗？"

"爱。"

"那么，孩子，我们所做的一切都值了。"

"妈，谢谢你……"

"傻孩子，你这么爱他，我跟你爸爸连反对你和路瑾言在一起都不忍心。眠眠，从现在开始，你要清楚，这段时间，路瑾言的视力一直都恢复得很好，没有下降的趋势，他眼睛之所以会突然失明，全都是因为顾昕若的酒瓶砸到了他。这一切都是顾昕若造成的，清楚了吗？"

安眠："清楚了。"

此时此刻，在医院的另一间病房里。

躺在安眠母亲办公室隔壁房间病床上的路瑾言，脑海里一直浮现着在倪斯清吧里发生的种种场景。他清清楚楚地记得是他亲手用力将顾昕若推离了自己的身边，也是他朝她大声吼着赶她走的，更是他决绝地不留任何余地地对她说——以后再也不想见到你。

——宁愿将你彻底伤到底，也不愿你看到失去光明的我。

酒瓶砸下来的瞬间，路瑾言清晰地听见玻璃镜片碎裂的声音，以及顾昕若带着担心和害怕的哭音。想要转过身，微笑着告诉她："别担心，我没事。"可是，细碎而微小的玻璃碎碴儿却已经猝不及防地跌入到他的眼睛内，甚至于，他已经能够感觉到眼睛内部的血液正在沸腾地想要冲向外面。

眼睛很痛，心也很痛。

之后，经过详细的检查和诊断后，最终，路瑾言的双眼被确诊完全失明。

路瑾言的母亲在得知这一消息的时候伤心地直接晕厥了过去，而路爸爸的双眼也蒙上了一层血丝，在一夜间苍老了许多。

病房里，路瑾言的父母看着病床上眼睛蒙着厚厚的白纱布却依然充满笑容的宝贝儿子，整颗心都酸透了。虽然一直都知道自己家的孩子与其他的小孩是不同的，在他的世界里，所有的事物都要透过厚厚的玻璃镜片才能够看得清晰，可至少，当光芒靠近的时候，他的眼里仍然是充满光明的。而现在，睁开眼和闭着眼对他来说都是毫无差别的。

"对不起，都是我们的错，是我们给了你一双这样的眼睛。"路妈妈伤心到怪罪起自己来。

"妈妈，你还记得你曾经跟我说过什么吗？"

"？"

"你说，眼睛是心灵的窗口，即使有一天眼睛会失去光明和色彩，可是心不能封闭起来。只要心没有封闭起来，光明和色彩就是存在的，希望也是存在的。"

"好孩子，好孩子……"

"好了好了，老路啊，瑾言这孩子这么懂事，你们也该感到欣慰啊。这人啊，不怕生病，就怕生病了自暴自弃。瑾言现在能够保持这样的心态，对他视力的恢复就是最好的良药。放心吧，还有我在呢。眠眠这么担心瑾言，我又怎么能让眠眠失望呢？"安眠的母亲安慰路瑾言的父母道。

"那，现在的情况是还有恢复的可能？这个几率大概是多少？"路瑾言的父亲进一步询问道。

"我找来了这里最专业最权威的眼科医生给瑾言做的检查，诊断显示，由于跌入的玻璃碎片细小尖锐，导致他的眼角膜受到伤害，加之瑾言从小就患有先天性的弱视，视力的恢复对他来说一直都是一个大难题。我现在的打算是先带他去国外看看，国外的技术比国内的先进，应该能够得到更好的治疗。"

"眼角膜受到损害，那是不是要换眼角膜？把我的眼角膜换给他，你看可以吗？反正我也活了大半辈子了，看得见看不见都没有关系，可孩子的人生才刚刚开始，这一瞎，什么前途都没有了啊。"路瑾言的母亲拉住安眠母亲的手，急切地哀求道，"用我的眼角膜，将我的眼角膜移植到瑾言的眼睛上吧！"

"妈……我不要你移植眼角膜给我……"

"唉，我国法律有明确的规定，任何活着的人在生前都不可以捐献自己的眼角膜，因为眼角膜捐献了眼睛也就看不见了，成了残疾人，这是有悖道德伦理的，所以不允许。但是可以填写捐献眼角膜的意向书，在死后将眼角膜捐献出来。所以，你们谁都不能给瑾言移植眼角膜。瑾言出事的时候，安眠这孩子还跟我吵着闹着要把她的眼角膜捐给瑾言呢。"

"妈……说这个干吗？"安眠嗔怪母亲道。

"那我们现在应该怎么办？"路瑾言的父亲问。

"一方面，先带瑾言去国外治疗，寻求其他的解决方案；另一方面，备案等待愿意捐献眼角膜的人。虽然眼库中心的眼角膜非常稀缺，成功的几率不大，但是任何一种办法我们都应该试试。就现在瑾言的情况来看，他还算幸运的，因为，解决的办法不单单只有死等眼角膜的捐献这一种。"

"安医生，谢谢，我们家瑾言遇到你，真是他三生有幸啊。孩子，来，快谢谢阿姨。"

"阿姨，谢谢你。"

"安眠一直都很担心你，这几天，她眼睛都没合上，一直陪着你做检查。我现在先带你父母去办下各种手续，你和她好好聊聊。孩子，保持好的心态，一切都会好起来的，啊。"

"嗯，谢谢阿姨。"

病房内，路瑾言凭着听力，朝安眠所在的方向张开了双手，安眠了然地靠近他，两个人拥抱在一起。

"谢谢你，小眠。"

"傻瓜。"

"傻瓜欢迎你回来。"

"我爱你，傻瓜。"

这样的对话显然是有些牛头不对马嘴的，可是路瑾言的双手却明显地颤抖了一下，因为他突然很不合时宜地想到了顾晰若。好像从来她都没有对他说过"我爱你"，可是他就是清清楚楚明明白白地知道，她是爱着他的，完全肯定，毫不怀疑。就像，他也同样爱着她，却从未对她说过"我爱你"。

他们之间，因为爱，已经不再需要任何语言。

病房外，路瑾言的母亲终于忍不住将心里的疑问说出来。

"为什么瑾言的眼睛在之前一点儿症状都没有，就连视力下降的趋势都没有，这样突然失明，会不会太奇怪了?"

"事实上，有一段时间他的视力是处于下降状态的，但是瑾言怕你们担心，所以央求我保守秘密。后来经过一段时间的治疗，他的视力又渐渐平稳后，这事也就没告诉你们。孩子不想让你们担心，也是因为他孝顺。"

"嗯，这孩子……"

"不过，这一次导致他失明的直接原因你们还不知道吗?"

"嗯?"

你 是 我 遥 不 可 及 的 梦

🌢

"瑾言这一次眼睛之所以会失明，是因为那个叫顾眄若的女孩将酒瓶砸到他的脸上，架在他鼻梁上的眼镜整个都被砸碎了，碎片跌入眼睛内才造成的。"安眠的母亲别有居心地说道。

"眄若？她为什么要砸瑾言啊？我们供她吃，供她喝，对她如对亲生女儿一样。老公，她为什么要砸瑾言啊？"

"可能这其中有误会吧。"安眠的母亲假惺惺地安慰道。

"误会？现在瑾言都瞎了，再大的误会……再大的误会，也不应该啊。我不会原谅她的……"

"老婆，眄若那孩子，你跟她相处了这么久，还不明白她啊？这其中肯定是有误会的。再说瑾言这孩子的眼疾也不是一天两天了。你也别急，回头问下瑾言，不就真相大白了？"

"我想不明白……我不会原谅她的……"

安眠的母亲一副看戏的姿态，表情虽然控制得很好，可心里却乐哈哈笑。哪个母亲会愿意看着自己的孩子受苦受难，受尽爱情的折磨？当初将安眠送出国，一方面也是希望安眠能够放弃路瑾言；另一方面，则是给安眠准备的退路，如果依然放不下那就选择偏执地抢夺。

将路瑾言的父母带到办理手续的地方，安眠的母亲转身回到了自己的办公室，和安眠的父亲聊了半个小时的电话后，心情变得更好了。

门外。

从路瑾言的病房门口一路跟随到手续办理处，再转到安眠母亲的办公室门口，短短一个小时内发生的一切以及所有的对话，他都清清楚楚地看到了和听到了。原本只是想找安眠的母亲帮忙请个更权威一点儿的私人医生去给病倒的父亲看个病的，却意外地撞到了这一切。

离开医院，坐在车里，李嘉禾冷静下来，努力将刚才看到的和听到的全部串联在一起。

很快，李嘉禾就得出了结论——那天在倪斯的酒吧里，路瑾言正是因为眼睛受伤了，所以才狠心推开了顾晞若。

再往前一点儿回忆，回到路瑾言曾经单独找到自己，问自己对顾晞若是否真心，是否愿意守护顾晞若，想必那时候路瑾言就已经发现了自己视力在下降。事实证明就是那一天，路瑾言检查发现自己的眼睛在未来随时都可能失明。

再到后来，路瑾言和自己签订"守护保证书"，也是因为他已经感觉到自己的视力越来越糟糕。所以，他希望，有生之年，即便他自己无法给予顾晞若未来，那么也一定要找一个可靠的深爱着顾晞若的人来替他守护好她，而这个人就是他李嘉禾。那么，这段时间，路瑾言想爱又不敢爱的姿态也完全可以理解了。路瑾言害怕在他给予了顾晞若全世界后，又会亲手毁掉他给予她的全世界，所以，他选择了以哥哥的姿态和身份暂时地陪在她的身边。并且，时不时地，路瑾言还会撮合李嘉禾和顾晞若，那么，他李嘉禾就是路瑾言为顾晞若找到的好归宿。

原来，路瑾言一直都是爱着顾晞若的，比李嘉禾想象的还要深爱着她。

李嘉禾颓然地靠在车座上，这一切来得太汹涌，汹涌到连他都失去了方向。

咚咚咚！

脑袋里的细胞好像在瞬间一个个崩裂开，头脑完全无法运作。

咚咚咚！

"呀，李嘉禾，你没出事吧？呀，哥哥你可别吓我啊。"

咚咚咚！

终于睁开了眼，原来是李沐禾在敲打着自己车窗的玻璃。将车窗摇下，清丽可人、笑容满满的脸庞映入眼帘。

"呀，李嘉禾，在想什么想得这么入神呢？"

"你怎么在这儿？这大包小包的，是要去旅游吗？"

"恭喜你，答对啦，加十分。"

"是……跟你旁边这位许清木先生一起去吗？"李嘉禾指指提着李沐禾大包小包的行李的许清木。许清木礼貌地朝李嘉禾点个头，微微一笑。

"嗯，又答对啦。呀，李嘉禾，你太聪明啦。"

"别跟我贫嘴，上车，李沐禾。"语气是凶巴巴的。

"干吗呀？"

"上车，我有话跟你说。"

无奈，李沐禾只好嘟着嘴坐上车。只不过，上车前她还特意跑到许清木的身边凑到他耳边安抚道："等我一会儿，我很快就下来，待会儿请你吃好吃的呦。"

"嗯，快去吧。"

待李沐禾上车后，李嘉禾果断地将车窗摇下来，然后开始了他的"家法伺候"。

"你和许清木现在是朋友的关系还是情侣关系？"

"暧昧关系。"

"什么叫暧昧关系？！李沐禾，给我严肃点儿回答。"

"所谓暧昧关系就是我仍然喜欢他，在等待他，而他也仍然对我没有男女之情。不过现在我们一起学习，一起摄影，相处挺好的，也会相互分享一些事情，分担一些事情。革命尚未成功，同志仍需努力。这样其实也挺好的，是吧！"

"你知道的，南西在他心里的位置是谁都取代不了的……你不难过？难过的话就放弃吧。"

"我不想取代谁，我就想做独一无二的李沐禾，以后也做他许清木独一无二的李沐禾就好。"

"好，有志气。那你们准备去哪儿？和家里说了吗？"

"南西生前一直都想要去西藏拍照，所以，这一次许清木是为了实现南西的愿望而去西藏摄影的，而我是去学习的。我想趁我还有勇气爱着的时候，跟他一起制造更多的回忆……家里那边我还没说，手机没电了，准备晚点儿再打个电话，还不知道他们允许不允许，不过我票都已经买好了。"

"家里那边我会替你告诉他们的。来，手机交给我。回头你妈不同意，可有的你闹得。好好去玩吧，有事用许清木的手机联系我。其他的，有哥哥在，放心。"

"呀，李嘉禾，你对我这么好，我真受不了。不过，有哥哥的感觉真好。"

"傻丫头，幸福一点儿。"

"嗯。"

远远地，李沐禾和许清木的身影变得越来越小，小到两道身影看过去几乎是重叠在一块儿的，勾画出着幸福的模样。

如果隐瞒可以让李沐禾能够暂时拥有美好的旅行和完整的回忆的话，李嘉禾愿意选择暂时的欺骗。瞒不了一世，但至少能够瞒过这一时，李嘉禾也就心满意足了。

但纸始终包不住火。

尘封在记忆里的那场酒驾事件还是不可避免地被公开了，甚至再一次登上了荧幕。而随着此次事件的曝光，商业局局长李启铭因涉嫌包庇罪、洗黑钱等一系列问题而被调查，这件事受到了各大媒体的关注和报道。一夜之间，平日里围着局长团团转的"朋友们""亲人们"。对其全部"敬而远之"，是一丁点儿也不愿意再与这位商业局局长扯上关系了。

这便是——人情冷暖。

/03/

李嘉禾疲惫地回到家，父亲仍然病倒在床上，好在之前一直给父亲看病的私人医生最终还是有情有义地来到了家里。在给父亲的药物里注入了少量的安定剂后，他终于安静地睡着了。

李嘉禾拉了把椅子，坐在父亲的床边，仔细地端详着父亲的模样。

在看到父亲即便是睡着了也紧蹙着的眉头和这几天滋生出来的无数白头发后，这个大男人，心疼地低下头呜呜地哭了。

夕阳西下，黄昏的时候，出去办事的后母回来了。而就在后母推开门的刹那，李嘉禾一瞬间完全呆住了。不久之后李家将会落魄不堪，商业局局长李启铭也只会成为世人嘲笑的对象，李嘉禾真的以为这个女人会在此刻带着她自己所有的财产卷铺盖走人的。

可是，她回来了。

后母回到家后，和往常一样，也没有和他多说什么，而是利落地拿出行李袋开始简单地整理自己的一些行李，很快她就收拾好了，最后她拿过李启铭床边摆放着的四人全家福，小心地放进行李袋里。一直默默坐在旁边的李嘉禾有些嘲讽地冷笑一声，心想：一切准备就绪，只差离开了吧。可是前一瞬，自己为何会以为这个女人会因为爱而留在他父亲的身边？李嘉禾啊李嘉禾，你还真是幼稚到好笑。

"咳咳咳……"偏偏这时候李启铭醒过来了。

李嘉禾和后母同时跑到桌边给李启铭倒水。临走前，也不忘把最后的戏码演好，李嘉禾不得不佩服后母的演技。

"爸……你醒了……"

"启铭……来，喝水吧……"

莫名的异口同声。

"佳凌……你怎么还在这儿？明天上头就会下令派人来清查家底了，说不定连我也会被一起抓走。我再也没有什么可以给你的了，收拾东西赶紧走吧，走得越远越好。我用李沐禾的身份证办的存折里还有一些钱，你带着，好好过，别苦着孩子。我这下半辈子只能在牢里度过了……"李启铭对李嘉禾的后母阮佳凌说。

"启铭，说什么傻话？你是顶天立地的一家之主，你怎么能说丧气话？你怎么能倒下？赶紧把身体养好，还有很多的事情等着你去处理，儿女的福分等着你去享受……被查的事情我都已经处理好了。没事的啊，放心养好身体，都会过去的。"

"处理？佳凌，你告诉我，事情是怎么处理的？你没做什么傻事吧？"

"都说有钱能使鬼推磨，这话一点儿都不假。启铭，这一次，就当我们破财消灾吧。你不会怪我把你毕生的积蓄都'破'掉了吧？"

"不会不会……破钱消灾，消灾就好。"

"那我们去吃饭吧，走，嘉禾，杨姨她今天特意做了几个大家都喜欢吃的菜，走，吃饭。"

可是，李启铭像是才发现了李嘉禾的存在般，冷冷地对他说："你还回来干吗？你不是为了她连老爸都可以出卖吗？你不是为了她连整个家都可以不顾吗？你还回来干吗？我们李家没有你这种不孝子，给老子滚！"

"爸，这件事与顾眆若无关。"

"无关？如果不是当年的酒驾事件突然被曝光，如果不是重新翻案，他们怎么会查到我，怎么能把所有的事情全部查清楚？时间都过去这么久了，他们想查都查不清楚了，如果不是你找人帮她忙，她一个小姑娘能查到什么？现在事情查清楚了，她因为母亲的车祸得到了大笔的赔偿金，你父亲现在却落个走私和包庇罪犯的罪名，你说她究竟存的是什么心啊？说不定从一开始，她接近你就是为了利用你，这个女孩子城府真的好深啊……"

"不是的，顾眆若不是那样的人。"

"不是怎样的人？这件事情与她是脱不了干系的。不是她调查公开所有事情的话，还有谁会这样做？李嘉禾，这么多年，我真是白养你了。"

"真的不是顾眆若，不是她……"

"滚，你滚！"李启铭气愤地吼道。

李嘉禾站起身，往门外走去，走到门口的时候又忍不住回过头对李启铭说："对一个六岁的小女孩来说，失去母亲是多么难受的一件事情，你了解吗？不，你不了解，就像当年母亲离开我的世界时，我心痛到无法呼吸，你仍然不管不顾，这些感受你当然不会了解……可是，如果当年，你没有一次次地包庇你的私人司机，你没有不断地帮他隐瞒罪证，坏人就会得到应有的惩罚，失去亲人的他们就不会在今天要重新讨个说法……往前一点儿说，如果当年不是你让你的私人司机在酒局之后，帮你将走私的货品运送到目的地，而是找人开车送他回家休息的话，事故就不会发生……退一万步讲，就算他已经开车撞到了那些无辜的人们，如果他愿意停下车将他们先送到医院的话，那些无辜的人们还是有救的，可是为了你的走私品，他选择了逃逸……如果你不昧着良心去做那些违法的事，你就一直会是我从小崇拜的父亲，可现在，你看不清事实，看不清自己……"

李启铭气急败坏地拿起阮佳凌先前端过来的水杯朝李嘉禾砸去："滚！我没有你这样的不孝子，你给老子滚，滚得远远的！"

"对不起，爸。"

砰！

转身，关门，李嘉禾隐忍的眼泪默默流下。

世界好大，大到前路漫漫，无处可去。

世界好小，一转身，李嘉禾就看到了此刻他最想见到的人——顾晗若。

看到李嘉禾伤感的眉角和疲惫的眼神，对东窗事发后的家庭战争，顾晗若已猜到八九不离十。她小心翼翼地走近他。可不知为何，对于这样的李嘉禾，顾晗若是害怕靠近的，她怕他不相信自己，怕他再也不会理会自己。可最终，害怕归害怕，顾晗若还是鼓起勇气，走到李嘉禾的身边，轻轻地抱住了他。她从来都不是那种很会安慰别人的小天使，所以，她选择给予他拥抱，从而将安慰传递给他。

"李叔叔……你父亲，现在还好吗？"

"嗯……"

"嘉禾，不是我，不是我说的。我不想让他们知道，让他们调查你父亲的。"

"我知道。"

"嘉禾……"

"嘘，不要说话，抱着我，我好累。"

酒驾事件的真相公开后，新闻媒体都报道了，顾晡若的确得到了一大笔赔偿金，可是她的赔偿金在拿到手的当天就已经被分成两部分处理掉了。其中一部分顾晡若以邮寄的形式寄给了路瑾言的父母，而另外一部分则通过慈善组织将它全部捐给了父亲顾之淳生前工作时所在的慈善幼儿园。从一开始调查，她想要得到的就不是赔偿金，她想要得到的只是真心的，完全出于真心的道歉。

"对不起，晡若，我代我父亲向你道歉，真心地道歉，希望你能够接受。"

"嘉禾，我、我没有责怪过叔叔的。"

"晡若，也谢谢你，在得知真相后要求我家管家对我隐瞒了所有真相。"

"不，不是，嘉禾，你别误会。我隐瞒真相是因为我不想调查了，我不希望将你父亲卷进来，不希望你和你父亲闹矛盾，不希望……"

"好吵啊。"李嘉禾用力将顾晡若拉入他的怀里。哪里来的丫头啊，真的好吵。

"嘉禾，我……"

"我知道，我都知道，你的矛盾和隐忍，你的退让和心伤，你的放弃和难过，你为我所做的一切，我都明白。可是，晡若，你低估了我的侦查能力，这些真相在你查到的时候我都已经查到了。"

"难道这一切都是你公开的？是你亲手抓的你父亲？"

"说什么呢，怎么会是我？"

"那会是谁？"

"安眠的父亲。"

"安眠的父亲？"

"嗯。这些年他一直都和我父亲有商业上的合作,他虽然表面上是某集团公司的老总,可事实上他还是个帮派的小头目。他隐藏得很深,后台很硬,几乎没人知道他这隐性的身份。我父亲本是清廉的好官员,认识他后,在他的威逼利诱下才渐渐迷失了自己。后来,我父亲想收手,可他不愿意,我父亲也不是怕人怕事的人,谁知,他一直都抓着我父亲的把柄,一步步地逼迫他。商场如战场,我父亲就是太过相信他,忘了握住他的把柄。多老奸巨猾的人啊……"

"真没想到会是他。可他为什么会突然间这么做呀?"

"我也不知道,大概是应了一句老话'商场如战场'吧。"

夜晚的小公寓,李嘉禾和顾昐若靠坐在一起,谁都没有说话。透过天窗,只见夜幕里的星星微微闪烁着,世界一派安宁。李嘉禾和顾昐若心里的忧伤随着时间的流逝,也在静静地流淌着,蔓延着,脑海里各自想着各自的心事。

安眠的父亲为何会在突然之间出卖他的老朋友呢?其实说到底还是为了他的宝贝女儿——安眠。当天在医院里,李嘉禾一直从路瑾言的病房门口一路跟随到手续办理处,再转到安眠母亲的办公室门口,就连她跟老公聊天时,他还一直站在门口偷听着。

李嘉禾不知道,安眠的母亲是否知道这一切,知道后她又会做出怎样的反应。因为,正是由那一通电话,李嘉禾才知道了所有的真相——李嘉禾的父亲李启铭想收手,却遭到了安眠父亲的拒绝,安眠的父亲将其走私的证据交公,出卖了李启铭。而安眠的父亲为什么会出卖老朋友李启铭,这其中其实还隐藏着一个原因,而这个原因就是安眠。

父亲李启铭落魄,儿子李嘉禾自然受牵连,儿子受牵连,与儿子有关的顾昐若必然会被抛弃。而偏偏整个酒驾事件又是与这丫头的母亲有关,那么"调查、公开、受难"这一系列事情的发生完全就可以自然而然地嫁祸到这丫头的身上。如此，公事私事，一举两得，简直是双赢。

李嘉禾自然是气不过的，当父亲冤枉顾昕若的时候，差一点儿他就说出了事情的真相。可是，他不能。父亲和安眠一家一直是有着"深厚"交情的，父亲是个重感情的人，当初若不是为了还安眠父亲的情意，他也不至于替他洗黑钱，更不至于沦落到走私犯罪。父亲现在已经病倒了，这件事就以后有机会的时候再告诉他吧。

和顾昕若躲在公寓里好几天，外面发生了什么事，他们一概不关心。

心血来潮地，顾昕若想要打开电视看一看中央台的考古节目，画面跳出来，却是城市台整点的新闻播报，不可避免地，一定会听到关于商业局局长李启铭的消息。

"商业局局长李启铭涉嫌走私、洗黑钱、包庇罪犯一事终于得到了最后的结果。经调查，商业局局长李启铭走私、洗黑钱一事是被人栽赃嫁祸的，而包庇罪犯一事也并不是其本人所为。调查显示，当年酒驾事件的肇事司机是李启铭第二任妻子的远方亲戚，整个包庇事件都是她在操纵的。但是……"

"果然，有钱能使鬼推磨。"李嘉禾嘲讽地说道。

"但是，调查发现李启铭自出任商业局局长以来，有过多次受贿行贿等不良行为，组织上是绝对不允许的。最终处置，李启铭第二任妻子阮佳凌因包庇罪即刻入狱，而李启铭则被撤销了商业局局长的职务，并被没收了名下的所有资产。"

"她是爱他的，我一直都错了。"李嘉禾用双手捧住自己的脸，后悔的泪水流入他的掌心。

顾昕若摊开他的双手，用她的双手轻轻地帮他拭去脸上的泪水。

"怪叔叔，不是你的错，是她爱得太偏执，偏执到蒙蔽了所有人的双眼。"

"我想去看看她。"

"嗯，我等你。"

"晡若，等我回来，我们一起去日本，离开这里。"

"……"

"我们去日本，晡若，好吗？"

呆若木鸡的顾晡若，在眼泪流下的瞬间，用力地点了点头。

"好。"

/04/

几天之后。

有老朋友给顾晡若打电话，约她去城市中央的茶餐厅小聚一下。顾晡若最初是打算拒绝的，可后来一思前一想后，最终还是决定赴约。还好，也真的只是"小聚一下"，刚刚好一杯茶的时间，该说的已说完，该聚的已聚完，剩下的便只有曲终人散。可是，就在顾晡若走到茶餐厅门口准备推门离开的时候，茶餐厅的驻唱歌手将他手中的吉他重新拿起，熟悉的旋律响起来……

忘了是怎么开始

也许就是对你有一种感觉

忽然间发现自己已深深爱上你

真的很简单

爱得地暗天黑都已无所谓

是是非非无法抉择

没有后悔为爱日夜去跟随

那个疯狂的人是我

OH，I love you

无法不爱你 baby

说你也爱我

OH，I love you

永远不愿意 baby，失去你

已经迈开的脚步又停在了原地，顾晔若知道，从她踏出这扇门的那一刻起，所有的坚持就真的崩落了，所有的一切也真的结束了。

她该怎么办？

是回过头跟老朋友说，抱歉，我们之前所做的约定作废；还是，继续推开门，往前走去？顾晔若不知道。也就是在这个时候，顾晔若的手机收到了一条短信，她身体有些僵硬地从包包里掏出手机，点开屏幕，一行清晰的字迹映入眼帘。

晔若，嫁给我，好吗？

发信人：李嘉禾

清冷的泪水打湿了屏幕，屏幕上的字迹越来越模糊。下一秒，顾晔若坚定地推开门，走了出去……

猝不及防地，遭遇了一场倾盆大雨。明明是可以选择待在原地的屋檐下躲雨的，顾晔若却不顾雨水的嘀嗒，冲进了雨中。也不知道她哪里来的兴致，突然就想要在这清冷无人的街道上来一场“雨中独步”。

或许，只是因为想到了记忆中熟悉的场景。

然而，睁开眼的时候，那个曾经脱下自己的大衣罩在两人头顶上的少年却早已消失不见。

城市中央的大屏幕里陌生的播报员正在播报着有关这一场酸度极浓的大雨，顾昉若揉揉自己疼痛的双眼，不满地唠叨道："原来是高浓度酸雨啊，难怪会感觉眼睛这么酸这么痛，好讨厌酸雨啊。"哪怕是一个人的时候，也要保持坚强的姿态，顾昉若还真是个无可救药喜欢逞强的小孩。而上一个瞬间，抬起双手触碰自己双眼的时候，顾昉若感觉到的明明就是她自己滚烫的高咸度的眼泪……

想念，溢满了整颗心脏。

仿佛，下一秒就会爆炸。

然而，这一秒却早已迷失了方向。

握在手心里的手机因为长时间被雨水淋湿的原因，已经开不了机，李嘉禾的短信顾昉若迟迟未回复。

发送短信的主人李嘉禾因为迟迟没有收到顾昉若的回复短信而高度紧张着，然而时间一分一秒地过去了，当李嘉禾仍然没有收到顾昉若的回信时，那种高度的紧张感渐渐地变成了万分的担心。而此时顾昉若的电话怎么拨里面传来的都是陌生女人的声音："对不起，您拨打的用户暂时无法接通。"

李嘉禾只好从一辆公交车转换到另外一辆公交车，如此，穿梭在整个城市间，不停地寻找着顾昉若。

最终，李嘉禾在路瑾言家楼下的角落里找到了她。见到她的时候，她正蹲坐在地上，将头埋在自己的双膝里，呜呜地哭个不停。

"很想很想他们的话，就上去看看他们，我陪你。"

摇头，然后又抬起头，向李嘉禾解释道："最后一次，以后，以后都不会再想念了。"

"傻丫头，楼上住着的一位是你最爱最喜欢的路妈妈，一位是对你最好最好的路爸爸，还有一位是最疼你最爱你的哥哥路瑾言，你有想念他们的权力。"

"你不会生气吗？"

"这些都是你告诉我的，我知道他们对你来说很重要很重要，所以，谁都没有权力剥夺你的想念，包括我。要不要我陪你上去？"

"不……不要了。"顾昤若有些闪躲地说道。

"昤若，你脸上怎么了？怎么有红印子啊？"

"没……没有啦，是被隔壁林老太家里的猫猫给抓伤的，好久没来这里，它当我是偷东西的贼了吧。"

"疼不疼？"

顾昤若没说话，只是摇头。

"那，我们回家吧。"

——我们回家。

这一句话，多么熟悉，顾昤若失了神，眼睁睁地望着李嘉禾，脑海里却闪出了另一个人的模样。像是丢了心魂的人，顾昤若呆呆地回答："嗯，我们回家吧。"

回到公寓，换了一身干净的衣服后，李嘉禾迫不及待地向顾昤若解释道："昤若，办理日本个人旅游签证，在职业地位和经济能力上有着一定的要求，而这些要求你暂时还没有达到。如此一来，我们一起去日本的话，就只能以陪读的形式过去。而去日本陪读所需要的条件之一就是婚姻公正，我们俩的年龄也刚刚好达到了婚姻法规定。这样一来，我父亲就可以同时做你的经济保证人。所以，昤若，只要你敢嫁，我就一定娶你。"

几乎是一口气将所有的话说完的，长这么大，李嘉禾从来没有这么不淡定过，顾昤若又怎会看不明白？

"我手机进水，短信回不了。"顾昤若解释道，末了，又补充了一句，"这件事，你问过叔叔了吗？"

"嗯，我已经把所有的事情都跟他解释清楚了，他同意了。这一次的事情，无论是对整个家，还是对他对我，甚至是对沐禾、阮阿姨，都是一次洗礼，都是一次重生。"

顾昤若牵起李嘉禾的手，紧握住，说："还有我，我一直都在。"

"嗯……昤若，虽然现在的我不能给你浪漫甜蜜的求婚，但是，到日本后，我会边读书边打工的，我答应你会补给你一个温馨的求婚仪式。"

"傻瓜，踏踏实实的幸福就好，其他的不重要。"

"对，幸福就好。"

之后，李嘉禾便开始忙碌地办理出国手续，而顾昤若则像是患了瘟疫的病人，躲在房间里，昏天暗地地睡。房间里厚厚的窗帘有气无力地垂在地上，整个世界都被遮得严严实实的。偶尔睡醒了，就呆呆地望着天花板发呆，望着望着眼泪就流下来了。

李嘉禾将一切手续都办好回到公寓时，正好撞见顾昤若蹲在厕所里哭到吐的情形。而这一次，李嘉禾并没有像往常一样，担心地询问她怎么了，而是站立在门口，无声地流下了眼泪。因为他清清楚楚地知道，顾昤若的病不是去医院，不是安慰就能解决的，她患的心病，只能用心药医治。

哭完吐完，顾昤若这才看到李嘉禾，便逞强地解释起来："这电影你说它好看吧，它偏偏让人看了恶心想吐；你说它不好看吧，它偏偏又让人看了感动落泪。刚好，你来了，我们换个片子看吧。"

"昕若，发生什么事了吗？"

摇头。

"手续都办齐了。"

"嗯。"

"我们下周一去日本。"

"嗯。"

"昕若。"

"我想见路瑾言……"终于，顾昕若哭出声，"去日本前，我想和他见一面。"

"好。"

接到"任务"后，李嘉禾首先和安眠取得了联系，在证实了他之前所猜想的一切都是事实后，他和安眠同时陷入了为难的境地。

路瑾言失明以来，对所有知情人唯一的要求就是：不要让顾昕若知道。

因为，路瑾言知道，一旦顾昕若知道了他失明的事实，她就一定会选择偏执而坚定地陪在自己的身边。就算全世界都反对，她也不会在乎。这样，就等于葬送了顾昕若一辈子的幸福，路瑾言又怎么会忍心亲手毁掉她的幸福？

顾昕若的世界已经不能再承受任何失去了。他路瑾言不怕看不见这个世界，他就怕看不见顾昕若幸福，怕自己会耽误她。

于是，安眠说："瑾言，不如找个借口推掉吧。"于是，李嘉禾说："瑾言，进行视频见面的话，发现的几率会小一点儿。"可是最终，已经在国外进行治疗的路瑾言还是坚持要回来和顾昕若见上这一面。

见面当天，路瑾言比约定的时间早到半小时，安眠将他扶到预订的餐桌旁等待顾昕若。安眠离开前，将深茶色的眼镜递给路瑾言，叮嘱他："待会儿我来接你，你安静地坐在这里等我。"

事实上，茶色眼镜，早到半小时，这些都只是路瑾言今天的"战略帮手"。

戴着茶色眼镜的路瑾言，和平时相比，只不过是换了一副新眼镜而已。而早到半小时，就可以顺理成章自然而然地一直待在座位上。如此，整个见面过程中，不需要走动，顾晔若肯定是看不出来的。半个小时后，顾晔若来到餐厅，向路瑾言走去。

失去视觉的人，往往听觉都会变得更为灵敏。

在听到顾晔若的脚步声即将靠近自己的时候，路瑾言扬起一个微笑，对顾晔若说："这儿，晔若。"

顾晔若深呼吸，调整好情绪，佯装淡定地说："嗨，瑾言，好久不见。"

开场白很简单，无非就是相互之间简单的问候。一切进行得都很顺利，直到路瑾言突然忘了"剧本"地询问顾晔若需不需要柠檬水，需要的话他帮她去拿时，局面才变得有些难以收拾。路瑾言询问这句话的时候，几乎是忘了他已经看不见的事实了，然而话已说出口，又不得不站起身，可是站起来后又发现真的好迷惘。

好在，顾晔若喊住了他："不用了，我今天不想喝柠檬水。"

时间一点一点流逝，顾晔若和路瑾言聊了很多，上到天文地理，下到生活琐事，彼此聊得很开心。直到准备离开的时候，气氛才变得有那么一些伤感，只因为路瑾言突然问顾晔若：

"你知道这个世界上最美的情话是什么吗？"

"是什么？"

"活着一分钟，爱你六十秒。"

十个字而已，却因为路瑾言说得很慢，听完这十个字，顾晔若感觉仿佛过了一个世纪。

路瑾言想要说给顾昑若听的就是这十个字。

顾昑若再也忍不住，眼泪汹涌而出，她真的忍了很久很久。可是，眼泪虽然拼命地在往下掉，她却忍着没有发出任何声音，她一如既往地安安静静地坐着，安安静静地听着路瑾言说话，安安静静任由眼泪爬满整张脸……

路瑾言说："昑若，你今天这身衣服搭得真好看，我家妹妹就是漂亮。"

顾昑若没吱声，却在心里大喊道："说谎！"

路瑾言说："昑若，将来无论遇到什么事情，你都要一直记得：只要你相信爱，便不会迷路。只要你相信温暖，世界便依旧色彩斑斓。"

顾昑若仍然没吭声，仍然在心里默念着她想要说的话："如果这是你想要给我的幸福，我会乖乖听话，不让你担心，不让你为我操心；如果我幸福就能够让你安心地去治疗，那么，我会告诉你，我很幸福。"

路瑾言说："昑若，不要想我。"

顾昑若用力地点头，又迅速地摇头。

路瑾言说："昑若，再见。"

顾昑若闭上眼，深吸一口气，为了不让路瑾言发现她在哭，勉强从喉咙里发出一个单音节词："嗯！"

这样的离别，就像是明天还会见面般，没有汹涌的不舍，没有永世的不见。就像明天，顾昑若和路瑾言还会见面般……

"到最后，连说'再见'的勇气都没有，顾昑若你真是胆小鬼。"转过身，离开的时候，顾昑若自言自语着。

——假装一切都不知道，是我现在唯一能够为你做的。

——请你安心，我会幸福。

{第十章}

我是你的眼

/01/

尘埃落定。

当飞机降落在日本领土上时，李嘉禾给了顾昕若一个大大的拥抱。从今以后，李嘉禾和顾昕若，彼此相依为命。

在日本的生活，是简单而纯粹的。

李嘉禾是标准的三点一线：家，学校，打工的餐厅。而顾昕若，由于日本政府对于陪读人员有着不能在日本谋职和打工的相关要求，她则成了标准的宅女和家庭小主妇。李嘉禾给她买了许多的电影碟片和菜谱，除开发呆时间和睡觉时间，顾昕若就是宅在家里看电影和学做菜。当然，她喜欢的美味和零食，李嘉禾也总是源源不断地供给着。

李嘉禾知道，在顾昕若的心底，除开“想要拥有一个温暖的家”这个梦想之外，还藏着一个愿望和一份喜欢。记不清从什么时候起，他发现了顾昕若对于电影有着近乎疯狂的喜爱和迷恋。而每一次顾眄若看电影的时候，不仅会加入许多她自己的想法和意见，还会假设性地尝试重新编剧情，再滔滔不绝地将编好的新剧情说给李嘉禾听。

最初李嘉禾只是感叹着这丫头脑袋里怎么会有如此多鬼马的想法，到后来，顾眄若亲口告诉他，她真的是很想很想要当一名编剧的时候，李嘉禾才理解了她对电影的热爱。知道顾眄若的心里藏着这么一个心愿的时候，李嘉禾当然不能袖手旁观。后来，通过父亲李启铭的关系，他找到了国内一家刚成立没多久的电影制片厂，并成功地将顾眄若的作品交给了那边。

好歹，顾眄若也是有些才情的女子，虽然她写的剧本不能全部用上，但其中某些点子和情节发展路线对电影制片厂来说还是有帮忙的，所以，后来顾眄若宅在家里又多了一件事——写剧本。如此，她也终于能够靠自己的努力赚点儿小钱，帮李嘉禾分担一点儿生活开销了。

平日里，李嘉禾和顾眄若就是这样，各自忙着各自的生活。节日到来的时候，他们才会把所有的时间都空出来，交给彼此。

春天的时候，李嘉禾会牵着顾眄若的手，在长长的唯美的樱花飞舞的小道上散步；夏日的时候，顾眄若会光着脚丫拉着李嘉禾的手去海边踏浪；秋季的时候，顾眄若会陪着李嘉禾安静地坐在树下看书，偶尔，靠在李嘉禾肩膀上的时候会歪着头喊他一起数落叶；寒冬的时候，李嘉禾会把顾眄若亲手织给自己的围巾一圈一圈围在脖子上，而后体贴地牵住她的手，将其放进他温暖的毛绒口袋里。

岁月安好。

春天散步，夏天看海，秋天数落叶，冬天暖融融。

顾眄若和李嘉禾这对小情侣的生活也过得有滋有味。生活如果一直循着这样的轨迹往前走，似乎也不错。可是，在法律上已经是夫妻的顾眄若和李嘉禾，却一直是分开睡的。偶尔，顾昁若被窗外的雷声吓到，李嘉禾也只是将她抱到自己的床上，而后安静地抱着她睡，直到天亮都没有丝毫的越界。

唯独有那么一次，顾昁若和李嘉禾坐在床上一起玩游戏……

李嘉禾给出上联"悲伤逆流成河"，让顾昁若来对下联。顾昁若想了很久，对了很久，始终都没有对上，便可怜兮兮地求助李嘉禾，李嘉禾只好又退步给出下联"寂寞泛滥成灾"。

"喏，轮到你出横批了。"

哪知，顾昁若猜了好几次，给出的答案又一次全军覆没，李嘉禾便玩味地对她说："呀，顾昁若小同学，你这样可不行，小脑袋不运转的话，输了可是要受惩罚的呦。"不服气的顾昁若气势汹汹地反问道："惩罚什么？我可不怕，愿赌服输，尽管放马过来。"

如此，正中李嘉禾下的小"圈套"。

"猜不到呀，猜不到我就公布答案了，等着受惩罚吧。"李嘉禾叫嚣道。

"哼，谁怕谁，接招！"

"横批就是——活该。"

"呀，李嘉禾，你故意的，这赤裸裸的一语双关啊。"

"天地作证，我可没有。"

"好吧，愿赌服输。说吧，什么惩罚？"

"亲我下。"

"什么？"

"顾昁若小同学，你可别装，我知道你听到了。"

顾昁若只好害羞地对李嘉禾说："那……你先闭上眼睛。"

下一秒，李嘉禾倒是乖乖地闭上了眼睛，可顾昁若却迟迟没有亲下去。她害羞地如蜻蜓点水般地掠过李嘉禾的眉，询问道："是不是亲这里就行了?"李嘉禾摇头，顾晞若又用唇掠过李嘉禾的脸蛋，问："那是不是这里?"李嘉禾又摇头。

最后，顾晞若将她的手移到李嘉禾的嘴唇上，问："该不会是这里吧?"李嘉禾一脸腹黑地笑着点点头。可是，顾晞若却迟疑了，她的脑海里突然就闪现出一个场景、一场雨，以及一个人的脸。李嘉禾见她迟迟没有动静，便睁开眼，一把吻住了她。

这个吻，由温柔转至热烈，顾晞若几乎快要不能呼吸。亲吻的那瞬间，李嘉禾是真的恨不得将顾晞若的全部都占有，也是真的恨不得将他的所有都交给顾晞若。

然而，这一次，也只不过是深吻而已，依旧没有越过雷池。

/02/

在日本的大多数时间里，顾晞若都是一个人宅在家里的，李嘉禾虽然没有"囚禁"她，但他也明确地告诉过她：不要一个人出去，除非有我在身边。通常情况下，顾晞若都是很乖很听李嘉禾话的，只有一次，鬼使神差地，她突然就想要一个人出去走走。

至于走到哪儿，去干吗，她一概不知。

出了房间门后，顾晞若沿着路一条直线往前走，心里想着，这样回来的时候就可以沿着直线往回走了。然而，顾晞若所居住的地方并不是一条直通到底的，而是有无数的小矮房连着小矮房，就像是迷宫一样，一不小心，她对眼前的道路就犯迷糊了。好在顾晞若远远地就看到了一家漫画店，这下就可以边看漫画打发时间边等李嘉禾下班来接她了。

背着嫩绿色小包包的她手舞足蹈地往前奔着，奔到交叉路口的时候，手里的包包却"嗖"的一下被人抢走了。

日语的"救命"应该怎么说？

日语的"抢劫"又应该怎么说？

这些李嘉禾都没有教过自己，站在路口处，顾昕若只能呆愣愣地站在原地。好在，能够联络通讯的手机一直握在她的手中。抢劫的小偷见顾昕若也没追过来，便放松了警惕，将包包里的钱包和值钱的东西扫荡一空后，便把嫩绿色的小包包嫌弃地扔在了地上。

好歹这个包包还是顾昕若在中国的时候在一家精品店淘了很久才淘到的心水包包，见小偷将包包扔在了地上，顾昕若连忙跑过去捡起来。可就在她拾起包包的时候，一张被超粉嫩的卡套包裹起来的生肖银行卡掉了下来，大概，刚才的小偷误以为这是什么精品店的打折卡了吧。

顾昕若拿着卡，突然思绪万千。

因为，这张银行卡是顾昕若十八岁生日时，路瑾言送给她的生日礼物。

顾昕若记得，生日当天，路瑾言用顾昕若的身份证给她办了一张生肖银行卡，然后将他身上所有的钱全部存进了卡里。顾昕若还记得，他办好卡后对她说："昕若，这张卡你留着，我会定期往卡里存钱，以备你应急之需。"

路瑾言一直都觉得他能够为顾昕若做的事情很少很少，而他真正为她所做的事情也真的不够多。所以，他总是想为她做更多更多的事情，而这只不过是其中的一件小事。

仍然是鬼使神差地，顾昕若拿着银行卡跑到日本国际银行的柜台，查询了一下卡里的余额和详单。查询的结果却意外到连顾昕若都不敢相信。从十八岁

🌢

生日那天到现在为止，几乎每个月都会有人往这张卡里存钱，并且卡里的余额也是顾昐若没有想到的数字。

默默存钱的人，无疑就是路瑾言。

顾昐若一直以为，路瑾言口中的定期是指一年或者两年甚至更久，可事实却是每个月。

泪水弥漫，想念蔓延。好久没有释放自己的情绪、宣泄想念的顾昐若，跌坐在漫画店的门口，眼前的漫画店招牌越来越模糊。

原本，来到日本后的顾昐若，性格上就发生了一些变化。变得不喜欢和李嘉禾抬杠，变得不会时不时地就和李嘉禾调侃几句，变得沉默了许多，越来越不爱说话。而自从这次抢劫事件之后，她就变得更加得沉默寡言了。

顾昐若虽然不说，可李嘉禾心里一直都明白：她是想路瑾言了，这种想念也从未停止。

不然，每当漆黑的夜晚来临时，顾昐若又怎会一次又一次地用布料蒙着她的眼睛，然后，颤抖地，小心翼翼地，慢慢地，挪着她的步子，往前走着？偶尔，走着走着，还会控制不住情绪地小声呜咽起来。而每一次，躲在黑暗中看着这样颤抖着前进的顾昐若，李嘉禾的心里除了心疼，还是心疼。

顾昐若一直以为这些都是只属于她自己的秘密，却不知李嘉禾一直都知道只是不忍心戳穿她。直到后来，李嘉禾越来越害怕，害怕失去顾昐若，甚至害怕她会放弃自己的生命。

因为，我国法律有明确的规定，任何活着的人在生前都不可以捐献自己的眼角膜，但是却可以填写捐献眼角膜的意向书，在死后将眼角膜捐献出来。

李嘉禾的逻辑思维和推断能力一直都很强。自然地，顾昐若如此诡异的举动，也是逃不出李嘉禾缜密的推断的。

黑夜里将眼睛蒙上厚厚的布，甘愿抛弃所有的光明而坠入黑暗。如此的举动，一定与牺牲和成全有关。将顾昕若嵌入这则理论里，再摊上一个路瑾言，便是牺牲顾昕若自己，成全路瑾言。努力地适应黑暗，适应失去光明和色彩的世界，然后，将自己的眼角膜捐出。如此，即便将来的自己会面对黑暗，也不会再惧怕黑暗。结论已经很明显，可是李嘉禾仍然不敢轻易下判断。不过，若是再加上他趁顾昕若不在家时，从她的箱底找到的那份"生前自愿捐献眼角膜"的医学申请书，答案就清清楚楚了。

这时候的李嘉禾，也大概猜到了顾昕若对于路瑾言失明的事实是知情的，她只不过是在假装什么都不知道。而事实证明，李嘉禾的猜测是正确，顾昕若一直都知道路瑾言已经失明了。

只是，在黑暗中，用厚厚的布蒙着自己眼睛的顾昕若，并不是为将来会失去光明的自己而做心理准备，她只是想亲身体验一下已经失去光明的路瑾言的感受，她只是想用这样的方式来告诉路瑾言："她顾昕若对他路瑾言，是不离不弃的。"

至于医学界和法律对于"活着的人生前是不可以捐献眼角膜"这一规定，顾昕若也是知情的。路瑾言失明之后，她查了太多有关失明、有关眼角膜、有关捐献、有关治疗的资料。

一个连死都已经不惧怕的人，哪里还会怕什么黑暗？

现在的顾昕若唯一害怕的就是面对李嘉禾。怕李嘉禾对自己失望，怕失去顾昕若的李嘉禾会伤心难过，怕再也给不了李嘉禾温暖，怕她下辈子都是会欠着他李嘉禾的。

也怕，从此她将失去李嘉禾。

事情终究该有个结果，也是时候，该真正地尘埃落定了。

只是，顾昕若似乎忘了，国内著名的眼科医生——安眠的母亲曾说过，对于路瑾言眼睛的治疗，是有两种治疗方案的，等待捐献的眼角膜只不过是其中一种。

有时候，太过偏执的爱，是真的很容易蒙蔽自己的双眼的。

/03/

周日的午后。

树影斑驳，春花灿烂。

阳光懒懒地穿透街道两旁的树木，原野奈奈子家的寿司店依然是整条街道上最热闹的地方。李嘉禾跟餐厅老板请完假后，便来到奈奈子家的寿司店里，给顾晰若买了两盒她最喜欢吃的招牌寿司。令人惊喜的是，李嘉禾还顺带得到了奈奈子赠送的一瓶陈年的上等红酒。

奈奈子的男朋友水野树与李嘉禾是老朋友了，在中国留学期间，水野树曾在李嘉禾家住过一段时间。李嘉禾来日本后，大多时候，排解心理压力和宣泄心事的方法就是喊上水野树去奈奈子家的天台喝上几杯。

然而，对于已经请了整个下午假，并且此时正在回家路上的李嘉禾，顾晰若完全不知情。她一如往日地宅在家里，阳光透过窗户落在她的脸上，可是，满眼的光似乎是刺痛了她的眼睛。下一秒，她将家里所有的窗帘全部拉下来，将家里所有的灯全部都关了，而后才满足地坐在地上，在黑暗的房间里将耳机的声音调至最大，一遍一遍沉沦地听着耳机里的音乐……

李嘉禾回到家里的时候，除了耳机里溢出来的声音，黑暗中，他什么都听不到。

"啪啪啪!"沿着墙壁,李嘉禾将吊灯按钮按下,再抬起头时,看到的便是顾昈若一脸诧异的表情。

"我还以为你不在呢。"

"餐厅下午放假吗?"

"没有,我请假了。"

"今天是什么特别的日子吗?"

"也没有,就是想和你一起好好吃顿饭。喏,原野奈奈子家的招牌寿司,水野树额外赠送的陈年红酒,还有新鲜的蔬菜和水果。"李嘉禾将寿司、蔬菜、红酒一起高高地举起来给顾昈若看,顾昈若抬起头放下耳机,高兴地站起身,跟着李嘉禾来到厨房。

"那得好好谢谢奈奈子和水野君。"

"已经谢过啦,顾昈若小同学。"

"嗯……做得不错,怪叔叔。"

厨房里,顾昈若负责洗水果和蔬菜,李嘉禾负责切水果和蔬菜,以及拌上沙拉酱。之后的整个下午,两个人就舒舒服服地窝在沙发上看电影,挑选的电影则是泰国人气超高的纯爱电影——《初恋这件小事》。

等整部电影播放完毕的时候,顾昈若突然打趣地询问李嘉禾:"初恋?啊!怪叔叔看完这部电影是不是想到了芊芊呢?"

哪知,小诡计没得逞,李嘉禾不回答问题,反而反问顾昈若道:"那,这位小同学,你看完这部电影想到的又是谁呢?"

顾昈若故作神秘地说:"嗯。这个,我得想想。"

"顾昈若小同学,你的初恋难道不就是我吗?这么简单的问题还得想这么久啊。"

"哈哈。什么初恋啊，二恋啊，现在恋啊，都是浮云。看完这部电影，每一位少女满脑子想到的应该都是那位帅气的男主角吧。"

"少女？这位小同学，你都已经步入妇女的行列啦。不准逃避问题，承认初恋是我很难吗？"

——你的初恋难道不就是我吗？

——我的初恋，好像是……好像是路瑾言吧。

其实，在李嘉禾问题抛出的一瞬间，顾昕若就已经想到了答案，可是，这样的答案，她只能在心里偷偷地回答。顾昕若保持沉默，李嘉禾也只好悻悻地转移话题："我刚回来的时候，你在听什么歌呢？是你常常听的那首歌吗？整个调子我都能哼出来了，可还不知道是谁唱的，是什么歌呢。"

"你不是不喜欢听那些台湾歌手的音乐吗？"

"原来是台湾歌手啊，我是不太喜欢听，不过，如果是你唱的话，我都喜欢听。"李嘉禾故意凑近顾昕若的耳边，调侃道，"来，唱给我听。"

"不要啦，我唱得不好。"

"难不成还害羞呀？来，唱一个，鼓掌。"

"我不要唱。"

"小气鬼，好吧，不唱也可以。那你告诉我是什么歌，回头我自己听去。"

"我不是小气鬼。"

"不要转换话题，是什么歌？"

"你今天干吗非执着在一首歌上啊？"

此刻，顾昕若越是不想说，李嘉禾就越想往下问。明明理智的李嘉禾告诉他不能再问下去了，可感性的李嘉禾又任性地不停地询问道："那你今天干吗非执着地不肯告诉我是什么歌呀？"

"我……"

"你总不能又不唱又不告诉我是什么歌的，对吧？"

"台湾歌手唱的，你不喜欢听的。"

"我一定要知道是什么歌。"

气氛陡然变得冷冽起来，顾晞若只好无奈地宣布答案："林宥嘉唱的，《你是我的眼》。"

"林宥嘉……台湾歌手？"

"嗯。"

"歌名是……《你是我的眼》？"

"嗯。"

听到歌名，李嘉禾直觉这首歌里的歌词肯定隐藏着许多的感情。此刻，他心里隐约的怒火正压抑不住地往上冒腾，他耍赖地对顾晞若说："《你是我的眼》，唱来听听。"

"不是说好不唱了的嘛。"顾晞若小声撒娇道。

"让你唱就唱。"

"我不要。"顾晞若本能地拒绝道。

"不要也得唱。"

"我不要。"

"快点儿。"

"我不要。"

平日里的李嘉禾在顾晞若重复说了"我不要"之后，一定会心软地听从她。可这一次，李嘉禾却不耐烦地朝她吼道："唱啊！"

从来都不会凶自己，甚至不会对自己大声说话的人，突然朝自己吼，顾晞若是真的吓到了，下意识地，只好开口哼起调来……

　　如果我能看得见

　　就能轻易地分辨白天黑夜

　　就能准确地在人群中牵住你的手

　　如果我能看得见

　　就能驾车带你到处遨游

　　就能惊喜地从背后给你一个拥抱

　　如果我能看得见

　　生命也许完全不同

　　可能我想要的我喜欢的我爱的

　　都不一样

　　…………

　　你是我的眼，带我领略四季的变换

　　你是我的眼，带我穿越拥挤的人潮

　　你是我的眼，带我阅读浩瀚的书海

　　因为你是我的眼

　　让我看见这世界就在我眼前……

歌词顾眆若唱得模模糊糊的，李嘉禾却出奇地全都听懂了，或者说，她隐藏的想念和感情，他全都听懂了。

　　难过、不甘、羞辱、愤怒，心如刀绞的感受一股脑儿地涌上李嘉禾的心头。那首歌的音调和歌词不断地浮现在他的脑内，他越想越觉得气愤和不甘心。以至于，失去理智的李嘉禾，像一头发怒的狮子冲到顾眆若的身边，直接将她抱起来丢到了床上。也不顾顾眆若的挣扎和哭喊，猛烈地将她身上的衣服一件一件地脱掉。顾昈若越是反抗，李嘉禾就越用力，用力扯掉她衣服上的纽扣，用力撕烂她用手护着的裙子……

李嘉禾现在满脑子里就只有一个念头，就是占有顾昈若，让她真真正正地全部属于自己，什么路瑾言，什么你是我的眼，通通都见鬼去。

"你要干吗？嘉禾，不要，不要这样对我。"

"我要对你怎样你难道不知道吗？"李嘉禾反问道。

"嘉禾，停下来，不要，我不要。"

"不要也得要。顾昈若，你是我李嘉禾的老婆，你就应该尽你该尽的'义务'。"

"不要这样对我……嘉禾，清醒点儿，听我解释，好不好？"

"解释？有什么好解释的？!"李嘉禾粗暴地朝顾昈若的唇角咬去。

"嘉禾，求你，求求你，停下来。"

"顾昈若，你求我也没用。听清楚了，你是我李嘉禾的老婆，只能想我，只能念我，只能属于我。"李嘉禾不顾已经满脸泪痕的顾昈若，疯狂地撕裂她的衣服，粗暴的吻从她的唇落到锁骨再埋入她的胸前……顾昈若越是反抗和挣扎，李嘉禾就越是愤怒和粗暴。

时间好似停止了。

顾昈若也不哭了。

终于，她停止了挣扎，放下反抗的姿态，任由李嘉禾的手在她的身上游走。闭上眼，她屈服地对李嘉禾说："对，我是你的老婆，这是我应该做的，我自己来。"这一秒，李嘉禾却停下了他游走的双手。他冷淡地将她推开，走下床，捡起一地狼藉的衣服，揉成一团，朝床上扔去。

"穿上。"

沉默。

"我说，把衣服穿上。"

依旧沉默。

"晰若，穿好衣服，我们谈谈吧。"终于，他还是放软了口气。

李嘉禾原本是想在一片和睦浪漫的气氛中友好地和顾晰若分手的，却因为这首歌，分寸大乱。此时哭累了的顾晰若正坐在床上紧紧地抱着被子发呆，李嘉禾怎么哄她都没用，衣服不肯穿，话也不肯说……这样的李嘉禾让顾晰若觉得好陌生好陌生。

"路瑾言失明了。"说完这句话，李嘉禾注意到顾晰若的眼睛转动了一下，他知道她在听，所以他又继续说道，"这件事情，我想你应该已经知道了。我想知道你是怎么知道的，你呢，想不想告诉我？"

"晰若？"

"嗯，我都告诉你。"

"你还记得来日本前我去会老朋友一事吗？"

"记得。"

"约我的人是安眠。她把所有的事情都告诉我了，路瑾言的失明，路瑾言为我所做的所有事情，以及路瑾言会失明的原因……当然，最初我是不相信的，可是在真相面前，我不得不相信。"

"那天晚上你脸上的伤痕，并不是被隔壁家的猫抓伤的？"

"嗯。我跑到路瑾言家去找他求证，他不在，只有路妈妈和路爸爸在。路妈妈不肯原谅我，我不怪她的，她打我骂我都是应该的。是我，路瑾言的失明全是因为我，这一切都是我的错，我是个罪人。可是，如果时间可以倒流，我宁愿这一切的灾难都发生在我身上……"

"所以，你宁愿放弃自己的生命，也要把你'欠'他的都还给他?"

"是。"

"那么，顾昤若，你把我当成什么了? 你把我李嘉禾当成了什么人? 呼之即来，挥之即去的傻瓜，还是蠢蛋? 想要的时候抱一下，不要了的时候就扔了?"

"不，不是……对不起。"

"爱情的世界里，光是一个人犯贱是不够的，那就让我这个单相思、犯贱犯到底的人来告诉你事情的真相。"

"嘉禾，不要这样说你自己，我……我会难过的。"

"顾昤若，听好了，路瑾言的眼睛不是因为你而瞎掉的，就算没有你的那一酒瓶的误砸，他也会失明。也就是说，从头到尾你都只是中了安眠的计。她告诉你事实，告诉你路瑾言为你所做的一切牺牲，只不过是想让你心甘情愿地离开路瑾言。至于你是打算自杀也好，捐眼角膜也罢，跟她没有半点儿关系。最后都只能证明你的死和你的牺牲毫无意义!"

"没有我也会失明，是什么意思?"

"水野树是东京医院附属眼科医院的实习生，虽说他的医术暂时还达不到安眠母亲的水平，但是对于视力一直处于下降状态突然之间又转回平稳状态这样的现象，他还是能够给出专业解答的，而答案就是——安眠的母亲在说谎。将路瑾言视力一直下降的事实隐瞒，直到真的失明那一天，路瑾言就会彻底属于安眠。安眠是个聪明人，路瑾言的心思她一猜就准，她知道失明了的路瑾言一定会主动选择离开你，因为他会觉得他已配不上你。而安眠，宁为玉碎不为瓦全，她宁愿看到路瑾言失明，宁愿他失明之后再陪在他身边，也不愿意看到你和路瑾言在一起。偏偏，你的那一记误砸成了导火线，将整个事件的发生时间缩短，她将这一切嫁祸给你自然也是顺理成章的。"

也许，一切都是天意。

当初在医院，李嘉禾听到了几乎所有的真相，却独独错过了几分钟前安眠和她母亲的谈话。可是，即便已经来到日本，他最终还是知道了真相。

"不……怎么会是这样？是我的酒瓶砸伤了他的眼睛，他才失明的。你怕我会做傻事，才编出整个故事来骗我的，是不是？"

"昕若，你相信我吗？"

"……我相信你，当然相信你。可是，我真的以为安眠变好了，她为了路瑾言牺牲了那么多……"

"安眠从小就把'宁可我负天下人，不可天下人负我'这句话当成她的座右铭，事实上，她的性格也的确是'宁为玉碎不为瓦全'的。并且，安眠她这不是牺牲，是自私，自私地剥夺了路瑾言选择的权力，自私地将路瑾言捆绑在了她的身边。"

"怎么会是这样？……"

"所以，昕若，即使我一直将你捆绑在我身边，结果只会酿成更大的悲剧。我放你走，我们，分手吧。"

"你没有捆绑我，是我自愿待在你身边的。"

"那一份生前自愿捐献眼角膜的文件，不就证明了一切吗？就算你现在陪在我的身边，总有一天，你也会选择放弃我，放弃自己的，不是吗？"

"我……"

"昕若，到日本后的第一个月，我就已经知道了路瑾言失明的真正原因。可是，我自私地以为，在这过去的一年多的时间里，你会爱上我，哪怕是一点点的动心。我期待着，希冀着，所以，我隐瞒了这一切，即便是我心疼地眼睁睁地看着你背着重重的包袱，背着莫须有的罪名，我依然自私选择了隐瞒。这样的话，我还有什么理由要求你留在我的身边？"

"你是说……你早就知道了？"

"你欠我感情，我欠你真相，我们两清了。再说了，现在不是你甩我，而是我要甩你。"

"嘉禾……"

"我已经帮你买好了机票，我会通知路瑾言去接你。他很幸运，有生之年等到了愿意捐献眼角膜给他的人。昳若，不管你这趟回国是回到路瑾言的身边，还是只是处理自己的感情，总之，我答应你，我会在日本等你一年。一年后，如果你没有回来，我会给你发离婚协议书，到时候，你就再也不是我李嘉禾的妻子，我也不是你顾昳若的丈夫，我们好聚好散。"

每个人的心里，都有一座伤城，都有着不能碰触的伤，一旦不慎触到，便是痛不欲生，不能自已。

顾昳若的心城里就藏着这么一个人，是谁都无法取代的。李嘉禾一直以为他可以，可最终他还是只能无能为力地选择投降。

/04/

这个世界，随时都要崩塌，地球都被调成了震动模式。

2011 年 3 月 11 日，顾昳若还未踏出日本国境，高达 9.0 级的地震便侵袭了日本国土，强震继而引发海啸，破坏性和毁灭性极强。

上一秒还风平浪静，下一秒已面目全非。

地面生生地裂开了口，房屋顷刻间轰然倒塌，逃跑中的人们惊慌失措，眼前的世界瞬间支离破碎。

来不及思考和逃离，在强烈的地壳运动和狂风的打击下，顾昐若失去了方向。

当地球恢复到安静的模样时，顾昐若在一阵剧烈的疼痛中睁开了双眼，眼前的一切对她来说完全是未知的。挣扎着想要爬起来，双腿却无法动弹，一块承载着许多重量的石板压在了她的腿上。值得庆幸的是，正因为这块石板将其他的石头、石块等建筑物崩落的物体承载住，顾昐若才得以活过来。

距离顾昐若躺着的地方不远处的位置，似乎有人在大口大口地呼吸，仔细听了听，不是搜救队，而应该是和顾昐若一样，遭遇了这场地震的人。

"喂？"

有微弱的喘息声传来。

"喂？"

"嗯？"

声音却不是从顾昐若喊过去的方向传来，而是从她的背后传来。她强扭着脖子往后看，便看到了一张扭曲的痛苦而绝望的脸，她的脸上有着厚厚的灰尘，如果不是她长长的辫子露出来了，顾昐若连她是男是女都分不清。

"你还好吗？"顾昐若问。

"累……"

"那不要说话了。那边好像有人在说话，搜救队应该很快就会过来的。"

"嗯。"

时间过得很慢很慢，却依旧阻挡不了夜晚的来临。疼痛和饥饿感一起袭来，顾昐若的上眼皮和下眼皮都在打架了，可她仍然强忍着，她害怕一旦闭上眼，就再也睁不开了。顾晞若将脖子扭到后面，又看了一眼在她背后的女孩，说：“我给你说个故事吧，我怕我会睡过去。”

“好。”

最开始，顾晞若也不知道要说什么，只是说着说着就说到了路瑾言，说到了南西、许清木，说到了李嘉禾、李沐禾。好像是要把这些年所有发生的事情都说给这个女孩听似的，顾晞若不停地说着，不停地说着。大抵也正是因为凭借了这样的意志力，她撑到了救护队的到来。

故事也刚刚好，还差一个结尾。

很快地，救护队分成两个小组来分别营救顾晞若和她身后的女孩。顾晞若的情况有些复杂，压在她腿上的石板一旦被抽出，整栋楼就会在瞬间倒塌，谁都逃不出来。可如果不抽出来的话，顾晞若就面临着锯腿的现实。

时间分分秒秒地朝前走着，顾晞若仍然无法做决定。最终，救护队和顾晞若决定赌一次。

由于整栋楼倒塌之后，在楼层顶部的中间位置形成了一个大窟窿，所以，使用吊车从楼房的中间位置将顾晞若腿上的石板先吊起，然后救护人员再快速地将顾晞若运出去的话，也不失为一种办法。危险性虽然相对地降低了，但是，两者的配合实在是太难。

这时候，和顾晞若一起遇难，已经被成功救出去，正打着点滴的女孩，突然向搜救队的护士小姐要求想陪在顾晞若的身边。

“我想陪着她，给她力量。”为了让顾晞若听懂，这个日本女孩用英语说道。

顾晞若这才明白，她们语言不通，原来，她一直都没有听懂自己的故事。可是听到她的鼓励后，恍惚中，顾晞若却以为自己是见到了南西，她干涩的双眼涌出一股热泪。而这十几个小时内，无论是面对疼痛、恐慌还是死亡，顾晞若都没有哭。

"可以告诉我你的名字吗?"女孩问。

"顾昉若。"

"你叫顾昉若?"正在做准备工作的护士小姐惊讶地问道。

"是。"

"原来你就是顾昉若啊,那我赶紧发推特给李嘉禾,告诉他你在这儿。"

"你怎么认识他?"

"不是我怎么认识他,是大家都认识他。现在推特上,关注度第一的就是名为'寻找顾昉若'的推特。而这条推特的发起人就是李嘉禾。他好像是中国来的留学生吧,据说因为一念之差,他离开了他的妻子,可是等到他妻子离开后,他又悔恨不已。地震发生的这段时间里,他每隔半个小时就会更新无数条推特来寻找她的妻子。喏,你看,他刚刚又更新了一条推特——求婚仪式已经准备好,我会一直等你。好像是因为结婚的时候他没有给他妻子准备求婚仪式吧,所以,他一直都想给她补上一个求婚仪式,多浪漫的人啊!这么说来……你是顾昉若,那么你就是李嘉禾要找的人?"

"求求你们,一定要把我救出去。"

有生之年,顾昉若第一次有这么强烈的求生欲望。

为了照顾到顾昉若的情绪,在计划实施前,医生先给她注射了全身止痛药和麻醉剂。很快地,顾昉若就闭上了疲惫的双眼……

恍恍惚惚中,顾昉若做了一个梦。

搜救队的医护人员和吊车的配合处理得很好,石板成功地从她的腿上移除,经过简单的伤口处理和止血后,她的腿便可以行动自如了。

护士小姐推给李嘉禾的推特他一字不漏地收到了。很顺利地,李嘉禾赶到了顾晞若的身边。将顾晞若接回家后，李嘉禾辞去了在日本的所有兼职，安心地在家陪着她。在他悉心的照料下，顾晞若震后所受到的心灵创伤也都很好地恢复了。

日本地震过后，余震仍然不断，李嘉禾答应补给顾晞若的求婚仪式就是在这样动荡的环境中进行的。还好，一切都进行得很顺利，就连原本一年后可能会派上用场的离婚协议书，顾晞若也将它全部撕碎了。

李嘉禾的求婚仪式别有一番新意，在大巴士上铺上红地毯，又请了一支乐队，全程奏礼乐。在他的安排下，顾晞若搭乘着那辆名为“顾晞若 & 李嘉禾，我们结婚了”的大巴士，来到了熟悉的小教堂。

梦中的顾晞若穿着长长的白婚纱，很美很美，在场所有的嘉宾都为之惊叹。

许清木和李沐禾坐在一起讨论着拍照的细节，这样一场幸福的盛宴，怎能缺了这两位专业摄影师的记录？而随意地谈话也能让周围的人感受到满满的恩爱和甜蜜的原野树和奈奈子也来到了现场。倪斯和芊芊彼此都是单独一个人前往小教堂的，却因为沾染了幸福的氛围，两人当即就交换了电话号码，成为了朋友。

顾晞若微笑着环视全场，一双清澈而温暖的眼睛突然撞入她的眼帘。他走向她，将她的手挽在自己的手上，然后跨过长长的红地毯，又将她的手抽离他的手，安心地将她交给李嘉禾。顾晞若的视线一直紧紧地跟随着转身离开的路瑾言，直到他走回到座位上，顾晞若的心才突然落空了。

好像缺了点儿什么……

路妈妈和路爸爸安静地坐在座位上，他们不再怪她，不再恨她，现在有的，满满的都是祝福她。

到底缺了点儿什么？

安眠。

对，安眠怎么不在路瑾言的身边？

梦境是自由的，顾眄若将之前的记忆嵌入了此刻的梦境中。

终于，她想起来了。

离开日本的前夕，李嘉禾告诉过她："路瑾言很幸运，有生之年，他等到了他的'眼角膜捐献者'，他的眼睛很快就会恢复光明，我会通知他来接你的。"再后来，在医院里，顾眄若问李嘉禾："嘉禾，告诉我，是谁。自愿将眼角膜捐献给路瑾言的这个人，已经知道他是谁了吗？"

"是安眠。"

"怎么……回事？"

"飞来横祸……"李嘉禾叹了口气，继续说，"两车相撞引发事故，安眠当时正在过马路，相撞后的车子失去控制，直直地朝安眠撞过去，人被撞飞到几米外……事后，在安眠的抽屉里，安眠的母亲找到了一份'死后自愿捐献眼角膜'的协议书。"

"撞得这么厉害，眼角膜没有损伤吗？"

"……也许，在车子撞过来之前，她就已经想到了最坏的结果。所以，直到送往医院被通知抢救无效之后，她的双手仍然在死死地护着她的双眼。这个姿势，一直到路瑾言对她说'安眠，安息吧'，她的双手才肯放下来。"

"安眠……不是飞来横祸，而是有预谋的自杀，对不对？"顾眄若哭着追问李嘉禾。

"警方已经证实了，这场事故只是一场意外。"

"可是，两车相撞的车主不是都说当时是因为安眠不守交通规则，他们为了保护她，才急打方向盘引发相撞的吗？"

"这事……你是怎么知道的？"

"路瑾言告诉我的。所以，安眠她是自杀的，对不对？"

"傻丫头，别多想了。"

"安眠之所以去送死，是不是全都因为我？因为我在邮件里拆穿了她的谎言，因为我威胁她我会回国把所有的真相都告诉路瑾言，因为我说我一定要把路瑾言从她的身边抢回来……她只不过是爱路瑾言，她只不过是害怕看到我和路瑾言在一起，她只不过是不愿失去路瑾言，对不对？"

"不对。晞若，你说得不对。因为，就算是你回国，我和你也不会在一起，我们永远都不可能在一起。"梦境中，路瑾言的脸突然浮现。最后这一句，就是路瑾言对顾晞若说的。明明知道是为什么，顾晞若却还是忍不住问路瑾言："为什么？"

"因为，我们再也回不到过去。"

思绪凝结。

所有的爱遗失在顺时针的遗忘里。

原来，我们回不到过去了。

终于，我们回不到过去了。

泪水沾湿了梦境，眼泪沾着睫毛微微颤抖，梦境终于消散。

顾晞若睁开双眼，世界一片空白。

一切都结束了。

一切都在重新开始……

miss

The Last.

I still miss you…